CATHOLIC MORAL TRADITION

IN CHRIST, A NEW CREATION

DAVID BOHR

Our Sunday Visitor Publishing Division
Our Sunday Visitor, Inc.
Huntington, Indiana 46750

Nihil Obstat:
Most Reverend Francis X. DiLorenzo, S.T.D.
Censor Deputatus
Imprimatur:
Most Reverend James C. Timlin, D.D.
Bishop of Scranton
September 28, 1989

The nihil obstat and imprimatur are official declarations that a book or pamphlet is free of doctrinal or moral error. No implication is contained therein that those who have granted the nihil obstat and imprimatur agree with the contents, opinions or statements expressed.

Scripture texts used in this work are taken from the New American Bible With Revised New Testament Copyright © 1986 Confraternity of Christian Doctrine, Washington, D.C. All Rights Reserved. No part of the New American Bible With Revised New Testament may be reproduced in any form without permission in writing from the copyright owner.

Vatican II documents appearing in this work are taken from Vatican Council II The Conciliar and Post Conciliar Documents, © 1975 and 1986 by Harry J. Costello and Reverend Austin Flannery, O.P., Costello Publishing Company, Northport, New York. All rights reserved.

The names of various publishers and individuals from whose works copyrighted material was excerpted are cited throughout this work. If any materials have been used inadvertently without proper credit, please notify Our Sunday Visitor in writing so that future printings can be corrected.

International Standard Book Number: 0-87973-439-6
Library of Congress Catalog Card Number: 89-62497

Published in the United States of America
Cover design by Rebecca J. O'Brien
439

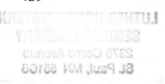

For
John V. Polednak
priest, friend, "companion on the journey"
who has encouraged me
every step along the way
not only to write
but also
to live as a new creation
in Christ

Catholic Moral Tradition
In Christ, A New Creation

David Bohr

So whoever is in Christ is a new creation: the old things have passed away; behold, new things have come. And all this is from God, who has reconciled us to himself through Christ and given us the ministry of reconciliation.
— 2 Cor. 5:17-18

Table of Contents

Foreword

It is a pleasure to introduce this book entitled *Catholic Moral Tradition*. This volume fills an important need for an introduction to moral theology that is both readable and reliable. It will prove useful to those who are approaching sustained theological studies for the first time and for those who desire to grow in the knowledge of their Catholic Faith. This book will also serve as a ready reference for the expert seeking an overview of the Church's moral teaching.

Monsignor Bohr presents the Church's moral teaching in full fidelity to the magisterium. At the same time, he synthesizes the best theological reflection on the Christian moral life. All this is presented so as to whet the appetite of the reader for an even deeper knowledge of what the Church believes and teaches.

The moral teaching of the Church shows all of us the true path to discipleship — not just in theory but in the practical decisions of everyday living. Perhaps the greatest service which *Catholic Moral Tradition* performs is to help us grow in living as true followers of Jesus.

James Cardinal Hickey
Archbishop of Washington
October 18, 1989

Preface

This current work attempts to develop a "theology of Christian living."
It is a major rewrite of class notes I originally put together over the past few
years for a course entitled "An Introduction to the Christian Spiritual-Moral
Life," which I present in our diocesan Religious Education Institute.
Founded in 1984 by Cardinal John O'Connor when he was Bishop of
Scranton, the Institute offers a formation program for adult Catholics who
minister as permanent deacons, pastoral associates, catechists, Catholic
school teachers, youth ministers, parish council and liturgy committee
members, etc. Some six hundred students enroll each year at a dozen centers
the Institute operates across the diocese.

The educational background of the Institute's participants ranges from
high school diplomas to graduate degrees. I have written this work with these
students foremost in mind. They are adults sincerely interested in learning
more about their faith. They are looking for substance, inspiration and
challenge, not academic degrees. My writing style thus tends to be more
casual than academic. With this work I am attempting to provide the reader
with a single-volume, introductory, yet holistic overview of the Catholic
Church's spiritual and moral traditions. As in all the courses offered at the
Institute, I try to break open the vast richness of our Catholic heritage and
delve into it, rather than go beyond it. Our goal is to better understand this
tradition so that we can better live it and share it with the contemporary world.

From the perspective of evangelization and catechesis, which have been
my principal areas of pastoral concentration the past fifteen years, I truly
believe that Catholic moral teaching will only appeal and make sense to our
contemporaries when it is perceived as offering a holistic vision of what it
means to be a genuinely integrated human person. Jesus Christ alone, "the
final Adam," provides us with that vision and with the transforming power,
or grace, to become "a new creation" and to live accordingly.

In this current work I turn to symbolic consciousness, as the method of
interpretation. It is the method most frequently found in Sacred Scripture, the
Fathers of the Church, our liturgical tradition, contemporary narrative
theology, and in the writings of Pope John Paul II. Many present day
Catholic moral theologians have shifted from classicism to historical
consciousness. While this latter approach rightly respects the actual concrete

situation, circumstances and empirical evidence — all of which the former virtually seemed to ignore — this modern historical approach, nevertheless, easily tends towards subjectivism and relativism and is, I maintain, just as one-sided and rationalistic as the classical methodology it has sought to replace.

The works of John Paul II and the more recent Vatican statements on Catholic moral teaching depend on a genuine theological anthropology rooted in Christian biblical revelation. Interpreted from a symbolic perspective, as they were originally meant to be, the major elements of our tradition are essentially preserved, but they are presented in a less preponderantly rationalistic manner and in a more personalistic and holistic way. Throughout this current work I attempt to contrast this Christian world-view or understanding of life constructed in this way with other opposing visions competing for our attention in today's society and culture. I also try to enter into dialogue with those contemporary voices within the sciences and humanities that tend to support this Christian vision of the total human person.

The author wishes to express special gratitude to Cardinal John J. Connor, Archbishop of New York, for his foresight, wisdom and determination to establish the Diocesan Religious Education Institute while he was Bishop of Scranton (1983-84), and for appointing me as its first Director. If it were not for that assignment and the need to find an appropriate textbook for the course I was to teach there, this book would never have been written. I also must thank Bishop James C. Timlin, D.D., our present Ordinary, for all his encouragement and support. When I commented to him that I was having difficulty in finding a text for the course, he readily suggested ''Why don't you write your own?'' Since then, he has frequently inquired about and personally expressed interest in its progress.

My gratitude goes out to all the staff, faculty, and students of the Religious Education Institute from 1984 to 1988 — to Rev. John V. Polednak, M.A., M.C.Sp., its spiritual director, who was always willing to listen to my musings and never let me give up on this task; to Dr. Rosalind Smith, Ph.D., then the assistant director and now the current director; to Sister Edward Ann Wierzalis, C.S.B., the diocesan Director of Religious Education (1984-89); to the other faculty members, including Rev. Vincent J. Grimalia, Rev. Kevin P. O'Neill, J.C.D., Rev. Paul M. Mullen, M.A., M.C.Sp., Rev. Leo J. McKernan, M.A., S.T.L. and Rev. Joseph F. Sica, M.Th. — all of whom have read the manuscript and used it, or parts of it, for their courses. I also want to thank Bishop Francis X. DiLorenzo, S.T.D., our auxiliary bishop and a moral theologian, as well as former Rector of St. Charles Borromeo Seminary, Overbrook, Pa., for all his encouragement and helpful reading of the text. A special word of thanks must go to Mrs. Jane Ludka, executive secretary of the Institute, who most ably saw to the printing of my class notes and prepared the manuscript for publication. Last but not least, I wish to thank all the students of the Institute who participated in my classes and contributed their questions and observations, which led to the development and refinement of these notes.

St. Pius X Seminary
Dalton, Pennsylvania
August 26, 1989

Abbreviations

AA *Apostolicam Actuositatem*, Second Vatican Council's Decree on the Apostolate of the Laity, November 18, 1965

AG *Ad Gentes*, Second Vatican Council's Decree on the Church's Missionary Activity, December 7, 1965

DH *Dignitatis Humanae*, Second Vatican Council's Declaration on Religious Freedom, December 7, 1965

DS H. Denzinger and A. Shonmetzer, *Enchiridion Symbolorum, Definitionem de Rebus Fidei et Morum*, 32nd or later edition, Freiburg, 1963

DV *Dei Verbum*, Second Vatican Council's Dogmatic Constitution on Divine Revelation, November 18, 1965

GS *Gaudium et Spes*, Second Vatican Council's Pastoral Constitution on the Church in the Modern World, December 7, 1965

LG *Lumen Gentium*, Second Vatican Council's Dogmatic Constitution on the Church, November 21, 1964

OT *Optatum Totius,* Second Vatican Council's Decree on Priestly Formation, October 28, 1965

PH *Personae Humanae*, Sacred Congregation for the Doctrine of the Faith's Declaration on Certain Questions Concerning Sexual Ethics, December 29, 1975

PO *Presbyterorum Ordinis*, Second Vatican Council's Decree on the Ministry and Life of Priests, December 7, 1965

RP *Rite of Penance*, Sacred Congregation for Divine Worship, December 2, 1973

SC *Sacrosanctum Concilium*, Second Vatican Council's Constitution on the Sacred Liturgy, December 4, 1963

UR *Unitatis Redintegratio*, Second Vatican Council's Decree on Ecumenism, November 21, 1964

Introduction:

Toward a Theology of Christian Living

If the self is defined by its ability to choose its own values, on what grounds are those choices themselves based? [For many Americans] there is simply no objectifiable criterion for choosing one value or course of action over another. One's own idiosyncratic preferences are their own justification, because they define the true self. . . . The right act is simply the one that yields the agent the most exciting challenge or the most good feeling about himself. — Robert N. Bellah et al., *Habits of the Heart*[1]

Faced with a moral problem or dilemma, a person almost instinctively asks, "What should I do?" A prior and more fundamental question is "Who am I?" or rather "What sort of person acts in this way?" My self-conception, my mental image of the "sort of person I am and am meant to become," matters spiritually and morally.

How I envision life and its meaning influences the way I act. If I see myself as all alone in a dog-eat-dog world, I am likely to be always on the defensive and suspicious of other people, afraid that somehow they may threaten my plans for success or even my existence. However, if I see myself as a member of a people or a community with a history and traditions, I probably have a deep sense of reverence and belonging which motivates me to preserve and share this rich heritage that I have been given. Furthermore, if I view myself as a child of God, created in his image and likeness and called to an intimate communion of life with him along with all my brothers and sisters who make up the human race, then my life takes on a whole new

7

meaning. These images that inhabit both my conscious and subconscious world provide the foundation for my attitudes and choices. "Who" I understand myself to be determines the way I respond to life, to the people and situations I encounter on my life's journey.

In a recent study of the self-understanding of Americans as a people, three sociologists, a philosopher and a theologian unveil the fierce individualism that undermines our capacity for commitment to one another. In the quotation above commenting on the results of their research, we see that the self-image of many Americans is defined by their "own idiosyncratic preferences" and not by an "objectifiable criterion." The authors thus conclude that "In the absence of any objectifiable criteria of right and wrong, good or evil, the self and its feelings become our only moral guide."[2] A soft-drink commercial broadcast frequently on American television during 1985 informed its viewers that "When one makes a choice, what is right is what *feels* right." While Pepsi-Cola certainly did not intend to establish a new morality, its commercial summarized the prevailing moral vision.

Modern individualism, nevertheless, is not the only strand feeding into the current ethical vision of the American people. Biblical religion inspired the first Puritans who landed on our shores. They sought to establish here the new "Promised Land." Governor John Winthrop (1588-1649), the first elected governor of the Massachusetts Bay Colony, considered true freedom or "moral freedom" to be the liberty to do only that which is good and not whatever one pleased. Success for these earliest settlers was not measured in terms of material wealth but was evidenced rather in "the creation of a community in which a genuinely ethical and spiritual life could be lived."[3] This biblical tradition remains a part of our cultural history.

As human beings we base our lives not primarily on reasoning and logic but rather on the stories, visions and dreams that capture our imaginations. We interpret our world first through stories and images long before we are even capable of abstract thinking. Childhood fairy tales, such as "Snow White and the Seven Dwarfs" and "Hansel and Gretel," are a powerful influence in developing a child's values. These classic stories, employing universal archetypes, provide vivid images of good and evil.[4] Before the philosophy of Plato and Aristotle, the early Greeks, along with other ancient peoples, developed mythology. Through these tales of gods and goddesses and their interaction with human beings, they attempted to interpret the meaning of life. In the gospels, too, we read that "All these things Jesus spoke to the crowds in parables. He spoke to them only in parables ...

'[announcing] what has lain hidden from the foundation [of the world]' "
(Mt. 13:34-35).

Unlike Europe in the Middle Ages, when practically everyone living in
that Age of Christendom subscribed to the same basic Christian story or
vision, we today live simultaneously in a number of different worlds. Each of
these communities or worlds (family, Church, ethnic community, sports,
politics, commerce, advertising, etc.) has its own story to tell. The world of
advertising, in so many different ways, relates the story that enough is not
enough; we always need the newest and most improved version. This vision
of consumerism, then, carries over into all other areas of life as it creates in
us an ever constant sense of insufficiency. Our spouse or friend is not "the
newest or most improved version," so we throw her or him away and get
another. Likewise, every autumn the world of college football shapes our
imaginations by the ritual quest to be "Number 1." The aggressive
competition it inspires soon begins to influence all our activities; whether in
schoolwork, business or interpersonal relationships, we must always be the
winner.[5] Which of these worlds and its stories most influences the way I live
my life? Is it the Christian story?

The Christian Story

With its roots in the Jewish scriptures, the Christian story tells us of one
God who created the world and everything in it. The pinnacle of creation was
man and woman, whom God made in his own image and likeness. God
breathed into them a part of himself, his spirit. He gave them consciousness
and freedom. Then he called them to share with him an intimate communion
of life. They, however, wanted to be like God and do things their own way —
that is, decide for themselves what is good and bad — so they refused to
listen to God's word. They sinned. They separated themselves from him and
thus broke their relationship with God.

Their sin had a sundering effect on all their relationships. Between
themselves, Adam points the finger of blame at Eve. Within their own hearts
they become ashamed as they discover they are naked. They must now till the
earth by the sweat of their brows. Their son becomes jealous and kills his
brother. Their descendants still want to make a name for themselves by
building a tower at Babel which would reach to heaven, but God scatters
them in their pride all over the earth and they can no longer speak one
language. Sin breeds disharmony. Relationships to God, to oneself, to one
another, to the earth and among nations, all begin to unravel.

9

Prior to the Fall, Adam was exactly what God intended humanity to be. The first in any series usually serves as the ideal pattern or exemplar for all the ones that follow. However, by his sin, Adam could no longer perform this role for the human race. This is why, as St. Paul tells us, God sent a New Adam, namely Jesus Christ who became "a life-giving spirit" (1 Cor. 15:45). "For Paul, Christ was in fact what Adam was destined to be. The 'life' that Adam lost is once again represented in the world and in it the divine intention for humanity becomes manifest."[6]

In Jesus Christ the sundering effects of sin were checkmated. "God was reconciling the world to himself in Christ" (2 Cor. 5:19), or as Paul explains it in his Letter to the Romans: "For just as through the disobedience of one person the many were made sinners, so through the obedience of one many will be made righteous" (5:19).

In Christ's paschal mystery we are being reconciled, made one again with all creation (see Eph. 2:7-10 and Col. 1:19-20). Indeed, through faith and baptism we become "in Christ . . . a new creation" (2 Cor. 5:17). This brings about the blessed result that "Hence, now there is no condemnation for those who are in Christ Jesus. For the law of the spirit of life in Christ Jesus has freed you from the law of sin and death" (Rom. 8:1-2).

This then, in sum, is the Good News, the Christian story line: God creates, we sin, God redeems us through a new creation in Christ. We now are expected to live our lives according to the Christ we have received (see Col. 2:6). In his Spirit, the Spirit of truth and of love, we are given the power for the development of our inner selves (see Eph. 3:16-19) and become a "spiritual person" (1 Cor. 2:15). We make Christ's attitude our own (see Phil. 2:5) and transform our behavior through this renewal of our mind, so that we "may discern what is the will of God, what is good and pleasing and perfect" (Rom. 12:2). We must "put on the new self, created in God's way in righteousness and holiness of truth" (Eph. 4:24). The Christian's spiritual and moral life rests on one's faith in Christ. Thus Jesus summed up his entire message in one line at the beginning of Mark's gospel account: "This is the time of fulfillment. The kingdom of God is at hand. Repent, and believe in the gospel" (1:15).

Contemporary Roman Catholic Spirituality and Ethics

In its Dogmatic Constitution on the Church (LG 39) the Second Vatican Council declared that "all in the Church, whether they belong to the hierarchy or are cared for by it, are called to holiness, according to the

10

apostle's saying: 'For this is the will of God, your sanctification' (1 Th. 3:3; cf. Eph. 1:4)." This teaching of the Council officially ended a nearly fifteen-hundred-year-old split in the Christian "way" of life that developed with the rise of monasticism. In the earliest centuries, the Christian's moral behavior flowed from the community's shared life in Christ's Spirit. With the growth of monasticism, however, a second, more perfect "way" of being Christian was held up to the faithful. Through the practice of the evangelical counsels, contemplative prayer and other ascetical works, a person could now embark upon a more spiritual "way of perfection." The average Christian was then left to traverse the "ordinary way" of observing the commandments; this split in the Christian "way" remained for nearly fifteen centuries.

A deep spiritual hunger is in evidence today. On one hand new spiritual movements have developed in recent years. The popularity of courses in spiritual discernment, journal keeping, religious cults and the success of Christian fundamentalism all attest to this fact. While on the other hand our heavily positivistic and technological approach to life in Western society and culture has ignored the needs of the inner world of the soul. In desperation many people turn to drugs, alcohol, sexual promiscuity, and even suicide and war to escape their inner emptiness and isolation. They seem incapable of recognizing the fact that God created us for himself alone and, as St. Augustine has observed, "Our hearts are restless until they rest in you, O Lord."

A number of developments arising out of Vatican II — including liturgical renewal, ecumenism, the rediscovery of the importance of Sacred Scripture, the reform and renewal of religious congregations, and a commitment to social justice — have given shape to contemporary Roman Catholic spirituality. Such movements as Cursillo, Marriage Encounter and Charismatic Renewal have flourished, in addition to the Emmaus Spirituality Program for priests, parish renewal programs, directed retreats and weekend youth retreats. A plurality of methods and programs with their roots in Scripture have all but replaced the "rosary-novena" style of devotional Catholicism. All of these developments in their own way have contributed to a new integration of the Christian spiritual and moral life.

Catholic moral theology received a mandate for renewal from the Second Vatican Council in its Decree on the Training of Priests (OT 16). It stressed that this discipline should have a livelier contact with the Mystery of Christ and the history of salvation. Its scientific presentation should draw more fully on the teaching of Scripture and highlight the vocation of the faithful in Christ and their obligation to bring forth fruit in charity for the life of the world.

In the first question of his *Summa Theologica*, St. Thomas Aquinas affirms the unity of all theology. For him the division between dogma and morality did not exist. Likewise for St. Paul. In nearly all his letters there are two parts. First he gives us a discussion of God's saving activity as revealed in Jesus Christ. Then he presents us with the imperative that these facts impose; he spells out their moral demands and the need for truly Christian behavior. After the Council of Trent in the sixteenth century dogmatic and moral theology became separate disciplines in the new seminary system that developed as a mandate of that council. Moral theology soon became allied with Canon Law and remained so until Vatican II.

Right after World War II, Father Bernard Häring, C.Ss.R., came from Germany to teach moral theology at the Academia Alfonsiana in Rome. His class notes for his seminary students were published in three volumes under the title *The Law of Christ*. This monumental work clearly emphasized the biblical, personal and dialogical character of the Christian life. The sacraments, here, were treated not merely as objects of regulations, but as means of a personal and spiritual encounter with the Risen Lord. Twenty-five years later in another comprehensive presentation of Catholic morality, entitled *Free and Faithful in Christ*, Father Häring would write that moral theology's first concern should not be with individually distinct acts nor with decision-making. "Its basic task and purpose is to gain the right vision, to assess the main perspectives, and to present those truths and values which should bear upon the decisions to be made before God."[7]

The majority of Catholic moral theologians, especially in the United States and Germany, seem to remain entrapped by the philosophical and legalistic residue of the earlier "manual tradition" which dominated Catholic morality in the post-Tridentine, pre-Vatican II era. A very few continue to operate almost as though the Second Vatican Council never happened. Many others have attempted to give a more pastoral orientation to this discipline by working with a different philosophical model of the moral agent and by stressing less the significance of moral absolutes and the legal character of moral theology.[8] There seems to exist among this latter group a tendency to separate, almost dualistically, the mysteries of faith and the gospel vision from everyday practical conduct. While clearly admitting that one's faith in Jesus Christ ("Christian intentionality") is the most important and decisive

12

element of Christian morality, they seem to concentrate almost exclusively on categorical conduct or normative ethics. The Good News, as "the power of God for the salvation of everyone who believes" (Rom. 1:16), does not really appear to adequately inform their moral deliberations.[9]

Criticism of the current state of Catholic moral theology has not been wanting. Father Enda McDonagh, a Catholic moralist from Ireland, claims that many contemporary Catholic moral theologians' "appeal to biblical and theological insights appear as a kind of paranetic overlay or the result of soft-headedness or muddleheadedness." In his estimation, their "categories and modes of argument . . . seem to owe nothing to Christian faith or theology."[10] Equally critical have been the observations of an American Protestant ethicist, Stanley Hauerwas. He has stated that "contrary to the dominant assumption, the call for a renewal of moral theology issued at Vatican II has not in fact taken place. . . . The attempt to make moral theology more 'nourished' by scriptural teaching, as Vatican II had requested, has been lost amid the concern to make ethics more pastorally responsive."[11] These are but two of the many voices that have been raised in dissatisfaction over the current state of affairs within Catholic moral theology.

Toward a Theology of Christian Living

The Second Vatican Council in its Pastoral Constitution on the Church in the Modern World (*Gaudium et Spes*) proposes an integrated vision of Christian life, based upon a coherent synthesis of scriptural teachings, doctrinal beliefs, spiritual and liturgical life, and moral behavior. Its first three chapters provide an outline of Christian anthropology, of what it means to be created "to the image of God" and restored to that image in Christ by the power of the Spirit. "Conformed to the image of the Son who is the firstborn of many brothers, the Christian," we are told, "receives the 'first fruits of the Spirit' (Rom. 8:23) by which he is able to fulfill the new law of love" (GS 22). The linking or reintegration of Christian spirituality and morality, thus, is evidenced in the Christocentric focus of the Council's teaching. Indeed, the Council Fathers clearly indicate that the Christian moral life flows from a genuine and vibrant spiritual life. Without explicitly naming it such, Vatican II presents us with a "theology of Christian living."

Through Christ and in the Spirit, Christian life is essentially a faith-response to the gift-call of divine revelation, for it is "through faith comes to contemplate and savor the mystery of God's design" (GS 15), and "Christ, the new Adam, in the very revelation of the mystery of the Father

13

and of his love, fully reveals man to himself and brings to light his most high calling'' (GS 22). This divine gift-call evokes our active, living response of faith. Thus, the Council Fathers assigned a renewed moral theology the task of showing ''the exalted vocation of the faithful in Christ'' (OT 16). The Christian spiritual-moral life constitutes our response to this exalted vocation.

Christian ethics is by nature revelatory and dialogical. It differs from the many and varied philosophical interpretations which attempt to explain the meaning of the moral life solely on the basis of human experience. Yet, some contemporary Catholic moralists ask if there exists such a thing as a specific Christian ethics or morality. In view of Vatican II's teaching on the universality of grace through Creation and the Incarnation (LG 16; GS 22), many Catholic theologians today maintain that all persons everywhere participate in the same gift-call. Dialogue, too, with humanists and other non-Christians has demonstrated that they most often share with us the same basic goals, attitudes and virtues. It is, therefore, the opinion of these moral theologians that there is no specific Christian ethics.

The question of whether or not there is a distinctive or specific Christian ethics is often complicated by semantic problems. A number of moralists have attempted to sift through the linguistic entanglements by carefully defining the terms. [12] In this work, henceforth, we shall distinguish ''specific'' (connoting exclusivity) from ''distinctive'' (connoting only a characteristic quality typically associated with a given reality), and between ''ethics'' (denoting and pertaining to first or fundamental principles) and ''morality'' (referring to actual human conduct derived from ethical principles). Further confusion arises from the frequent use of ''moral theology'' within Catholic circles to designate the bringing together of both ethics and morality, while the Protestant tradition labels this same process ''Christian ethics.''

Only on the most universal level of general precepts and norms where, in the words of Vatican II, ''Those who, through no fault of their own, do not know the Gospel of Christ or his Church, but who nevertheless seek God with a sincere heart, and, moved by grace, try in their actions to do his will as they know it through the dictates of their conscience'' (LG 16), is it possible to maintain that there is no specific nor distinctive Christian ethics and morality. On this most fundamental level the Church accepts the fully human as its starting point, but as the Council Fathers add, ''faith throws a new light on all things and makes known the full ideal which God has set for man, thus guiding the mind towards solutions that are fully human'' (GS 11). Faith in

14

the Good News of Jesus Christ explicates the inner demands of grace, shedding a new and fuller light upon what is human and reasonable. Thus, evangelization or the explicit proclamation of this gospel is "the essential and primary mission of the Church."[13]

A false understanding of Vatican II's teaching on the universality of grace has bred confusion, as well, in other segments of Catholicism. Some missionaries question the very need of explicitly proclaiming the Gospel. Is it not a direct infringement upon the freedom and conscience of the nonbeliever? Likewise, some Catholic educators will maintain that the Catholic school's primary task is to offer quality education, and not to evangelize. Such issues surface whenever we lose sight of the Trinitarian nature of divine revelation and dualistically separate faith from practice.

The Christian believes that ultimate Truth or Reality is a Trinity of Persons. This Divine Mystery, furthermore, is revealed to us through the double mission of the Son and the Holy Spirit. St. Irenaeus, in the second century, described this double mission as "the two hands of the Father"[14] that makes the discovery of God in history possible. The mission of the Spirit, the universality of grace, reaches out to all men and women of every time and place. The Holy Spirit calls them in their heart of hearts and seeks to transform them into images of the New Adam, Jesus Christ, even if they are in ignorance of him or his Church. But this mission is only one hand.

Perhaps if it were not for original sin, which mars our human nature, God very well might have saved us with just one hand. But somewhere back there, before recorded time, it all began to unravel. Sin negatively affected not only our relationship to God, to one another, and to all of creation, but deep within us our hearts were pulled asunder and tossed into confusion by unruly desires, longings, drives and passions, all seeking their own independent way. In such a state our eyes became blind to God's plan. Our hearts grew cold to the transforming power of his love, his grace. God now needed, so to speak, his other hand, the mission of the Son, the Word-made-flesh, who came into the world to be its light, a light that "the darkness has not overcome" (Jn. 1:5). God thus wants all men and women to arrive at full awareness of his plan of salvation.

Jesus reveals "the way and the truth and the life" (Jn. 14:6). He clearly unveils God's other hand, the creative, unifying hand of grace, the mission of the Spirit, that has always been at work in the world, but whose presence great numbers of the human race could only see through a mirror darkly. The Word is both revelation and power. In the Old Testament the word of God

15

(*dabar* in Hebrew) possesses both noetic and dynamic elements. On the one hand, it creates the world and sets history in motion, and on the other, it manifests God's will, His salvific plan.[15] The Good News is "the power of God for the salvation of everyone who believes" (Rom. 1:16). It is a grace, a gift-call to live our lives according to the Christ we have received.

Christ as the Concrete Norm of Christian Life

First and foremost Christian life is an adherence to neither a doctrinal system nor to an ethical code. It is a matter of discipleship, of a personal following of Jesus Christ. It is a matter of abiding in him, of living in his love. "If you keep my commandments, you will remain in my love, just as I have kept my Father's commandments and remain in his love . . . This is my commandment: love one another as I love you" (Jn. 15:10, 12). By making his attitudes our own (Phil. 2:5) we imitate Christ (Jn. 13:15); we "put on the Lord Jesus Christ" (Rom. 13:14). We share in the living reality that is Christ not only by an external association but by an interior transformation. We are united with him like branches on a vine (Jn. 15:1-5).

Our imitating Jesus' total self-surrender to the will of the Father (Heb. 10:7-10) leads to a mystical identity with him so that we could say with St. Paul that "yet I live, no longer I, but Christ lives in me" (Gal. 2:20). Only by following Jesus in his passover through death to life can we come to the Father and share in the very life of the Trinity, for it is through obedience to God's will in imitation of Christ that the Holy Spirit is also given to us (Acts 5:32). Christ is, thus, our supreme law, not as a set of external norms for us, but because he gives us the inner capacity to transform our lives in conformity with the Father's will for us.

Conformed to Christ in the power of the Spirit, we are led to the Father. The Trinitarian nature of Christian life implies that "there is a certain parallel between the union existing among the divine persons and the union of the sons of God in truth and love" (GS 24). Created in the image of God (Gen. 1:27) who is a Trinity of persons, we are social beings. Restored to that image in Christ (see 2 Cor. 3:18 and 4:4), our communal vocation becomes clear. Through baptism we become members of his Body (1 Cor. 12:13, 27), and in the Eucharist "we, though many, are one body" (1 Cor. 10:17). Christ, as our concrete norm, thus reveals the essential communal, and thereby ecclesial, dimension (see Eph. 1:23; 5:23, 30) of Christian life.

The belief that Christ gathers us together through word and sacrament into his Church, furthermore, brings to the fore the missionary nature of our life in him. The marks of the early Church "gathered together" (*ekklesia*) in Acts 2:42 — teaching, fellowship, breaking bread, and prayer — served to make the disciples "witnesses" of the Risen Lord (see Lk. 24:48 and Acts 1:8). The Church, his Body, exists to continue Jesus' mission of proclaiming "the gospel to every creature" (Mk. 16:15). Indeed, the salvation of our souls depends on our willingness to spend our lives in the service of Christ and his gospel (see Mk. 8:35). Accepting Christ as the norm of our lives requires dedicating ourselves to the "ministry" and "message of reconciliation" (2 Cor. 5:18, 19), so that, in the words of Jesus to his disciples at the Last Supper, "they may all be one, as you, Father, are in me and I in you, that they also may be in us, that the world may believe that you sent me" (Jn. 17:21).

The New Testament clearly gives evidence to the fact that for the earliest Christians the most basic source of morality was not primarily the sayings of Jesus, "but the very Person of Jesus himself, who is the *center-point* as well as the *end-point* of the relationship between God and man."[16] Jesus Christ, in other words, is both our deontological and teleological norm. As the "image of God" (2 Cor. 4:4; Col. 1:15), Jesus Christ fully reveals to us our human nature; he clearly shows us what it truly means to be a human being.[17] At the same time he makes known to us the purpose or goal (*telos*) of human nature which is to become "like God" (deification, or *theosis*).[18]

Christ, furthermore, is the universal objective norm of human existence. While standing before Pontius Pilate, Jesus maintained that "For this I was born and for this I came into the world, to testify to the truth" (Jn. 18:37). He said to Thomas, "I am the way and the truth and the life" (Jn. 14:6) and to Philip, "Whoever has seen me has seen the Father" (Jn. 14:9). Jesus is the Word of truth, who reveals the Totally Other. Absolute Truth as revealed by him is "Abba, Father"; it is a person. Indeed, it is a Trinity of persons, for as we have just seen Jesus himself is the truth (Jn. 14:6), and he and the Father send the Spirit of truth (Jn. 14:17). "All truth in the created world is suffused with the holiness of this truth of the intimate divine life."[19]

God is, however, incomprehensible, and He is not "grasped" like any other object of knowledge. The great mystics who "saw God" thus "speak of their knowledge as an 'entrance into unknowing,' and John of the Cross described the object of his search and his finding simply as 'I-don't-know-what' (*no sé qué*)."[20] The authentic revelation of God, therefore, is not first and foremost a matter of the intellect but a matter of spirit, a dialogue of love between persons. "*Cor ad cor loquitur*" ("heart speaks to heart''). God's pure and absolute subjectivity is what constitutes his very objectivity, which finds expression in his Word-made-flesh, Jesus Christ, who is incarnate truth.

Divine truth, as revealed in and by Christ, becomes the norm of our lives. The Second Vatican Council in its Decree on Religious Liberty thus maintained that "the highest norm of human life is the divine law itself — eternal, objective and universal, by which God orders, directs and governs the whole world and the ways of the human community according to a plan conceived in his wisdom and love. God has enabled man to participate in this law of his so that, under the gentle disposition of divine providence, many may be able to arrive at a deeper knowledge of unchangeable truth" (DH 3). This eternal law is the will of God, or God himself under the aspect of the lawgiver.

Contemporary Western civilization, which has its roots in the post-Enlightenment philosophies and sciences, shuns an objective moral order in its turn to the existential subject and the immediacy of experience. An evolutionary view of human life and the universe, analyzed from the perspective of the positive sciences, allows no place for absolute and immutable laws. Continuing flux and process are the only absolutes. "Progress is our most important product." In a technological society, even human behavior is mechanically interpreted and therapeutically fixed or managed. There is no room for interiority. Creative autonomy is considered the only proper expression of a freedom based upon individual rights and subjective feelings. Vestiges of all these trends have infiltrated contemporary Christian ethics to various extents. Some Catholic moralists, too, seem to have succumbed to them in varying degrees in their attempts to correct the excessive legalism and objectivism of the pre-Vatican II manualist tradition.

The above observations on the current status of post-Vatican II developments within the areas of Christian spirituality and ethics have now, for all practical purposes, come full circle. Although admittedly outlined with broad, sweeping strokes, a clear focal point emerges, namely, our life in Christ Jesus, a life lived in the Spirit of truth and love transforming us into a whole new creation. In the succeeding chapters of this work we shall look systematically at the various elements that comprise this truly magnificent reality to which each one of us has been called through faith and baptism.

As suggested by conciliar documents, our starting point in Part I will be divine revelation as handed down to us through sacred Scripture and the teachings of the Church. It would be wrong, however, to label this approach as an "ethics from above," since it is rooted in the fully human, as concretely and historically lived in the person of Jesus Christ. After looking at the biblical themes and vision of faith that provide the foundation for our study, we will survey the historical and cultural elements that have influenced our understanding of the Christian life through the centuries.

A study of the principal elements or categories that constitute our response to God's call for an intimate communion of life with him will be the subject matter of Part II and comprise the major portion of this work. This will provide a new look at what in the "manualist" or neo-Scholastic tradition was called "*De Principiis*," a study of the fundamental elements. Again, attempting to be faithful to the direction given by the Second Vatican Council, we will anchor our examination of these principal elements in the gospel of Jesus Christ and the mysteries of our faith.

The graced reality of the person "in Christ," called to live in him as a whole new creation, will provide our starting point in this section. The gift-call of conversion, or repentance for sin, will show forth the nobility of our Christian vocation that is lived out in a faith-response of love and hope. This "yes" of faith then requires that we live according to the law of Christ, the grace of the Holy Spirit, planted deep within our heart of hearts, our soul, our conscience. There we always remain free, either to grow in Christian maturity and virtue or to refuse God's gift-call of grace and thus sin, alienating ourselves from God, one another, creation and our own deepest identity.

For our study of each of these elements we will turn to the sacred Scriptures, the Fathers of the Church, and our theological tradition. We shall take as our starting point Christian biblical revelation and the great mysteries of faith — the Trinity, Creation and the Fall, redemption through Jesus Christ's incarnation and paschal mystery, and the mystery of the Church as a sacrament of communion of life with God. Following a genetic-historical approach in the development of the themes, we will strive primarily for convergence and synthesis. We hope to capture the full gospel vision of life's meaning and see how we can best live the Christian story. We want to bring into focus, as it were, a bird's-eye view of the entire forest, where we can pinpoint the individual trees that comprise this gospel world-view, the one divine plan.

To arrive at this end, we shall employ the insights and findings of the secular sciences, especially those schools or approaches that find an easy congruence with the existence of transcendent and spiritual realities. We will enlist the aid of other Christian theological traditions where helpful, especially Orthodox Christianity, an ancient and rich tradition that is often overlooked by contemporary Roman Catholic moralists. The major shift in theological method that occurred at Vatican II was not merely a shift from the deductive, static and abstract methodology of medieval and renaissance classicism to the inductive, dynamic and more evolutionary world-view of historical consciousness, as some theologians would today maintain. It was in fact, as we shall see, a rediscovery of symbolic consciousness, of a more wholistic sacramental world-view which sees earthly and historical realities as revelatory of the deeper Mystery that brings into being, underlies and sustains all that exists. It is this symbolic worldview that gave shape to the Scriptures, the development of the Christian Liturgy and the writings of the early Church Fathers.

After our exposition of the principal elements which provide the foundation for our spiritual and moral lives, we will look in Part III at three areas of special ethical concern: sexual ethics, biomedical issues, and Catholic social doctrine. Our study will make no attempt to be exhaustive. It is the author's intention to offer only an introductory summary of contemporary Roman Catholic spirituality and ethics based upon the vision of renewal proposed by the Second Vatican Council.

Notes

1. Robert N. Bellah et al., *Habits of the Heart: Individualism and Commitment in American Life* (Berkeley, Los Angeles and London: University of California Press, 1985), pp. 75-76.

2. Ibid., p. 76

3. Ibid., p. 29.

4. See Andrew D. Thompson, "Toward a Social-Psychology of Religious Valuing," *Chicago Studies* 19, No. 3 (Fall 1980), p. 278.

5. See Richard M. Gula, S.S., *To Walk Together Again: The Sacrament of Reconciliation* (New York/Ramsey, N.J.: Paulist Press, 1984), pp. 160-165.

6. Jerome Murphy-O'Connor, O.P., *Becoming Human Together: The Pastoral Anthropology of St. Paul* (Wilmington, Del.: Michael Glazier, Inc., 1982), p. 43.

7. Bernard Häring, *Free and Faithful in Christ* (New York: Seabury Press, 1978), vol. 1, p. 6.

8. See Norbert J. Rigali, S.J., "The Future of Moral Theology," *Chicago*

Studies 20, No. 2 (Summer 1981): 160 and Stanley Hauerwas, "The Demands of a Truthful Story: Ethics and the Pastoral Task," *Chicago Studies* 21, No. 1 (Spring 1982), pp. 59-62.

9. Joseph Fuchs, S.J. — in "Is There a Christian Morality?" *Readings in Moral Theology No. 2: The Distinctiveness of Christian Ethics*, eds. Charles E. Curran and Richard A. McCormick, S.J. (New York/Ramsey, N.J.: Paulist Press, 1980), p. 5 — writes: "Scripture speaks unambiguously and frequently about transcendent and Christian attitudes, making quite clear that they are *specifically Christian attitudes* [emphasis in original]. Scripture speaks more rarely about particular, categorical approaches to the various spheres of life (social attitudes, family and conjugal morality, etc.), and is less clear about their meaning and application to various historical periods." Fuch's statement perhaps attempts to explain his and other moralists' almost exclusive deliberation being given to categorical conduct or normative ethics. Nevertheless, for someone seeking to live a life informed by gospel faith, such moral exposition, concentrating solely on the categorical element without hardly a reference to the transcendental, appears devoid of faith. The practical integration of these two basic elements of Christian morality in the writings of this group of Catholic moralists is less than obvious. Their rational exposition of ethical norms seems to give only lip service to biblical and spiritual insights.

10. Enda McDonagh, "Orthopraxis and Moral Theology," *Proceedings of the Catholic Theological Society of America*, ed. Luke Salm, F.S.C., vol. 35 (June 11-14, 1980), p. 17.

11. Stanley Hauerwas, "The Demands of a Truthful Story: Ethics and the Pastoral Task," *Chicago Studies* 21, no. 1 (Spring 1982): pp. 60-61.

12. See especially James J. Walters, "Christian Ethics: Distinctive and Specific?" for *Readings in Moral Theology No. 2*, pp. 90-110, whose distinctions are employed here; also, Richard A. McCormick, S.J., "Does Religious Faith Add to Ethical Perception?" *ibid.*, pp. 156-173.

13. Paul VI, "Evangelization of the World: essential mission of the Church," address during the general audience of October 30, 1974, quoted in *L'Osservatore Romano* (English ed.), 45 (November 7, 1974), p. 1.

14. "Against the Heresies" 5, 36, 2 (SC 153, 458, 460) as cited by Kilian McDonnell, O.S.B., in "A Trinitarian Theology of the Holy Spirit," *Theological Studies* 46, no. 2 (June 1985), p. 206.

15. See René Latourelle, S.J., *Theology of Revelation* (New York: Alba House, 1966), p. 30.

16. George V. Lobo, S.J., *Guide to Christian Living: A New Compendium of Moral Theology* (Westminster, Md.: Christian Classics, Inc., 1984), p. 111. Emphasis mine.

17. See Murphy-O'Connor, op. cit., p. 36.

18. See especially Stanley S. Harakas, *Toward Transfigured Life* (Minneapolis, Minn.: Life and Light Publishing Co., 1983), pp. 27-28, wherein he states: "Human purpose and human nature (human ontology) are related to the fundamental fact of our human *telos* to become 'like God.' This also points to an additional reason why attempts to base the ethical good on nature or empirical human nature are bound to fail: because of sin (original and committed) we are not fully human. Therefore, attempts to argue from what man is to what man ought to be are bound to fail as starting from an inadequate base."

19. Häring, op. cit., vol. 2, p. 10.

20. Joseph Powers, *Spirit and Sacrament* (New York: Seabury Press, 1973), p. 6.

Part I

Beginnings and Background

Chapter 1

Biblical Foundations

"All biblical ethics is based on the call of the personal God and man's believing response." — Hans Urs von Balthasar[1]

In our attempts to live the Christian life, to determine what is right and wrong, some tell us we need only turn to the Bible. There we shall find all our answers. Many others strongly disagree with this literalist approach of fundamentalist evangelical Christianity. The situation ethicist Joseph Fletcher accuses morality based upon specific scriptural guidelines of being a "prefab morality." In simplifying moral decisions, the Bible, he suggests, becomes a kind of neurotic security device. Certain twentieth-century philosophers, such as Bertrand Russell, Jean-Paul Sartre, Julian Huxley, and Herbert Marcuse, would applaud Fletcher's judgment. In light of the work of the Swiss psychologist Jean Piaget, they would argue that Christian ethics with its emphasis on submission to external moral authority promotes only an "infantile" morality.[2] Opinions as to the exact place of the Bible in Christian ethics run the gamut from absolute divine command to psychological crutch. Among Christians there is no general agreement on how Scripture should be used in a systematic ethics.

Catholic theology does not see the Bible as being first and foremost a book of ethics. Although considered to be divinely inspired, it does not provide us with God's own list of right and wrong. Its ethical prescriptions cannot be taken literally in many areas. For instance, parents would certainly be ill advised to follow Deuteronomy's directives for dealing with a rebellious teenager.

"If a man has a stubborn and unruly son who will not listen to his father and mother, and will not obey them even though they chastise him, his father and mother shall have him apprehended and brought out to the elders at the gate of his home city. . . . Then all his fellow citizens shall stone him to death" — (Dt. 21:18-21).

We would find repugnant, too, the way some of the prophets summoned the people of God to exterminate their enemies, even women and children. While we today value hospitality, our sensitivities are repelled by the manner in which Lot was willing to sacrifice his daughters for the sake of it (see Gen. 19:7-8). In the Old Testament, furthermore, polygamy, legalized concubinage and divorce are morally accepted practices. Even the New Testament St. Paul would be surprised by our modern abhorrence of slavery.

Scripture in Catholic Tradition

The belief that God reveals himself, creates and conserves all things in existence, and summons us to salvation by his Word provides the axis of the Catholic theological tradition. The doctrine of divine revelation manifesting the mystery of God's will finds its completion in the Word-made-flesh. Immediately prior to Vatican II a widely held thesis maintained that there were two sources of revelation: Scripture and Tradition. Since certain doctrines of the Roman Catholic Church were not readily detectable in the New Testament, this thesis proposed that these doctrines were passed on orally as part of the living tradition of the Church. The Second Vatican Council, however, rejected this two-source theory.[3] In its Dogmatic Constitution on Divine Revelation (*Dei Verbum*) Vatican II stated that "Sacred Tradition and sacred Scripture make up a single sacred deposit of the Word of God, which is entrusted to the Church" (DV 10).

"The word of God is living and effective" (Heb. 4:12). Sacred Scripture is part of the living apostolic tradition that "makes progress in the Church, with the help of the Holy Spirit. There is a growth in insight into the realities and words that are being passed on" (DV 8). Furthermore, "the task of giving an authentic interpretation of the Word of God, whether in its written form or in the form of Tradition, has been entrusted to the living teaching office of the Church alone" (DV 10). Indeed, the New Testament is the Church's book. Tradition itself determined the full canon of sacred Scripture, as over the centuries the successors of the apostles, the bishops in council, identified those writings that were truly inspired.

The faith tradition of Israel and of the early Church gave birth to the sacred Scriptures, not vice versa. This historical fact is often overlooked by evangelical Christians. At the same time, Vatican II clearly teaches that the "Magisterium is not superior to the Word of God, but is its servant. It teaches only what has been handed on" (DV 10).

The Bible is an anthology of sacred literature, not a systematic presentation of doctrine and ethics. It is a compilation of writings that recount God's relationship with his people throughout salvation history. In attempting to understand the intention of a sacred writer, the Council Fathers tell us that we must pay attention, among other things, to "literary forms for the fact is that truth is differently presented and expressed in the various types of historical writing, in prophetical and poetical texts" (DV 12). In addition, "due attention must be paid both to the customary and characteristic patterns of perception, speech and narrative which prevailed at the age of the sacred writer" (DV 12).

The Scriptures, in fact, arise out of an oral/audial culture that relies more upon stories, symbols and images for interpreting reality than it does upon abstractions, theory and principles. These latter are the tools of a literary culture whose language is a form of logic originating from cognitive skills. An oral culture depends on memory and imaginative skills; it is rooted in history and experience. The Bible is full of stories, parables, poetry and various other forms of non-discursive language. The role of imagination in these sacred writings is far more pervasive than we are accustomed to admit.

The gospels, indeed, report Jesus communicating Christian existence in parables. Telling a story is a way of "imaginatively objectifying" one's experience; "it can be a window into the way things objectively are."[4] The biblical scholar, C.H. Dodd, furthermore, defines a parable as "a metaphor or simile drawn from nature or common life, arresting the hearer by its vividness or strangeness, and leaving the mind in sufficient doubt about its precise application to tease it into active thought."[5] Most of the non-discursive language in the New Testament functions to capture the imagination, to tease the mind, and thus to motivate to action. Its fundamental purpose is to challenge, invite and even coax the hearer to do God's will.

The Bible was never intended to be a textbook of ethics and morality. A quotation from Scripture can never solve a moral problem. As scholarship today highlights the diversity of biblical voices, we have come to understand more clearly that the Bible, in fact, is better at challenging one's decision than it is at providing solutions. Scripture does, however, offer us a new way of envisioning life. The New Testament authors present us with "images of the Christian life which imply new ontological structures grounding new modes of human ethical conduct."[6] Analyzing these images can give us deeper insights and a better understanding of scriptural teachings. At the same time, when searching for pertinent biblical evidence we must always keep in mind Vatican II's directive that "no less attention must be devoted to the content and unity of the whole of Scripture, taking into account the Tradition of the entire Church and the analogy of faith'' (DV 12).

Contemporary Catholic Bible scholars thus describe "Christian biblical revelation" as "that written history and recollected experience, not only as it has been recorded in the Bible, but also as it is *now* being appropriated (continuing revelation) in the human and religious experience, knowledge and understanding of those living in a Christian faith community, i.e., in people attempting to live according to the reality and consequences of these divine entrances into the realm of the human."[7] The way the Church comes to understand the Bible in its life, liturgy and theology constitutes the true "biblical meaning" as distinct from either its "literal sense" or its "canonical sense."[8] Just as the early Christian communities had to formulate their own specific rules of conduct in light of the new life "in Christ" which they believed they were called to live, so too, today, contemporary moral issues must be approached within the whole context of "the full and living Gospel" (DV 7).

Old Testament Elements

Christian biblical revelation finds its spiritual and moral roots in the tradition of Israel. The books of the Old Testament contain numerous law codes, commandments and norms that give detailed prescriptions relating to the practice of ethics, cult and religious customs. What is primary, however, is not the specific directives but the overall vision that gives us the basic framework and structure upon which the religious and moral lives of God's chosen people were built.

God's Word and Call. The book of Genesis relates that God creates through the power of his Word. God spoke, and so all things came to be. God made human beings in his own image and likeness, giving them freedom and thus the ability to respond to his Word. He gave man and woman dominion over all subhuman creation, making them responsible for it. Adam and Eve, however, did not listen to God's Word. Exercising their freedom negatively, they wanted to decide for themselves what was good or evil. As proven by their sin, they refused to be responsible.

Out of a sinful world God called Noah to faith and salvation. "The story of Noah symbolizes God's abiding concern for the salvation of humankind: salvation through an exodus of repentance and trust."[9] God, then, calls Abraham and promises to make him the father of many nations (see Gen.

17:4-6). As described by Father Hans Urs von Balthasar, "In the solitary dialogue-encounter with God, Abraham, in virtue of his mission, becomes the founder of a community whose laws governing horizontal relationships all depend, in the biblical testimony, on the founder's or mediator's vertical relationship with God or on God's founding act (Ex. 22:20; 23:9; Dt. 5:14f.; 15:12-18; 16:11f.; 24:17f)."[10] Abraham is our father in faith, which is a clinging to God's promise and trusting in his fidelity. God next called Moses into the desert where he personally experienced God's powerful presence. God's call sent Moses to lead his people, the descendants of Abraham, up from slavery in Egypt.

The Covenant and the Law. God's call to Noah, to Abraham, to Moses and to all of Israel issues in the establishment of a "covenant" (*berith* in Hebrew; *diatheke* in Greek). At Sinai God made this agreement with Israel: "You have seen for yourselves how I treated the Egyptians and how I bore you up on eagle wings and brought you here to myself. Therefore, if you hearken to my voice and keep my covenant, you shall be my special possession, dearer to me than all other people, though all the earth is mine" (Ex. 19:4-5).

A covenant is a solemn agreement or treaty between two parties establishing a personal relationship of love and fidelity between them. Israel, of course, is not an equal partner on the same level as God. The entire initiative is God's alone, yet this special divine election carries with it an awesome responsibility. It calls for an unconditional obedience: "You shall therefore hearken to the voice of the LORD, your God, and keep his commandments and statutes which I enjoin on you today" (Dt. 27:10). All of Israel's morality is a covenant morality. This special, privileged relationship serves as the foundation of Israel's religious and moral life. "If Israel enjoys His special favor it must also respond to this initiative in its whole way of life. God's self-giving demands a corresponding human response."[11]

The covenant provides the motive for observing the Law or Torah. In Old Testament revelation the Law specifies the pattern of life appropriate for God's people. Eventually the Torah's 619 commandments ordered the whole life of Yahweh's faithful, for God's will had to be done in every detail. The Law, however, was always considered to be a grace or a gift. It spelled out for the people the nature and content of their loving response to God's all-merciful and faithful love (*hesed*), which characterized his covenant with them.

The Ten Commandments. The Decalogue or Ten Commandments (Ex. 20:2-17 and Dt. 5:6-21) is the core of the Mosaic Law or Torah. They summarize the fundamental demands of God regarding his covenanted people. "The meaning of the decalogue can best be determined from the *context of its revelation,* from its being bound up with the Passover, the double central event of salvation history in the Old Testament — the liberation from the bondage of Egypt, and the covenant on Sinai."[12] Its observance is meant essentially to be an act of love. It warned the recently liberated people of forms of slavery infinitely more subtle and pernicious than those experienced in Egypt.

As recorded in sacred Scripture, the Ten Commandments express the will of God for the *community* of Israel. Divided onto two tablets, they formulate the most basic duties toward God and the other members of the community. They are not meant primarily to be a code of individual conduct, for one participated in the covenant only inasmuch as one was a member of the covenanted people. Thus individual sin was more than the transgression of a law; it was a breaking of the community's covenant with Yahweh.

Founded upon the permanent relationship of God with his people, the Decalogue is itself a revelation of God's holiness, as well as of what he wills his people to be. "Be holy, for I, the LORD, your God, am holy" (Lv. 19:2). In this sense, the Ten Commandments also have a universal significance, transcending the social conditions of a desert people. They relate God's salvific purpose as it corresponds to the constitutive structure of human nature and thus are valid for all times and peoples.

The Prophets. As the centuries wore on, the covenant, which had bound the people by ties of love and loyalty to Yahweh, far from acting as a restraining influence on them, actually became the occasion for moral perversion. God's steadfast love and faithfulness to his promises were taken for granted, seen as guaranteeing in themselves protection from harm and assurance of national glory. "The moral stipulations that were the necessary part of their response to the covenant were forgotten, and in their place there was substituted a ritual worship which was vitiated by formalism."[13] Scripture, indeed, records how the sons of Eli debased the priestly office and acted contemptuously with the people. We read, too, of Samuel's sons, whom he appointed judges like himself, of how they "did not follow his example but sought illicit gain and accepted bribes, perverting justice" (1 Sam. 8:3).

In the midst of this spirit of social irresponsibility and moral degeneration, when pagan elements and open idolatry infiltrated the people's worship, the prophets appeared to remind them of their covenant commitment and ancient ideals. Convinced of the unity of history, a unity determined by God's overriding plan, the prophets looked to a future that shared the absolute certainty of the past. From this perspective they sought to arouse the people's hardened hearts with a sense of hope and turn them to God once more.[14]

The prophets insist on the sincerity of religious practice being proved by right conduct (see Amos 5:21-24). They plead for justice and active social responsibility (see Is. 1:15-17; 58:6-7; Mic. 6:6-11; Jer. 7:8-10). The later prophets, Jeremiah and Ezekiel, will promote the interiorization of the law that will change the very heart of a person and effect a total intimacy with God. There will, then, be no need for external instruction or constraint. "The days are coming, says the LORD, when I will make a new covenant with the house of Israel and the house of Judah. . . . I will place my law within them, and write it upon their hearts; I will be their God, and they shall be my people. No longer will they have need to teach their friends and kinsmen to know the LORD. All, from the least to the greatest, shall know me" (Jer. 31:33-34; see also Ezk. 36:26-27).

Wisdom Literature. After the Babylonian captivity, in the post-exilic period, Israel's scribes carried on an international correspondence with the intellectual elite at the court circles of neighboring nations.[15] This phenomenon gave rise to a body of literature that was more philosophical than theological. Reference to the great events and heroes of salvation history is absent. The wisdom writings are more concerned with the individual person than with the community of faith and religious institutions. They offer maxims and insights based on the reasonableness of human nature and are thus free from any trace of Hebrew particularism.

The wisdom writers did not begin with revelation to explain the meaning of human existence. Instead, the human capacity for intelligence, discipline and moral behavior became the springboard for their discussions. Placed within the context of Israel's faith, their writings mediated the Law and the prophets to the common folk in their daily lives. They taught the young how to avoid greed, selfishness and opportunities, and thus succeed in life. They reflected upon the serious questions about the meaning of life, suffering and death. Wisdom itself was personified as the source of life and divine nourishment. She was a special gift of Yahweh. By accepting her guidance

30

and instruction Israel shared in God's own life. "In this way natural insights contribute to deepen the awareness and understanding of Yahweh's plan of salvation and His will for the community."[16]

The religious life — that is, the spiritual-moral life, of the Old Testament period — revolved around an understanding of God's self-gift and call through his word in creation and in his intervention in salvation history (revelation) and the people's affirmative, obedient response (faith). This call and response established a graced covenant, a personal relationship of love and fidelity between God and his people. The Law or Torah, summarized in the Ten Commandments, was God's gift to Israel. It showed the people, plunged into darkness by Adam's sin, how to walk according to God's ways and keep his covenant. As time wore on, Israel's heart grew cold. The people turned to other gods, giving only lip-service to Yahweh through religious formalism. God sent the prophets to call them back to their covenantal relationship. Later, Israel's sages drew upon the natural insights of neighboring nations, and within the context of faith these wisdom writers provided prudent and practical advice to direct an individual's behavior. Thus the Old Testament period came to a close demonstrating the congruency and combined effectiveness of divine Revelation and human reason in shepherding human concerns.

The New Testament

The writings of the New Testament record the normative faith experience of the early Christian Church. "From his fullness we have all received, grace in place of grace, because while the law was given through Moses, grace and truth came through Jesus Christ. No one has ever seen God. The only Son, God, who is at the Father's side, has revealed him" (Jn. 1:16-18). Jesus Christ, the Son of David and the Son of God, is himself the new covenant. The Word of God-made-flesh, he incarnates the perfect divine-human relationship. Adam's "no" is reversed by Jesus' perfect "yes" to the will of the Father (see Heb. 10:9-10).

The Teaching of Jesus. By his words and deeds, Jesus fully reveals the will of God the Father. He makes known God's plan for our salvation; he unveils the "original grace" that was at work in the world even before Adam's sin. "For it is in him that it pleased the Father to restore all things (cf. Eph. 1:4-5 and 10). To carry out the will of the Father Christ inaugurated

31

the kingdom of heaven on earth and revealed to us his mystery; by his obedience he brought about our redemption" (LG 3).

1. Jesus began his public ministry proclaiming, "This is the time of fulfillment. The kingdom of God is at hand. Repent, and believe in the gospel" (Mk. 1:15). The "**kingdom of God**," or "the kingdom of heaven," is the central image of Jesus' teaching. He announced a new intervention of God, like his intervening in Egypt to deliver the ancient Israelites from slavery. This Good News is both a gift and a call, demanding here and now a response of faith.

The kingdom is the dynamism of God's love erupting in time. It is a nonterritorial, eschatological reality that is already here in Jesus and yet not fully accomplished. The kingdom is God's plan, his dream, his vision for the human race, which through his Word and Spirit he is already working to bring about. "Go and tell John what you hear and see: the blind regain their sight, the lame walk, lepers are cleansed, the deaf hear, the dead are raised, and the poor have the good news proclaimed to them" (Mt. 11:4-5). The forces of sin and evil may play havoc with God's plan, they can delay it, but they can never prevent it from coming to fruition. Jesus' victory over sin and death clearly demonstrates this fact.

2. Proclaiming the kingdom of God, Jesus calls those who hear him to reform their lives. He announces the Good News of repentance for the forgiveness of sins. Indeed, God's readiness to forgive is limited only by this one condition, repentance.[17] This **call to conversion** or **repentance** (*metanoia*, in Greek) is the key that opens the door of the kingdom of God. It is the grace or gift which allows us to look at the world through God's eyes rather than through our own narrow and limited vision.

Sin has blinded us to God's plan, his will for us. We can no longer clearly see his presence and creative action among us. We have hardened our hearts with selfishness and closed our ears to his call, but Jesus is the eternal Word-made-flesh empowering us to return to the Father. He is the true Light that shines in the darkness of our sin and its confusion. He is the one who shows us the way. Through conversion, the radical transformation of our heart, mind and will, we keep the divine law and change our lives to conform to God's will, his plan; we enter his kingdom (see Mt. 5:20; 7:21; 18:3, 21:31; 22:12; 23:13; Mk. 9:47; Jn. 3:5).[18] Faith is our positive response, our acceptance, of the gift-call of conversion.

3. For those who accept Jesus' invitation, he is the new Moses. Just as Moses brought the old law from Mount Sinai, so in Matthew's **Sermon on the Mount** Jesus proclaims the new law. The Sermon (Mt. 5-7) serves as a "handbook for disciples," detailing the moral implications for all those who answer Jesus' call to follow him personally. Here, "he re-lays anew the foundations of ethics as such, by making the moral value of an act depend only on inner disposition of heart."[19] The interiorization of the Law foretold by the prophets (see Jer. 31:31-34; Ezk. 36:26-27) arrives at its fulfillment. Yet, Jesus in no way despised external action. In the final parable of the Sermon, about the house built on rock, he calls the disciples to put his words into action (Mt. 7:24-27).

The Beatitudes (Mt. 5:3-12) comprise the prologue to the Sermon. They describe the basic attitudes and dispositions that should characterize the life of a disciple who in following Christ "wills to make himself or herself an act of love and who will share in the Passion of Christ to deliver humankind from its suffering, its alienation and sin. . . . They are blessings for the disciples who will fulfill the words of the Covenant by being identified with Christ."[20] The Lord's Prayer (Mt. 6:9-13) constitutes the theological center, the heart, the "outline" of the Sermon. It expresses the Fatherhood of God as a gift and sonship as a promise — a gift and promise that oblige a brotherhood of love toward all (see Mt. 5:43-48).[21]

In the Sermon on the Mount, Matthew's message is that a new level of existence is given by God in Jesus. As children of the Father we can love as God loves his children. This gift, indeed, makes it possible for us to "be perfect, just as your heavenly Father is perfect" (Mt. 5:48). Thus the radical demands of the Sermon are intended to throw light on the primordial will of God, unrestrained by the conditions and difficult circumstances of this world, regardless of human weakness and hardness of heart.[22] In view of the Christ-event we now live in a new age; the eschatological clock has struck. Because Jesus came, died and rose, things are now possible which would have been impossible before. Raised to a new kind of divine level, we dare pray and strive, as Jesus taught us, that the will of our Father be done.[23]

4. All of Jesus' moral teaching is centered on the **Great Commandment of love** of God and one's neighbor (Mk. 12:28-34; Mt. 22:34-40; Lk. 10:25-28). Love is the form and essence of Christian perfection. "This Christian perfection in love is different in kind from the Greek ideal of perfection. Its aim is not the attainment of a harmonious personality, morally

faultless, self-contained, but of 'holiness,' as God is holy (cf. Lev. 19:2; 1 Pet. 1:16)."[24] Such holiness involves a love that completely surrenders the individual ego and imitates God's incomprehensible love for everyone, including sinners. Jesus, indeed, gives himself as a model of fraternal love (Jn. 13:34 15:12) by laying down his life for our sake (Jn. 15:13; Mk. 10:45).

The double commandment of love receives a threefold distinctive note in Jesus' teaching: "He revealed the indissoluble interior bond between these two commandments; he showed clearly that the whole law could be reduced to this and only this chief and double commandment, and he reinterpreted 'neighbourly love' as 'love of the nearest person,' that is he interpreted it in an absolutely universal sense."[25] Love of God, as Jesus understood it, means fulfilling in faith and obedience all that God requires for entering into his kingdom. It involves prayer, religious acts properly so called, and forgiveness of one another.

Authentic love of God is found in loving concern for others. In the parable of the Last Judgment (Mt. 25:31-46) Jesus shows us the concrete implications of the Great Commandment. The traditional "corporal works of mercy" find their origin here. This parable, in a certain sense, provides us with the questions we will be asked on life's final exam. It gives us the "bottom line" of Christian existence. Christian love is a direction of attitude and concern which has to do with our will, rather than with our emotions or feelings. It is totally related to who God is and how God deals with us. Since God continues to look out for our welfare, the least we can do is look out for the welfare of others, whether we feel a natural affinity toward them or not. Most interesting to note, too, is the fact that in this parable those condemned for not doing these loving deeds are not even aware they never did them. Lack of sensitivity to the needs of others is just as serious a violation of the Great Commandment as is cold-hearted selfishness.

5. Following Christ requires on our part a willingness to imitate him. Throughout the gospels Jesus employs parables, metaphors and images to illustrate the **demands of discipleship**. He encourages people to leave home, take up their cross and follow him (see Mk. 8:34-35). While free of the more strenuous asceticism of John the Baptist, Jesus warns of the dangers of wealth (Mt. 6:19-21, 24; Lk. 16:9). He esteems marriage as an arrangement of creation (Mt. 19:3-9), and yet teaches celibacy for the sake of the kingdom of heaven (Mt. 19:12). He speaks reservedly of fasting as a legal achievement (Mt. 16:6; Lk. 18:24), but he himself fasted for forty days before beginning

his mission (Mt. 4:2). Jesus tells his listeners that they must "Strive [in Greek, *agonizomai* = to compete strenuously, to struggle] to enter through the narrow gate, for many, I tell you, will attempt to enter but will not be strong enough" (Lk. 13:24).

The disciple, indeed, must leave everyone and everything behind (Lk 5:11; 9:58; 14:26; Mk. 2:14), and proclaim the Kingdom of God (Lk. 9:59-60). This expectation is portrayed also in the parables of the pearl and the hidden treasure in the field (Mt. 13:44-46). Other sayings of Jesus also make rigid demands. No matter what the circumstances, obedience to God is even more important than the members of one's body. A disciple must be willing to cast away even a hand, foot and eye if they become an enticement and occasion of sin (Mt. 5:29ff.; 18:8f.; Mk. 9:43-48).[26] Identification of the disciple with the suffering of the Master is a necessity that will lead to participation in his triumph (Lk. 22:28-30). In the end, "This is how all will know that you are my disciples, if you have love for one another" (Jn. 13:35).

The Church in the New Testament. In the light of the faith experience of the primitive Christian Church the writers of the New Testament recorded for future generations the conduct and words of Jesus. In addition, they preserved for us the apostolic teaching and tradition, which sustained by the Spirit of the risen Lord (2 Cor. 3:1-18) is itself normative in its formulation of spiritual and ethical precepts. The principal elements of this tradition laid the foundations for their understanding of the new Christian "way."

1. The Pentecost event (see Acts 2) gave birth to a new "way" (Acts 9:2; 18:25; 19:9, 23; 22:4; 24:14, 22) of life under the **influence of the Holy Spirit**. Through faith and baptism, the Holy Spirit, the creative and unifying power of God's love, is given to the baptized in order to overcome the corrupting influence of the "flesh," that is, human nature inclined toward sin. Jesus disclosed to Nicodemus that the rebirth in water and Spirit makes entry into the Kingdom of God possible: "What is born of flesh is flesh and what is born of spirit is spirit. Do not be amazed that I told you, 'You must be born from above' " (Jn. 3:6-7). Through the Spirit the believer is created anew; he or she becomes a whole new creation. Christian life thus does not primarily consist of obedience to rules, but is a living out of the life of the new creature in Christ's Spirit. The moral life now flows from the spiritual ontology of the new creature.

The same Holy Spirit is recognized as the real guide of the community of faith (Jn. 14:26), as the "Spirit of truth" (Jn. 14:17; 15:26; 16:13; 1 Jn. 4:6), who will teach the disciples and be their Advocate, their comforter and enlightener. With the gift of the Spirit the moral teaching and commands of Jesus become gospel, truly Good News, because they no longer work unto sin and judgment as in the Old Testament, but instead impart the capability of fulfilling what is demanded.[27]

In his epistles St. Paul provides us with a well-developed theology pertaining to the Holy Spirit's power within the lives of the faithful. Through the Spirit we become "spiritual persons" (1 Cor. 2:15); we receive the power to develop our inner selves (Eph. 3:7), and we become children of God (Rom. 8:14). The Spirit is the new "law" (Rom. 8:2); showing us the "way" to live (Gal. 5:18f.). Christian existence, the spiritual-moral life, is ultimately the way of love and service (Rom. 13:8-10; Gal. 5:14; 6:2), and the Spirit is the unifying principle of the Christian community, which is the Body of Christ (1 Cor. 12:12-13). This gift of the Spirit, however, remains only a warrant or pledge (2 Cor. 1:22) within the baptized. It inaugurates the transformation of the Christian which is in actuality a lifelong process.

2. In the power of the Holy Spirit the first Christians realized they **shared a communion of life** (*koinonia*, in Greek) with the risen Lord and with one another. Through faith and baptism all are "one in Christ Jesus" (Gal. 3:28). As in the Old Testament, God entered into a covenant with his "chosen people," so the primitive Church saw itself as the new Israel (Gal. 6:16), the people of the new covenant. For them Christian existence was a way and style of life based upon a common sharing of the riches of the "new life" of Christ. "They devoted themselves to the teaching of the apostles and to the communal life, to the breaking of bread and to the prayers. Awe came upon everyone.... All who believed were together and had all things in common" (Acts 2:42-44). Theirs was an ethics of *koinonia*, or a communal ethics. Its primary concern was relationships, both vertical and horizontal, that is, with God and with one another.

3. Having received the pledge of the Spirit at baptism and having been incorporated into the Body of Christ, the believer must grow or mature in Christ by continuing to share his paschal mystery. Such a living out of our baptismal commitment gives birth to the **dying/rising ethics** of St. Paul. For him, everything a Christian is and does derives its being, its power and its significance from the death and resurrection of Jesus Christ.[28] "We were

indeed buried with him through baptism into death, so that, just as Christ was raised from the dead by the glory of the Father, we too might live in newness of life'' (Rom. 6:4). In Johannine theology as well, Jesus' example of self-emptying service (see Jn. 13:15) associated with his paschal mystery gives rise to his commandment that we love one another as he has loved us (13:14) by laying down his life for us (15:13).

4. The Church in apostolic times, reflecting upon the meaning of Christ's death and resurrection, arrived at a **deeper understanding of the Great Commandment**. For St. Paul, charity is the bond of perfection (Col. 3:14), and love of neighbor fulfills the whole law (Rom. 13:8; Gal. 5:14). In his ''hymn to charity'' (1 Cor. 12:31-14:1) love is the better way, the greatest charism; it is the sovereign among the theological virtues. According to St. John effective fraternal love is the criterion of true discipleship (Jn. 13:35; 1 Jn. 2:10-11). One proves one's love by keeping the commandments and thereby enters into the very mystery or inner life of the Trinity (Jn. 14:15-24; 17:23-26; 1 Jn. 3:23-24). This exercise of the divine gift of charity implies that one is begotten by God and lives in communion with him who is love (1 Jn. 4:7-12).[29]

5. In early preaching, the final coming of Christ in glory was used to stimulate the faithful to holiness of life. This **eschatological perspective** generated a twofold developmental pressure within Christian existence. ''From above, the power of the dawning kingdom with the reappearance of Christ presses in upon the world of time. And from within there is the pressure of the spiritual power of Christ, which is in the Christian, and in which Christ wants to take shape.''[30] Thus, on one hand, the person ''in Christ'' is already a ''new creation'' (2 Cor. 5:17) and his or her actions are expected to flow from this reality (*agere sequitur esse*). ''If we live in the Spirit, let us also follow the Spirit'' (Gal. 5:25). Still, on the other hand, ''we ourselves, who have the firstfruits of the Spirit, ... groan within ourselves as we wait for adoption, the redemption of our bodies'' (Rom. 8:23; see also 2 Cor. 5:2). This deliberate tension is again seen in the fact that we are already delivered from the bondage of sin and death by the free gift of God (Rom. 5:12-17), but nevertheless, we must work out our salvation in fear and trembling (Phil. 2:12).[31]

The early Church's sense of the impending catastrophic end made everything in this world provisional (1 Cor. 7:20, 31). The events of the last days are not only doctrines to be recited and professed at the end of the Creed, but truths that impose obligations. The Christian's pilgrim status serves as "a perpetual summons to vigilance and sobriety, to responsible action in the world, to combat and struggle against the destructive powers of evil and to living hope and joyful confidence."[32] There is an overwhelming amount of material in Paul's letters foretelling a strict testing by the final judge and requital for one's acts (see 2 Cor. 5:10; Rom. 14:10). Yet, in the end, a sure and lively hope in the final fulfillment of God's plan, his kingdom, must lead Christians to live in joy and peace.

The New Testament portrait of Christian existence flows from the teachings of Jesus as seen in the light of the apostolic tradition of the primitive Church. This tradition has preserved for us Jesus' proclamation of the Kingdom of God, his call to conversion and discipleship, and all that this entails. The faith experience of the early Church gave witness to Christ's victory over sin and death in his paschal mystery. Through baptism the believer shares in Christ's new life and becomes a member of his Body, the Church. Gathered therein, the faithful, having received the pledge of the Spirit, continues to "put away . . . the old self" and "put on the new self, created in God's way" (Eph. 4:22, 24). This comes about through the keeping of Christ's new commandment to "love one another . . . as I have loved you" (Jn. 13:34), through which "all will know that you are my disciples" (13:35).

For the Christian there exists a constant tension between what has already been accomplished (namely, the deontological aspect of being a "new creation" and a member of the Body of Christ) and what still awaits fulfillment (that is, the teleological or eschatological aspect of the coming judgment with its reward or punishment).[33] The New Testament thus presents us with different types of biblical morality: the eschatological type of moral law developed especially in the Synoptic gospels; the categorical type found especially in Paul; and the more transcendental type of moral law common to the writings of John. In reality all three types are complementary. They are equally inspired and part of the canon of Scripture. "We cannot favor one to the detriment of the others: this would be tantamount to setting up one's own canon within the single canon of the Church."[34]

Biblical morality, furthermore, is not unrelated to natural and philosophical ethics. St. Paul accepted the then current concept of the natural law (see Rom. 2:14-15) and taught that reason is able to recognize God's divinity (Rom. 1:18-25). Nevertheless, reason has become perverted and given way to foolishness by failing to recognize God's glory and the moral law. People became idolators (Rom. 1:23), and all, Jews and Gentiles alike, stand subservient to sin (Rom. 3:9-20).[35] Biblical morality, however, because it is guaranteed by Revelation remains the faithful and abiding mirror of human morality, correcting where necessary the indications that come from reason.[36]

Fidelity to the fundamental kerygma provides the Christian theologian with the ultimate criterion for moral action. "When Paul tells us that a particular way of acting runs counter to the fundamental kerygma, that a particular behavior of the baptized person — fornication, for instance — is incompatible with one's union with Christ, that those who act in this manner are excluded from the heavenly kingdom, then it seems that we are dealing with rules that are still valid today."[37] Christianity is primarily a proclamation of God's action and grace reversing our sinfulness and weakness. Christian existence, our spiritual-moral life, is a matter of our active cooperation with God's will, his plan to restore us to "original grace" and bring about a whole "new creation" by transforming us in Christ, the Second Adam, into a new humanity. Today, our continuing search for God's will in the concrete circumstances of everyday life demands fidelity to God's word made known to us through divine Revelation and human reason.

Notes

1. Heinz Schürmann, Joseph Cardinal Ratzinger, and Hans Urs von Balthasar, *Principles of Christian Morality* (San Francisco: Ignatius Press, 1986), p. 89.

2. See Richard J. Mouw, "Commands for Grown-Ups," *Readings in Moral Theology No. 4: The Use of Scripture in Moral Theology*, eds. Charles E. Curran and Richard A. McCormick, S.J. (New York/Ramsey: Paulist Press, 1984), pp. 67, 68 and 77.

3. See Raymond E. Brown, *Biblical Exegesis & Church Doctrine* (New York/Mahwah, N.J.: Paulist Press, 1985), p. 30.

4. *Christian Biblical Ethics. From Biblical Revelation to Contemporary Christian Praxis: Method and Content*, written and ed. by Robert J. Daly, S.J., with J.A. Fischer, C.M., T.J. Keegan, O.P., and A.J. Tambasco, et al., in consultation with the CBA Task Force (New York: Paulist, 1984), p. 13 with reference to Amos Wilder, *New Testament Faith for Today* (London: SCM, 1956), pp. 59-77.

5. C.H. Dodd, *The Parables of the Kingdom* (New York: Charles Scribner's, 1961), p.5 cited in *Christian Biblical Ethics*, p. 223.

6. *Christian Biblical Ethics*, p. 54.

7. Ibid., p. 14.

8. See Raymond E. Brown, *The Critical Meaning of the Bible* (New York/Ramsey, N.J.: Paulist, 1981), pp. 34-35.

9. Häring, *Free and Faithful in Christ*, vol. 1, p. 9.

10. Ratzinger, Schürmann and von Balthasar, op. cit., p. 90.

11. Lobo, *Guide to Christian Living*, p.24.

12. Ibid., p. 27.

13. Eugene H. Maly, *Prophets of Salvation* (New York: Herder and Herder, 1967), p. 25.

14. See ibid., pp. 20-24.

15. See John F.X. Sheehan, S.J., *The Threshing Floor: An Interpretation of the Old Testament* (New York/Paramus, N.J./Toronto: Paulist Press, 1972), pp. 179-181.

16. Lobo, op. cit., p. 40.

17. See Rudolph Schnackenburg, *The Moral Teaching of the New Testament* (New York: Herder and Herder, 1965), p. 27.

18. See ibid., p. 20.

19. Ibid., p. 63.

20. Jean-Marie Cardinal Lustiger, *Dare To Believe: Addresses, Sermons, Interviews (1981-1984)* (New York: Crossroad, 1986), p. 104.

21. See Frederick E. Schuele, "Living Up To Matthew's Sermon on the Mount: An Approach," in *Christian Biblical Ethics*, pp. 205-206.

22. See Schnackenburg, op. cit., p. 80.

23. See Schuele, op. cit., p. 207.

24. Schnackenburg. op. cit., p. 108.

25. Ibid., p. 95.

26. See Karl Hermann Schelkle, *Theology of the New Testament* (Collegeville, Minnesota: The Liturgical Press, 1973), vol. 3: "Morality," pp. 162-166.

27. Ibid., p. 39.

28. See Terence J. Keegan, O.P., "Paul's Dying/Rising Ethics in 1 Corinthians," in *Christian Biblical Ethics*, p. 220ff. Also see, Ratzinger, Schürmann, von Balthasar, op. cit., pp. 20-23.

29. Lobo, op. cit., pp. 56-58.

30. Schelkle, op. cit., p. 50.

31. See Keegan, op. cit., pp. 228-230.

32. Schnackenburg, op. cit., p. 195.

33. See Ratzinger, Schürmann, von Balthasar, op. cit., p. 68 with footnote no. 16.

34. Edouard Hamel, "Scripture, The Soul of Moral Theology?" in *Readings in Moral Theology No. 4*, p. 119.

35. See Schelkle, op. cit., p. 26.

36. See Hamel, op. cit., p. 110.

37. Ibid., 124.

Chapter 2

Historical Perspectives

". . . the history of the past ends in the present; and the present is our scene of trial; and to behave ourselves towards its various phenomena duly and religiously, we must understand them; and to understand them, we must have recourse to those past events which led to them. Thus the present is a text, and the past its interpretation." — John Henry Newman[1]

Only those who stand upon the shoulders of preceding generations are able to get a clear lay of the land and peer into the distant horizon. To study history is to remember both victory and defeat. The story of Christianity begins with the faith experience of the risen Lord, Jesus Christ's victorious triumph over the forces of sin and death. This story unfolds as the community of his followers, the Church, struggles through the centuries to remain faithful to Jesus' call to share his new life. This struggle has known both success and failure, saints and sinners. At times, political, economic and social factors beyond the Church's control have given shape to the Christian religious, spiritual and moral life. They influenced the evolution of ecclesiastical institutions, the development of doctrine, and the relationship of the Church with the secular world.

The study of history allows us to learn from both successes and failures. It relieves us of the burden of having to constantly reinvent the wheel, while helping us better understand our present situation. A certain hubris, however, seems to be adrift in contemporary American society. We have naturally assumed that since we are the latest generation of the human race, living in the most scientifically and technologically advanced society in the world, we thereby must be the most improved, the best and the brightest. History, therefore, has nothing to teach us. Those who have lived before us are looked upon as being more primitive, less knowledgeable and less wise.[2] Yet, Jesus offers praise to his Father "for although you have hidden these things from the wise and the learned you have revealed them to the childlike .... No one knows ... who the Father is except the Son and anyone to whom the Son wishes to reveal him'' (Lk. 10:21-22). The Old Testament, too, witnesses to the fact that succeeding generations after Moses, instead of growing wiser, became more and more stiff-necked and stubborn of heart.

Our nearly two-thousand-year journey through Christian history will not excite the trivia buff. This chapter, rather, will divide that history into four major periods, each of which exhibits an important change of focus in understanding how one should live the Christian life. Since incarnation is really the primary law of Christian revelation, we want to see how each of these periods sought to enflesh the gospel in the differing social, economic and cultural environment of their particular time. From this historical survey we hope to better understand the present state and task of the theological renewal already underway within the Catholic Church relating to the spiritual and moral life.

The Age of the Fathers (ca. A.D. 100 to 700)

The primitive Church had basically no ecclesiastical structure. The gospels had not yet achieved their final written form. There were no formally defined doctrines, no distinction between clergy and laity, no church buildings. The first followers of Jesus gathered in the houses of friends to celebrate the Lord's Supper. They were convinced that the end of the world and the Lord's coming in glory were just around the corner. But as the decades passed, they began to realize that the world was showing no signs of coming to an end and that the Church might continue to exist for generations, perhaps even centuries.

Concerns over safeguarding the orthodoxy of the faith arose, which led to the development of the concept of apostolic succession. With all the apostles now dead it was considered important for Church officials to be able to trace an unbroken link between themselves and the apostles. Thus, in the immediate post-apostolic period the bishop emerged as the elder with the primary responsibility of proclaiming and defending the authentic message of Jesus in the local Church. From the preaching and teachings of these early bishops, as well as of some priests and articulate laypersons, grew a huge body of sound theology, known as patristic literature or the writings of the Fathers of the Church.

Antiquity, holiness of life, orthodox teaching and ecclesiastical approval are the four criteria traditionally employed to determine who is listed among the Fathers of the Church. They include writers down to Gregory the Great

(+604) or Isidore of Seville (+636) in the West, and John Damascene (+749) in the East. Their proximity to the New Testament era allows them to give us an authentic interpretation of apostolic faith and its subsequent adaptation to changing historical and cultural circumstances.

Fundamental Elements. Despite their geographical spread and reaching across several centuries, a number of fundamental elements characterize the patristic writings. They make no real distinction between doctrine and morals. Christians are expected to put into practice the faith they profess. Christian living involves appropriating Jesus' paschal mystery to one's daily life. The Fathers make constant reference to sacred Scripture as they portray Christianity as a new "way" of life centered upon belief in the risen Lord and the celebration of the Eucharist. The unity of the faithful in creed, code and cult was of utmost importance since it manifested the Church's special ethos as God's unique Kingdom of the Last Days. Moral failures were seen primarily as failures to maintain the "concord and harmony" of the community. The Fathers of the Church, in other words, continued to keep alive the rich and deep spiritual vision of the apostolic era.

Moral Teaching and Concerns. The Church Fathers, the same as sacred Scripture, do not provide a systematic presentation of Christian morality. Their concerns were immediate and practical, such as, how does one live as a Christian in the midst of a pagan society and culture. After the Constantinian embrace of the Church in the fourth century, new practical questions would arise concerning the pursuit of spiritual perfection and the relationship of Church and state among others.

1. The writings from the early **post-apostolic period** are mainly homiletic and epistolary treatises offering moral catechesis and instruction. The earliest non-biblical document is the *Didache*, or "Teaching of the Twelve Apostles" discovered at Constantinople in 1873. Although its date of composition is unknown, it is clearly a late-first-century work. Based on the sayings of Jesus it offers a compendium of moral teaching for the Christian convert.

Two ways there are, one of life and one of death, and there is a great difference between the two ways. 1.2. The way of life is this: First, love the god who made you; then, love your neighbor as

44

yourself. Do not do to another what you do not wish to be done to you . . . — *Didache* 1,2.[3]

The *Didache* warns against idolatrous practices, superstition and fornication, while encouraging the Christian to provide for the needy and share everything with his brother.

"The Letter of the Pseudo-Barnabas," considered by some early Christians to be part of the inspired word of God, was attributed to the disciple, Barnabas, but its author is actually unknown. It accents the need of meditative prayer and participation in the Christian community in order to grow in the spiritual and moral life.

Associate with those who fear the Lord, with those who meditate on the precise sense of the words they have heard, with those who have the Lord's commandments on their lips and observe them, with those who realize that meditation is the labor of joy and therefore ruminate on the Word of the Lord. — "Letter of Barnabas" 10[4]

For this author we were "created all over again" and made the "temple of God" through the forgiveness of sins and believing in the Name. He also sets forth the particulars of his ethical teaching by appealing to the image of the Two Ways, a methodological device probably taken from the Qumran community.

"The Letter of Clement of Rome," written about A.D. 97 to the Church of Corinth, is primarily a moral exhortation calling for peace and unity after a rebellion by the younger members of the Corinthian Church. He presents penance and conversion as the virtues that will lead to peace and order. In his seven letters, Ignatius of Antioch (ca. 108-117) develops the Pauline and Johannine teaching of life (*zoe* vs. *bios*, in Greek) in and with Christ which brings about a complete transformation of mentality and leads to a share in divine existence guaranteeing immortality. For him, union in the love of God and the imitation of Christ constitutes the Christian community. Only those who accept Christ in the person of his Church with its teaching and commandments may receive "the bread of God." For Ignatius, the Eucharist is the source and center of Christian life. Every Christian, furthermore, has an obligation to spread the gospel by his or her prayer and conduct.

2. In the second half of the second century, the **Greek Apologists** defended the Church against the charges of immorality leveled by the

educated classes and civil rulers in pagan society. Justin Martyr (+165) was a philosopher and convert from paganism who founded a school of Christian philosophy in Rome. Against a background of pagan vices he defends the ideal of Christian virtue.

> And those not living thus as he [Jesus] taught, should not be considered Christians; nor should those who profess the doctrines of Christ only with their tongue; for he said that not they who confess him, but they who do his works will be saved ... We would even desire that they who say they are Christians but do not live in accordance with this doctrine should be punished by you. — "First Apology" 16[5]

St. Irenaeus of Lyons (+ca. 200) came from Asia Minor and was a disciple of Polycarp of Smyrna. He elaborated a Christian anthropology that has its roots in Pauline theology. The perfection of human nature consists of the cultivation of the image of God within. Through baptism, the new Adam is substituted for the old.

3. The third-century **African Fathers** commented on the burning issues posed by living in a pagan society and culture: pagan worship, the fashioning of idols by Christian artisans, the lewd theater, fashions, cruel circuses, military service, flight from persecution, virginity and so forth. Tertullian (+220), born in Carthage the son of a Roman centurion, was a lawyer and the first of the Fathers to write in Latin. His theology is filled with legal terms such as, debt, guilt, satisfaction and compensation. The gospel is our law, repromulgating and perfecting the precepts of the natural law. Sin consists in breaking the law. Rebelling against the moral mediocrity of Catholics, Tertullian would defect to the more rigoristic Montanists in his later years.

Cyprian of Carthage (+258) was a famous rhetorician who, two years after his conversion to Christianity, was chosen Bishop of Carthage. A student of Scripture and the writings of Tertullian, he found himself in the middle of Novatian's rigorous schism. Novatian was a Roman priest who set himself up against the Bishop of Rome, Cornelius, over the question of readmitting the lapsed. Cyprian maintained that only the bishops legitimately ordained in succession from the apostles have the power to forgive sins, to confer the Holy Spirit by imposing hands, and to sanctify the Church. Cyprian's was a social view of the Church. He insisted: "Thus when someone prays, it is not for the self alone. For we do not say 'My father who is in heaven,' nor 'Give me today my daily bread'. . . . Our prayer is public and communal'' (''On the Lord's Prayer''8).[6] The works of these first two Latin Fathers would give a decidedly legal and institutional, rather than mystical bent to the theology of the Western Church.

4. **Clement of Alexandria** (+214) is the first of the great Greek or **Eastern Fathers**. A philosopher and Christian convert, he was a teacher in the Alexandrian School which was founded as a preparation for martyrdom as well as baptism. He integrates what is best in Greek philosophy with the Christian moral ideal, justifying speculative reason as essential to the proper understanding of faith. For him Christ is the ''pedagogue'' sent to correct our evil tendencies brought on by our intemperate desire to achieve knowledge and experience, obscuring the image of God in which we are created. Total self-mastery is the ideal that motivates the Christian art of living. Clement refers to ''deification'' as the supreme state in which we come to know God by loving as he loves. He defends marriage as a way of salvation against Gnostic hostility toward the married state.

Origen (+254), Clement's successor as the Alexandrian theologian, taught the vocation of all Christians to holiness and may be considered the creator of spiritual theology. Against the philosophical currents of his day which gave a cyclic explanation of human existence, Origen insisted uncompromisingly on the existence of human free will. While he believed that human beings were made in the ''image'' of God in their original condition, the perfection of God's ''likeness'' in us only comes about in the end through our striving to imitate God. He was eventually condemned as heretical for his optimistic view that even devils might be converted and all evil annihilated at the end of time.

In the fourth century, Cyril of Jerusalem (+386) wrote the ''Mystagogical Catechesis'' as an instruction for the newly baptized.[7] In keeping with the practice of the Eastern Church it provided moral instruction derived principally from the liturgical texts. The moral life clearly appears as flowing from the baptismal life in Christ. John Chrysostom (+407) is the most renowned of the Greek Fathers as a preacher and moralist. Appointed Patriarch of Constantinople, he held up the ideal of evangelical perfection as within the reach of all Christians — for the laity as well as for monks, for the clergy and virgins. He insisted that the practice of prayer and contemplation, beginning with meditation on sacred Scripture, was within the reach of all. He maintained that in the Sermon on the Mount Christ was reinforcing the

47

Ten Commandments by attacking the roots of evildoing, whereas Moses merely condemned external sins.

A clear social consciousness is evident in John Chrysostom's works. For him the egotistical search for salvation was impossible.

> Many imagine that it suffices for their virtue to assure their own salvation; and that in regulating their lives honestly, they lack nothing. This is an error, as the parable of the talents shows. . . Do not think it is enough to work for your own welfare, for thus you can run to ruin.[8]

Furthermore, Christians must aid the poor and needy because Christ is identified with them. "Do you really wish to pay homage to Christ's body? Then do not neglect him when he is naked. At the same time that you honor him here with hangings made of silk, do not ignore him outside when he perishes from cold and nakedness" ("On Matthew: Homily," 48.9).[9]

5. In the last decade of the fourth century, Ambrose and Augustine, considered among the great Latin or **Western Fathers**, vigorously attack the excessive accumulation of private property in the hands of the rich. In the midst of worsening social and economic conditions in the Empire, they denounced the love of money, the luxurious lifestyle of the rich and the lack of concern for the poor.[10] Ambrose of Milan (+397) received a legal education and was an imperial official when he was chosen as Bishop of Milan by public acclamation in 373. The will of God as elucidated in the Scriptures provides the foundation of his moral teaching. At the same time he accepts the classic Stoic pattern of upright living and discusses the Christian life under the four classic virtues of prudence, justice, fortitude and temperance. Laying down the various duties for his priests in his *De officiis ministrorum*, he provides the first case-approach to moral theology.

Augustine of Hippo (+430), baptized by Ambrose, is the greatest of the Latin Fathers and one of the greatest theologians of all time. After a youth spent in sensual indulgence and a period of intellectual wandering, he became a Christian and later Bishop of Hippo in northern Africa. His *City of God* and *Confessions* remain Christian classics. In his homilies, tracts and letters he elaborated on subjects like marriage, virginity, truth and the theological virtues. He penetrated doctrinal truths that form the basis for Christian morality — grace and freedom, divine love and concupiscence, the Kingdom of God and the kingdom of Satan, original sin and the restoration of grace, faith and works, natural law and revealed law.

Much of the knowledge uncovered by modern depth psychology was anticipated by Augustine. In the trinity of mind, love and knowledge he saw imprinted in human nature the image of the triune God. He stressed the importance of "motive" and "discerning the conflicting spirits" in moral life. Freedom of will does not exclude determination through factors that may condition, but in no sense dictate, the final decision of the will. Augustine acknowledges the effects of temperament, experience, education and ignorance. His own youthful experiences and Manichaean background left a great deal of ambiguity in his treatment of sexual ethics. Marital relations even for the sake of procreation, could hardly ever be indulged in without passion causing at least venial sin.

Towards Mystical Communion. The word "spirituality" is not common in patristic literature. Looking forward to the final eschatological fulfillment, sharing in the fullness of Divine Life with the glorified Christ is, however, viewed as the final goal of Christian existence.

1. During the first centuries when persecution of the Church was frequent, **martyrdom** was seen as a personal identification with the sacrificial death of Christ in dedication to the Father. The martyr was one who was able to experience ahead of schedule the final eschatological event. When the persecutions ended, however, Christians began to look for other ways to arrive at complete union with God in Christ. Origen maintained that a life of complete self-sacrifice was a kind of unbloody martyrdom, and Clement of Alexandria taught that every death was a kind of martyrdom provided one approached it with the proper dispositions.

2. **Prayer** was looked upon by the early followers of Jesus as a way of communion with God. Origin listed four types of prayer: supplications, prayers, intercessions and thanksgivings. He and Clement were to explain that this vocal prayer would become purified and interiorized to go "beyond itself into the prayer of silence, characterizing the state of union with God in liberation from the body. Then prayer becomes vision, but it is a vision of love. . . ."[11] A number of observances were also recognized in the early Church as expressions of prayer and communion with God. Among these were, first of all, observance of the Lord's Day and of Christ's Resurrection. Other "observances" included fasting and almsgiving. Cyprian called

"barren" (*sterilis oratio*) a prayer which did not "go hand in hand with alms." "Other forms of asceticism included freely chosen austerity of life, manual labor — particularly in monasteries, pilgrimages to shrines and holy places, a spirit of poverty and humility in following Christ."[12]

3. The origins of **monasticism** can be traced to ascetics within the Church, living alone or in groups, who appeared in the Near East and Africa in the second century and in the West at the end of the third. Origen depicts their basic traits as constant meditation aiming at mystical vision of God, renunciation of the world by embracing sexual abstinence, poverty, and the perfection of certain virtues, especially humility, self-denial and continence. The first hermits or anchorites led a solitary form of existence usually in the desert. This was considered the highest possible level of following Christ, free from all distraction and temptation.

Later in the fourth century when large numbers were suddenly becoming Christian after the Constantinian embrace of the Church, a desire to imitate the primitive Church as described in Acts 2:42 led to the development of cenobitism, a modified form of community existence. Basil the Great (+379) was opposed to the total isolation of the anchorites on the grounds that it left no possibility of fulfilling the commandment of love of neighbor. The growth of monasticism in the West was sparked by *The Life of St. Anthony* written by Athanasius of Alexandria (+373). The typical Latin monastery was usually a cenobitical community established near a city. John Cassian (+435) provided a collection with commentaries on the most important sayings of the Desert Fathers. Thus the notion of contemplative vision, as striven after by the anchorites, gained entry into Western monasticism. By the seventh century the Rule of St. Benedict became predominant within the West, gaining for Benedict of Nursia (+550) the title of "Father of Western Monasticism." This second more perfect "way" of being Christian, the "way of perfection," would eventually leave ordinary Christians traversing the lesser way of keeping the Ten Commandments. The original single "way" of Christian living proposed by the New Testament and early Fathers would be irreparably split in two for nearly fifteen centuries.

The Middle Ages (700 - 1500)

Pope Leo III's crowning of Charlemagne as emperor of the Romans and protector and defender of the papacy on Christmas Day, 800, formally inaugurated the era of Christendom, a period of Germanization and legalization within the Roman Catholic Church. It is difficult for us to imagine the deleterious effects that wave upon wave of migration and invasion had upon the Roman Empire over the centuries. The Germans came in the fifth and sixth centuries. Rome was sacked in 410. Then came the Moslems in the seventh and eight centuries. Roman civilization was left in ruins. The networks of transportation and communication, government, the military, the system of education — all were devastated or destroyed. Large cities became small villages. The Church was the one institution that survived, because it had its own system of government and administration and was not considered a threat to the invaders.

The Privatization of the Sacrament of Penance. During the patristic era the Sacrament of Penance had a canonical or public form. It was often referred to as a "second baptism" and was required only for the most grievous sins. Since sin was social and ecclesial, repentance had to be social and public. This canonical and liturgical form of penance, however, could only be undertaken once in a person's lifetime. In other words, it was not repeatable.

Canonical penance was never established in the Celtic and Anglo-Saxon churches of the British Isles. Perhaps the peculiar situation where the abbot's role largely overshadowed the bishop's explains why. The pastoral need, furthermore, to provide Christian formation for individuals who had been baptized without first having been evangelized and catechized and to reassure people who were fearfully preoccupied with hostile supernatural powers gave way to the development of a new repeatable and privatized form of penance. Influenced by the secular legal system with its tariffs (fines) and commutations (substitute penalties) as satisfaction made for crimes, the new form of penance led to the human relationship with God being seen largely in legal and commercial terms. Severe types of *paenitentia* characterized Celtic penance, including exile, pilgrimage, fasting, nocturnal singing and even more bizarre forms.[13]

Moral theology thus became attached to the specific needs of confessors. Penitential books were developed to aid the generally uneducated clergy in levying the appropriate tariff or penance for a given sin. The *Penitential* of Burchard, for example, lists some twenty varieties of homicide, each with its own appropriate penance determined according to the social rank of the person who was killed.[14] These books did not focus on the Christian "way" of life, but only on the varieties and types of sin. Christian life itself became essentially a matter of avoiding sin, rather than following Christ and living the Good News. Emphasis was placed increasingly upon the nature of the individual moral act.

The Systemization of Theology in the New Universities. In the darkest period of the ninth and tenth centuries, it was the Church that became the agent of civil order and human culture when civil authority and structures were weak and unstable. What formal education existed was provided by parochial, cathedral and monastic schools. Out of the cathedral schools in the twelfth century developed the new universities, such as those at Paris, Oxford and Montpellier. Between 1150 and 1500 some eighty such universities were set up across Europe. The Crusaders brought back to Europe the impact of Jewish and Arab influences including the rediscovery of Aristotle's works, which contributed immensely to the intellectual revitalization of Europe.[15]

The new university systems had faculties of arts, theology, medicine and law — canonical and civil. Trained philosophers and theologians among the new orders of friars, the Dominicans and Franciscans, developed the new systematic, scholastic methodology for grappling with key theological issues. The great scholastics made no distinction between doctrinal and moral themes. They treated moral questions in their presentations on Creation, the Fall, the Incarnation and the sacraments. Even Albert the Great's (1193-1280) commentary on Aristotle's *Nicomachean Ethics* gives no indication of attempting to develop a special theological discipline.

The two greatest figures of this period are Bonaventure (1221-1274) and Thomas Aquinas (1223-1274). Bonaventure of the Franciscan school maintained that theology exists not merely "to serve contemplation, but also to make us holy; in fact, its first purpose is to make us holy."[16] Thomas Aquinas in his *Summa Theologica* presents a magnificent and unified conception of the whole of theology. For him there could be no separation of doctrinal from moral theology, because there is no separation of truth from behavior. The three pillars of Thomas's moral vision are: first, the human person's relationship to creation and to one's last end; secondly, the fact that we are made in the image and likeness of God; and thirdly, the humanity of Christ as our way to God.[17] While integrating Aristotelian thought into the Christian vision, Thomas draws his principal nourishment from the Scriptures and the Fathers. For him the New Law is primarily the grace of the Holy Spirit, which is given to those who believe in Christ. Written codes and commandments are only secondary principles helping us to use the grace of God correctly.

The following century saw the development of Nominalism based on the metaphysics of William of Ockham (1290-1359), which denied the Greek concept of essences or universals. For Ockham there is no such thing as human nature, only individuals exist, and no fact about any object in the universe can be used to prove anything about any other object. His theological system focused on God's omnipotent will. God can do whatever he pleases and is not bound by such human concepts as wisdom or rationality.[18] His moral system thus stressed the importance of the individual moral act with its concrete circumstances rather than the observance of universal rules or the cultivation of virtues, that is, basic attitudes (*habitus*) as emphasized by Thomas Aquinas. This led to the development of individualism, voluntarism and legalism, as well as relativism and "situation ethics" in later centuries.

For the most part the scholastic developments of these centuries did not penetrate pastoral practices, which continued to be directed by canon law and pastoral handbooks called *summae confessariorum*. These latter were mostly alphabetically arranged reference books for confessors, containing questions of canon law and doctrine, along with solutions to cases of conscience. After the publication of Gratian's *Decretum* (1140), the first major collection of Church laws, canon lawyers began to treat a number of moral questions, producing lasting confusion between the moral law imprinted in the heart and positive law.

Pursuit of the Spiritual Life. During the early Middle Ages monasticism was the mainstay of religion and civilization. The monks generally provided a high ascetical ideal and example of Christian life for clergy and laity alike. Entire Germanic tribes were often baptized en masse before being evangelized or catechized. These tribal peoples exhibited a more primitive stage of religious development. For them the Holy was often localized in sacred objects and rites. This introduced a certain externalism into Christian spirtuality. "Germanic" traits became evident: love of the tangible evidenced in the Eucharistic controversies, juridical interests, veneration of relics and tombs of the saints, self-flagellation, emotional and individualistic devotions. Nevertheless the monks continued to promote a deep reverence for sacred Scripture and a love of the Liturgy.

By the ninth and tenth centuries the monasteries themselves became particularly vulnerable to the worst abuses of the feudal system. In attempts to gain control of Benedictine estates and revenues, young noblemen and even children were appointed abbots. Just shortly after the tenth century the monastery of Cluny was founded some sixty miles north of Lyons. Independent of all authority except the pope, it offered a way of life that appealed to those desiring to practice Christian virtues in the purest possible manner. The Cluniac reform spread with lightening speed across Europe. Within two hundred years well over a thousand communities placed themselves under its stricter discipline.

The associating of monasteries begun with the Cluny reform led to the founding of the first religious orders. In Cistercian theology developed by Bernard of Clairvaux (1091-1153) the interpretation of Scripture played a central role in the growth of individual mysticism. Conforming oneself to the word of God can restore the soul to its intended perfection, an intimate union of love with Christ the interior Lover. The piety of the new mendicant orders was a more active type. Dominic (Domingo de Guzman, 1170-1221) founded the Order of Preachers to provide the Church with articulate, well-educated domestic missionaries who could fight the false asceticism of the Albigensians (Cathari, "the pure"). At the same time Francis of Assisi (1181-1226) exhibited an almost obsessive devotion to Lady Poverty. His first rule was a collection of texts from the Gospel. He loved nature because it was another manifestation of the beauty of God. The heart of his spirituality was living the Gospel, summed up in Jesus' love for us as perfectly expressed in the Eucharist.

A trend toward interiorization is clear in a new current of spirituality that took root in northern Europe in the fourteenth century. In England, Julian of Norwich (1342-1416) writes about her own mystical experiences. God's all-embracing love is at the center of Julian's fourteen visions which she had at the age of thirty while seriously ill and at the point of death. "The Cloud of Unknowing" by an anonymous English author envisages readers who have already made progress in the spiritual life and have reached the state of contemplative prayer — this "meek stirring of love," without images or discursive thought.

At this same time mysticism flourished in the Low Countries and the Rhineland. Inner union with Christ, bridal mysticism, devotion to the Trinity, eucharistic and Christocentric piety, along with teaching on the development of the life of prayer were characteristic elements of this movement in the Low Countries. Jan van Ruysbroeck (1293-1381) published his masterpiece,

Spiritual Marriage, whose title summarizes the contents and goal of all his literary activity. The Brethren of the Common Life, reacting against both scholastic speculation and the mysticism of the late fourteenth century, was a lay movement that aimed at the development of a Christ-related daily life of asceticism, solitude, meditation and devotional reading. Active as teachers and publishers they fostered the "*Devotio Moderna*" and aided the spread of Christian humanism. This movement produced "The Imitation of Christ," the spiritual classic often attributed to Thomas à Kempis (+1471).

Lack of intellectual insight and a strain of anti-intellectualism brought with it many dangers in the realm of popular piety. Superstition and witch-hunting, copious accounts of visions and ignorance of the Bible were commonplace. Superficiality, moralizing in preaching, and devotional excesses were predominant. There existed, also, an inordinate fear of the afterlife and of God's judgment.

Renaissance, Reformation and Counter-Reformation (1500-1800)

The Italian Renaissance marked the "rebirth" of classical art and literature. It ushered in the birth of a new humanism centered on human reason and human needs. The invention of the printing press allowed its ideas to be disseminated across the continent with breathtaking speed. Humanists foresaw the establishment of a new golden age. It was a time of optimism and confidence.[19] By the middle of the fifteenth century, many devout Christians were rejecting the sterile and superstitious ritualism of popular religious practice. They turned toward the cultivation of an inner spiritual life rooted in individual prayer and meditation upon the Scriptures. Erasmus (1466-1536) flooded Europe with his writings castigating the clergy for their immorality and greed while he ridiculed the idea that salvation can be gained through external ritual and the purchase of indulgences. Martin Luther (1483-1546), an Augustinian monk, composed his Ninety-Five Theses objecting to the whole theory of indulgences and many of the other abuses attacked by Erasmus and posted them on October 31, 1517, to mark the beginning the Protestant Reformation.

Classical Moral Theology — The Manualist Tradition. Although a Thomistic revival occurred at the beginning of the sixteenth century, it was the decrees of the Council of Trent (1545-1563) regarding the administration of the sacrament of Penance that gave shape to Roman Catholic moral theology for the next four hundred years. Trent also established the seminary system for the training of future priests. Out of a concern to prepare good confessors who could help the penitent properly confess all mortal sins according to their number, species and circumstances as required by the council, an order of studies was established which separated doctrinal lectures on the *Summa* of Thomas Aquinas from "cases of conscience" in moral matters.

An independent and self-contained field of moral theology emerged. Its one concern was to ascertain whether or not the penitent had sinned. Several authors, beginning with John Azor (1536-1603), prepared a new handbook (*Institutiones Morales*) which followed a basic pattern of presentation that remained unchanged in seminary training until after the Second Vatican Council (1962-1965). The first part gave general principles of the moral life, which were followed in order by the commandments of God and the Church, the sacraments, censures and indulgences, and finally the particular obligations of the various states of life.[20] All these "manuals" were heavily influenced by the individualistic tendency of the age out of which they were born.

With moral theology concerned only with the tract on the judgment of conscience (*De conscientia*) during this period, discussion about the role of subjective factors in determining moral imputability became quite lively and bitter. Laxist tendencies were evident in the espousal of "probabilism," in which system all kinds of subtleties were invented to cast some doubt on and thus excuse from the obligation of most laws. Probabilists maintained that a person could follow the more lenient opinion as long as it was held by at least one reputable theologian. Rigorists, such as the Jansenists, countered with "probabiliorism" which held that between two probable opinions one must always choose the safer course by adopting the more probable one. Alphonsus Liguori (1696-1787), the founder of the Redemptorists and patron of moral theologians, proposed the via media of "equiprobabilism" requiring that the two conflicting opinions should have equal support among the experts. A genuine pastoral sense and spiritual realism pervaded his teaching as a whole. An understanding and appreciation of the concrete circumstances of the moral action always prevails in his writings over a mechanical employment and application of formula, no matter how correct or justifiable the formula might be.

Christian Spirituality. While Protestantism rejected the excesses of medieval spirituality with its emotionalism, superstition and veneration of relics, it promoted even further its underlying strain of individualism. Martin Luther, greatly influenced by Nominalist philosophy, stressed the uniqueness of the individual believer's relationship with God and the role of personal conscience. His recourse to Scripture alone (*sola Scriptura*) signified a direct personal approach to Christ. Catholic tradition, on the other hand, has always maintained that the believer's relationship with God is a mediated relationship — *mediated* through the community of faith, the Church, in which the Word of God is proclaimed.

A reaction to contemplative excesses developed within Catholicism. Ignatius of Loyola (1491-1556), founder of the Society of Jesus, emphasized the unity of prayer and action in his classic *Spiritual Exercises*. His mysticism reached the degree of conscious reflection where he could formulate reliable rules for discerning the movements of the soul. At the same time, Ignatius' affirmation of the world springs not from a naive optimism, but from a true grasp of the cross. Through the worldwide efforts and missionary imagination of the Jesuits the Catholic Counter-Reformation became a success.

The mystical way continued to flourish in Spain. Teresa of Avila (1515-1582) found the comfortable and sheltered environment of the Carmelite convent of the Incarnation at Avila adverse to spiritual progress. She set about to establish a small community that would live according to the ancient Carmelite ideals. In time her reform movement led to the development of a new religious order called the Discalced Carmelites (literally, "unshod," wearing sandals to symbolize their commitment to poverty). Urged by her spiritual advisors to record in writing her mystical experiences, Teresa wrote her great masterpiece, *The Interior Castle*, in which she describes the human soul as a castle containing seven concentric dwelling places, the innermost inhabited by God. This last is the level of "spiritual marriage." These spiritual experiences, Teresa maintained, give the person a greater interior calm, allowing one to endure greater external turmoil and thus serve others better. At the end of this spiritual journey a person is united not only with God, but also with oneself.[21]

John of the Cross (1542-1591) was a Carmelite priest, poet and mystic who met Teresa of Avila and who, like her, vowed himself to the primitive rule of the Carmelites. His "Spiritual Canticle" describes the ecstasy of union with God. His prose works describe the cost of discipleship. If you want to save your life, you must lose it. Uniquely and strongly he underlines

57

the Gospel paradox: the cross leads to resurrection, agony to ecstasy, darkness to light, abandonment to possession, and denial of self to union with God.[22]

Spirituality in Italy and France was given to more practical concerns. Philip Neri (1515-1595) and Charles Borromeo (1538-1584) promoted the renewal of the interior life and priestly ministry. The situation in France was complicated by controversies between Jansenism and Quietism, the former overstressed the Lordship of Christ and the corruption of the flesh, while the latter maintained the powerlessness of the human person to do anything at all towards salvation. Francis de Sales (1567-1622), Bishop of Geneva, writing against the Jansenists, emphasized the gentleness of God. His *Introduction to the Devout Life* developed the teaching that laypersons of whatever occupation and social rank are called to be saints. In France, Cardinal Pierre de Berulle (1575-1629) founded the French Oratory, which placed the Mystery of the Incarnation at the center of the spiritual life. Here too, the sacraments as signs of grace and love occupied a fundamental place in the Christian life of all the baptized — clergy, religious and laity.

In the world of secular learning and philosophy the Enlightenment originated in the Netherlands and in England in the middle of the seventeenth century. Rejecting the Christian interpretation of life, it gave birth to the Age of Reason and Science. It influenced every area of life and culture by its striving for mathematical abstraction, rational clarity, order and progress. Espousing an optimistic view of the world and human nature, it endeavored to usher in an era of utopian perfectionism. The Enlightenment gave birth to modern subjectivism and individualism, for which Nominalism and humanism had first paved the way. Its influence continues to pervade Western civilization and culture through scientific rationalism, materialism, positivism and communism.

The Nineteenth Century and Early Efforts at Renewal (1800-1960)

Moral Theology. In Germany under the influence of the Enlightenment and, then, in the Romantic movement and the first early vestiges of ecumenism, a reform of Catholic moral theology was attempted at the University of Tübingen. John Michael Sailer (1751-1832) and John Baptist Hirscher (1788-1865) were inspired by the renewal in biblical studies and offered a systematic presentation of the perfect ideal of the Christian way. Hirscher, in particular, based his moral theology entirely on the central gospel image of the Kingdom of God. Both theologians, however, displayed an uncritical interpretation of Scripture and little appreciation for the work of the great scholastics.

Political tensions in Italy regarding the status of the Papal States would prevent the German efforts at renewal from reaching the Roman universities. Pope Pius IX's "Syllabus of Errors" attacked the fruits of the Enlightenment, especially the spread of democratic liberalism, by stating that the pope "cannot and should not be reconciled and come to terms with progress, liberalism, and modern civilization." The First Vatican Council (1869-1870) was held and defined the doctrine of the infallibility of the pope. A general atmosphere of hostility and suspicion existed between German and Italian scholars.

Not until after World War II, when two German moralists, Bernard Häring, C.SS.R. (1912-) and Joseph Fuchs, S.J. (1912-), were sent to teach at the pontifical universities in Rome, would the renewal in Catholic moral theology — begun in Germany a century before — finally reach Rome. In most countries, however, including the United States the highly individualistic, legalistic and casuistic approach of the "manuals" continued to be presented in seminaries until after the Second Vatican Council (1962-1965). This council mandated the renewal of moral theology:

> Its scientific presentation should draw more fully on the teaching of holy Scripture and should throw light upon the exalted vocation of the faithful in Christ and their obligation to bring forth fruit in charity for the life of the world. (OT 16)

Taking their direction from the Enlightenment, liberal Protestant theologians in the twentieth century gave birth to "situation ethics." More a widespread trend than an actual system, it gives primordial importance to the situation and only a minor place to norms. Joseph Fletcher has been the leading proponent of situationism in the United States. The foundations of his approach are personalism, positivism, pragmatism and relativism. He is not afraid of saying that "only the end [of love] justifies the means." He further insists that every rule has its exceptions. Fletcher takes the Nominalism of William Ockham to its ultimate conclusion.

Traditional Roman Catholic ethics has always been situational, recognizing that circumstances, such as ill health or defending innocent human life, can alter the morality of a particular action. Situation ethics itself, however, was condemned by Pope Pius XII in 1952, and on February 2,

1956, the Holy Office (now the Sacred Congregation for the Doctrine of Faith) issued an instruction against it. This latter document condemned pure subjectivism and relativism which does not recognize "the objective right order determined by the law of nature."[23]

Catholic Social Doctrine. The Industrial Revolution and the popularity of Marxist philosophy among the European working class led to the development of a discernible body of official Church teachings on the social order in its economic and political dimensions. Based on the dignity of the human person created in the image of God, Catholic social doctrine expounds upon the human rights and duties that protect this dignity. Espousing the radical social nature of human existence, this teaching also explains the Christian concept of society and of the State and the interrelationship between the two as represented in the balancing of the principles of subsidiarity and socialization.

Pope Leo XIII's encyclical *Rerum Novarum* ("On the Condition of the Working Man"), written in 1891, marks the beginning of a systematic presentation of Catholic social ethics. This first stage comprised the Church's response to the Industrial Revolution and is concerned primarily with workers' rights and the economy. During World War II a second stage emerged confronting the growing material interdependence of the world. This era of internationalization of Catholic social doctrine is reflected in the addresses of Pius XII and in the encyclicals of John XXIII and Paul VI through *Populorum Progressio* ("The Progress of Peoples") in 1967, as well as in the documents of Vatican II and the Third International Synod of Bishops (1971). A third stage began in 1971 with Paul VI's *Octagesima Adveniens* ("The Eightieth Year"), which addressed the problems of society in a post-industrial, technological age.

Christian Spirituality. The nineteenth century inaugurated a transition from a medieval to a more contemporary spirituality. Individualism and regimentation continued to hold sway in a large number of institutionalized devotions: the Sacred Heart, Mary, the Eucharist, the Sacred Wounds, the Apostleship of Prayer, etc. A more organic notion of theology arose out of the Tübingen School. This corresponded with renewal in liturgy, historical studies and social ministry. Developments in psychology and sociology along with scientific and technological advances blazed new trails for Christian spirituality into the twentieth century.

In England, Cardinal John Henry Newman (1801-1890) was the driving force behind the Oxford Movement, the first example of the modern spiritual renewal that would find genuine expression in the documents of Vatican II. Newman's was a Christocentric spirituality, stressing the Incarnation as the foundation for an active Christian life in the world. In France, Thérèse Martin (1873-1897) entered the Carmelite convent at Lisieux, where she lived a cloistered life of obscurity. Her autobiography, *The Story of a Soul*, (explained her "little way" to countless readers. In her quiet redemptive suffering (she died from tuberculosis at the age of twenty-four), she is one of the great examples of the gospel paradox that we gain our life by losing it.

Between 1900 and 1950 the manuals of ascetical and spiritual theology, such as Adolfe Tanquerey's *The Spiritual Life* and Reginald Garrigou-Lagrange's *The Three Ages of the Interior Life*, were based, for the most part, on neo-scholastic presuppositions and were highly individualistic in their approach. Spirituality continued to be treated as a separate and independent discipline from moral theology. A new focus on the historical understanding of human existence began to shape Catholic theology and spirituality in the 1950s — in works by such authors as Pierre Teilhard de Chardin, Hubert van Zeller, Thomas Merton, and Josef Goldbrunner.

The fifth chapter of Vatican II's Dogmatic Constitution on the Church (*Lumen Gentium*) was entitled "The Call of the Whole Church to Holiness." It finally laid to rest the centuries-old split in the Christian "way," as it emphasized that the fullness of Christian life and the perfection of charity is the vocation of all the baptized, and not just of priests and religious. In the Council's vision spirituality is rooted in the mysteries of creation and redemption, in the presence of the Holy Spirit, and in the mission of Christ and the Church. It is shaped by one's situation in life and finds its summit and foundation in the sacred Liturgy.

In conclusion, the vision and teaching of Vatican II brings us full circle from the New Testament and patristic eras, which were marked by a vivid awareness of life in Christ and his Spirit, celebrated in sacrament and shared in the community of faith. It presents us, once again, with an integrated and holistic understanding of the Christian life, which in a very real sense was lost because of historical events and cultural circumstances in the early Middle Ages. During this period of Germanization, western civilization regressed to an almost primitive stage of existence. It was the Church alone that preserved it from total destruction and provided the basis for its growth and flowering in the Renaissance and beyond. Germanic influences, nevertheless, introduced a certain legalism and individualism into the Christian life.

The great scholastics in the new universities of the thirteenth century did recapture for a moment the earlier holistic understanding of the Christian life, but this never seeped down to the uneducated clergy and the populace at large. Soon Nominalism would appear within the schools and provide a philosophical basis for voluntarism, legalism and individualism. The Protestant Reformation would build its theology and spirituality on this latter philosophical system. Spiritual renewal within the Catholic Church frequently blossomed forth in contemplative and mystic tendencies which appeared in various monastic and lay movements over the centuries. It was evidenced in the apostolic initiatives and missionary endeavors of the new religious orders established in the thirteenth century and afterwards.

While the Council of Trent (1545-1563) was indeed a great reform council for the Catholic Church, in the wake of it the curriculum of studies devised for the new seminary system unfortunately separated the study of the moral life from courses on doctrine. This served to continue to make the confession of sins the focus of Christian life, much as it had been in the Middle Ages. Resolving questions of conscience and determining the degree of sinfulness became the major preoccupations of moralists in the post-Tridentine period. Such spiritual masters as Teresa of Avila and Francis de Sales described for the common folk the way to intimacy with God. In the nineteenth century the first attempts were made to reintegrate theology into an organic whole at the University of Tübingen, but another century would pass before these endeavors at renewal would cross the German border. In the 1950s, renewal in liturgy, biblical studies, and the social apostolate combined with new insights from psychology, sociology and scientific studies to promote a new and more integrated vision of human existence. This holistic vision, then, found its way into the documents of Vatican II.

Notes

1. John Henry Newman, *Essays Critical and Historical* (New York, 1897), vol. 2, p. 250.

2. See especially Stanley S. Harakas, *Toward the Transfigured Life*, p. 50, where he writes: "It was not long after Darwin that a number of persons began to explicate the philosophical consequences of evolutionary theory, including many who sought to develop ethical theory on the basis of

evolutionary concepts. Common to all these views is the idea that conduct at a later stage in history is, by necessity, more evolved conduct and therefore 'good' and 'right.' The inadequacy, however, of identifying the good with anything that is chronologically later is evident."

3. SC 248, 140-142, as cited in Francis X. Murphy, C.Ss.R, *The Christian Way of Life, Message of the Fathers of the Church*, 18 (Wilmington, Del.: Michael Glazier, Inc., 1986), p. 23.

4. SC 172, 158 quoted in ibid., p. 32.

5. *Florilegium Patristicum*, 2. 28-38, ed. Rauschen as quoted in ibid., p. 69.

6. CSEL 3, 1, 271 as quoted in ibid., p. 136.

7. The authorship of the "Mystagogical Catechesis" is actually disputed. This series of sermons is attributed by one school of thought to Cyril's successor, John II, the opinion favored by the *Clavis patrum qraecorum*. See Daniel J. Sheerin, *The Eucharist*, Message of the Fathers of the Church, 7 (Wilmington, Del.: Michael Glazier, Inc., 1986), p. 64.

8. PG 58, 601 as quoted by Murphy, op. cit., p. 173.

9. As quoted by Peter C. Phan, *Social Thought*, Message of the Fathers of the Church, 20 (Wilmington, Del.: Michael Glazier, Inc., 1984), p. 39.

10. Ibid., p. 37.

11. Louis Bouyer, *The Spirituality of the New Testament and the Fathers*, trans. Mary P. Ryan, History of Christian Spirituality I (New York/Tournai/Paris/Rome: Desclée and Company, Inc., 1963), p. 299.

12. Agnes Cunningham, SSCM, *Prayer: Personal and Liturgical*, Message of the Fathers of the Church, 16 (Wilmington, Del.: Michael Glazier, Inc., 1985), p. 28.

13. See James Dallen, *The Reconciling Community: The Rite of Penance*. Studies in the Reformed Rites of the Catholic Church, 3 (New York: Pueblo Publishing Co., 1986), pp. 103-110.

14. See Häring, *Free and Faithful in Christ*, vol. 1, p. 56 citing Migne, PL 140, 853 DC.

15. See Rodger Charles, S.J. with Drostan MacLaren, O.P., *The Social Teaching of Vatican II* (Oxford: Plater Publications, and San Francisco: Ignatius Press, 1982), p. 35.

16. Bonaventure, *Prologue to the commentary on the Book of Sentences*, p. 3, Quarachi ed., I, 13 cited in Bernard Häring, C.SS.R., *The Law of Christ*, General Moral Theology, vol. 1 (Cork: Mercier Press, Ltd., 1963), p. 11.

17. Ibid., p. 12.

18. See William A. Herr, *Catholic Thinkers in the Clear* (Chicago, Ill.: Thomas More Press, 1985), pp. 130-132.

19. Herr, op. cit., pp. 139-140.

20. Häring, *Law of Christ*, I, pp. 19-20.

21. See Herr, op. cit., pp. 177-179.

22. See Leonard Foley, O.F.M., ed. *Saint of the Day* (Cincinnati: St. Anthony Messenger Press, 1975), p. 334.

23. *Acta Apostolicae Sedis*, 48 (1956), 144-145 as cited in Lobo, *Guide to Christian Living*, p. 209.

Part II

Fundamental Elements

Chapter 3

Christian Anthropology: The Person "In Christ"

> *Christian moral behavior is distinctive precisely because it is Christian, i.e., what one does follows upon what is (agere sequitur esse). How we talk about what a Christian does will therefore depend on how we talk about what a Christian is.* — Terence J. Keegan, O.P.[1]

"Who am I?" is the fundamental question of human existence. A person's search for self-knowledge is the basic quest of life. This question today is all that more intense because of the cultural pluralism that abounds especially in contemporary American society, but which is also rapidly spreading across the globe. Since the beginning of time people have clung together in homogeneous groupings determined by culture, lifestyle, mentality and religion. During the Middle Ages, for example, everyone in Christendom basically thought alike and held the same values. Parents taught their children at home and passed on their knowledge and wisdom from one generation to the next. The lack of mobility along with the absence of the communications media prevented the broadcast of differing world-views. Today, television, radio and the press bring the world into our living rooms each day. With the simple touch of a button one can visit every culture and society on the face of the earth.

The secularization of Western culture, along with the increased mobility and communications technology of modern times, has presented people with the opportunity to choose between any number of viable options in philosophy, lifestyle and belief systems. Each one of them, whether hedonistic, utilitarian, atheistic, materialistic, evolutionary, secularistic, oriental, Christian, or whatever, proffers its own vision of human existence and the good life. Contemporary society has become a veritable marketplace of ideas and world-views competing for attention, as well as for new adherents and disciples. The advent of psychology, sociology and anthropology has also given us a new look at ourselves.

In such a pluralistic environment, how do we sort through the maze? How do we find the truth? The history of the human race has provided us with three basic approaches to the interpretation of reality — the magical, the metaphysical and the scientific. All three approaches were in evidence in our historical survey of the Christian spiritual and moral life. The metaphysical predominated. Anchored in the classical mind-set of ancient Greek philosophy and Renaissance thought it associated truth with Being. The magical appeared in the superstitious practices and popular piety of the Middle Ages. On an intellectual level, however, the Age of Enlightenment marked the beginning of the shift from metaphysical thought patterns to the development of the empirical sciences which equated truth not with Being, but with fact.

Methods of Theological Interpretation

Theology is a child of the thought patterns of its time. For understanding the New Testament, we need to know the Hebrew mind. In the first to third centuries the gospel was explained in Hellenistic terminology by the early Fathers. The influences of Roman law and empire would affect the Church in the fourth century, as would the class and hierarchical structure of feudal society in the Middle Ages. Without grasping the shift from the classical mind-set of the post-Tridentine manualist tradition to the genetic or historical mentality of many contemporary Catholic theologians, one cannot adequately understand the status of Roman Catholic theology today.

The Classicist World-view. The theological manuals which served as seminary textbooks in the post-Tridentine era adopted the classicist world-view. Influenced by Scholasticism and the Renaissance's rediscovery of ancient Greek thought, the classical mind turned to metaphysics and deductive reasoning in its attempts to interpret reality. It accepted as a premise an objective, ideal order in Nature or the universe that was perfect in every aspect. The seeker of truth had only to discover this perfect order by extracting its immutable essences, which in turn provided universal principles for the governance of human actions.

Its method was deductive, moving from the universal to the particular. One could progress in knowledge up to a point — that point being "perfection." Once the ideal order was found, the principal virtues were stability and fidelity. Any significant change becomes a threat to the follower of this world-view, because it would destroy order and beauty. After all, how could anyone improve upon what is perfect? Thus the great scholastic systems of theology have been compared to the Gothic cathedrals of that time. Their ideas were "chiseled to no less exacting measures than stones used for houses of worship, and their internal balance was not less precarious than that of the soaring arches. . . . Stone buildings, beautiful as they look, closed systems of thought, fascinating as they are, have no life in them. . . . They do not grow."[2]

According to the classical mind-set we can know reality as it is by abstracting its essence. Human nature or "man," for example, is defined as a "rational animal." In the scholastic manuals definitions predominate. This transmission of knowledge by means of universal concepts tacitly assumes that we can place ourselves outside the flow of history. Conceiving ourselves as standing at an immovable point in the universe, we can know all events and thoughts with an absolute exactness that remains valid forever. Our conclusions are always accurate and complete as long as our deductive logic is correct. Abstract, universal, eternal, necessary, essential and static are adjectives characterizing this particular world-view.

The Historical World-view. The equation of truth with fact, rather than with Being, led to the development of a historical mentality. With the dethronement of the metaphysics of Being, history and mathematics became the only true knowledge left as the Enlightenment progressed throughout eighteenth-century Europe. Every field of learning began to be considered from a historical perspective. Philosophy, theology, economics and the natural sciences, all took on a historical slant. Soon the combination of mathematical thinking with factual thinking would give birth to the scientific method. A new technological age began in which the new empirical sciences became the primary interpreters of reality.

The person who is of a historical mind-set does not believe that we can absorb concepts or essences, but only data. We cannot possess the fullness of truth, only fragments. Furthermore, we ourselves are part of the historical process, part of the universal movement that penetrates the whole created world. We live in time and cannot step out of it. We can shape history, but we are also shaped by it. Life means movement, change and growth. Life is viewed from an evolutionary perspective. Vatican II thus noted: "The accelerated pace of history is such that one can scarcely keep abreast of it. . . . And so mankind substitutes a dynamic and more evolutionary concept of nature for a static one, and the result is an immense series of new problems, calling for a new endeavor of analysis and synthesis" (GS 5).

Concerned only with facts and data, historical consciousness as a cognitional theory employs the inductive method. It begins with the experience of the particular, the concrete, and its conclusions are as accurate as the evidence will allow. It provides us with descriptions, rather than definitions. Thus our movement through history has been compared to flying in an airplane and watching the earthly objects roll by. Information pours in through the small windows, the windows in this case being our senses. What reaches us, however, is only a small part of all that can be grasped and assimilated. Yet we must work with this limited data, all the while aware that there is much more beyond. Life is a never-ending process of knowing and wanting to know more.[3]

It has been said that "it is no accident that history and the historical approach grew up precisely in the atmosphere of Christian belief."[4] Christianity, anchored by its belief in the Incarnation, lives in a specific way on the plane of history, and is concerned with facts and historical circumstances. The revision that has taken place in Catholic moral theology since Vatican II has been an attempt to incorporate the insights and advantages of this historical approach. It allows for the integration of biblical teaching and the mysteries of faith with moral deliberation. It views moral life as always incomplete and in need of conversion, while respecting the uniqueness of the person and the ambiguities of historical circumstances.

Most Catholic "revisionist" theologians see a need to preserve the clarity, consistency and precision of the classicist world-view while working with the advantages and insights of historical consciousness. Many of them are aware that this latter approach tends toward subjectivism and relativism. Indeed, there exist many different types of each world-view and different degrees to which persons and Church documents reflect them. The revisionists, nevertheless, tend to depend exclusively on the inductive method by always beginning with a consideration of the concrete data provided by human experience and the empirical sciences.[5]

The Re-emergence of Symbolic Consciousness. Both the classical and historical mindset, however, follow a rationalistic approach that came to the fore in the Western intellectual tradition with medieval Scholasticism. The rediscovery of Aristotelian philosophy by the new universities founded in France and Italy in the eleventh century provided a basis for modern scientific exploration and theological thought. Aristotle firmly held that the only two ways human beings can know reality are by sense experience and rational thought. This limiting of experience to some indisputable datum of the senses eventually gave birth to that "technological spirit which encourages endless manipulation of the surface of reality but is insensitive to its depth."[6]

Prior to this turn to theory — to the detached, disinterested, pure, abstract categories of science, of philosophy, of speculative theology — Christianity in its Western cultural form depended on powerful images and symbols to give intellectual expression to its self-consciousness. The etymology of the word "symbol" reveals that it comes from the Greek "*symballein*," which means literally to fall together, to throw together. It refers to the two corresponding halves of a ring or tablet that were used as tokens of identity for guests, messengers or partners of a treaty. A "symbol" is something which points to its complementary other half creating mutual recognition and unity.[7] Symbols, like signs, point to another reality, but unlike signs, they also participate in the reality to which they point. A symbol makes present that to which it points; it is, in other words, sacramental.

The Scholastics believed that by replacing symbolic consciousness (*mythos*) with rational theory (*logos*) they were bringing Christianity out of the Dark Ages and into the modern world. Even today, staunch adherents of both the classical and historical world-views look upon the symbolic as a less developed stage of thought that is found among children and primitive peoples. Mircea Eliade, the twentieth-century historian of religions, however, has observed:

> Symbolic thinking is not the exclusive privilege of the child, of the poet or of the unbalanced mind: it is consubstantial with human existence, it comes before language and discursive reason. The symbol reveals certain aspects of reality — the deepest aspects — which defy any other means of knowledge.[8]

Symbols alone enable us to comprehend Mystery, as the language of Scripture, the Church Fathers, and the great mystics so eloquently attest.

The sciences themselves are leading contemporary Western society to a rediscovery of symbol. Ethnology or cultural anthropology first brought late nineteenth-century Europeans into contact and dialogue with non-European peoples, such as Oceanians, Africans and others, who continued to depend upon symbol as the primary instrument of knowledge. Quantum physics pointed out that the deeper we probe into the structure of matter the more we find ourselves in contact with the whole. Beyond atoms and molecules we come not to infinitesimal building blocks but to pockets of energy composed of particles or waves depending on the position of the beholder. These subatomic entities behaved as particles when the observer was looking for particles, and behaved as waves when the observer was looking for waves. Niels Bohr suggested that both realities were true at the same time, according to what he called his theory of complementarity. The isolated particles, he concluded, were but abstractions. In reality, he said, their properties could only be defined as they relate or interact with other systems.[9]

The psychologist Carl Jung, who spent most of his time probing the inner life of persons through the study of dreams, discovered that much of a person's inner life is unconscious. He concluded too that this inner reality is a creative energy that continually seeks to express itself through our actions and behavior. The world and civilization we humans have created are but the outer manifestation of our inner dreams and images. Thus life itself is not a series of unrelated parts but an intricately interdependent whole. Furthermore, the experience of time in the inner world of dreams is remarkably different from our day to day conscious reality. We know that a dream that feels like an hour in duration may have occurred in a split second. Psychologists today have demonstrated that the right side and the left side of our brain function differently. The left side orders the world in a linear and manageable way; the right side does not think in space-time continuums. The latter is the realm of art, symbol, play, mystical experience and Being; the former is the realm of logic, theory, technology, historical/empirical data and doing/making.[10]

Contemporary Roman Catholic theologians have rediscovered the importance of symbolical consciousness through the renewal in biblical, liturgical and patristic studies and through contact with the above-mentioned sciences. The sacramental or symbolic reality of both Christ and the Church have been explored and have found expression in the teachings of Vatican II.[11] Indeed, this Council's Dogmatic Constitution on the Church has recourse to symbols and images, rather than definitions, in making known to us "the inner nature of the Church" (LG 5). Revelation as symbolic disclosure has received wide popularity among twentieth-century Christian theologians. Avery Dulles draws a parallelism between the properties of symbolical communication and revelation. These properties, he proposes, are fourfold: 1) symbolic consciousness gives not speculative but participatory knowledge, luring us to situate ourselves within the universe of meaning and value which it opens up to us; 2) it involves the knower as person and has a transforming effect; 3) it has a powerful influence on commitments and behavior; and 4) it introduces us into realms of awareness not normally accessible to discursive thought.[12]

Symbolic consciousness does not desert the concrete, the historical, but rather sees it as revelatory of deeper meaning. With the classicist it equates truth with Being, or more preferably Mystery, because with the historical mind-set it maintains that all perception is from within. In the words of the narrative theologian John Shea, "There is no vantage point from which to spy on Mystery."[13] It is the permeating context of all being and activity. Symbolic consciousness, furthermore, of its very nature, is relational. Because it always points beyond itself to its "other half" and because it finds its first expression in stories and myths, which are always the properties of communities, the symbolic overcomes the individualistic and objectivistic tendencies of the rational approaches. The symbolic is primordial. It is common to all peoples and to individual persons in their earliest stages. Only at a certain point in development does it open up to abstract reasoning, which must always remain connected to its roots in the symbolic and not strive to replace it. A holistic approach would seem to demand that we now attempt to balance the right-side and left-side functioning of the human mind.

The classical mind-set that gave birth to the manualist tradition in moral theology after the Council of Trent began its study of morality by analyzing the "human act." This act was judged according to the "law" in one's "conscience," which was informed by knowledge of the law. If the "human act" was contrary to the "law," it was considered to be a "sin." If it was in accordance with the "law," it was considered good and conducive of "virtue." In this very simplified description of the moral process as developed in the manual tradition, we find the five fundamental categories ("*De Principiis*") which come into play in any moral decision — human act, law, conscience, sin and virtue.

Placed, however, within the biblical context of the mystery of Christ, salvation history and our Christian vocation, as recommended by Vatican II (see OT 16), the starting point for our study of the spiritual-moral life becomes Christian anthropology or the PERSON-IN-CHRIST who has received the grace (gift-call) of CONVERSION and has given one's affirmative FAITH-RESPONSE IN LOVE AND HOPE (i.e., DISCIPLESHIP). This

	CLASSICAL MENTALITY — BEING	HISTORICAL WORLD-VIEW — FACTS / DATA	SYMBOLIC CONSCIOUSNESS (Christian Biblical Revelation) — MYSTERY (Trinity of relationships)
1) Equates TRUTH with	BEING	FACTS / DATA	MYSTERY (Trinity of relationships)
2) Interprets REALITY by	Metaphysics and deductive reason abstracting essence	Empirical science and inductive reason examing data	Symbols pointing beyond themselves while participating in the reality
3) Concept of NATURE	Static, immutable, ideal order	Dynamic, evolving historical process	A relational order of opposites
4) Basis of NORMS	Absolute, universal principles	Empirical evidence corresponding to historical circumstances	Narratives revealing mystery (Gospel = Christ/love as supreme norm = the eternal relational order at core of all creation)
5) Tends toward	Objectivism, legalism and authoritarianism	Subjectivism, utilitarianism and relativism	Integration of complementarities and relational maturity
6) Type of KNOWLEDGE	Categorical, speculative, intellectual (left-brain)		Participatory, holistic; categorical and non-discursive (both left-brain and right-brain)
7) Views KNOWER as	Agent / observer who learns facts		Person who grasps both speculative truths and spiritual values which transform knower
8) Approach	Rationalistic / individualistic (logos)		Holistic / communal (mythos)
9) Leads to	Intellectual conversion / information		Total conversion evidenced by moral transformation

"faith-response" requires one to live according to the LAW OF CHRIST, the law of grace, revealed in one's heart, one's CONSCIENCE, where a person always remains free to mature in VIRTUE or to reject God's offer of love, and thereby SIN. Within this context the "human act" becomes the incarnation, the enfleshing, the symbolization, of an interior personal relationship or withdrawing from it, rather than the starting point of some objectivistic or legalistic analysis.[14]

Created in the Image of God

We act according to who we are and, even more fundamentally, believe ourselves to be (*aqere sequitur esse/credere*). Our contemporary pluralistic society, as we have already noted, gives us any number of options in this particular category. For those who accept biblical revelation, the very first pages of Scripture inform us that God created us in his image (see Gen. 1:26). This is the basis of human dignity. We mirror his image in our rationality, freedom and capacity for personal relationships.[15]

By Reason of Creation. Gifted with intelligence and freedom, the human race is created "through the Word" (Jn. 1:3) for sharing in the fullness of love (Jn. 1:16). In the Word spoken by God we are created as "response-able" beings, "called to participate in truth and love."[16] This "response-ability," planted deep within the core of our being, is experienced as an unquenchable thirst and hunger for understanding and love. We continually question the meaning of life and search for an unconditional love. Called forth into existence by God's word and spirit, we are restless, as St. Augustine so perceptively observed, until we rest in eternal Truth and infinite Love.

Good is that which ultimately satisfies our deepest thirst and hunger. In the gospels Jesus tells the rich young man, a seeker of truth in action, who asks "What must I do?" that "No one is good but God alone" (Mk. 10:17; also see Mt. 19:17; Lk. 18:19). Offering "living water" to the Samaritan woman at the well who had failed five times at love, Jesus relates to her that "true worshipers will worship the Father in Spirit and truth" (Jn. 4:23). Indeed, Jesus reveals to us that God, the Good, ultimate reality, is not an idea, principle, force or other inanimate existence, but is rather Father, Son and Spirit — Trinity — interpersonal relationship.[17]

God, the Creator, as revealed by Jesus is not the "*Esse Subsistens*" (Subsisting Being or Supreme Being), nor the Prime Mover of Greek philosophy. He is rather "*Relatio Subsistens*" (Subsisting Relationship) as designated by the Scholastics. He is a Trinity of personal relationships or Tri-unity. The "three persons" are not individual substances or personalities in the modern sense but pure relatedness.

> Relationship is not something extra added to the person, as it is with us; it only exists at all as relatedness. Expressed in the imagery of Christian tradition, this means that the First Person does not beget the Son in the sense of the act of begetting coming on top of the finished Person; it *is* the act of begetting, of giving oneself, of streaming forth.[18]

Made in God's image, human beings most perfectly mirror that image in the quality of their relationships, in their self-giving. Adam-before-the-Fall was the exemplar of what the human race was meant to be: living in relationship, in peace and harmony with God, within himself, with others and with all creation. This primordial importance of relationship is also accented by many contemporary schools of philosophy, the social sciences and even quantum physics (as noted previously).

By Reason of Redemption. After Adam's Fall, God sent a "new Adam" (see 1 Cor. 15:45), Jesus Christ, to be a "life-giving spirit." By Christ's paschal mystery we are reconciled to God and restored to the level of sonship by being reborn in the Spirit and "predestined to be conformed to the image of his Son" (Rom. 8:29). In the true biblical sense "Adam" is a corporate personality; this word encompasses the whole human race. Likewise, Paul's employment of the image "new Adam," along with "body of Christ," has the same corporate inference. For John, too, the open side of the new Adam (Jn. 19:34) repeats the creative mystery of the "open side" of Adam in Gen. 2:21ff. From the lance-thrust side of Christ a new Eve is formed: "it is the beginning of a new definitive community of men with one another, a community symbolized here by blood and water, in which John points to the basic Christian sacraments of baptism and Eucharist and through them to the Church as the sign of a new community of men."[19]

Through the paschal mystery, Christ redeems us by reconciling us with God, with ourselves, with one another and with all of creation. He reverses Adam's sin and restores the "original grace" that was lost through the Fall. Incorporated into Jesus' dying and rising through faith and baptism we are *called* to "pass over" with Christ to the Father (Rom. 6:5-11). This is a real incorporation, not just symbolic. We are "divinized" in the language of the Greek Fathers; we may in fact "come to share in the divine nature" (2 Pet. 1:4).

This *call* to share in the divine life, it must be pointed out, is both an ecclesial and sacramental reality. We share in it only as members of the Body of Christ, the "new Adam." Living Christ's paschal mystery, which we re-present and celebrate in sacrament, we are united with his self-emptying and self-giving love. We truly become "sons in the Son," children of God, by giving ourselves, and with ourselves the whole visible world, to God.[20] For Paul, authentic humanity is something we achieve by bringing the creative love of God in Christ to others. Paul is highly selective in the way he uses "image of God"; he applies it only to Christ as the new Adam (2 Cor. 4:4). As regards believers, he will only say that we "are being transformed in the same image from glory to glory" by the Holy Spirit (2 Cor. 3:18). He holds forth the hope that one day we may *become* the "image of God."[21]

By reason of both creation and redemption each of us is constituted as a *person-in-Christ*, for "in him were created all things in heaven and on earth" (Col. 1:16). Christ is indeed "the Alpha and the Omega, the first and the last, the beginning and the end" (Rev. 22:13). "Christ is the beginning of the future, the already inaugurated finality of the being 'man'. This idea was expressed in the language of scholastic theology by the statement that with Christ revelation is concluded."[22]

As persons we truly participate in the very Mystery of God. Just as in biblical literature God is perceived as a paradox — Creator and Destroyer, Lover and Judge, Father and Son, Warrior and Husband, male and female, hidden and close, etc. — so too, persons are perceived as paradoxes. Each human being is a complexus of disparate qualities, drives, abilities, weaknesses, strengths, etc.[23] When it comes to the Mystery of God, the person, and spiritual realities, we today realize that "we must not look, in the Aristotelian fashion, for an ultimate concept encompassing the whole, but must be prepared to find a multitude of aspects which depend on the position of the observer and which we can no longer survey as a whole but only accept alongside each other."[24]

We cannot stand outside mystery and peer at it as a mere observer. We can only experience it by entering into it. Pure objectivity is unobtainable.[25] Just as modern physicists have developed the law of complementarity in order to report their studies of subatomic realities, so scientific theology from

FUNDAMENTAL ELEMENTS

In
THE CLASSICAL MORAL MANUALS
(from Trent to Vatican II)

Primary focus: Is this action a sin or not?

HUMAN ACT

LAW

CONSCIENCE

VIRTUE

SIN

Characteristics: act-centered / law-centered; an objective analysis was attempted by taking the "human act" as the starting point for

For
A THEOLOGY OF CHRISTIAN LIVING
(from the gospel mystery as proposed by Vatican II)

Primary focus: What sort of person am I becoming?

PERSON "IN CHRIST"

CONVERSION

FAITH-RESPONSE IN LOVE AND HOPE

LAW OF CHRIST

CONSCIENCE

VIRTUE / SIN = HUMAN ACT

Divine-human dialogue (basic dynamic)

CALL

and

RESPONSE

Characteristics: person-centered / Christ as supreme norm; the "human act" is the visible fruit or symbol of

Augustine to Luther to Heidegger (to mention only a few) has frequently resorted to literary paradox as a principal tool. Bonaventure and Nicolas of Cusa developed the *coincidentia oppositorum*.[26] As we seek now to better understand "who we are" in the light of Christian biblical revelation we too will take this same route.

1. The person "in Christ" is both **fallen and redeemed**. Revelation makes known to us that the image of God in which the human race was created has become distorted by sin from the very dawn of history. Human persons experience a lack of inner wholeness; they know a division and split exists within themselves. All human life, whether individual or collective, shows itself to be a dramatic struggle between good and evil. We feel unable to overcome the assaults of evil successfully on our own. "But the Lord himself," Vatican II teaches us, "came to free and strengthen man, renewing him inwardly and casting out the 'prince of this world' (Jn. 12:31), who held him in the bondage of sin" (GS 13).

"Through the incarnation, God gave human life the dimension that he intended man to have from his first beginning; he has granted that dimension definitively. . . . In the mystery of the redemption man becomes newly 'expressed' and, in a way, is newly created. He is newly created!" (*Redemptor Hominis*, nos. 1 and 10). Thus, as St. Irenaeus wrote in the second century, "On account of His great love, He became what we are, that He might make us what He is."[27] Through redemption in Jesus Christ, human nature is raised up to the supernatural level of divine life. "*Man lives in God and by God*: he lives 'according to the Spirit', and 'sets his mind on the things of the Spirit' " (*Dominum et Vivificantem*, 58).

Different theological traditions have understood redemption in various ways. Classical Protestant theology has stressed the individual's sinful condition even after responding in faith to God's loving gift in Jesus Christ. In this view, God looks at Christ's perfect act of obedience which veils, as it were, the wretched sinfulness of the believer. The Christian remains "*simul justus et peccator*," incapable of doing good works on one's own. In the Church, Christ becomes present to the individual as redeemer and exemplar. Emphasis is placed on the personal, individualistic aspects of character formation in light of biblical teachings, while the sacramental and mediational role of the Church is virtually ignored.

Catholic theology lays emphasis on the basic goodness of the human person even after the Fall. It stresses our inner transformation through grace.

We are created anew. We are divinized by Christ and become a whole new creature, and we are expected to live and act accordingly. When we are incorporated as members of Christ's Body through faith and baptism, Christ becomes present through the sacramentality of the Church. The Catholic tradition thus emphasizes the ecclesial, social aspects of redemption. Healed and transformed through grace, we remain weakened by the wound of sin, but through membership in Christ's Body we continue to be strengthened and to grow in him.

2. "Man, though made of body and soul, is a unity" (GS 14). Biblical thought recognizes no division of **body and soul**. A human being is not a body, and in addition, a soul. The human person is a totality, an embodied spirit. In the New Testament "body" (*soma*), "flesh" (*sarx*), "soul" (psyche) and "spirit" (*pneuma*) refer to the entire human person. The opposition between "flesh" and "spirit" refers simply to the unredeemed and redeemed states of human existence. When "spirit" is distinguished from "body," it means that the spiritual order transcends the material, but it in no way implies that a human being is composed of two parts.

An ancient Greek anthropology espoused by Plato and his followers considered the body as the prison of the soul. The human being, in their view, was composed of two parts — a body plus a soul, much like a container with its contents. This dualistic understanding affected many of the Greek Fathers of the Church and has led to the popular, individualistic preoccupation with "saving one's soul." Under Stoic influence, a false asceticism developed which looked upon the body as depraved and which sought to repress all passions and emotions. The provincial Council of Constantinople in 543 condemned the teaching, held by the followers of Origen, that the human body is a degrading place of exile to which pre-existing souls have been consigned.[28]

Contemporary Western culture has moved to the opposite extreme in denying the very existence of the "soul." Scientific positivism allows no room for spiritual realities. Theology, still reacting to the individualistic and dualistic tendencies associated with the classical religious imperative "to save one's soul," tends to sidestep the issue. Modern translations of Scripture prefer to use the words "life" or "self" rather than "soul" (see Mt. 16:26 — Revised Standard Version, The Jerusalem Bible, New American Bible). Yet, there is a real difference between "life" and "soul." We tend to think of the former in terms of physical existence or of the external conditions surrounding us. The "soul," however, is an inner psychic reality which connects one's consciousness to one's inner depths.[29] Thus, Vatican II reminded us that when someone "recognizes in himself a spiritual and immortal soul, he is not being led astray by false imaginings that are due to merely physical or social causes. On the contrary, he grasps what is profoundly true in this matter" (GS 14).

The existence of this inner spiritual realm of the human person is attested to by Jungian psychology. The psychoanalyst Carl Jung (1875-1961) referred to this inner realm as the "unconscious," which he saw as composed of two layers. The upper layer is rationally explainable and consists of material that we have artificially made unconscious. Underneath, Jung maintained, we find the absolute unconscious in which psychic activity goes on completely independent of the conscious mind and upper layers of the unconscious. This deeper layer of supra-individual activity he called the "collective unconscious."[30] This interior realm possesses a structure common to all members of the human race as the universality of archetypes, images and symbols attests.[31] These latter, in fact, witness to an inner reality that is just as objective and universal as a human being's anatomical and physiological structure.

What a number of psychologists now refer to as the Self emerges from the peculiar relationship of the body to conscious and unconscious (internal) information. This Self is a dynamic center of motivating energy capable of functioning outside the space-time continuum, as in the example of dreams. This energy source requires a physical body to be fully operational, and it becomes more conscious and focused as we develop through life's stages to maturity. The Self is believed to be neither male nor female, the determination of which seems to be strictly physical. In the end, however, the fully developed human being must integrate both components into the Self. Its perpetual existence after the death of the physical body is a central tenet of Christian faith.[32] Many of the early Fathers of the Church, along with the great mystics such as Teresa of Avila, John of the Cross and Catherine of Siena, moved around in this inner world of the Self, or soul, with a knowledge and competence similar to contemporary medicine's mastery of the human body.

Physicians who advocate a holistic approach to healing the body are today also exploring the link between the physical and the spiritual. Bernie S. Siegel, M.D., writes in *Love, Medicine & Miracles*:

The physical benefits of meditation have recently been well documented by western medical researchers, notably Dr. Herbert Benson. It tends to lower or normalize blood pressure, pulse rate, and the levels of stress hormones in the blood. It produces changes in the brain-wave patterns, showing less excitability. These physical changes reflect changes in attitude, which show up on psychological tests as a reduction in the over competitive Type A behavior that increases the risk of heart attack. Meditation also raises the pain threshold and reduces one's biological age.[33]

The psychosomatic unity of the human person and its vital importance to the individual's total health and well-being are more and more being affirmed by contemporary research in medicine and psychology.

3. This peculiar relationship of the physical and spiritual within the human person allows one to experience both "Becoming" and "Being," both **time and eternity.** The shift from classical to historical consciousness has caused Western civilization to think only in terms of linear time, of the scientific time-space continuum. This horizontal passage of time corresponds to the realm of progress and Becoming, to human growth and development, to what "ought to be." It is Greek "*chronos*" or chronological time. Scripture, however, informs us of a vertical time, of the "today" of God or the Greek "*kairos*." It is the realm of Being, of what "is," of the eternal "now." "Behold, now is a very acceptable time; behold, now is the day of salvation" (2 Cor. 6:2).

"The vertical 'today' is suspended in and over the horizontal 'now'; it cannot be anchored in it as something future which is at hand (for horizontal time passes away and cannot be anchored), nor can it be regarded as something timelessly suspended above it, for the 'future of God' is not a timeless idea, but an event of divine freedom breaking in."[34] It is this tension between the temporal and the eternal, between what "already is" and "is not yet fully" that constitutes the ethical imperative. The in-breaking of the Kingdom of God, present already in what is, calls us to completion, wholeness, fullness. The distance between "what is" and "what is not yet fully" is bridged by what we call "duty" (or "responsibility" or "obligation"). Failure to respond accordingly produces "guilt."

Psychological research, furthermore, has discovered that the left and right side of the brain function on different views of time. The left side operates on linear time, ordering the world in a manageable way. The right

81

side of the brain, on the other hand, does not think in space-time continuums. It sums up its experience of time in a moment, as often occurs in a dream state where a long sequence of events happens in a split second. Developmental theories of the human personality operate out of the horizontal or linear experience of time. Existentialist psychology analyzes the deep structure of the now of Being experienced by the right side of the brain. It is becoming clear that both views are correct. The truth is a blend of both. Time within human experience is both linear and non-linear.[35]

In her study of the mystics, Evelyn Underhill has pointed out that well integrated persons are those who develop both the qualities of Being and the constant reality of Becoming.[36] The modern predominance of historical consciousness within Western society and culture has placed almost total emphasis on scientific and technological progress with an accompanying concern for developing the Doing values of work, management, competition, achievement and success. The Being values of worship, joy, play, beauty, art and intimacy have been eclipsed. The cultivation of these latter values allows us to experience the inbreaking of eternity into our daily lives and promotes holistic health and integration within the human person. They help us to face the central issues of life, of contingency, birth and death. In the words of Hans Urs von Balthasar,

> . . . time up to death cannot be dammed up, and the kingdom of God "grows" through this void, not visibly, but through removing treasure and laying it up in the kingdom above, away from moth, rust, and thief. . . . To be in historical time means to journey in a foreign land. Not because God has not providentially impregnated everything with his presence, but because the form of temporality itself, by its lack of unity, is an absence of the creature from unified eternity.[37]

The mission and task of the Church, of the members of Christ's Body, is to become ever more fully the sacrament and proclaimer of this Good News, of this in-breaking of the Eternal into time. By such an evangelization process it alone becomes possible to transform the world of historical time.

4. The human person, furthermore, is both a **unique individual** and a **social being**. The very first pages of Scripture tell that God created us in his image as social beings, "male and female he created them" (Gen. 1:27), for

"It is not good for the man to be alone" (Gen. 2:18). Biologically, from the first moment of union of sperm and ovum a human being is the fruit of mutual interaction, yet at that same moment, too, a new individual human life is given, distinct from that of the father and mother, with a unique, never-to-be-repeated genetic code. Psychologically and sociologically to meet a human person is to encounter a community which has formed him or her and of which he or she is a member (see GS 25). Born into a given, particular community, a human person is a cultural being who is influenced, although not wholly determined by prevailing modes of thought, economic conditions, social structures, etc. Such influences are diachronic and synchronic, that is, historical and cultural.

Biblical revelation attests to the primary social nature of the human person. Vatican II tells us that God has "willed to make men holy and save them, not as individuals without any bond or link between them, but rather to make them into a people who might acknowledge him and serve him in holiness" (LG 9). In the Old Testament, God enters into a covenant relationship with the community of Israel, the people he delivered from bondage. Violation of the covenant by an individual — for example, someone committing murder — was seen as a threat to the very existence of the community. The death penalty was exacted, not just as retribution, but as a "radical excommunication," purging the stain that invites God's wrath and menaces the sanctity and cohesion of the community (see Dt. 19:13). The prophet Ezekiel was one of the first to develop the notion of personal responsibility, rejecting the "proverb that you recite in the land of Israel: 'Fathers have eaten green grapes, thus their children's teeth are on edge' " (Ezk. 18:2).

This sense of a communitarian vocation, or corporate solidarity, is also manifest in the New Testament. The Pauline images of the "new Adam" and the "body of Christ," as we have already noted, designate a corporate personality. Likewise, Paul never speaks of "new men" but only of "the new self" as in Col. 3:9-11 or Gal. 3:28: "There is neither Jew nor Greek, there is neither slave nor free person, there is not male and female; for you are all one [person] in Christ Jesus." The variety of spiritual gifts which contribute to the organic unity of the Body (1 Cor. 12:4-31; Rom. 12:3-8; Eph. 4:1-6) and the array of social virtues (see Gal. 5:22-23; 1 Cor. 13:4-7), which in the concrete constitute the being of the Body, are but facets of love, that creative power which animates "the new man."[38] The Great Commandment of love clearly indicates, furthermore, that God intends that

83

we need to love and to be loved. One cannot be an authentic human being and be alone.

Within the context of Christian biblical revelation, moral judgment is also a community effort. "The 'mind of Christ' is a perspective proper to the New Man of whom individuals are only members [1 Cor. 2:6]. . . . whatever the corporate mind tests and finds to be 'good, acceptable and perfect' is in fact the will of God [see Rom 12:2]."[39] Individuals are directed by "the Spirit of Christ" only inasmuch as they are truly rooted "in Christ," that is, in "the empowering love which creates the organic unity of the community."[40] Inspired by the self-giving love of Christ, an authentic moral decision both is rooted in and builds up the unity of the community.

Authentic individuality, in the viewpoint of Paul and the early Church, is constituted by being a dependent and completely integrated member or *part* of the Body of Christ. Unlike a fine arts club, for example, which comes into being because of the individuals who form it for a specific purpose, the Church preexists the members who belong to it. Rather than being brought into existence by its members, "the Christian community brings its members into being, the new being of authenticity."[41] The Christian's individuation occurs paradoxically the more perfectly one functions as the unique member he or she was called and gifted to be. Just as a hand does not have its true existence separated from the body, although it may be considered separately, likewise "in the Body of Christ the members do not have separate existences, but can still be considered separately. This would seem to be the only way to make sense of Paul's very obscure formulation in 1 Cor. 12:27, which can be paraphrased, 'You are the Body of Christ and, considered separately, members of it.' "[42]

When the tension between the individual and social aspects of our human existence is not kept in a balanced perspective, we can easily lapse into the extremes of collectivism and individualism. By instinct, human beings are group animals. Our collective nature gives way to a herd psychology, whereby we easily shirk responsibility for our personal growth and choices in life. Conforming to popular opinion, succumbing to peer pressure, and directing one's life by the customs and prescriptions of conventions undoubtedly make things simpler. It is this corporate orientation or herd mentality that Paul speaks of in Rom. 1:28 when he writes that "God delivered them up to their own depraved sense [or 'debased mind'] to do what is unseemly."[43] In the gospels Jesus warns us to counteract this collective tendency and to "enter through the narrow gate; for the gate is wide and the road broad that leads to destruction, and those who enter through it are many'' (Mt. 7:13; also Lk. 13:24). The "wide gate" is the path of least resistance and mass identity. The "narrow gate" demands that we pay close attention and grow in spiritual consciousness, lest we fail to enter the kingdom of God.[44]

Ironically individualism has become the primary "group consciousness" of contemporary American society. In *Habits of the Heart* the sociologist Robert Bellah writes that "By the end of the eighteenth century, there would be those who would argue that in a society where each vigorously pursued his own interest, the social good would automatically emerge."[45] The life of Benjamin Franklin became the purist image of this "utilitarian individualism." Along with it there arose an "expressive individualism" which saw an American's ultimate independence take flesh in the freedom of a virtually uninhibited self-expression, as witnessed in the life of the poet Walt Whitman (1819-1892). The result of all this is that today "much popular writing about the life course (Gail Sheehy's *Passages*, for example), as well as much of the thinking of ordinary Americans, considers the life course without any reference to any social or historical context, as something that occurs to isolated individuals."[46]

In the moral sphere this now ontological individualism, according to Bellah, means that "the objectified moral goodness of [Governor] Winthrop [of the Massachusetts Bay Colony] obeying God's will or [Thomas] Jefferson following nature's laws turns into the subjective goodness of getting what you want and enjoying it. Utility replaces duty; self-expression unseats authority. 'Being good' becomes 'feeling good.' "[47] Such an individualistic stance, furthermore, "finds it hard to comprehend the social realism of the church — the idea that the church is prior to individuals and not just the product of them."[48] Within this American context hundreds of Christian sects have been born which view the Church as primarily a voluntary association of believers. For St. Paul, however, individual autonomy does not constitute the essence of freedom but rather is characteristic of inauthenticity.

5. On the categorical level, moreover, one's freedom of choice is often experienced as limited by **external predeterminations**. Yet, because a human person is gifted with *radical freedom* on the deepest transcendental level, he or she experiences the tension, the pull, between these *coincidentia oppositorum* ("coincidences of opposites"), such as we have just been

considering. Awareness of various categorical limitations has even moved some philosophers and therapists to deny the very existence of human freedom. Indeed, we know we were given no choice about our being born, nor about the time and place of our birth. We were not allowed to select our parents or siblings, nor our physical characteristics, ethnicity, social and economic level. We came into this life with so many factors predetermined for us. Commitment to prison, a concentration camp, or a health care facility can further limit one's freedom of choice and mobility. The behaviorist school of psychology, therefore, subscribing to a positivistic and materialistic interpretation of human behavior, denies the very existence of human free will; all our categorical decisions, it maintains, are solely the results of conditioned reflexes.

Christian biblical revelation, however, rests on the fundamental belief that God freely chose to create. Creation is not an accident, nor something God had to do. And in creating us in his image, God bestowed on us a share in his creative freedom. Love itself of its very nature demands freedom, or else it is not love. God has gifted us with a radical — that is, transcendental — freedom in order that we might enter into a personal and loving relationship with him. Through this gift the human person is capable of self-transcendence and personal fulfillment by becoming the person God's loving call invites him or her to be. Such freedom is acquired through the radical acceptance of the gift of the Spirit, the gift of grace (see 2 Cor. 3:17). Our positive response to this gift thus makes us one with God, sharing a communion of life with him, and thereby truly free.

This gift of radical freedom means that at the deepest core of our being, in our non-categorical, unreflexive consciousness, we stand open to the Transcendent, to God himself. All knowledge which comes through the use of our senses is categorical and reflexive. Our senses detect the categories of size, shape, color, form, etc., and mediate this information to our consciousness where images are formed impressing upon us knowledge of the reality in question. Our spirit, as it were, reaches out in search of truth and returns to us with an image of the reality it has encountered in its seeking process. Such knowledge is called "objective" inasmuch as it reflects back to the individual subject knowledge of reality beyond the immediate Self. This "objective" knowledge, nonetheless, is also subjective because it is received according to the condition of the perceiving subject.

Within the human person there also exists the possibility of non-categorical, unflexive consciousness — that is, knowledge which does not depend on categories and the process of reflection. Such knowing rises to the surface of consciousness in mystical experience, but it always remains at the deepest core of our being where God and the Self meet one another as co-subjects. We cannot reflect upon this encounter, for in that very moment it becomes objectified in categories and we immediately distance ourselves from it. It is truly a transcendental process of which we can have no adequate knowledge. For this reason the Council of Trent taught that "no one can know with a certitude of faith which cannot be subject to error, that he has obtained God's grace" (DS 1534).[49] At this core level no one can take our freedom from us. It is strictly a matter between God and the individual subject, a matter of accepting or refusing the gift of grace.

On the level of categorical options, freedom of choice is frequently identified with individual autonomy. Within the context of American cultural individualism, "freedom turns out to mean being left alone by others, not having other people's values, ideas, or styles of life forced upon one, being free of arbitrary authority in work, family and political life."[50] Such individual autonomy reaches mythical proportions in American literature and contemporary television, from James Fenimore Cooper's *The Deerslayer* and Herman Melville's *Moby Dick* to the Lone Ranger and the mystique of the American cowboy and the modern hard-boiled detective. These latter heroes tell us something important about the nature of American individualism. "The cowboy, like the detective, can be valuable to society only because he is a completely autonomous individual who stands outside it."[51]

The notion of individual autonomy cherished by so many contemporary Americans, however, flies in the face of the Christian concept of freedom.

> For Paul there is no such thing as human autonomy. All human existence involves slavery. What is to be determined is to what we are enslaved. "You who were once slaves of sin . . . having been set free from sin, have become slaves of righteousness (Rom 6:17-18). Paul speaks of himself as a slave of Jesus Christ (Rom 1:1). He warns the Galatians not to distort the Christian notion of freedom into Greek freedom. "Do not use your freedom as an opportunity for the flesh, but through love be slaves to one another" (Gal 5:13).[52]

In the perspective of the New Testament freedom does not mean being free *to* do whatever one chooses. Since the Fall, human beings, whether they know it or not, have lived enslaved to the powers of sin and death, operative through the Law. Only by remaining in his word of truth does the Son set us free (Jn.

87

8:31-36). Real freedom is to be free *from* law, the flesh, sin and death *for* the gospel, the Spirit, grace and life. Freedom is a matter of the Spirit's presence (2 Cor. 3:17).

The power of the Spirit produces genuine freedom as it unites us with the community of the Church, Christ's Body, through the reception of baptism (see Rom. 6:1-6). "Individuals, therefore, enjoy 'freedom *from*' only to the extent that they belong to an authentic community."[53] As members of Christ's Body we are delivered from the bondage of sin and receive the power, encouragement and support to become the person God is calling us to be. The community of faith provides the environment necessary to heal the wounds of sin and selfishness. This alone frees and transforms us so that we can become "slaves of God" (1 Pt. 2:16) and serve one another in imitation of Jesus Christ (Jn. 13:14-15). For the Christian, "Freedom consists of being able to choose who your master will be."[54]

The classical "manual" tradition in Catholic moral theology was concerned with the human person only inasmuch as he or she was a "doer of action," a performer of the "human act." As such, the individual was treated as an object to be analyzed. He or she could be known categorically and reflexively. The human person was thus little more than a particular instance of "humanity" distinguished only through his or her own individual knowledge and freedom.

Returning to Christian biblical revelation and the history of salvation, as suggested by Vatican II (OT 16), the human person is first of all seen as created in the "image of God" and as participating in the Mystery of Christ. As such, he or she is a subject, a mystery that cannot be fully known as a direct object of categorical reflection. Yet, persons as subjects have a certain *awareness* of themselves, a sense of their own identity. They are unique, and they precede, ground, transcend and perdure the life-span of any individual action.

This self-awareness, verified by human experience and divine revelation, informs us that we are at one and the same time children of Adam and children of God. We are both fallen and redeemed, we are body and spirit capable of participating in both time and eternity. We are unique individuals, yet thoroughly social or relational beings who also experience ourselves as both predetermined and radically free. Such are some of the many complementarities that constitute the person who receives the divine gift-call to conversion and discipleship, "the exalted vocation of the faithful in Christ . . . to bring forth fruit in charity for the life of the world" (OT 16).

Notes

1. In Robert J. Daly, S.J., ed., *Christian Biblical Ethics*, p. 221.

2. Ladislas Orsy, S.J., *The Evolving Church and the Sacrament of Penance* (Denville, New Jersey: Dimension Books, 1978), p. 101.

3. See ibid., 103.

4. Joseph Ratzinger, *Introduction to Christianity* (New York: Herder and Herder, 1970), p. 38.

5. See Richard M. Gula, S.S., *What Are They Saying About Moral Norms?* (New York/Ramsey, N.J.: Paulist Press, 1981), pp. 18-23. The revisionist preference for the historical approach, for example, is expressed by Orsy, op. cit., p. 112: "In moral theology, too, there is a need to turn from the classical to the historical approach. . . . From the secure position of definition of essences, we must move to the humble process of increasing our understanding, as much as we can, through the data and information that is available to us."

6. John Shea, *Stories of God: An Unauthorized Biography* (Chicago: The Thomas More Press, 1978), p. 22.

7. Ratzinger, op. cit., p. 62.

8. Mircea Eliade, *Images and Symbols: Studies in Religious Symbolism* (New York: Sheed and Ward, 1969), p. 12.

9. See Brian P. Hall, *The Genesis Effect: Personal and Organizational Transformations* (New York/Mahwah, N.J.: Paulist Press, 1986), pp. 11, 32-33; also Ratzinger, op. cit., p. 123, fn. 27 where it is pointed out that in introducing the law of complementarity into physics Niels Bohr referred to the complementarity of God's justice and mercy as presented by theology.

10. See Hall, op. cit., pp. 10, 31-32.

11. See Avery Dulles, S.J., *Models of Revelation* (Garden City, New York: Doubleday & Co., 1983), pp. 158-159.

12. Ibid., 136-137.

13. Shea, op. cit., p. 19.

14. See the author's doctoral dissertation *Evangelization in America* (New York, N.Y./Ramsey, N.J./Toronto, 1977), chapter 5, "Fundamental Evangelical Categories for Contemporary Christian Living," pp. 157-197, where he initially developed these categories within the context of a gospel world-view, relating them to the summary of Jesus' preaching found in Mk. 1:15.

15. See John Paul II's fifth encyclical letter *Dominum et Vivificantem*, ("Lord and Giver of Life"), no. 34: ". . . man in his own humanity receives

as a gift a special '*image and likeness*' to God. This means not only rationality and freedom as constitutive properties of human nature, but also, from the very beginning, the capacity of having *personal relationship* with God, as 'I' and 'you', and therefore the *capacity of having a covenant. . . .*'' (italics in original) Thomas Aquinas maintained that Christian life or morality meant realizing the image of God within us. This divine image, he maintained, is reflected by the fact we are intellectual beings, having dominion over our actions, and is most perfectly manifested in our practice of charity.

16. *Dominum et Vivificantem*, no. 37.

17. Harakas, *Toward Transfigured Life*, p. 26.

18. Ratzinger, op. cit., 131-132.

19. Ibid., p. 180.

20. See John Paul II's second encyclical letter, *Dives in Misericordia*, (''Rich in Mercy''), no. 7. See also Robert J. Daly, S.J., *Christian Biblical Ethics*, pp. 69-70: ''This is the heart of our Christian ethics, that we perceive ourselves and all men and women as called to 'pass over' with Christ. This means a call to self-transcending love of God and neighbor, of neighbor and God.''

21. Murphy-O'Connor, O.P., *Becoming Human Together*, p. 54, 76-77.

22. Ratzinger, op. cit., p. 198.

23. Daly, op. cit., p. 107.

24. Ratzinger, op. cit., p. 124.

25. Ibid., p. 125.

26. Daly, op. cit., p. 104.

27. *Treatise Against Heresies*, 5 pref., *Early Christian Classics,* ed. H.R.M. Hitchcock, (London: S.P.C.K., 1916), Vol. 2, p. 89, as cited in Lobo, *Guide to Christian Living*, p. 82.

28. J. Neuner, S.J. and J. Dupuis, S.J., eds., *The Christian Faith in the Doctrinal Documents of the Catholic Church*, revised ed. (New York: Alba House, 1982), p. 118, no. 401/1 (DS 403).

29. John A. Sanford, *The Kingdom Within: The Inner Meaning of Jesus' Sayings* (New York/Ramsey, N.J.: Paulist Press, 1970), pp. 160-161, 156.

30. Hall, op. cit., p. 36.

31. Sanford, op. cit., pp. 20, 49.

32. Hall, op. cit., p. 50.

33. Bernie S. Siegel, M.D., *Love, Medicine & Miracles* (New York: Harper & Row Publishers, 1986), p. 150.

34. Hans Urs von Balthasar, *A Theological Anthropology* (New York: Sheed and Ward, 1967), p. 35.

35. Hall, op. cit., pp. 31-32. The author here tells of an experiment with time in the use of biofeedback during meditation states: "Itzhak Bentov . . . noted that when a person produces Theta waves, which is a deep meditative state, and keeps his or her eyes open and on a clock with a second hand, the second hand slows to a point of almost stopping."

36. See Eveyln Underhill, *Mysticism* (New York: Meridian Books, 1955), p. 41.

37. Urs von Balthasar, op. cit., pp. 38-39.

38. See Murphy-O'Connor, op. cit., pp. 182, 185.

39. Ibid., pp. 213-214.

40. Ibid., p. 215.

41. Ibid., p. 181.

42. Ibid., p. 182.

43. Ibid., p. 213.

44. Sanford, op. cit., p. 65; also pp. 64, 80ff.

45. Bellah, et al., op. cit., p. 33.

46. Ibid., p. 82.

47. Ibid., p. 77.

48. Ibid., p. 244.

49. J. Neuner, S.J. and J. Dupuis, S.J., op. cit., p. 560, no. 1936.

50. Bellah et al., op cit., p. 23.

51. Ibid., p. 146.

52. Keegan, op. cit., p. 231.

53. Murphy-O'Connor, op. cit., p. 161.

54. Harakas, op. cit., p. 106 giving a reported statement of Bishop Gerasimos of the Greek Archdiocese of North and South America.

Chapter 4

Conversion

*The beginning of the spiritual life is conversion, an attitude of
the will turning towards God and renouncing the world. . . . "The
world" signifies here a dispersion, the soul's wandering outside
itself, a treason against its real nature.* — Vladimir Lossky[1]

Jesus began his public ministry proclaiming the Good News: "This is the
time of fulfillment. The kingdom of God is at hand. Repent, and believe in
the gospel" (Mk. 1:15). With these words Jesus announces that the promised
intervention of God has arrived. God's power is now definitively at work
removing our hearts of stone and putting within us a "new heart" (Ezk.
11:18f.). This radical transformation, or conversion, is all God's doing; it is a
grace and a gift (see Acts 5:31; 11:18). Conversion is a gift which calls us to
the Kingdom of God, to participate in truth and love. It is an invitation to turn
away from the alienation and darkness of sin and to come home to the love of
God, who is eternal life. It is allowing God to act on us, to endow us with his
gifts. "Therefore, the very call to repentance is a gospel, and the call to
conversion is a call to joy."[2]

Conversion and repentance constitute the fundamental theme in the
preaching of the prophets, John the Baptist, Jesus, and the apostolic Church.
It is the key which opens the door to the Kingdom of God. Conversion,
turning towards God and away from sin, is the cornerstone of Christian life.
Yet it was not even mentioned in the manuals of moral theology that were
used to train candidates for the priesthood in the post-Tridentine, pre-Vatican
II era. The separation of moral and ascetical theology in the new seminary
system that emerged after the Council of Trent relegated the dynamics of
ongoing conversion, although it never used the term, to the latter discipline.
For all practical purposes, this wrenched the heart and soul from the body
(concrete moral behavior) of Christian life.

As part of the Christian vocabulary, "conversion" virtually disappeared
after the Constantinian embrace of the Church. Baptism itself became

synonymous with conversion. Thus, when infant baptism became commonplace, all talk of conversion ceased for it was taken for granted that a person who was baptized, even as an infant, would naturally live a Christian life. Today, the understanding of conversion varies among the different Christian traditions. A Puritan and fundamentalist approach to conversion has left its stamp on our American consciousness. From Jonathan Edwards and the Great Awakening through powerful preachers from Billy Sunday to Billy Graham, the "born-again" experience of accepting Jesus Christ as one's personal Lord and Savior has shaped our common perception of conversion.

The fundamentalist understanding of conversion becomes quite questionable, however, when confronted with the ancient tradition of the Church. Revivalism is extremely individualistic in its approach, concentrating for the most part on private sins and demonstrating virtually no awareness of the communal nature of the Church. Research indicates that most of those who come forward for the "altar calls" at these evangelistic campaigns are either deeply committed Christians already or they have only transient church involvement in the months afterwards.[3]

This is not to infer that conversion is never marked by an abrupt, powerful religious experience which turns one's life in a totally new direction. Conversion, however, can often be a very long, slow and laborious process. St. Augustine, in a way, is an example of both; "over thirty years, he slowly but surely moved toward Christian life, but he needed that sudden voice calling to him to make it happen."[4] Our liturgical tradition from the ancient catechumenate to the new Rite of Christian Initiation of Adults clearly indicates that conversion is a continuing process, a spiritual journey, which unfolds within an ecclesial and sacramental context.

Biblical Perspectives on Conversion

Conversion is a central theme of sacred Scripture. The Greek word *metanoia* means "to change one's mind" and "to regret." It translates the Hebrew or Aramaic concept which suggests making an about-face after having discovered one is traveling in the wrong direction. The Old Testament term *shub* is an action word; it implies an actual turning away from one's former path, correcting one's course and heading off in a new direction.

The Old Testament *"Shub."* All the prophets of the Old Testament call the people to repentance with the word *"shub."* Conversion in the prophetic tradition is a call to turn away from the worship of idols, from false gods, and to return to the true God. It is a call, too, to turn away from injustice, immorality and from contempt for the commands of God. "Thus says the LORD of hosts, the God of Israel: Reform your ways and your deeds, so that I may remain with you in this place. . . . Are you to steal and murder, commit adultery and perjury, burn incense to Baal, go after strange gods that you know not, and yet come to stand before me in this house which bears my name and say: 'We are safe; we can commit all these abominations again'?'' (Jer. 7:3, 9-10).

Refusal to be converted to God on the part of the people and their leaders brings a threat of punishment. A feigned repentance is to no avail: "Your piety is like a morning cloud, / like the dew that early passes away. / For this reason I smote them through the prophets, / I slew them by the words of my mouth; / For it is love I desire, / not sacrifice, and knowledge of God rather than holocausts" (Hos. 6: 4-6). The mere external observance of penitential practices such as fasting, dressing in sackcloth and ashes and making lamentations is wholly insufficient. "Rend your hearts, not your garments, / and return to the LORD, your God. / For gracious and merciful is he, / slow to anger, rich in kindness, / and relenting in punishment" (Joel 2:13).

Penance in the Old Testament is a religious and personal act which has as its aim love and surrender to God. It involves the whole person. Conversion to God must be expressed in one's whole conduct and especially in works of justice and charity. True "fasting" that is pleasing to God involves setting free the oppressed, feeding the hungry, sheltering the homeless and clothing the naked (see Is. 58:6-7). The later prophets would see the whole history of Yahweh's dealings with his people as God's call to repentance and conversion (Zech. 1:3; Mal. 3:7). This call to conversion is always a gift of God; it never comes about simply through human effort (see Jer. 31:18).

The New Testament. In the gospel, John the Baptist continues the prophetic tradition by calling the people to repentance. He "appeared in the desert proclaiming a baptism of repentance for the forgiveness of sins" (Mk. 1:4). His preaching was aimed at the moral reformation of the Jewish nation. His call to sinners, typified as tax collectors and soldiers, demanded a turning away from greed and power and a turning to God. He also warned the followers of the Law, the Pharisees and Sadducees, to produce the appropriate fruits as evidence of their repentance (Mt. 3:7-9). The motive of his preaching was that they might escape the threatening judgment of God's wrath.[5]

94

Despite its outward similarity to John's preaching, Jesus' call to repentance had a deeper significance. It combined a command to believe the Good News. For Jesus, conversion is an expression of joy and confidence in salvation. It is a grateful response for God's loving action, a coming home to a merciful Father. Indeed, Jesus informs us that God's readiness to forgive is limited only by one condition, repentance. In the parables of the prodigal son (Lk. 15:11-32) and the Pharisee and the tax collector (Lk. 18:9-14), Jesus teaches us that only when a person recognizes and regrets one's sinfulness, placing one's total trust in God's mercy, is genuine conversion present.

For Jesus, all have need of repentance. In God's sight we are always "unprofitable servants" (Lk. 17:10); we are always his debtors (Mt. 6:12). But if we realize this, then the saying will be proved true in us that "the one who humbles himself will be exalted" (Lk. 18:14). Self-righteousness and contempt for others are the main attitudes that militate against repentance. Furthermore, there is an urgency in Jesus' call to conversion, the refusal of which brings a threat of judgment that inevitably follows for the unrepentant (see Lk. 10:13-15; 13:1-5). Such judgment does not in the least imply that God actively inflicts evil; rather the punishment is truly self-inflicted. God offers us life, healing, reconciliation. By remaining unrepentant a person chooses instead the way of death and self-dissolution. Finally, Jesus warns against recanting and backsliding. Conversion demands a total commitment of an undivided heart. "No one who sets a hand to the plow and looks to what was left behind is fit for the kingdom of God" (Lk. 9:62).

While St. Paul's use of *"metanoia"* is infrequent, the idea of conversion or an about-face in one's life is clearly evident in the terms "new creation" (2 Cor. 5:17; Gal. 6:15), "newness of life" (Rom. 6:4; 2 Cor. 5:15), and "new person" (Eph. 2:15; 4:24). Through baptism one dies to the "old self," one dies to sin and lives for God (see Rom. 6:1-11). This is all God's work, but it demands that we do not conform ourselves to the ways of that world which has no knowledge of God (see Rom. 12:2). This conversion or personal transformation is an ongoing process, for in Paul's own words, "our inner self is being renewed day by day" (2 Cor. 4:16).

In place of "conversion," which does not appear at all in the Gospel according to John, we find pairs of antithetical terms: light and darkness, truth and lies, love and hate, life and death, God and world. Hearing Jesus' word, believing the Good News, involves a turning from one to the other (Jn. 5:24). Seeing the Kingdom of God and entering it demands our rebirth, our "being born from above" (Jn. 3:3-7). Again, this is all God's doing, for in the words of Jesus as cited by John, "no one can come to me unless it is granted him by my Father" (Jn. 6:65).[6]

The early apostolic Church saw conversion as a spiritual rebirth accompanying faith and baptism as prerequisites for membership. This initial conversion celebrated by baptism is the primary focus of the New Testament authors. Yet the later writings deal with a second conversion, which becomes the fundamental theme of the Book of Revelation (see Rev. 2:4-5; 3:3, 19; etc.). There the seer, expecting an imminent parousia, challenges the still young churches to repent of their waning fervor and weakening love. For these early Christians there can be no turning back from conversion. The faithful disciple must make ever greater progress in the new life Christ gives.

Conversion in the New Testament is a definite about-face, a turning *from* sin and evil *to* the mercy and love of God. The follower of Christ "must turn from evil and do good" (1 Pet. 3:11). St. Paul is very clear on the necessity of actively rejecting evil as an outgrowth of our baptismal entrance into the life of the Holy Spirit. Russian Orthodox theologian, Stanley Harakas, writes

> Much of St. Paul's moral exhortation is toward encouraging his readers to avoid specific vices: "Do not be conformed to this world;" "hate what is evil," "do not be haughty . . . never be conceited," repay no one evil for evil;" "Beloved, never avenge yourselves;" "Do not be overcome by evil but overcome evil with good;" are such injunctions from just one of St. Paul's chapters.[7]

While no longer "in slavery to sin" (Rom. 6:6), the baptized person still has to activate his or her new status and relationship as a member of "the household of God" (Eph. 2:19). The grace and power of God is given the believer, yet "every athlete exercises discipline in every way. They do it to win a perishable crown, but we an imperishable one" (1 Cor. 9:25).

Conversion in Theological Tradition

The writings and liturgical practice of the post-apostolic era constantly convey the necessity of avoiding evil and turning to God, of choosing the "way of life." The *Didache*, or Teaching of the Twelve Apostles, which was a late-first-century moral instruction for converts from paganism, presents the "two ways," one of life and one of death. The "way of life" involves the shunning of evil and everything resembling it, avoiding anger, lust, superstitious practices, lying, love of money and grumbling. Baptism, which celebrated one's conversion, included from ancient times the rite of exorcism requiring a conscious, deliberate rejection of evil: "Do you reject satan?... and all his works...?"

The Patristic Era. While rejoicing in the new life of Christ given us at baptism, in the forgiveness of sins and the power of God's grace, the Fathers of the Church seem to give an equal amount of attention to the believer's need to avoid and shun evil. The Letter of Clement of Rome to the Church at Corinth, exhorting peace and unity after an outbreak of rebellion among the junior members of the Corinthian church, pleads:

> Let us then give up those empty and futile aspirations, and turn to the glorious and venerable rule of our tradition. Let us attend to what is noble, what is pleasing, what is acceptable in the sight of our maker. Let us fix our gaze upon the blood of Christ, and understand how precious it is to the Father, because, poured out for our salvation, it brought the whole world the grace of conversion.[8]

Conversion is an exercise of human free will cooperating with God's grace, with the power of Christ's paschal mystery, which enables the Christian to turn from evil and attend to what is noble, pleasing and acceptable in the eyes of God.

In the second century Justin Martyr in his *First Apology* informs us that admission to baptism was subject to three very precise requirements: sorrow for sins, faith in the Church as the teacher of truth and transformation of life.[9] Origen viewed the long catechumenal preparation for baptism as a spiritual journey comparable to Exodus.[10] Tertullian in the third century in his tract *On Penitence* "stresses the necessity of repentance for sin, as well as participation in the redemption through Baptism and the continual imitation of Christ by a life of mortification, almsgiving and prayer."[11] As infant baptism became commonplace, the mention of "conversion" virtually disappears from Christian writings. A developing interest in the practice of asceticism takes its place. Rufinus of Aquileia (345-410), for example, in translating into Latin the nine *Homilies of Origen on the Psalms* explains his reason for choosing this particular work:

> These Homilies offer certain precepts for an emended way of life, and teach the first ways of penance and conversion, then that of purgation and progress.[12]

While a Stoic and Neo-Platonic dualism, which primarily views the body as a prison for the soul, influences some of the ascetical practices called for in the writings of the later Fathers, a clear understanding of the gospel's demands also underlies these same works.

The Greek Fathers, from Clement of Alexandria to John Damascene, speak of the necessity of overcoming our "passions," that is, those egotistic desires and actions which are opposed to our true nature. These are usually divided into passions of the soul and passions of the body. John Damascene lists fifty-four of the former including impiety, blasphemy, anger, bitterness, gossip, hypocrisy, ingratitude, insensitivity, flattery, etc., and thirty-four of the latter, such as hedonism, drunkenness, fornication, homosexuality, theft, murder, magic, laziness, gambling, etc. Basil of Caesarea, however, warned that when dealing with the sinner or wrong-doer one must show compassion and patience.

> It is not possible to strive for perfection from the start. Nor is it right to tell someone still given to evil doing that he should do good; rather he should be encouraged to recede from vice. For it is only when he has had his full of wrong-doing that he becomes capable of doing good and becoming involved with good works.[13]

The rejection of passions, sin and evil deeds bridges the gap between God and ourselves. These ascetical struggles mark the milestones of our spiritual journey, of our ongoing conversion, to unity with God. Central to this part of the message of the Fathers is "the realization that there nests within us, in addition to all the good elements of the divine image, a disordered disharmonious tendency, ever ready to interfere with the life appropriate and fitting to a child of God growing in the divine image. . . ."[14]

Classical Theology. The classical understanding of conversion in the post-Tridentine, pre-Vatican II period emphasized the intellectual and objective character of faith. To become a convert meant to accept the truths of divine revelation as authoritatively presented by the Church. The determining feature was ecclesiological, becoming a member of the Church. While "convert" and "convert-making" remained part of Catholic vocabulary, the term "conversion" itself had practically disappeared. Missing, too, were the Christological and anthropological aspects of conversion, the radical transformation of the person in Christ. The biblical renewal, which began in the nineteenth century in Europe, once again brought attention to the central importance of *metanoia* in the Christian life.

The Liturgical Renewal. The Second Vatican Council's Constitution on the Sacred Liturgy stated that "Before men can come to the liturgy they must be called to faith and to conversion" (SC 9). In referring to the re-establishment of the catechumenate, the Council's Decree on the Church's Missionary Activity states:

> Under the movement of divine grace the new convert sets out on a spiritual journey by means of which, while already sharing through faith in the mystery of the death and resurrection, he passes from the old man to the new man who has been made perfect in Christ (cf. Col. 3:5-10; Eph. 4:20-24). This transition, which involves a progressive change of outlook and morals, should be manifested in its social implications and effected gradually during the period of the catechumenate (AG 13).

Conversion, as viewed by the Council Fathers, is clearly a continuing process involving Christological and anthropological dimensions.

The new Rite of Christian Initiation of Adults (RCIA) promulgated by Paul VI in 1972 incorporates the Council's understanding of conversion. An analysis of the introduction and prayers of the RCIA reveals that conversion is, first of all, understood as an entrance into a covenantal relationship to which God calls us. It is, secondly, Christocentric since the transformation to which we are called finds its fundamental pattern in the paschal mystery of Jesus. We are called to "put on" the Lord Jesus (Gal. 3:27). Thirdly, conversion is a sacramental experience whereby the believer embodies, or "sacramentalizes" in his or her own life this interior spiritual transformation, and also celebrates in ritual this inner journey. The celebration of the liturgical rites articulate the elements or stages of this developing conversion and support their continuing development as well. They express and effect what they signify. Conversion, fourthly, is essentially an ecclesial event. The Christ to whom we turn is found in his body, the Church. It is not just "Jesus and me," nor a matter only of accepting Jesus as my personal Lord and Savior. The RCIA stresses that the entire faith community must accompany and support the new member by sharing their own conversion journey. Fifthly, conversion is viewed as a spiritual journey. The transformation involved is developmental; it is not just a one time event, but a continuing process. Lastly, the RCIA reminds us that conversion involves every dimension of the human person. It is a comprehensive reality involving the transformation of the whole person.[15]

The new Rite of Penance promulgated in 1973 sheds further light on the Catholic understanding of conversion. Here, reconciliation, contrition and doing penance or satisfaction for sin are described as integral components of conversion. In the Introduction to the rite we read:

> "We can only approach the Kingdom of Christ by *metanoia*. This is a profound change of the whole person by which one begins to consider, judge, and arrange his life according to the holiness and love of God, made manifest in his Son in the last days and given to us in abundance" (see Hebrews 1:2; Colossians 1:19 and *passim*). The genuineness of penance depends on this heartfelt contrition. For conversion should affect a person from within so that it may progressively enlighten him and render him continually more like Christ.[16]

In his commentary on the new Rite of Penance in *Reconciliatio et Paenitentia* (1984), Pope John Paul II urges us to look upon conversion and contrition in light of the Good News. He writes:

> ... we do well to recall and emphasize the fact that *contrition and conversion* are even more a drawing near to the holiness of God, a rediscovery of one's true identity which has been upset and disturbed by sin, a liberation in the very depth of self and thus a regaining of lost joy, the joy of being saved, which the majority of people in our time are no longer capable of experiencing.[17]

The new rite is more than a private guilt-shedding event. It is a celebration of ongoing conversion in the life of the believer. Also called the Rite of Reconciliation, it is a celebration of our returning to the love of God, of our being reconciled in our relationships with God, with self, with one another, and with all of creation.[18]

The liturgical renewal undertaken by the Second Vatican Council has returned to the biblical understanding of conversion and placed it, once again, at the center of Christian life. Its pivotal importance for our spiritual and moral development is distinctively accented and celebrated in the new rites. The Church today in its liturgy teaches us that conversion is an ongoing process of transformation in Christ which flows from God's covenant love. As such, it involves the whole person in all his or her relationships and has essential ecclesial and sacramental dimensions.

Conversion involves recognizing God's mercy, faithfulness, and love. It involves turning away from our sins and turning towards the love of God. Oftentimes, we hear God's love calling us, attracting us, but we find ourselves tied down or pulled in other directions. This is why Paul VI reminded us in his *Paenitemini* (1966) of the necessity of penitential practices, which have been held in such high regard by Scripture, the Church Fathers and the monastic tradition.

> This exercise of bodily mortification — far removed from any form of stoicism — does not imply a condemnation of the flesh which sons of God deign to assume. On the contrary, mortification aims at the "liberation" of man, who often finds himself, because of concupiscence, almost chained to his senses.[19]

While conversion is a grace, a divine gift-call to an intimate communion of life, it is a call we can drown out with the noise of the world in which we live. Through penitential and ascetical practices we "tune in" or "set our dials," as it were, on God's grace, thereby predisposing ourselves to receive his gift. Finally, through acts of worship, charity, mercy or reparation, we manifest the quality and depth of our transformation in Christ and heed John the Baptist's command: "Produce good fruit as evidence of your repentance" (Mt. 3:8).

The Transformation of the Whole Person

Conversion happens as we allow God's all-merciful, reconciling love to transform us into a whole new creation. It means that we give God the permission to restore us by the power of his creative mercy to true humanity. We let him raise us up in Christ to new life, to that righteousness whereby every aspect of our being is at one, in harmony with his will, his plan for all of creation. Conversion is a turn about from the alienating effects of sin, from the self-satisfaction of mere existence subjected to the law of entropy and spiritual inertia.

Taking into consideration the many complementarities that constitute the human person, described in the previous chapter, conversion is the grace which keeps them in their proper relationship by empowering us to overcome the tendency of simply abandoning ourselves to our natural center of gravity. God's grace, his divine energies, break forth through the core of our being and radically transform us so that we can grow in all ways "in Christ." Such

101

Christian maturity demands total conversion, a fourfold conversion which is at one and the same time religious, intellectual, affective and moral.

Religious Conversion. The desire and thirst for ultimate meaning and love is written deep within the core of our being. Bernard Lonergan thus writes that "Religious conversion is being grasped by ultimate concern. It is other-worldly falling in love."[20] We hear deep within our hearts the call of the Other, the Mystery in whom "we live and move and have our being" (Acts 17:28). Religious conversion is simultaneously a drive toward ultimate Transcendence and a being embraced by God. "It is a total and permanent self-surrender without conditions, qualifications, or reservations. As a dynamic acceptance of our vocation to holiness, it precedes all our individual actions."[21]

In religious conversion the power of God's grace breaks forth in our lives filling us with joy and thus making us capable of every renunciation. It brings into harmonious relationship the complementarities that constitute who we are. It empowers us now to overcome the effects of Adam's sin and to live as children of God, to put off our old fallen nature through our redemption in Christ, to renounce the things of the "flesh" and become spiritual persons who share even now in eternal life. In religious conversion God is reconciling all our relationships and making us truly free to become the unique persons he has called us to be from all eternity.

Religious conversion is the gift-call of the "eternal now" (*kairos*) in our lives. It is the breaking in of God's kingdom, the bursting forth of the favorable time.[22] As such it is ontological, existential and non-developmental. It is God's love flooding our hearts and making us holy. It can be given to a person at any stage of intellectual and affective development, as is evidenced by the instances of truly holy children, for example, a twelve-year-old St. Maria Goretti, or a seven-year-old child afflicted with a terminal illness, or even by a mentally handicapped adult.

The mystics regularly speak of the mysterious Other who appears in our experience as "no-thing," One whom we cannot name, who exceeds all our understanding.

Fixed upon One whom they love who surpasses all finite reality, they are willing to leave creation behind, since in God they will recover everything as joy. Knowing their own limited status in the world, they experience this humility as exuberant gift. Finally, progressively detaching themselves from specific loves, they center upon the Other in a vital union of intersubjective love in which they can truly say that they and God are one without erasure of their own identity.[23]

On our part, religious conversion is an exercise of transcendental freedom, of our fundamental, core freedom. It is our "yes" of faith to God's gift-call. Through religious conversion we gratefully and joyfully place ourselves in God's hands. We accept his rule and kingdom as Absolute in our lives; there is no other God but him. In poverty of spirit we seek his will in all things, in every aspect and detail of our daily existence. While, as a free gift of grace, God can give such conversion in whatever degree and measure he chooses, most often on the human side within our temporal existence it grows progressively as we advance in wisdom and age.

Intellectual Conversion. The way we experience things is mediated by insights we have had and networks of theories which have been, since birth, constituting our "world-view." Human persons construct such world-views or imaginative perceptions in order to understand and cope with the world they live in. New experiences and insights at times may necessitate a change in one's perception of reality. They may require that one alter or even totally reconstruct his or her way of viewing the world. Such a re-imagining or change in a human being's perception of reality is what is called intellectual conversion. It is actually an ongoing, developmental process that involves a turning away from what seems to be to what is.

In the realm of Christian faith intellectual conversion marks a continuing turning away from ideologies, misconceptions and false images of God to the one true God as revealed to us by Jesus Christ, for "no one knows the Father except the Son and anyone to whom the Son wishes to reveal him" (Mt. 11:27). The eighteenth-century French writer, Voltaire, it is said, once commented that "God made man in his image and likeness, and ever since man has been returning the favor." We human beings have picked up our images of God from the way we have been taught about God and especially from the way we have been treated in his name. One of the most common images of God is the Heavenly Policeman, the Just Judge, or the Great Lawgiver. This is the "gotcha" God most often invoked by frustrated parents, teachers, and even pastors. This God constantly watches us, keeping tabs on every time we trip up, and holds over our heads the eternal imprisonment of hell if we ever get too far out of line. Then, there is the "God of the Gaps" or the great Aspirin-God to whom we turn when all else fails; this God fills in all the answers and makes all things better.[24] There is also the Superman-God or "*Deus ex machina*" who jumps in on cue at the appropriate moment to make everything right. The Loner-God stays in his heavens as the Great Self-sufficient Individualist who never interferes with our desire for privacy and for control over the affairs of this world. These and other false images of God combine with many idols and ideologies to supersede the rightful place of the true God in our lives — idols and ideologies such as economic success, power, fame, careerism, sex, materialism, conservatism, liberalism, etc.

Empowered by the grace of religious conversion we can turn away from false and rudimentary images of God to an ever greater knowledge of the Mystery that calls us in and through Jesus Christ (see 2 Cor. 4:6). Those who have studied the psychology of religious development suggest that our concept of God passes through three principal stages. The first is a primitive stage of magical understanding or systemic control, where the sacred is identified with or localized in exterior objects or ritual actions. The religious awareness of individuals and entire peoples begins at this stage. Little children first grasp reality in very concrete terms. The Church is "God's house," Jesus lives in the little host in the tabernacle, and so forth. For primitive peoples, too, the sacred is present in certain objects and localities, sacred spaces, altars, trees and rivers. The cult of relics within Christianity, for example, developed in the Middle Ages upon the conversion of the primitive German tribes.

A second, more developed stage of religious understanding is sometimes referred to as the stage of idealization. Here the sacred is an ideal to be imitated, but it still remains something completely external to us. Children in their early teens tend to imitate their heroes and idols, dress like them, copy their mannerisms, etc. In the Middle Ages some Christians practiced self-flagellation and had themselves nailed to crosses in literal imitation of Christ. Jesus and the saints at this stage of religious development are models to be imitated and copied.

The third, most mature stage of religious understanding is that of personal process whereby one realizes that his or her life shares in the very mystery of Being. Here a person comes to an awareness of the immanent-transcendent Mystery with whom one shares a communion of life. For the Christian at this stage, Christ's death and resurrection is an ongoing process in which one participates; it is the very pattern of one's existence and participation in life itself. This is the dynamic understanding that characterized the writings of the Fathers of the Church and the great mystics.[25]

These stages of religious understanding pertain to the order of human growth and development. In this century, developmental psychologists, such as Jean Piaget, have sought to uncover the structural characteristics of human development. Lawrence Kohlberg and James Fowler have taken Piaget's research on cognitive development and applied it to show how our moral and religious lives grow. These structural developmentalists, while articulating the operational rules or laws which the mind follows in reasoning or making judgments, run into valid criticism from other schools of thought for overlooking some important factors that constitute truly integrated development. The psychoanalytic and social-learning schools of development, represented by Carl Jung and Erik Erikson, see the growth process as a series of struggles and integrations between the inner psychic forces and the external demands of the social world. Human development for them is psychosomatic, tied to the physical development of the body on one hand and the emotional-imaginal on the other.[26]

Affective Conversion. Cognitive development alone is insufficient to explain the dynamics taking place in religious and moral conversion. Affective conversion describes the transformation that occurs within the realm of our feelings and emotions through the power of the imagination.

> Affective conversion occurs in the appropriation of our images and symbols. Each of us has an internal language by which we communicate to ourselves; it primarily emerges in dreams. We can be unconsciously governed by these symbols or we can learn how to make them our own. Under one aspect of the about-face that occurs in this realm, we move away from images that express our narcissism, our self-interested feelings, and our affective impotence to attach ourselves to valuable persons, places, or things within a network of relationships, loyalty to a community, and faith in our capacity to change human destinies.[27]

Affective conversion describes the change of values that takes place within a human person as he or she turns away from narcissistic love, or a totally self-centered, atomistic individualism, to a self-giving love of others and to fully relational living.

Just as concepts and insights provide for intellectual perception, so symbols and images constitute our affective orientation. "A symbol is an image of a real or imaginary object that evokes a feeling or is evoked by a feeling,"[28] It obeys not the law of logic but of image and feeling. Feelings in turn must be distinguished as to whether they are nonintentional states and trends or intentional responses. Nonintentional states would include feelings of fatigue, irritability, bad humor and anxiety, all of which, as such, have causes. Feelings arising from nonintentional trends all have goals, such as hunger, thirst and sexual discomfort. As intentional responses, however, feelings always occur at the level of symbolic imagination; they answer to what is intended, apprehended or represented in the symbol.[29] Because symbols pull together and embody both what we know and feel about a given reality they constitute values, which alone because of their attraction have the power to motivate us to action.

Negative feelings that arise from nonintentional states and trends tend to evoke symbols or images that motivate us in the direction of self-absorption and selfish preoccupation. Such natural concupiscence, the result of original and actual sin, pulls us in the opposite direction of grace, or the spirit of God's love within us reconciling us and drawing us into relationship. One of the first steps, then, in counteracting these negative pulls is the cultivation of the virtue of simplicity or "poverty of spirit," the first of the Beatitudes (Mt. 5:3). Through ascetical practices and the pursuit of detachment, the "purgative way" in classic spirituality, one receives the gift of "self-control," a fruit of the Spirit (Gal. 5:23). The great spiritual traditions, including eastern mystics like Buddha, have consistently recognized that attachment to any desire or need prevents growth. Detachment, they maintain, is the key to enlightenment, or the "illuminative way."

In affective conversion our intentional responses, or positive feelings are all directed to the order of charity (*ordo caritatis*), as formulated in the writings of St. Augustine and St. Thomas Aquinas. In these classical formulations we see that, after love of God, persons are the primary value to be loved.[30] The all-encompassing symbol in Jesus' preaching for this "order of charity" is the Kingdom of God. This inbreaking of God's reign gives us hope, the basis of affective conversion. For a follower of Christ such a conversion is the central dimension of the Christian call. "What it means for a disciple of Jesus is to love the neighbor without restrictions, and for Jesus that includes even love of our enemies" (Mt. 5:43-48; Lk. 6:27-28, 32-36).[31]

For the Christian, affective conversion means accepting God's rule and kingdom as Absolute in one's life. His will is to be sought in every phase and aspect of human existence. We thus cannot compartmentalize our existence and relegate his sovereignty to Sunday observance alone. God's order of charity is to be sought and applied to all spheres of economic, social, cultural, political and personal life. Accepting God's rule and kingdom as Absolute in one's life allows no room for nourishing and clinging to false securities, for setting up "defensive blocs" against the dizzying demands of Christlike love.

Moral Conversion. The fundamental human drive to seek ultimate meaning and love propels our intellectual and affective development. Such personal growth, or self-transcendence, finds concrete expression on the plane of moral behavior. Moral conversion is a shift or transposition from the level of thought and feeling to the level of decision and action. Moral conversion requires that we be responsible, that we do the truth as we personally perceive or understand it. This moral understanding, like our religious understanding, passes through stages from extrinsic legalism to personal appropriation. At whatever stage, however, moral conversion involves putting our understanding of what is right and good into action. It bridges the gap between what currently is and what *ought* to be, between the "already" and the "not-yet."

In the classical Christian perspective, once again, moral conversion pertains to the order of goods for persons' needs (*ordo bonorum*). It involves the recognition of oneself as a free and responsible subject with the ability to make decisions for action that are based not on personal satisfaction but on value.[32] Experiencing persons as values is also to experience the necessity of satisfying human needs in a way that enables people to flourish. It is fundamentally a matter of justice. From the biblical perspective of St. Paul, "living the truth in love, we should grow in every way into him who is the head, Christ, from whom the whole body . . . builds itself up in love" (Eph. 4:15-16).

As Christians, the truth we are called to live is the Absolute Good revealed to us in Jesus Christ as self-emptying love. Indeed, Jesus does not just tell us that God loves us, he demonstrates and proves it by his death on the cross. The U.S. bishops, when speaking about conversion in their 1976 pastoral reflection on the moral life, have thus called us "to live the paschal mystery, which we proclaim at Mass: 'Dying, He destroyed our death and, rising, He restored our life.' This paschal mystery is central to Christ's life and mission and to ours as His disciples."[33] Christ's paschal mystery constitutes the fundamental rhythm and pattern of the disciple's daily life (see Lk. 9:23). Moral conversion is an ongoing process of "putting on" Christ; it is a matter of making ever greater progress in our love for one another (see 1 Th. 4:10).

Christian *metanoia* is a total transformation of the human person brought about by religious, intellectual, affective and moral conversion. Religious conversion, turning to God's merciful and reconciling love flooding our hearts is primary. This fundamental about-face is an exercise of our transcendental or core freedom, and takes place on the level of non-categorical, non-reflexive consciousness in our heart of hearts. It is a turning to eternal life, the eternal "now," and as such is purely ontological, non-developmental. It is pure gift, pure grace, an abandoning of oneself to the creative, reconciling Love in whom we live, move, and have our existence.

The dynamics of Christian conversion flow from the very nature of the Triune God revealed to us through Jesus Christ in the power of the Holy Spirit. The God who calls us by giving us a share in his very own life is internally (*ad intra*) a permanent tri-unity of personal relationships, a community of persons in oneness. God, therefore, who is the Absolute Good, is no objective, impersonal good, but rather interpersonal good. This all-loving, interpersonal Mystery encounters us on the non-categorical, intersubjective level of our existence and draws us into his own eternal life. Our fundamental "yes" to this divine gift-call reconciles us to God making us his children and gifting us with redemption. Our "yes" on this core level reverses the dissolution and corruption of sin as it works to restore harmony to the various complementarities that make up our human nature, as described in the previous chapter.

On the external (*ad extra*) or categorical level, the Triune God is revealed through the missions of the Son and the Spirit, the sending of the Word of truth and the Spirit of creative, reconciling love. These missions correspond to the human heart's desire for ultimate meaning and love. They are eternal realities active, indeed even enfleshed, in time, in created realities. Intellectual and affective conversion come under the influence and direction of these two divine missions, the action of God within historical time. Religious conversion, on this categorical level of human understanding and practice, and moral conversion are fundamentally dependent upon intellectual and affective conversion. As such they are continuing processes, they are developmental. They reach to the fullness of the Eternal Life that calls and beckons them.

The ultimate convergence of these multifold conversions is "*theosis*" or deification, the ontological end (*telos*) of human nature. Jesus referred to this ultimate end as the Kingdom of God, which again is a matter of interpersonal communion because it is a sharing in Divine Trinitarian Life. Communion with the Trinity, traditionally, is not only a religious mystical experience, it is a religious ethical experience as well.[34] The ancient monastic tradition along with a range of Eastern and Western mystics witness to the fact that the "unitive way" of mystical communion follows upon the "purgative way" (affective conversion) and the "illuminative way" (intellectual conversion), all of which is preceded by and built upon an underlying religious conversion. These three conversions also precipitate a religious ethical or moral conversion, reminding us of Jesus' words of exhortation: "Remain in my love. If you keep my commandments, you will remain in my love, just as I have kept my Father's commandments and remain in his love" (Jn. 15:9-10).

Notes

1. Vladimir Lossky, *The Mystical Theology of the Eastern Church* (Crestwood, New York: St. Vladimir's Seminary Press, 1976), pp. 199-200.

2. Schelkle, *Theology of the New Testament*, vol. 3, p. 77.

3. See Dean R. Hoge, "Using Sociology for Effective Evangelization," *Catholic Evangelization Today: A New Pentecost for the United States*, ed. Kenneth Boyack, C.S.P. (New York/Mahwah: Paulist Press, 1987), p. 161.

4. Stephen Happel and James J. Walter, *Conversion and Discipleship: A Christian Foundation for Ethics and Doctrine* (Philadelphia: Fortress Press, 1986), p. 23.

5. See Schnackenburg, *The Moral Teaching of the New Testament*, p.26.

6. See Schelkle, op. cit., pp. 80-81 for the understanding of "conversion" in Paul and John.

7. Stanley Harakas, *Toward Transfigured Life*, p. 242 with reference to Romans 12.

8. "Letter of Clement 7," SC 167, 110-112 as cited in Murphy, *The Christian Way of Life*, p. 42.

9. Michel Dujarier, *A History of the Catechumenate: The First Six Centuries* (New York/Chicago/Los Angeles: Sadlier, 1979), pp. 38-39.

10. Ibid., p. 56.

11. Murphy, op. cit., p. 125.

12. CCL 20, 251 as cited in ibid., p. 188.

13. "Homily on Psalm 1,4''; PG 29, 218 cited in Murphy, op. cit., p. 154.

14. Harakas, op.cit., p. 244.

15. See Robert D. Duggan, "Conversion: The Underlying Dynamic of Evangelization," *Catholic Evangelization Today*, pp. 103-105.

16. *The Rite of Penance* (New York: Catholic Book Publishing Co., 1976), "Introduction, 6, a.,'' p. 11, citing Paul VI, Apostolic Constitution *Paenitemini*, February 17, 1966: AAS 58 (1966) 179.

17. John Paul II, *Reconciliation and Penance* (December 2, 1984), no. 31, III.

18. See ibid., no. 8.

19. Paul VI, Paenitemini (Apostolic Constitution on Penance), in *Vatican Council II: More Post Conciliar Documents*, vol. 2, general ed., Austin Flannery, O.P. (Northport, New York: Costello Publishing Co., 1982), p.5.

20. Bernard Lonergan, *Method in Theology* (New York: Herder and Herder, 1972), p. 240.

21. Happel and Walter, op. cit., p. 20.

22. See Hans Urs von Balthasar, *A Theological Anthropology*, p. 35: " 'Today' is the present of vertical salvation time, which 'in itself' is presence for man and the world, but is taken hold of by man and the world undergoing *conversio* and must be changed into a 'for-itself.' ''

23. Happel and Walter, op. cit., p. 46.

24. See Gula, *To Walk Together Again*, pp. 53-58.

25. See Cornelius van der Poel, *The Search for Human Values* (Paramus, N.J.: Newman Press, 1971), pp. 15-20; and Tad W. Guzie, *Jesus and the Eucharist* (Paramus, N.J.: Paulist Press, 1974), pp. 128-144.

26. Hall, *The Genesis Effect*, p. 89.

27. Happel and Walter, op. cit., p. 21.

28. Lonergan, op. cit., p. 64.

29. Happel and Walter, op. cit., p. 108.

30. Ibid., 38-39.

31. Ibid., p. 40.

32. See Lonergan, op. cit., p. 240.

33. National Conference of Catholic Bishops, *To Live in Christ Jesus* (Washington, D.C.: USCC, 1976), p. 7.

34. Harakas, op. cit., p. 237.

Chapter 5

Discipleship:
Faith-Response in Love and Hope

> *"Through faith Mary continued to hear and to ponder that word, in which there became ever clearer, in a way 'which surpasses knowledge' (Eph 3:19), the self-revelation of the living God. Thus in a sense Mary as Mother became the first 'disciple' of her Son...."*
> — John Paul II[1]

Faith, hope and love comprise the content of conversion. In the classical tradition they are called the theological virtues. Collectively they constitute a person's fundamental "yes" to the divine gift-call of conversion. They are supernatural, infused ontological energies that emanate from the grace of the Holy Spirit flooding our hearts. As such, they form the basic attitudes that place us in a personal relationship with God, and through him, with one another and all creation. In the gospels the concept of "discipleship" incorporated this reality of complete dedication to the will of God, to his kingdom, as it was manifested in the life and teaching of Jesus.

Faith-hope-love describes a single fundamental stance. These three virtues are integrally connected. St. Paul tells us that "through the Spirit, by faith, we await the hope of righteousness" (Gal. 5:5), and St. John informs us that through faith we have come to know the love God has for us (1 Jn. 4:16). From the perspective of our response to these gifts all that counts is "faith working through love" (Gal. 5:6). In the New Testament, faith is the way and love is the goal, that is why St. Paul concludes: "So faith, hope, love remain, these three; but the greatest of these is love" (1 Cor. 13:13).

In this chapter we want to explore the dimensions of this faith-response in love and hope. As we look at the theological virtues individually, we shall see that the actual dynamics of their infusion and unfolding within us corresponds to the nature of the conversion process. Their infusion occurs in the deepest core of our being on the non-categorical, non-reflexive level; this in classical terminology is the "*fides qua*" or the "faith by which" we respond to God's grace. Their unfolding or development in our lives occurs on the categorical level and comprises the *"fides quae"* or the "faith which" (the content) we believe. After looking at each of the theological virtues individually, we shall consider some practical questions concerning the relationship of faith to prayer and ecumenism, as well as various dimensions of the refusal to believe.

The "Obedience of Faith"

St. Paul frames his epistle to the Romans within the phrase "obedience of faith" (Rom. 1:5; 16:26). The English word "obedience" has its roots in the Latin verb *"obediere"* meaning "to listen, to heed." For Paul, obedience is a synonym for faith (see Rom. 6:16; 10:17; 15:18; 2 Cor. 10:5; 2 Th. 1:8); it is acceptance of Jesus' own mode of existence through which he "humbled himself, becoming obedient to death, even death on a cross" (Phil. 2:8; also Rom. 5:19). Faith for the Christian essentially means hearing God's call to conversion addressed to us in Jesus Christ and responding to it with all our heart (Mt. 22:37). The Second Vatican Council thus teaches us that before a person commits one's entire self to God in faith, he or she "must have the interior helps of the Holy Spirit, who moves the heart and converts it to God, who opens the eyes of the mind and 'makes it easy for all to accept and believe the truth' " (DV 5).

Faith in Sacred Scripture. The Old Testament tells us that "Abram put his faith in the LORD, who credited it to him as an act of righteousness" (Gen. 15:6). Abraham believed God who promised him a son in his old age. He put his complete trust in God's word and promise. Thus, he has been designated "our father in faith" (see Rom. 4:12). In the New Testament, Mary becomes *the* model of faith in God and of Christian discipleship. Her faith is compared to the faith of Abraham when in Luke's gospel account Elizabeth exclaims: "Blessed are you who believed that what was spoken to you by the Lord would be fulfilled" (Lk. 1:45). Mary's obedience of faith reverses the disobedience of Eve and brings forth the incarnation of the Son of God.[2]

In the Gospel according to John, Mary points the way to Christian discipleship when at the wedding feast in Cana she introduces her Son's "hour" by telling the servants, "Do whatever he tells you" (Jn. 2:5). The rich archetypal symbolism here must not be lost; the "marriage feast" is symbolic of communion of life, here it is communion of life with God

112

through following Jesus. The "wine" is symbolic of both blood and eternal life, which Jesus gives through his paschal mystery, his blood poured out for the life of the world. Discipleship for the Christian comes about through the obedience of faith which makes the believer one with Jesus' paschal mystery. As did Mary, the Christian disciple thus shows solicitude for the needs of others and points out "those things which must be done so that the salvific power of the Messiah may be manifested" in our world.[3]

The apostolic community's interpretation of faith in the mind of Jesus is portrayed in the story of Peter's walking on water (Mt. 14:28-31). Here the word of the Lord prepares the way. Peter trusted Jesus' word and "began to walk on the water toward Jesus" (Mt. 14:29). Faith accepts more the word which promises that water will support one than it does practical experience. "To believe means to depend upon a reality which is more real than the world itself."[4] Such an act of faith is not just a one time event that holds good forever. It is a commitment that must be continually renewed, as evidenced by Peter's beginning to sink when he becomes frightened by a strong wind. The bond of faith must be constantly affirmed anew. Faith is existence amid fear and doubt, but without fearing ("Take courage, it is I") and without doubting ("O you of little faith, why did you doubt?").

Christian faith is a decision to heed God's word revealed in Jesus and to put it into action. It is based on God's love for us and our love for Christ (Jn. 16:27) which we demonstrate by keeping his commandments (Jn. 14:15). Faith, which is full and genuine, is always "working through love" (Gal. 5:6). Faith, also, has a content that must be embraced, as St. Paul clearly attests to when he writes, "For I handed on to you as of first importance what I also received: that Christ died for our sins in accordance with the scriptures; that he was buried; that he was raised on the third day in accordance with the scriptures; that he appeared to Kephas, then to the Twelve" (1 Cor. 15:3-5). Biblical faith is always first and foremost a response to God's word, a personal act of confidence in God revealing, which also necessarily includes an acceptance of the truths or teachings revealed.

A Theological Vision of Faith. After the Council of Trent, Catholic theology spoke of faith almost exclusively in terms of its doctrinal content and a person's acceptance of these truths as definitively taught by the Church. Protestantism, at the same time, tended to describe faith more in terms of its subjective, personal elements. The history of dogma demonstrates, however, that the great teachers of the faith, such as Augustine

DISCIPLESHIP / TOTAL CONVERSION

RELIGIOUS CONVERSION (Gift–call to divine communion of love = eternal life)	FAITH	HOPE	LOVE	Non-categorical response (*fides qua*)
CONVERSION / Categorical response (*fides quae*)				
INTELLECTUAL (conviction/content) — Faith	Doctrinal truths	Scriptural images	Trinity (of personal relationships)	
AFFECTIVE (trust) — Hope	Word / promise of another	Covenantal communion	Self-giving love	
MORAL (commitment) — Love	Orthopraxis ("doing the truth") / evangelization	Work of reconciliation / peace-making	Living Christ's paschal mystery / keeping Two Great Commandments / Doing God's Will	

114

and Thomas Aquinas, described both the personal, subjective elements of trust and confidence, as well as the objective truths or contents to be believed.

1. At its deepest core **faith is a total surrender** to the ultimate graciousness of the Mystery in which we live, move and have our existence. It is an entering into a totally loving relationship with this Mystery whose love and mercy reconciles us, heals and energizes us. Through the act of faith made at this transcendental, non-categorical level we are restored to a level of intimate relationship with God. Motivated by the Spirit of God, through faith, we have "received a spirit of adoption" through which we dare address this Mystery in our heart of hearts as " '*Abba*, Father!' The Spirit itself bears witness with our spirit that we are children of God" (Rom. 8:15-16). This "faith by which" (*fides qua*) we live is ultimately a matter of "*cor ad cor loquitur*" ("heart speaking to heart").

Because of the effects of original sin, the human person's natural center of gravity draws one toward what is visible. Our hearts, in other words, readily look away from the infinite Mystery that calls us; we are distracted now by a wide variety of finite loves. A person thus needs to turn around inwardly to see that at the very core of human existence there is a point that cannot be nourished and supported by the visible and tangible. Indeed faith is the conversion in which we discover that we are following an illusion if we devote ourselves only to the tangible and the visible.[5] Such faith, which is pure grace, a gift of the Spirit, overcomes the alienation between God and us that was first introduced by original sin. Faith at this level offers the possibility of salvation to "all men of good will in whose hearts grace is active invisibly" (GS 22).

2. On the level of categorical consciousness **faith is a synthesis of conviction, trust and commitment**. It is the conjunction of intellectual, affective and moral conversion. Here the "faith which" (*fides quae*) we assent to gives expression to the universal divine presence through symbol, image and language. It is a responding in mind, heart and action to what now cannot be escaped.[6] As a process of religious growth and development, faith finds itself concretely enfleshed in creed, cult and code. Christian faith, indeed, leaps beyond the purely human assumption of the worthwhile character of human existence by which we all function, striving for truth, justice and love. "It is the act of surrendering to God in Christ, who is the one faithful witness to the way the world can be."[7]

As **conviction**, faith seeks understanding. Faith has content, that is, truths to be grasped and become convinced of. Such conviction results from an inner illumination of consciousness by which we are able to comprehend reality in a whole new light. Indeed, the Christian fully accepts Jesus' testimony that "I am the light of the world. Whoever follows me will not walk in darkness, but will have the light of life" (Jn. 8:12). Historically, the Christian "creed" or "doctrine" finds its first formulation, its original setting, in the baptismal ceremony. There the triple answer to the triple question, "Do you believe in God . . . in Christ . . . in the Holy Spirit?" gives form to the first Christian creed. It is the positive corollary to the triple renunciation that precedes it: "I renounce the devil, his service and his work." The Creed, thus, is not the acceptance of theories about some unknown and invisible realities; rather, it signifies an about-turn by the whole person.[8] The Christian "creed," and thus doctrine, is anchored in the very act of conversion by which we are incorporated into Christ's paschal mystery.

Faith on the cognitive level, also, involves the element of **trust**. It involves an affective conversion whereby we accept as true the word or promise of another over and above what is now immediately verifiable and evident to ourselves. Such was the faith of Abraham when he trusted God's promise that he would have a son in his old age, of Mary who trusted the angel's word that she would conceive a son without "knowing" man, and of Peter who trusted Jesus' word to "come" to him by walking upon the water. Trust is accepting the testimony of a witness as valid; it is believing the story of the eyewitness. Thus Jesus answers those who claim his self-testimony is invalid: "Even if I do testify on my own behalf, my testimony can be verified, because I know where I came from and where I am going" (Jn. 8:14).

Christian faith involves trusting the eyewitness testimony of the apostolic community. We believe the Christian story as "handed down" to us through the faith of the apostles (see 1 Cor: 15:3-5) and through their successors, the bishops (see DV 7). This is a communal faith, which is not the property of any sole individual. It is entrusted to the ecclesial community, the Body of Christ, the New Adam. Only inasmuch as we are incorporated as members of Christ's Body through faith and baptism do we really enter into the Christian story. We thus turn away, are converted, from the false and incomplete stories, ideologies and philosophies "the world" accepts as true and enter "the mind of Christ" (see Rom. 12:2). The American scripture scholar,

Jerome Murphy-O'Connor describes it in this way:

> As the community deepens its commitment to the ideal, the
> existential attitude of Christ (Cf. Phil 2:5) becomes progressively
> more manifest, primarily in the community and as a derivative in the
> individuals who constitute it. To the extent that the community
> exemplifies the authentic humanity manifested by Christ, it judges
> from the standpoint of Christ. . . .
> Only in this perspective does it become possible to understand
> how Paul can define "the will of God", which is the object of the
> corporate mind's activity as "the good and acceptable and perfect"
> (Rom 12:2). . . . What Paul means, then, is that whatever the
> corporate mind tests and finds "good, acceptable and perfect" is in
> fact the will of God.[9]

Through the element of trust the Christian believer categorically accepts the
truth of faith as it is presented to us by the ecclesial community, by the
tradition of the Church. He or she accepts the Christian story as it comes to us
in Creed and sacrament, which is our symbolic, yet real, insertion into
Christ's paschal mystery.

The moral dimension of categorical faith is summed up by **commitment**.
Genuine orthodoxy necessarily includes orthopraxis, or "living the truth in
love" (Eph. 4:15). This aspect of our faith-hope-love response will be treated
later when we look at the primacy of love. It is appropriate for us here and
now, however, to consider the moral implications of our commitment to the
truth of the "faith which" (*fides quae*) we believe. Convinced of the validity
of the apostolic witness handed down to us through the Catholic Church,
believers have the right and duty to participate in ecclesial life, in its worship
and mission.

The Church exists primarily to continue Jesus' evangelizing mission.
Jesus gathered his disciples together for the purpose of sending them forth to
proclaim the Good News.[10] The proclamation of the gospel is necessary for
salvation; it partakes of the incarnational dynamic of divine revelation. Thus,
St. Paul explains in his Letters to the Romans, "For 'everyone who calls on
the name of the Lord will be saved.' But how can they call on him in whom
they have not believed? And how can they believe in him of whom they have
not heard? And how can they hear without someone to preach? And how can
people preach unless they are sent? As it is written, 'How beautiful are the

feet of those who bring [the] good news!' '' (Rom. 10:13-15).

Summarizing the vision of Vatican II, Paul VI wrote that "Evangelizing is in fact the grace and vocation proper to the Church, her deepest identity."[11] The Council, indeed, had pointed out that everyone within the Church has the basic duty to be involved in the work of evangelization (AG 35; LG 33). Through faith and baptism we become members of Christ's Body, and as such, we are united in him and with him in continuing his mission of revealing and incarnating the Father's self-emptying and reconciling love.

Being one with Christ and his mission requires ongoing religious, intellectual, affective and moral conversion on our part. It requires that we are attentive to our own evangelization process as we commit ourselves to Christ's continuing mission. In the words, once again, of Paul VI:

> The Church is an evangelizer, but she begins by being evangelized herself. She is the community of believers, the community of hope lived and communicated, the community of brotherly love; and she needs to listen unceasingly to what she must believe, to her reasons for hoping, to the new commandment of love. She is the People of God immersed in the world, and often tempted by idols, and she always needs to hear the proclamation of the "mighty works of God" which converted her to the Lord; she always needs to be called together afresh by Him and reunited.[12]

Participating in the Church's worship and mission, and conscientiously attending to our own growth in knowledge of the faith give evidence of the quality of our faith commitment. The same as Mary at Nazareth, the disciple of Jesus must continue to hear and ponder God's word in his or her heart and let it take form in him or her; with Mary at Cana we must point Jesus out to others and invite them to "do whatever he tells you." These are specific moral responsibilities incumbent upon the Christian believer.

Hope in God's Promises

"Hope is faith and love on pilgrimage; it is not something apart from faith and love."[13] Hope corresponds to the affective dimension of our total faith-response. It constitutes the internal motivational dynamism of faith in this in-between time. It is a solid trust and assurance that God's promises will be fulfilled, based upon what he has already done for us in Christ. Hope is a conviction beyond any doubt that God's kingdom will indeed come. As such,

Christian hope is a communal hope based upon God's covenant with his people.

In the classicist tradition between Trent and Vatican II, hope was defined as an elevation of the will, made possible by grace, by which we could expect eternal life and the means to obtain it. Hope was thus narrowly conceived and interpreted individualistically as *my* hope for *my* salvation. Sins against hope were primarily despair, the anticipation of failure, and presumption or anticipated success. Christian biblical revelation, however, presents us with a richer and more encompassing picture of hope.

The Biblical Vision of Hope. In the early Old Testament period hope proceeded from faith in the Covenant and was directed toward God promising the land and the messianic kingdom of the final age. This was primarily a communal hope valid for the individual insomuch as he was a member of God's people. After the collapse of the northern and southern kingdoms, the prophets promise that God will establish a new covenant, that the Messiah will purify and redeem his people, and Yahweh's kingdom will then be established over Israel and the whole world.[14] In the New Testament the promise of the Kingdom of God and its blessedness is the motive Jesus puts forth for his radical demands of discipleship and obedience to God's will (see the Beatitudes: Mt. 5:3, 10).

New Testament hope is founded on the belief that God has in fact established the promised new covenant in Jesus Christ by his life, death and resurrection. God's promises are fulfilled as Jesus reveals the new and everlasting covenant between God and us, sealed in the blood of his paschal mystery. We are thus assured of God's acceptance and his forgiveness of our sins. The powers of sin and death have been defeated through the Spirit of God that dwells in us (see Rom. 8:9-13). "For in hope we were saved" (Rom. 8:24), St. Paul tells us. Believers thus do not look forward to someday being saved, for "in hope" they are *already* saved, "in that by God's doing, they are already promoted into the expectation of the future."[15] Hope is always directed to the future.

The hope inspired by Christ's death and resurrection finds expression in the disciple's patient endurance. In the synoptics Jesus forewarns that "You will be hated by all because of my name. But the one who perseveres to the end will be saved" (Mk. 13:13; also Lk. 8:15). Other attitudes are bound up with hope, which together give shape to the Christian life. Hope is the well-spring of joy (Rom. 12:12), and of bold candor (2 Cor. 3:12). It is the source of confidence for our future glorification in Christ (Phil. 1:20), inspiring both gratitude and vigilance, as well as readiness for change or continuing conversion (see Eph. 5:14-17). Hope gives us reason for practicing asceticism, for "training us to reject godless ways and worldly desires and to live temperately, justly, and devoutly in this age" (Titus 2: 12-13). Finally, hope embraces all of creation as it "awaits with eager expectation the revelation of the children of God" (Rom. 8:19).

Theological Perspectives on Hope. On the level of our heart of hearts, the non-categorical, non-reflexive level of consciousness, hope is one with faith and love. This "hope by which" (*spes qua speratur*) one hopes is, like faith, a pure gift of the Spirit, for as St. Paul writes: "For through the Spirit, by faith, we await the hope of righteousness" (Gal. 5:5). Hope on this level describes the fiducial confidence that is an integral part of the gift of faith. On the categorical level the "hope which" (*spes quae*) we embrace is capable of development over time and is comprised, again like faith (*fides quae*), of cognitive, affective and moral elements.

The cognitive content of Christian hope is summarized in Jesus' image of the Kingdom of God. Just as doctrinal statements incorporate the intellectual content of faith, so biblical imagery, eschatological and apocalyptic, opens up for us the content of our hope. Paul reminds us that "What eye has not seen, and ear has not heard . . . God has prepared for those who love him" (1 Cor. 2:9); and that "hope that sees for itself is not hope. For who hopes for what one sees?" (Rom. 8:24). Hope thus looks to what is unseen, to the eternal (2 Cor. 4:18), which can only be made known to us through symbols, images and parables. Jesus, therefore, taught about the coming of God's invisible and eternal kingdom through the use of images and parables (Mt. 13:34-35). Hope is the affective element of faith that appeals to our imaginations rather than to our intellects. For the imagination, whether functioning on the natural level or on the level of supernatural revelation, is "the gift that envisions what cannot yet be seen, the gift that proposes to itself that the boundaries of the possible are wider than they seem."[16]

As an element of affective conversion, Christian hope is "an anchor of the soul" (Heb. 6:19). It is that interior dynamism which exudes confidence, perseverance, peace, joy and serenity in the midst of life's storms. Rooted in Christ's paschal mystery it is a turning from selfish preoccupation for one's individual safety and security to a covenantal relationship and corporate solidarity as a member of Christ's Body, the Church. Christian hope is a communal hope based upon our incorporation in the Last Adam, who has overcome the power of sin and death and made us a new creation. It is anchored in God's forgiving and reconciling love manifested in Christ. Even on the natural plane, hope is a common act of "imagining with." Despair lies in the constriction of the private imagination, for "what happens in despair is that the private imagination . . . reaches the point of the end of inward resource and must put on the imagination of another if it is to find a way out."[17] Christian hope thus is a participation in the imagination of the Last Adam; it is a shared confidence, in the words of Paul VI, that "Only the kingdom therefore is absolute, and it makes everything else relative."[18]

The moral dimension of Christian hope finds expression in the work of reconciliation. "Blessed are the peacemakers, for they will be called children of God" (Mt. 5:9). Nurtured by their hope in Christ, believers actively pursue reconciliation in all its forms: with God, within themselves, with neighbor, and with all creation. They spend themselves in promoting works of peace and justice, in bringing hope to the hopeless, in protecting the environment and advancing ecology. This is why the Council Fathers at Vatican II reminded us that

> Far from diminishing our concern to develop this earth, the expectancy of the new earth should spur us on, for it is here that the body of the new human family grows, foreshadowing in some way the age which is to come. That is why, although we must be careful to distinguish earthly progress clearly from the increase in the kingdom of Christ, such progress is of vital concern to the kingdom of God, insofar as it can contribute to the better ordering of human society (GS 39).

Christian hope is the motivational force that bridges the "already" and the "not-yet." It seeks to enflesh in the "already" of temporal affairs concrete images of an eternal and universal kingdom "of truth and life, a kingdom of holiness and grace, a kingdom of justice, love, and peace."[19]

The Primacy of Love

"So faith, hope, love remain, these three; but the greatest of these is love" (1 Cor. 13:13). Love is the greatest of all virtues. It is both the origin and goal of faith. It summarizes all the commandments (Mt. 22:40; Rom. 13:10). In the writings of St. Thomas Aquinas, too, charity is the mother, basis and root of all the virtues. In our day, the Second Vatican Council stated that "Love of God and of one's neighbor, then, is the first and greatest commandment. Scripture teaches us that love of God cannot be separated from love of one's neighbor" (GS 24, with cf. Rom. 13:9-10, and 1 Jn. 4:20).

The word "love" in the English language, unfortunately, suffers inflation from overuse. We "love" everyone and everything — God, our spouse, children, friends, cat, dog, car and apple pie, etc. While the human concept of love always connotes a movement toward that which is recognized as valued and filled with worth, the ancient Greeks, for instance, distinguished such movement by the object intended. They thus used four words, where popular English today tends to use only one, "love." The Greeks used "*epithemia*" for sexual love, for that desire with the connotation of lust. "*Eros*" designated passionate love, a drive toward union which brings about personal fulfillment; its object can be a person, or even a thing or idea. "*Philia*" signifies the affectionate inclination that exists between siblings and friends. Finally, the Greek word "*agape*" described the total dedication to another's welfare regardless of sacrifice or personal cost; it is a total movement of the will independent of sentiment or feeling. Such is the love that Jesus revealed on the cross.

Love in Sacred Scripture. The commandment to love God is the first commandment in both the Old and New Testaments. Israel's Lord is "a merciful and gracious God, slow to anger and rich in kindness and fidelity, continuing his kindness for a thousand generations, and forgiving wickedness and crime and sin" (Ex. 34:6-7). In view of the Covenant, therefore, Israel must return God's love as the essence of its relationship with him. Thus, is heard the commandment: "Therefore, you shall love the Lord, your God, with all your heart, and with all your soul, and with all your strength" (Dt. 6:5). For these ancient Israelites, "fear of the LORD" and "love of God" were one and the same (Dt. 10:12). Love of God includes both obedience and service.

Israel also read in its Law: "You shall not bear hatred for your brother in your heart. . . . Take no revenge and cherish no grudge against your fellow countrymen. You shall love your neighbor as yourself. I am the LORD" (Lv. 19:17-18). In the later development of the Law, love of neighbor was extended even to strangers who dwelled in the land (Lv. 19:34; Dt. 10:19). The obligation of hospitality to a guest was of highest importance (Gen. 18:1-8; 19:1-8), and the law of reprisal (*lex talionis*) sought a just, rather than a revengeful, compensation for violated rights: "A life for a life! . . . Limb

122

for limb, eye for eye, tooth for tooth" (Lv. 24:18,20).

The New Testament speaks of the primacy of God's love for us: "In this is love: not that we have loved God, but that he loved us and sent his Son as expiation for our sins" (1 Jn. 4:10). In the gospels Jesus insists that the old commandment of the love of God still holds true (Mk. 12:28-34). Our love for God is evidenced in keeping his word (1 Jn. 2:5) and in showing love to our brother in need (1 Jn. 3:17). Jesus unites love of God and love of neighbor. It is in love of neighbor that obedience and love of God are authenticated. Furthermore, Jesus extends love of our neighbor to include everyone, even our enemies (Mt. 5:44-45). Christian love is not founded on an emotional bond or on feelings, rather it is a matter of the will that reaches out to everyone in need. It is truly *"agape."*

Christian love has its roots in our intimate participation in the life of God who *is* love (1 Jn. 4:8, 16). In the Johannine writings this new spiritual reality of sharing life in Christ means bearing fruit in love, like branches on a vine (Jn. 15:1-17) and following his example of self-emptying service (Jn. 13:15). In Paul's letters this means sharing in the paschal mystery by which Christ handed himself over to death and therefore was raised up by the Father (Phil. 2:5-11). Love is the law of discipleship: "This is my commandment: love one another as I love you"(Jn. 15:12, 17). Christ, then, is the model of love through his life of service (Mk. 10:45) and through his self-giving, even to the point of crucifixion (Jn. 15:13).

A Christian Theology of Love. Bernard Lonergan has stated that "Faith is the knowledge born of religious love."[20] God's creative and reconciling love flooding our hearts is both the origin and goal of our faith and our hope. In our heart of hearts, at the transcendental core of our being, God's love becomes an invitation to us to enter into a divine communion of love. We accept his love there in an exercise of core freedom, which remains non-categorical and non-reflexive. In classical theology this act, celebrated in the sacraments of baptism and penance, places us in "the state of grace."

On the categorical level of salvation history, God's love for us is manifested in creation and in God's saving deeds. Thus St. Paul reminds us that "God proves his love for us in that while we were still sinners Christ died for us" (Rom. 5:8). The supreme depth of God's self-giving love is fully manifested in Jesus' paschal mystery. At the same time, Jesus returns the human race's perfect response of love and reverses the First Adam's sin. Reconciled "in Christ" to God and neighbor, we become children of God

123

and thereby brothers and sisters to one another. Love of God is thus only genuine when it proves itself in love of one another (1 Jn. 2:5; 3:17). "It need scarcely be mentioned that a violation of love of neighbor cannot be covered over by an ostensible love of God. . . . To shun one's neighbor on the pretext of devotion is to build a temple to false gods."[21] Our growth in Christian love, like faith and hope, therefore has cognitive, affective and moral components which are integrally linked with the ongoing conversion process.

Through Christian biblical revelation we have come to know that the *content of Christian love* is the Triune God, a tri-unity of personal relationships. The Ultimate Good that calls us, attracts and draws us, is the immanent-transcendent Mystery of creating and unifying Love that holds all things in existence, in relationship, through a permanent act of self-giving. It is not *eros* which reaches out in love in order to find self-fulfillment, but *agape* which gives itself totally "for" the enhancement of the other. This transcendent Good which is the origin and source of all that exists lies intimately close at the heart of created reality, seeking a response of obedient faith that will allow its glory to shine forth. Only the refusal of faith, as a personal exercise of the gift of created freedom, can prevent its manifestation. This Absolute Good, this personal Triune God, however, in mercy and faithfulness never stops working to bring about a "new creation" through the gift of reconciliation and cooperation with His will in and through Jesus Christ.

The New Testament reveals that Jesus is the incarnation and revelation of the God who is Love (*agape*). In taking on our human nature "he emptied himself" and became "obedient to death, even death on a cross" (Phil. 2:8). He thereby surrendered existence-for-himself and entered the pure movement of the "for." In his incarnation and paschal mystery, "he who does not cling to himself but is pure relatedness coincides in this with the absolute and thus becomes lord."[22] Jesus Christ in his life, death and resurrection reveals to us the content of genuine Love, which is a being-for-others that brings about oneness or communion, a being in relationship. Jesus' paschal mystery reveals the very pattern and rhythm of human existence and constitutes the content of Christian love.

"Being a Christian means essentially changing over from being for oneself to being for another."[23] The affective dimension of Christian love involves a *movement* away from narcissistic love *to a self-giving love.* Such conversion or movement requires of the disciple that he or she turn away

124

from those attitudes, dispositions and vices which make loving relationships and community unattainable. St. Paul occasionally drew up lists of these traits which made self-giving impossible (Rom. 1:29-31; 13:13; 1 Cor. 5:10-11; 6:9-10; 2 Cor. 12:20-21; Gal. 5:19-21; and Col. 3:5, 8). They all overlap to some extent but include anger, arrogance, carousing, covetousness, dissension, immorality, jealousy, selfish ambition, slander, stealing, tale-bearing, unruliness, and so forth. His ''vice-lists'' differ from other contemporary catalogues which were heavily weighted with individualistic vices, such as ignorance, tastelessness, awkwardness, pessimism, instability, etc.[24] Paul contrasts the social vices to that Christ-like love which exhibits the ''fruit of the Spirit'': love, joy, peace, patience, kindness, generosity, faithfulness, gentleness, self-control (Gal. 5:22-24), and which makes community life and genuine relationships possible.

"Living the truth in love" (Eph. 4:15) is the goal of Christian faith. The moral dimension of Christian love involves *doing the will of God* (Mt. 7:21), listening to Jesus' words and acting upon them (Mt. 7:24). It means manifesting the Absolute Good as revealed by Jesus Christ in our daily lives, in the quality of our relationships. This we do primarily by opening ourselves up to Christ's paschal mystery and making it the foundation and pattern of our lives. It means manifesting God's self-giving love in all our actions, and loving one another as Jesus has loved us. "Living the truth in love" involves becoming "perfect" (Mt. 5:48) or "merciful" (Lk. 6:36) like our heavenly Father. Love is "the bond of perfection" (Col. 3:14). Indeed, God's perfection is his boundless love. We therefore live the truth by keeping the commandment of love of God and love of neighbor.

1. Our **love of God** proves itself in love of neighbor. Jesus testifies to this in the Last Judgment scene in Matthew's gospel, when he says: "Amen, I say to you, whatever you did for one of these least brothers of mine, you did for me" (Mt. 25:40). At the same time, however, love of God must be nurtured in our hearts through religious practices, through reverence, prayer and worship. St. Thomas Aquinas held that religion is one of the "potential parts" of the virtue of justice, which is defined as rendering another his due. Justice restores equality, but since there obviously can be no equality between God and us, religion is only something like justice in that it renders God his due. "Religion" denotes a relationship to God. It is not for God's sake but for ours, since by the very fact that we revere and honor God our

minds are subjected to him. A thing is thus perfected by being subjected to its superior.

Reverence and adoration are attitudes which arise from genuine humility and the recognition of our total dependence upon God's love. These attitudes orient our lives to gratitude and praise for all his gifts, for the beauty of his creation and the joy of salvation. Adoration leads to the contemplation of God's own beauty which is "itself the primordial source of our joy, our strength, our love and our fellowship with all of his children."[25] Through reverence, adoration and contemplation we open ourselves to the eternal "Now," to Being itself, and our whole existence acquires a new direction as we let God endow us with his gifts. We come to realize that we are stewards of God's gifts. We are free to enjoy them, to share them and to use them responsibly but not free to squander and abuse them.

Religion's central elements of creed, cult and code correspond respectively to our ongoing intellectual, affective and moral development in faith. Thus we read in the New Testament of the earliest Christian community that "They devoted themselves to the teaching of the apostles and to the communal life, to the breaking of bread and to the prayers" (Acts 2:42). The Letter to the Hebrews reminds Christians that "We should not stay away from our assembly, as is the custom of some, but encourage one another" (Heb. 10:25). Celebrating Sunday for the early Christians was a commemoration of the fact of creation, as well as the resurrection. It was truly "eucharist," thanksgiving. In Christian worship we do not place before God our human achievements, but rather we become totally receptive and allow ourselves to be completely overtaken by him. "Letting God act on us — that is Christian sacrifice."[26] Religion is the outward expression of our love for God, the giving of ourselves to him as members of Christ's Body. The Letter of James, however, does not let us forget that "Religion that is pure and undefiled before God and the Father is this: to care for orphans and widows in their affliction and to keep oneself unstained by the world" (James 1:27).

2. **Love of neighbor,** in the end, is the "bottom line" of Christian faith and love. Jesus, as we have seen, combines the two Old Testament commandments of love of God and love of neighbor into a single twofold commandment. The Johannine community phrased it this way: "If someone who has worldly means sees a brother in need and refuses him compassion, how can the love of God remain in him? Children, let us love not in word or

126

speech but in deed and truth'' (1 Jn 3:17-18). The Second Vatican Council thus teaches that the community of Christians must be a sign of God's love to the world. ''Every benefit the people of God can confer on mankind during its earthly pilgrimage is rooted in the Church's being 'the universal sacrament of salvation,' at once manifesting and actualizing God's love for men'' (GS 45).

Vatican II distinctly links the celebration of the sacraments to the worship of God and the practice of charity (see SC 59). The Decree on the Apostolate of the Laity reminds us that

> In the early days the Church linked the ''agape'' to the eucharistic supper, and by so doing showed itself as one body around Christ united by the bond of charity. So too, in all ages, love is the characteristic mark. . . . That is why mercy to the poor and the sick, and charitable works and works of mutual aid for the alleviation of all kinds of human needs, are held in special honor by the Church.
>
> Today these activities and works of charity have become much more urgent and worldwide. . . . Charitable action today can and should reach all men and all needs. Wherever men are to be found who are in want of food and drink, of clothing, housing, medicine, work, education, the means necessary to leading a truly human life, wherever there are men racked by misfortune or illness, men suffering exile or imprisonment, Christian charity should go in search of them and find them out, comfort them with devoted care and give them the helps that will relieve their needs (AA 8).

Love of neighbor in all its forms gives flesh to our love of the God whom Jesus Christ has revealed as a community of self-giving love.

Christian love, which mirrors the permanent and faithful love of the Trinity, primarily means ''staying in relationship.'' It is a love which reaches out in the power of the Spirit to forgive, reconcile, heal and create anew. It is a love rooted in Christ's paschal mystery, which St. Paul reminds us is also the foundation of Christian marriage (Eph. 5:25-33). Christian love is the bond and mark of discipleship (Jn. 13:35). It demonstrates the breakthrough of God's kingdom into history, imparting a specific Christological element to the human behavior of believers. The gift-call of Christian faith-hope-love alone

... explains the summons to a self-renunciation that goes to the

127

extreme of martyrdom (Mk 8:35 passim), the command to love one's enemies (cf. Mt 5:43-47), to renounce one's rights (cf., e.g., 1 Cor 6:1-8), not to countenance divorce (Mk 10:2-12; 1 Cor 7:10f.). It also facilitates and colors the characteristic Christian relationship to the world, which is both distanced and involved (cf. 1 Cor 7:29ff.) and calls for voluntary self-denial and poverty (cf. 2 Cor 6:4-10), separation from family (Lk 14:26), and celibacy (cf. Mt 19:12; 1 Cor 7).[27]

Christian discipleship involves responding to God's grace transforming us "by the renewal of [our] mind, that [we] may discern what is the will of God, what is good and pleasing and perfect . . . each according to the measure of faith that God has apportioned" (Rom. 12:2-3).

Prayer

Prayer is essential to the life of faith, to the development of our spiritual-moral life. It alone establishes that personal communication with God without which genuine growth in faith-hope-love is impossible. When communication between spouses or friends breaks down, the relationship begins to fall apart. The same occurs in our relationship with God. Indeed, the way we pray, or do not pray, speaks volumes about our own personal understanding of who God is and of his place in our lives.

The gospels are full of accounts of Jesus praying (Mk. 1:35; Mt. 11:25; Lk. 22:41; Jn. 17; etc.). He continually exhorted his disciples to pray (Mk. 9:29; Lk. 11:5-13), and taught them how to pray correctly (Mt. 6:5-13; Lk. 11:1-4). He instructed his disciples: "In praying, do not babble like the pagans, who think they will be heard because of their many words. Do not be like them. Your Father knows what you need before you ask him" (Mt. 6:7-8). He taught them to address God as "*Our* Father," and to pray that his will be done. The early Church faithfully followed Jesus' commands (Acts 4:23-30; 12:5) and handed them on as precisely as possible (Eph. 5:19-20; Col. 3:16; Heb. 13:15).

Prayer is a conversation with God, that is, a listening and a responding to his word. It is a dialogue God always begins. It involves listening to the various forms His word assumes: his cosmic word evident in the marvels of creation, his written word in the Scriptures, his incarnate word in Jesus Christ, his word addressed to us in the needs of our neighbor, etc. Prayer is a grace, a gift, which opens us to the presence of the Mystery in whom we live. Prayer makes us receptive to the Spirit of Truth, the Spirit of the paschal

Christ present and active in our world. Persons pray when they are inwardly and outwardly recollected. Self-discipline is thus a prerequisite in order for one to take time, indeed make time, for prayer.

Two classical definitions of prayer are "speaking to God" and "raising the soul to God." Direct address or speaking to God is the most common form of prayer. The danger inherent in this form is that we end up saying prayers, rather than actually praying. Indeed, we can often do so much of the talking here that in reality we are telling God how he ought to run the universe. We tell him to find us a better job, to make the sun shine, to cure our neighbor of cancer, etc. As Jesus told us, "Your Father knows what you need before you ask him"(Mt. 6:8). Prayer is for our sake, not for God's. Our speaking to God must be sparked by an attitude of loving dependence which seeks first the Father's will in all things. "Your kingdom come; Your will be done, on earth" (Mt. 6:10).

When speaking to God in prayer we should incorporate all the traditional elements of adoration, thanksgiving, contrition and petition. Our prayers should, first of all, voice his praises. They should well up out of our gratitude for his gifts of love and mercy. Having received the Good News of salvation in Jesus Christ and experienced it in our lives, we dare to say "Our Father." Then, we should confess to God that we are sinners who are much in need of his mercy (Lk. 18:13). Although we already know beforehand that he will forgive us, we must bring ourselves to admit our complete dependence upon his all-merciful love. Finally, we address to God our petitions, not to tell him how to run the world but to seek discernment of his will in our many needs and daily concerns. In the Garden of Gethsemane, Jesus petitioned: "My Father, if it is not possible that this cup pass without my drinking it, your will be done!"(Mt. 26:42). Here we have the model of every prayer of petition.

Prayer is listening to God, as well as speaking to him. We "raise our souls to God" in meditation and contemplation. In meditation I ponder life and the events of life, looking to identify God's presence and action in my own life and in human history. Meditation can lead to contemplation, which may be described as the experience of encountering God, real though obscure, in all the dimensions of human life. It may be likened to standing spellbound before some awe-inspiring panorama of nature or being enveloped by an all-pervasive feeling of harmony or peace. Such a contemplative experience of the divine is described in the opening lines of the First Letter of John: "What was from the beginning, / what we have heard, / what we have seen with our eyes, / what we looked upon / and touched with our hands / concerns the Word of life" (1 Jn. 1:1).

Prayer in all its forms is both individual and social. The theological reason for this is the unity of the Spirit given to the Church, as well as to the individual members of Christ's Body. The Christian both praises God in the fellowship of prayer and prays to the Father "in secret" (Mt. 6:6). Such individual prayer, however, is rooted in the fact that one's encounter with Christ is mediated by the Church through Scripture and tradition. The Eucharist is the Church's prayer par excellence; it is the center to which all Christian prayer is directed and from which it flows. In addition to liturgical prayer other communal forms of prayer include the Liturgy of the Hours, or breviary, paraliturgical celebrations, popular devotions and prayer groups of various types. Whether their prayer is communal or individual, Christians are encouraged by St. Paul to "Pray without ceasing" (1 Th. 5:17).

Ecumenism

At the Last Supper Jesus prayed to the Father for his disciples that "they may be one, as we are one, I in them and you in me, that they may be brought to perfection as one, that the world may know you sent me, and that you loved them even as you loved me" (Jn. 17:22-23). In the gospels Jesus places the unity of his disciples among themselves in the form of a prayer, rather than as a statement of fact. Christian unity is first and foremost unity with Christ, "the Son" whose very being is a being "from" the Father and "for" others. In fact, "it is the nature of Christian existence to receive and live life as relatedness, and thus to enter into that unity which is the ground of all reality and sustains it. . . . All not-at-one-ness, all division, rests on a concealed lack of real Christlikeness, on a retention of individuality which hinders the coalesence of unity."[28]

The Second Vatican Council in its Decree on Ecumenism addressed the centuries-long separation that exists between the Catholic Church and other Christian communities by stating that "often enough, men of both sides were to blame. However, one cannot charge with the sin of separation those who at present are born into these communities and in them are brought up in the faith of Christ, and the Catholic Church accepts them with respect and affection as brothers" (UR 3). In 1943, Pope Pius XII in his encyclical *Mystici Corporis* maintained that the Body of Christ and the Roman Catholic Church are one and the same.[29] Evidencing the thaw brought about by the

130

ecumenical movement, Vatican II teaches that the Church of Christ "subsists in the Catholic Church" and adds that "many elements of sanctification and of truth are found outside its visible confines"(LG 8).

Undertaking efforts that promote unity is a specific moral obligation of Christ's followers. It is a constitutive element of our Christian faith-hope-love response, of our Christian discipleship. The dialogue currently taking place between the Christian churches, as well as between them and the other major world religions is an essential component of the Church's fidelity to Christ's continuing mission. Since we are all called in our heart of hearts to partnership in Christ's paschal mystery, in a way known to God alone (see GS 22), we must constantly strive to give concrete expression to that call in an ever growing oneness of faith.

The Refusal To Believe

Because of the divine gift of freedom, both on the transcendental and categorical levels of human consciousness, persons can refuse the gift of faith. Such a refusal may take the forms of doubt, atheism and agnosticism, as well as formal repudiation through heresy, apostasy and schism.

Doubt in Faith. We can identify at least three types of doubt related to faith. A certain kind of questioning doubt is actually healthy for the life of faith. This *creative doubt* gives expression to a most earnest and sincere search for a deeper and more illumined faith. At its heart is an authentic desire to understand more fully divine revelation, Church teachings, rites and practices. Contrary to "heretical doubt" its goal is to overcome certain deficiencies in a person's faith commitment. Correspondingly, there can also exist a *sinful lack of doubt*, which is characterized by an unwillingness to grow in one's knowledge of the faith. Sometimes, the external appearance of a firmness of faith masks an underlying security complex or even an obstinate refusal to learn more. *Sinful doubt* can arise from spiritual laziness or even scornful arrogance and pride.[30] Although faith is a divine gift-call it is like a hidden "treasure buried in a field" (Mt. 13:44). Thus, Jesus tells us in the gospels, "Ask and it will be given to you; seek and you will find; knock and the door will be opened to you" (Mt. 7:7).

Atheism. The Second Vatican Council stated that atheism must "be regarded as one of the more serious problems of our time" (GS 19). Atheism is a denial of the existence of God, which can take place on either or both the transcendental and categorical levels of human consciousness. Thus, we can identify the "pseudo-believer," who professes faith with the lips but in his or her heart ignores the call to communion with God. There can also exist the "pseudo-atheist," who denies God's existence on the categorical level but existentially searches for truth and is willing to put it into practice. Then, there is the "authentic" atheist who has fully and consciously made a decision against God.[31]

There are different forms of atheism. Political or "militant atheism" is the official doctrine of the Communist Party and of the government of the Soviet Union since its establishment in 1917. Dialectical materialism, a philosophical form developed by Karl Marx, adheres to a scientific socialism based upon an analysis of economic, social, cultural processes, relationships and interdependencies. It promises a perfect society which will produce a perfect humanity. It is quasi-religious, offering an earthly version of the Servant-Messiah, collectively understood. Furthermore, in the "age of science" many people contend that everything can and will be explained by scientific reasoning, or that there is no absolute truth.

While speaking about the different kinds of atheism, Vatican II concluded that it does not naturally arise from the heart of man, because of the attraction of the divine gift-call.

> It springs from various causes, among which must be included a critical reaction against religions and, in some places, against the Christian religion in particular. Believers can thus have more than a little to do with the rise of atheism. To the extent that they are careless about their instruction in the faith, or present its teaching falsely, or even fail in their religious, moral, or social life, they must be said to conceal rather than to reveal the true nature of God and of religion (GS 19).

Others, such as the French existentialist, Jean-Paul Sartre, see the existence of God as a threat to human freedom, or are convinced that Christianity is doomed to remain an unfulfilled hope which has failed in its quest for universal love. Vatican II, also, points out that "Not infrequently atheism is born from a violent protest against evil in the world" (GS 19), from those who mistakenly believe that God is the source of evil. "How could God let it happen?" they continually ask.

Agnosticism. A widespread phenomenon of our day is the assertion, made by many, that we can know absolutely nothing about God. Such agnosticism, which neither denies nor affirms the existence of God, has many causes. It arises "when scientific methods of investigation, which of themselves are incapable of penetrating to the deepest nature of things, are unjustifiably taken as the supreme norm for arriving at truth" (GS 57). Linguistic analysis, as developed by Ludwig Wittgenstein, argues against the God question from a philosophical viewpoint. Contemporary materialism and a one-sided success orientation, which reduces people to consumers and producers, has also spawned a complete lack of interest in God.

Repudiation of the Faith. The 1983 Code of Canon Law lists and defines three types of formal repudiation of the Christian faith.

> Heresy is the obstinate post-baptismal denial of some truth which must be believed with divine and catholic faith, or it is likewise an obstinate doubt concerning the same; apostasy is the total repudiation of the Christian faith; schism is the refusal of submission to the Roman Pontiff or of communion with the members of the Church subject to him. (Canon 751)

As canonical realities, when public, manifest and formal, they can lead to loss of ecclesiastical office and excommunication. Subjective moral culpability in these matters must be judged with utmost prudence. "The sin of apostasy is committed only if one, through baptism and evangelization, had the real opportunity to come to faith and was a believer, and yet turns totally away from the Christian faith."[32] If a person, however, was evangelized and baptized but never made a fundamental commitment of faith through his or her own fault, such a person would be guilty of the sin of infidelity. Heresy and schism today on the part of the average "baptized Catholic," living in a pluralistic and secularistic society, could more easily be a material, rather than a formal sin. Such errors would have to be knowingly, consciously and intentionally espoused with full cognizance to be formally sinful.

Another traditional sin against faith is superstition. A practice is superstitious when it proposes to control God's actions or the heavenly forces upon which a person feels his or her own existence mysteriously depends. Superstition distorts God's absolute sovereignty. We need to be very careful in making a judgment in this matter. What is superstitious for one person, such as performing a certain ritual or reciting a novena of prayers, can very easily be a deep expression of faith for another person.

Traditional sins against hope, despair and presumption, have already been mentioned, as have sins against love when we considered St. Paul's lists of vices detrimental to community life. Other sins against hope and love arise out of our lack of compassion and insensitivity to others' needs, as well as out of our failures to work for reconciliation, justice and peace. Neglect of prayer and meditation, of making time for the things of the spirit, can readily be the source of much hopelessness and lovelessness in our world. They also demonstrate our lack of faith, for in the end all sin arises out of the failure to believe (see Jn. 16:9), out of the failure to remain in God (1 Jn. 3:6).

Notes

1. John Paul II, *Redemptoris Mater*, Encyclical Letter (March 25, 1987), no. 20.

2. See ibid., nos. 12-19.

3. Ibid., no. 21.

4. Schelkle, *Theology of the New Testament*, vol. 3, p. 87.

5. Ratzinger, *Introduction to Christianity*, pp. 24-25.

6. See Shea, *Stories of Faith*, p. 98.

7. Happel and Walter, *Discipleship and Conversion*, p. 48.

8. Ratzinger, op. cit., pp. 54-55.

9. Murphy-O'Connor, *Becoming Human Together*, p. 214.

10. See Bohr, *Evangelization in America*, pp. 98-99.

11. Paul VI, *Evangelii Nuntiandi* (apostolic exhortation, December 8, 1975), no. 14.

12. Ibid., no. 15.

13. Bernard Häring, C.Ss.R., *Hope Is the Remedy* (Garden City, N.Y.: Image Books, Doubleday & Co., Inc., 1971., p. 41.

14. Schelkle, op. cit., pp. 99-100.

15. Ibid., p. 102.

16. William F. Lynch, S.J., *Images of Hope* (New York/Toronto: A Mentor-Omega Book, 1965), p. 27.

17. Ibid., p. 19.

18. Paul VI, *Evangelii Nuntiandi*, no. 8.

19. Preface for the Feast of Christ the King.

20. Lonergan, op. cit., p. 115.

21. Schelkle, op. cit., p. 120.

22. Ratzinger, op. cit., p. 164.

23. Ibid., p. 190.

24. Murphy-O'Connor, op. cit., pp. 132-135.

25. Häring, *Free and Faithful in Christ*, vol. 2, p. 106, with reference to St. Augustine, *De civitate Dei*, XXI, 29-33 PL 41, 796-804.

26. Ratzinger, op. cit., p. 215.

27. Ratzinger, Schürmann, von Balthasar, *Principles of Christian Morality*, pp. 22-23.

28. Ratzinger, op. cit., p. 135.

29. Pius XII, *Mystici Corporis* (encyclical, June 29, 1943), *AAS* 35 (1943), 201-202.

30. Häring, *Free and Faithful in Christ*, vol. 2, pp. 262-263.

31. Ibid., pp. 334-335.

32. Ibid., p. 236.

Chapter 6

The Law of Christ

> *That which is preponderant in the law of the New Testament, and wherein all its efficacy is based, is the grace of the Holy Spirit, which is given through faith in Christ. Consequently, the new law is chiefly the very grace of the Holy Spirit.* —Thomas Aquinas[1]

The gift of faith establishes us in a covenantal relationship with the infinite Mystery that calls us and embraces our whole existence. Such faith, which is pure grace, makes known in our heart of hearts, our conscience, the one, eternal Absolute who calls us to "Be holy, for I, the LORD, your God, am holy" (Lv. 19:2). This inner call to holiness, God's Word, took flesh in Jesus Christ and thus visibly and tangibly entered the categorical realm of human history. By his incarnation and paschal mystery, Jesus fully manifested God the Father's will, his plan, for the human race. Through the power of the Holy Spirit, Christ continues to be present as *the* norm for human living. The gospel thus reveals not an external law as such, but rather a dynamic inner principle derived from our spiritual being in Christ.

The "law of Christ" is not a systematized legal code, but an inner, spiritual power through which we realize the deepest aspirations of our innermost being. It is a reality we live "in" much like the law of gravity. Unlike the latter, however, to which material bodies are subject by necessity, the "law of Christ," or the moral law, leaves us free to obey or violate it. Obedience to this law, then, makes us one with Christ in doing the Father's will and establishes us in a communion of life, or friendship with him (see Jn. 15:14). This is what St. Thomas Aquinas is referring to in the quotation above, when he tells us that "the new law is chiefly the very grace of the Holy Spirit." Formulated commands or written precepts are but secondary elements disposing us, who through original sin are distracted by a wide variety of finite loves, to use the gift of grace correctly.

We Americans tend to think of law primarily in terms of written codes. In the absence of a common culture and religious faith our commonality is based upon a written constitution and codes of law. Our government is a government of laws arrived at by a democratic process designed to protect the rights of the individual from the infringement of others, including the government itself. Based upon the modern philosophy that human beings possess inalienable rights to life, liberty and property (the product of their labor), government and laws exist to protect the "enlightened" self-interests of each individual. The only recognized absolute is "freedom and equality," which over the course of years has become radicalized by relativism as the only acceptable moral postulate.

Laws, rules and regulations are determined and changed by public pressure and political processes reflecting no higher truth than the will of the majority. In such a cultural atmosphere even Catholics find it difficult to accept the Church's teaching, rooted in Christian biblical revelation itself, which regards the eternal, objective and universal divine law as "the highest norm of human life" (DH 3).

Ancient civilizations appealed to higher divine or eternal orders as the source of their legal codes. The Greeks identified reason with the divine creative principle within the human person, and Roman jurisprudence attempted to establish its enduring basis in the concept of natural law. The concept of individual autonomy was as foreign to them as it was to the early Christians.

In the New Testament, St. Paul informs us that while we "were once slaves of sin" now in Christ we "have become slaves of righteousness" (Rom. 6:17-18). "For the law of the spirit of life in Christ Jesus has freed you from the law of sin and death" (Rom. 8:2). Any society which does not get its values from a source other than positive law "must be prepared to accept, sooner or later, arbitrariness and tyranny—because it is only an appeal to an unchanging standard which enables us to judge law as good or bad."[2]

Christian biblical revelation provides us with such an unchanging standard in the person of Jesus Christ. In this chapter, therefore, we shall first look at Christ as *the* norm of Christian living. Next, we shall explore the Church's natural law tradition, comparing it to the Enlightenment's theory of natural rights and the scientific laws of nature. We also want to consider the natural law's relationship to the law of Christ. We shall then study the interrelationship between values and norms, and finally, examine the significance of human, positive laws.

137

Christic: THE Norm of Christian Living

In the Gospel according to John, Jesus presents himself as the norm of Christian discipleship when he commands us, "As I have loved you, so you also should love one another" (Jn. 13:34). St. Paul in his Letter to the Romans tells us to "put on the Lord Jesus Christ" (Rom. 13:14). The New Testament leaves no doubt that Jesus himself is the model and pattern of human perfection. "[A]s the Son of the Father, he carried out the entire will of God (i.e., every 'ought') in the world."[3] Sharing our nature he offered the human race's totally adequate response to God's absolute summons to holiness.

Jesus reverses the effects of Adam's sin. In Adam we grabbed for the fruit of "the tree of the knowledge of good and bad" (Gen. 2:17), trusting the tempter who claimed, "God knows well that the moment you eat of it your eyes will be opened and you will be like gods who know what is good and what is bad" (Gen. 3:5). Thus St. Paul exhorts us to be one with the attitude of Christ Jesus, "Who, though he was in the form of God, / did not regard equality with God something to be grasped. / Rather, he emptied himself, / taking the form of a slave, / . . . becoming obedient to death, even death on a cross" (Phil. 2:6-8). United with Jesus Christ in his paschal mystery, we ourselves become one with "the last Adam a life-giving spirit" (1 Cor. 15:45). We are thus made participants in the new and eternal covenant which brings the forgiveness of sins through obedience to God's will (see Heb. 10:1-18). In Christ, we trust the truth of God's word more than the Tempter's illusions.

An Inner Dynamic Principle. Christ becomes our supreme "law" not as an external norm of action, but as a dynamic principle giving us the inner capacity to be conformed to him. We have not so much to copy him externally as to follow him personally, to enter into a personal communion with him. St. Paul speaks of us being not under the law of Christ, but "within the law of Christ" (in Greek, *ennomoi Christou* — 1 Cor. 9:21). Father Hans Urs von Balthasar thus states,

Christ is the concrete categorical imperative. He is the formally universal norm of ethical action, applicable to everyone. But he is also the personal and concrete norm, who, in virtue of his suffering for us and his eucharistic surrender of his life for us (which imparts it to us — *per ipsum et in ipso*), empowers us inwardly to do the

Father's will together with him (*cum ipso*).[4]

Through the sacramental liturgy of the Church we celebrate and effect our mystical identity with Christ. Established within the paschal mystery the liturgy is inseparable from our spiritual-moral life.

The Eucharist, indeed, is the bread of eternal life. It nourishes us in the very mystery of the divine-human encounter that has taken flesh in Jesus Christ. In him, we witness at one and the same time both the divine self-outpouring (i.e., the self-giving love of God, divine creative love drawing all things into relationship) and the perfect human self-surrender (i.e, the prototype of perfect obedience to God the Father). Through faith and sacrament our inner transformation to this Christ becomes real in our own lives. We are united with him as branches on a vine (Jn. 15:1-5), as members of the one body, baptized in one Spirit (1 Cor. 12:12-13).

The paschal mystery is the inner dynamic core of Christian living. Christian ethics is of its very nature cruciform (i.e., vertical and horizontal at the same time). It is summed up in the inseparability of the Two Great Commandments as taught by Jesus. "Dialogue between human beings, if it is to be morally in order, presupposes a dialogue between God and man, whether or not man is explicitly aware of this."[5] Conversely, the human person's relationship with God points expressly to dialogue at a new and higher level between human beings. Overcoming the alienation of sin and restoring relationships of love involves crucifying action. For this reason, then, Christ himself is the sole norm in every particular relationship, in every concrete situation. For through him, in him and with him alone is Eternal Love manifested in temporal, historical existence.

The Gift of the Spirit: the Law of Grace. Christ's paschal mystery finds its completion in the gift of the Spirit. Just as Moses ascended the mountain of the Lord and brought down the two tablets of the Law, so Christ, the New Moses, ascends into heaven and sends down the Holy Spirit, our new law (Gal. 5:18). This sending of the Spirit marks the fulfillment of what the prophets Jeremiah (31:31-33) and Ezekiel (36:26-27) foretold regarding the Lord imprinting his law within our hearts in a new covenant. The Spirit is the "spirit of Christ" (Gal. 4:6; Phil. 1:19), who, in Jesus' words, "will teach you everything and remind you of all that [I] told you" (Jn. 14:26).

Thus Christ, who is the supreme norm of Christian living, continues to communicate his life to us through the grace of the Holy Spirit. This grace becomes our new "law," not as some extrinsic gift, but as an inner elevating and transforming power. It illuminates our minds to understand God's call and moves our wills to put love into action. It sharpens our perception of moral values, purifies our motivation and sensitizes our consciences to the will of God by allowing us to share in the divine life itself. Grace is thus not a thing, but rather God's personal self-gift to us. It is the indwelling of the Triune God within our hearts, an intimate sharing in the interpersonal relationships in the Blessed Trinity. Grace is both a gift and a call, requiring a personal response on our part. It invites us to come to the "full stature of Christ" (Eph. 4:13) by "living the truth in love" (v. 15).

1. As a gift of the Holy Spirit, the "law of grace" is **primarily creative or unifying**. It constitutes relationships. Even at the very beginning of Creation, the Book of Genesis tells of the "spirit of God" hovering over the chaos, the primal abyss, and bringing about order and harmony (i.e., proper relationships) in response to God's word (see Gen. 1:1-3). At the first Pentecost the gift of the Spirit makes possible a new oneness of the human race by addressing people from all over the world in a single language they can all understand (see Acts 2:5-13). St. Paul tells us that "in one Spirit we were all baptized into one body, whether Jews or Greeks, slaves or free persons, and we were all given to drink of one Spirit" (1 Cor. 12:13). The "law of Christ" is, indeed, the law of love (Gal. 5:14), which is fulfilled when we "bear one another's burdens" (Gal. 6:2).

The outpouring of the Holy Spirit of the Father and the Son *is* the sending of the Spirit of the divine "We" into the hearts of believers. Such mutual inherence has an explicitly ecclesial dimension. It is this "being-for-one-another" that constitutes precisely the meaning of Jesus' new commandment that we love one another as he has loved us. The Christian ethical task is the implementation of this personal awareness of being a "we," of being members of Christ's Body. Paul in his Letter to the Galatians thus addresses the inaccurate perception of those who thought that the sign of the presence of the Spirit was a complete freedom in their actions. Christian freedom, he explains, is not a freedom to gratify the "desires of the flesh," but a freedom for service.

St. Paul points out that "the desires of the flesh" which war against the Spirit are more than just bodily inclinations such as for food, sex, pleasure, etc. They are those longings or cravings that breathe dissension, discord, separation because they are impersonal and not conducive to relationships.

140

Among the "works of the flesh," he lists impurity, idolatry, hatreds, acts of selfishness, factions, envy, drunkenness, etc. He contrasts these with the "fruits of the Spirit" which are personalizing and socializing, such as love, joy, kindness, gentleness, self-control, etc. (see Gal. 5:16-26). The presence of the Spirit breaks down every separating barrier whether built on race, sex or social status, and every genuine gift of the Spirit is meant to build up the entire community.[6] Even creation itself awaits the manifestation of the first fruits of the Spirit in the children of God, in order that it too may "be set free from slavery to corruption" (Rom. 8:19-21).

2. The gift of the Spirit also accentuates **the teaching function of grace** (Jn. 14:26). The Holy Spirit "teaches" what Jesus taught and causes it to enter into our hearts. The Spirit does not bring a new gospel. His role is completely subordinate to the revelation brought by Christ. "There is, therefore, a perfect continuity in revelation: coming from the Father, it is communicated to us by the Son, but it attains its fullness when it enters into the most intimate part of our being through the action of the Spirit."[7] He is the "Spirit of truth" who will remain with the disciples after Jesus' departure (Jn. 16:13), who will convince the world that there is sin, righteousness and judgment (Jn. 16:5-11).

Through the mission of the Holy Spirit, as Counsellor and Spirit of truth, "the Son, who 'had gone away' in the Paschal Mystery, 'comes' and is continuously *present in the mystery of the Church*, at times concealing himself and at times revealing himself in history, and always directing her steps."[8] Through the Spirit, the risen Lord who is "the way and the truth and the life" (Jn. 14:6) continues to be present and teach in his Body, the Church, which "in Christ, is in the nature of a sacrament— a sign and instrument of intimate union with God and of the unity of the whole human race" (LG 1). The "law of Christ," which is the very grace of the Holy Spirit, is a dynamic inner gift-call orientating us toward ultimate communion of life with the Triune God. It applies to us the reconciliation, or redemption, won in Christ, drawing us into his life and thereby reversing the de-creation begun by sin. "In the law of Christ" (Paul's *ennomoi Christou*) the Holy Spirit's creative and unifying power continues the work of transforming us into a whole new creation.

Natural Law

The symbolic or sacramental consciousness of the early Church readily saw creation itself as an *expression* of the wisdom and creative power of God, of the divine *Logos* ("Word"). The goodness, harmony and beauty of creation are but a manifestation of the Good "which gives in an inexpressible way: as *bonum diffusivum sui*, as *creative love.*"[9] The Book of Genesis shows God's word mediating the divine plan into an external and recognizable form. It is God's vision of creation and humanity that is mediated through God's spoken word to become the created order.[10] The beauty and harmony of creation are true reflections of the proper relational order intended by the divine Logos. All that is good and meaningful in life faithfully corresponds to this divine wisdom and creative power, this divine ecology written deep within the heart of all created reality. Evil is that which de-creates, which is destructive of the proper relational order intended by God's word.

Created in the "image and likeness of God," all human beings likewise have the capacity for sharing in the divine plan or vision (which Jesus referred to as the "kingdom of God") and for allowing it to find expression in our own unique and individual personhood. Gifted with radical freedom, though, we can grasp for equality with God and eat of "the tree of knowledge of good and bad," thereby forging our own limited plans independent of God's will. Such hubris, however, is non-relational, revealing the fearful alienation and shame roused by such naked independence (see Gen. 3:8-12). Because of the human race's attempt to exercise its freedom in just this way, in the name of Adam and Eve we have become virtually incapable on our own of doing *the* good, which our minds and hearts can still dimly see lying attractive as if behind a veil.

History of the Natural Law. Western civilization's early attempts to comprehend in some rational way the meaning and purpose of human life and earthly existence posited a principle of order in the universe itself. The ancient Greeks detected through experience and observation that the visible universe was indeed a "cosmos," a harmonious whole governed by some immanent principle of order. Thus the Stoic philosophers developed a concept of "natural law" that was the practical equivalent of the laws regulating the physical order of the universe. In human beings, they associated this immanent principle (*Logos*) with reason itself.

Later, Roman jurists noted certain common elements which they found among the wide variety of laws and customs of the different peoples and nations that came under the control of the ever expanding Roman Empire.

142

These common elements, acknowledged to be the work of human reason, they referred to as the "law of nations" (*ius gentium*) and thus used it as a unifying and integrating force in the Empire. However, ultimately they would accept the Hellenistic basis of the natural law (*ius naturale*) and equate it with that law which governs animals and human beings apart from any intervention of human reason. Such a concept, as proposed by the famed Roman jurist Ulpian, for all practical purposes identified natural law with brute natural tendency.[11]

1. **Early Christianity** adopted the term "natural law" from the Greeks and Romans, but transformed the idea. In his Letter to the Romans, St. Paul wanted to emphasize the universal need for salvation in Jesus Christ. So, he set out to demonstrate that both Jews and Gentiles have ignored God's plan or law and thereby have sinned. The Jews have failed to keep the Mosaic Law, and "the Gentiles who do not have the law by nature (*physis*) observe the prescriptions of the law . . . written in their hearts, while their conscience also bears witness and their conflicting thoughts accuse or even defend them" (Rom. 2:14-15). This early Christian interpretation of "natural law" is clearly concerned more with what is specifically human than with what belongs to the physical and animal world.

2. A survey of the **Fathers of the Church** indicates their interest in natural law. Justin Martyr recognizes that in some cases both Christians and pagan philosophers teach the same truth, because of the "seeds of truth" (*spermata aletheias*) present in the human capacity for reason and contemplation. These "seeds" are made manifest in human reason (*logos*) through its participation in the pre-existent "Logos" (reason, word), Jesus Christ. St. John Chrysostom saw the "law of nature" (*nomos physeos*), as he called it, being general, eternal and immortal. It is the moral teacher of the human race. "God placed in man the inborn law, to serve as does the captain over a ship, or the charioteer over the horse."[12] He points out its relational and social character when he refers to the natural moral commandments as "necessities which hold together our lives."[13]

St. Augustine links the Greek concept of an immanent principle of order (*Logos*), which was virtually mechanical, with the Christian belief of a personal God creating through his eternal Word, as found in the Johannine "Prologue." Nature itself is thus seen as dependable because it is the expression of God's dependable will. While the Eastern or Greek Fathers situated their understanding of the natural moral law within their theological context, the treatment of this concept in the Western Latin tradition under the influence of Roman jurisprudence received a more autonomous and legalistic bent. Isidore of Seville, writing in the seventh century, went back to Ulpian's definition of natural law as that which is common to all animals and knowable through right reason. This definition was taken up by Gratian's *Decretum* and so influenced all medieval treatment of the subject.

3. The great **Scholastic synthesis** on natural law was provided by Thomas Aquinas. He defined it as "the participation of a rational creature in the eternal law."[14] It is a personal participation in God's plan, his providence and wisdom, for the eternal law is God himself as the source of moral law and obligation in our world. Eternal law is God under the aspect of law-giver, while natural law is human nature under the aspect of inherent obligations.

> Natural law, according to St. Thomas, consists in certain fundamental moral judgments acquired intuitively and not by deductive reason. These self-evident principles of the moral order can be reduced to "Good is to be done, and evil is to be avoided." Only these first principles are absolutely universal. Other general laws derived from these, may perhaps admit of exceptions because of accidental circumstances.[15]

Thomas made a distinction between the natural law according to the "order of reason" (*lex naturale*), that is, human reason providing guidance and direction for human affairs, and the natural law according to the "order of nature" (*ius naturale*), namely, those basic tendencies and inclinations that human beings share in common with animals.[16] His treatment of these two interpretations, however, was not without ambiguity. After St. Thomas, the rise of Nominalism introduced a strong voluntaristic trend that attributed natural law to the positive will of God. Later, the manualists reduced natural law to the given aspects of the "order of nature" and tended to downplay the role of reason.

4. On the whole, **Protestantism** rejected the concept of natural law. Protestant theologians very often look upon "nature" as describing the original state of humanity unspoiled by sin. Because of their view that sin has brought about the total corruption of everything human, reason can no longer serve as a source of ethical knowledge. In some Anglican circles the natural

law theory has survived under the concept of "created orders," and "God-given or natural intentions." Lutherans, too, talk about "orders of creation," but shy away from the term "natural law."

5. Since the Renaissance in the fourteenth century, **modern philosophy** has consistently moved away from the idea of an absolute, objective and eternal law. There arose instead the concept of the autonomous individual, rejecting any norm of morality other than the prompting of one's own conscience. Liberalism, as a philosophic movement, was by definition subjective. It rejected any need for authoritarian guidance and "taught us that the only danger confronting us is being closed to the emergent, the new, the manifestations of progress."[17] The Enlightenment which it spawned sought to dethrone every authority hostile to reason as the highest principle in political life.

Thomas Hobbes (1588-1679) and John Locke (1632-1704) proposed that the human being's self-preservative desires were the only valid basis upon which to build political society. Enlightened selfishness replaced Christian virtue. Following the new method of the natural sciences, nature is viewed only as matter in motion devoid of all higher purposiveness and incapable of providing us with any ethical imperatives. Concern with comfortable self-preservation alone makes a human being law-abiding and productive. Reaction to this scientific view of nature as matter in motion, which can be conquered for the sake of human needs, was twofold: "a return to the notion that nature is good, but only the brute nature of the fields, forest, mountains and streams in which beasts live contentedly; or a transcendence of nature altogether in the direction of creativity."[18]

Auguste Comte (1798-1857) proposed a theory of positivism, whereby the only mature scientific outlook was one concerned with observable data. When developed by others it asserted three central principles: "1) that all human thought is conditioned by history so that no norm or judgment is universally valid; 2) that the domain of facts alone allows of objective certitude: values are purely subjective; and 3) that there are no objectively founded moral values — only a choice between adjustment to the environment or suicide."[19] Charles Darwin's (1809-1882) theory of evolution saw human beings as evolving from the lower animals and concluded we were not created in the image and likeness of God and are not bound by the moral law as traditionally understood. The philosophical premise of historicism, coupled with Darwin's theory, in turn led Frederick

Nietzsche (1844-1900) to propose a cultural relativism which considered the human person to be pure becoming unlike any other being in nature.

In the field of ethics Jeremy Bentham (1748-1832) developed a utilitarian theory in which the guiding principle determining moral decisions was the seeking of pleasure and the avoidance of pain. An act whose consequences were pleasurable was good; if it produced pain it was bad. Sigmund Freud (1856-1939), the founder of modern psychiatry, viewed sexual love as the greatest human pleasure fulfilling our longing for love and happiness. For him, God was an illusion, a Father-figure, born out of our sense of insecurity, and the human psyche itself was in some sense bestial, sexual and animal. Thus modern times have given birth to a number of disparate systems, whose conflicting mass of opinions are united only in their rejection of the idea of an absolute, objective and eternal law written within the human heart.

Contemporary Interpretations. Most Catholic moralists today, especially in the United States and Western Europe, have rejected the "physicalist" (strictly "order of nature") interpretation of the natural law presented in the Pre-Vatican II moral manuals, which many claim continues to guide the magisterium's teaching on sexual and bioethical issues. They instead tend to opt for the rediscovered "order of reason" approach, found both in Thomas Aquinas' works and the Church's social teaching over the past century. In varying degrees this recent widespread approach to the application of the natural law in ethical situations demonstrates the pervading influence of modern philosophical trends, the influence of scientific positivism, historicism and relativism. The very use of human reason itself, they maintain, effects human nature, which is ever changing, and hence too the natural law.

It is the rare Catholic moralist who still today espouses a strict "order of nature" approach. The Second Vatican Council offered a decidedly personalistic interpretation of the natural law "by stressing the finality of the free subject with its interpersonal relationships and personal ends."[20] For instance, when addressing the issue of responsible parenthood, the Council Fathers stated:

> When it is a question of harmonizing married love with the responsible transmission of life, it is not enough to take only the good intention and the evaluation of motives into account; the objective criteria must be used, criteria drawn from the nature of the

human person and human action, criteria which respect the total meaning of mutual self-giving and human procreation in the context of true love (GS 51).

Here, "mutual self-giving" and "the context of true love" are not mere subjective elements, but objective criteria. The official teaching of the episcopal magisterium today, in treating issues involving the human person's physical, biological structure, i.e., sexual and bio-medical ethics, accepts the fact that we are embodied spirits who must keep in proper balance or interrelationship both the "order of reason" and the "order of nature."

Science and technology, the use of reason, have made possible in recent centuries the great advancements and marvels which have promoted health, communication and our overall general comfort and physical well-being. They have brought us to the point where we can begin to perceive the fact that all nations and inhabitants of this spaceship earth are indeed one human family. In the negative column, the atom bomb as well as our polluted air, streams and rivers are the resultant products of this same scientific use of reason. The ecology movement of recent years has arisen out of concern for technology's untrammeled intrusion into our human environment, for its lack of respect for the delicate balances or interrelationships existing among nature's elements within the biosphere of plant and animal life. The magisterium, without employing the current movement's terminology, has always tried to promote an "ecological awareness" of the human person's spiritual-corporeal nature through its teaching on the natural law. Its concern today continues to be the proper use of reason (the Scholastic "*recta ratio*") in carefully examining "to what extent a particular intervention into the biological processes would amount to a loss of human values or undue manipulation of the human person so that there would exist an objective moral evil."[21]

The secularistic and pluralistic spirit of contemporary American society shies away from any inherent, universal and spiritual principles of order either within the world or within ourselves. We are the heirs of the Enlightenment who recognize individual freedom as the only absolute. Everything else, including truth itself, is relative. We create our own values and lifestyles according to what makes us happy or provides us with the most pleasure and least amount of pain. Whoever I am and whatever I do is good, as long as I do not infringe upon anyone else's rights. As an American social philosopher, Allan Bloom, recently observed:

147

The same people who struggle to save the snail-darter bless the pill, worry about hunting deer and defend abortion. Reverence for nature, mastery of nature — whichever is convenient. The principle of contradiction has been repealed. . . . The male and female sexual organs themselves now have no more evident purposiveness than do white and black skin, are no more naturally pointed toward one another than white master and black slave, or so the legend goes.[22]

Our contemporary secular society views human nature in a Rousseauistic perspective whereby the human person is born whole but has been corrupted by societal influences. Through correctives ranging from revolution to therapy, human beings can become whole once again, "but there is little place for the confessional or for mortification of the flesh."[23]

The Content of Natural Law. Although the natural law tradition accepts as a premise God writing his law within the human heart, the will of God always transcends any idea we may have of it. The divine law cannot be objectified and defined. This imprinting in the heart only means that human beings have been given the radical capacity for self-reflection and thereby can discern how they should act in particular situations. God's will remains there always as a summons to a point which always lies beyond our grasp, a call to perfect love.

On the whole, Catholic tradition has identified the Ten Commandments, especially the second tablet or last seven, as being precepts of the natural law. Yet, neither in the Old Testament nor the New do the Ten Commandments appear as a codified system of law. Their character is more revelatory than legal. The Septuagint referred to them as the "Decalogue" or "ten words" thus emphasizing the revelatory character of word.[24] Christian Orthodox theology interpreting the patristic tradition has likewise identified the content of the natural law, in large part, with the Ten Commandments. It views the natural law as a common denominator ethics, i.e., "a very elemental moral law which articulates the absolutely necessary modes of behavior for the maintenance of the human community."[25] Thus its content is seen solely as addressing basic social relationships which permit and protect the existence of human society. In the Orthodox tradition, natural law does not consider our human physical make-up nor our relationship to the rest of creation.

Within the Roman Catholic tradition, St. Thomas Aquinas distinguished between *primary* and *secondary precepts* of the natural law.[26] The primary precepts are universal, unchangeable and absolute. They include transcendental precepts, or very general norms having no specific material content, such as "Do good and avoid evil," "Love your neighbor" and "Give everyone his or her just due." St. Thomas also maintained that "the precepts of the decalogue themselves, inasmuch as they contain the quality of justice, are immutable."[27] Furthermore, negative precepts of the natural law interpreted according to the "order of nature," i.e., certain physically defined actions which may never be used as a means even for a good cause, are considered by him to be absolute. Thus he condemns fornication, direct killing of an innocent person, taking property one has no right to, divorce and polygamy. He states, for example, that "The end of the act itself [fornication] by its nature is disordered even if the person acting could be intending a good end. The end does not suffice to excuse the act, just as is clearly the case with the one who steals with the intention of giving alms."[28] Secondary principles, or conclusions drawn from common principles, are the same for most people ("*ut in pluribus*") but their desire or awareness of what is right may be lacking. St. Thomas thus recognized that historicity is part of the natural law as far as its "material" or secondary precepts are concerned, but not in its "formal" or primary principles.

In the end, Thomas Aquinas himself is not precisely clear as to what precepts pertain to the primary or the secondary aspects of the natural law. Besides, he recognizes that God has transferred a certain authority to human beings, such as empowering civil government to condemn a criminal according to the law. In view of this lack of clarity, many Catholic moralists today, following the trends in modern philosophy, deny that there exist any moral absolutes according to the "order of nature," or that certain physically defined actions are intrinsically evil. For them, our contemporary cultural situation values human freedom to such a degree that it is quite clear that in our age the "order of reason" alone determines what is in accordance with the natural law.

At the same time, as we have already alluded to above, the ecology movement today is warning us that "we cannot manipulate our cosmos or our societies or ourselves at will and still survive. . . . For when you cheat on nature in a serious and chronic way, you are enfeebled, you sicken and die."[29] There is an immanent universal principle of order or relationship written into the very heart of all physical reality, which when manipulated, and not respected, works against us in destructive ways. The social sciences, too, continue to discover universal patterns of behavior that are irrespective of geography and culture. The developmental psychologists, such as Jean

149

Piaget, Erik Erikson and Lawrence Kohlberg, have claimed to have discovered patterns of personal growth that transcend geographical and social boundaries. The structural anthropologist Claude Levi-Strauss has studied the "universal" in human behavior. In linguistics Noam Chomsky has proposed the radical thesis that the underlying ways of human thinking and speaking are not really relative to culture nor malleable by human intervention but rather appear to be intrinsic to the constitution of the human person.[30]

The person-centered approach to morality called for by the Second Vatican Council does not see the content of the natural law as being some extrinsic limitation arbitrarily imposed upon us by religion or society. It strives, rather, to place before us our intrinsic nature as embodied spirits living now in the dual realms of time and eternity, of "becoming" and "Being." The natural law sets before us the call to *total* personal integration which comes about through the proper ordering of the complementary tensions (physical-spiritual, temporal-eternal, individual-social, etc.) that constitute the dynamic core of what it means to be a human person. Father George V. Lobo, S.J., a Catholic ethicist from India, recently wrote:

> Hence, to affirm moral absolutes regarding certain basic human values like life and sexuality does not necessarily imply a physicist or biological view of the natural law. Those who make such remarks may themselves be revealing an overly spiritualistic or disincarnate view of man. They may be implying, without being aware of it, that man is merely spirit and that the morality of his activity is determined wholly by his spiritual intentionality, whereas, in fact, man is essentially an incarnate spirit and, hence, his earthly life and other basic values have a determinant role in his moral life.[31]

The content of the natural law, therefore, is absolute, universal and immutable in its very core, i.e., inasmuch as it participates in and gives expression to the call of Transcendence, the Eternal Law, written within our very being. Its basic principles, recognized even by the weakened power of human reason after the Fall, call us to relationships of justice in all interactions with the human and physical order, i.e., the "order of reason" and the "order of nature." Specific, concrete formulations of natural law precepts deduced from its basic principles can, however, be affected by historical circumstances and thus be in need of better formulation with the passing of time. The precise meaning, for example, of the commandment "You shall not kill" continues to receive further specifications in each historical age.

The Natural Law and the Law of Christ. Sacred Scripture informs us that the world was created according to the will and plan of God. Creation itself is revelatory of "his invisible attributes of eternal power and divinity" (Rom. 1:20). God alone is Absolute Good (see Lk. 18:19), a Trinity of Persons in perfect relationship to one another. The variety, harmony and beauty of the created order is but an expression of the one Good. Thus all creation participates in the supernatural order. All is graced. But original sin tended to blind us to the presence of the spiritual and the eternal. We thereby naturally perceive reality only in terms of the physical and temporal, of what we can see and touch.

The natural and the supernatural, though, are not really two distinct and separate orders. As such, there is no purely natural order that is the subject of moral experience. There exists only the one divine plan according to which we have all been created. The natural law is simply the way human reason, unaided by revelation, comes to know this plan. The "law of Christ" is the full revelation of the divine plan. It makes known to us what unaided human reason in its present fallen state cannot inerrantly comprehend. Their interrelationship is analogous to the divine and the human in Jesus Christ, which although inseparable in reality may be distinguished reflectively. St. Paul thus spoke of once knowing "Christ according to the flesh, yet now we know him so no longer" (2 Cor. 5:16). Through the eyes of faith the "law of Christ" remains the completion and the judge of the natural law. Indeed, the natural law itself points to the relational order manifested in Christ's commandment of self-giving love (Jn. 13:34).

Values, Norms and Laws

Although the primary source of Christian living is the interior grace of the Spirit of Christ, the New Testament makes it "fairly obvious that the early Church had no hang-ups about rules. Laws and regulations were at the heart and soul of early Christianity."[32] Much of St. Paul's teaching oscillates between the indicative reality of our living "in Christ" with its corresponding demands and relatively trivial rules and regulations designed simply to maintain order in the community. For Thomas Aquinas, the positive law (*lex scripta*) pertains to the new law of grace only in a secondary way. In the form of prohibitions it warns us of our sinfulness and our constant need of grace. Helping to guard against the danger that carnal persons may falsely and egotistically interpret the movement of the Spirit, positive law teaches us how to use grace correctly.[33] Law is thus the

151

expression of an intrinsic value, be it the call of God or some transcendent principle. Law is also a demand, but a demand that flows from a value, and the emphasis should be clearly on the value.

Values. A value is some reality we recognize as possessing an intrinsic worth. It is something we prize and cherish, and are willing to act upon. Yet, a value is but the mediator of a deeper inner reality. It is an image, often unconscious, of what that value represents, namely, a person's world-view. In the words of Brian P. Hall, "Values then are information technology mediating the inner world, and enabling it to express itself outward in daily activity."[34] They are analogous to God's "spoken word" in Genesis effecting his plan for creation. Thus, by the use of symbolic consciousness, human beings recreate the world in which they live from their inner vision which is mediated in turn by values. Hall calls this process "The Genesis Effect."[35]

Anchored within the existential relationship of faith, within the context of our personal response to God's gift-call, values mediate that inner reality allowing it to find enfleshment in the temporality of our everyday lives. Values are relational priorities inherently given, which potentially exist in all persons. They are not some rational set of norms and rules that everyone must abide by, as proposed by traditional classicism, nor are they just private individual priorities as maintained by the subjective camp of historical relativism. Values mediate and give expression to the multiple aspects or qualities that flow from our faith relationship, deep within our heart of hearts at the unreflexive level of consciousness, with the Absolute Good, the personal Triune God. They are constitutive of our relational existence as human beings. Through our personal choice and internalization of value priorities, each one of us opens our lives to creative growth and maturity, becoming the unique person we are "called" to be in Christ. Thus, as Hall states, "To believe in Jesus Christ really means to be energized by the same value clusters that he was energized by, as an aspect of our personal relationship to him."[36]

Since our faith relationship with the immanent-transcendent Mystery of the Triune God is at one and the same time both eternal and temporal, the values expressive of this covenant of love may likewise be divided accordingly. Thus we may speak of eternal or "being" values and temporal or "doing" values. The "being" values are spiritual ones that open us up to the eternal, such as poverty of spirit, detachment, contemplation, intimacy,

152

play, beauty, art, harmony, companionship, etc.; they are values we must always attend to and seek to realize as much as possible within our lives. The "doing" values are moral values that we must enflesh in our temporal, everyday lives, such as seeking truth, justice, reconciliation, peace; showing reverence, mercy, compassion; striving to be obedient, chaste, honest, responsible, creative, helpful, diligent, productive, etc. The undue neglect of either sphere of values throws our lives out of balance. A proper attention given to both spheres fosters our "becoming," our vocation, who we are called to be.

Because values are constitutive of our relational existence, the person is the basic value, being both the center and the bearer of values. The entire spectrum of human rights and duties exists to safeguard and promote human dignity which is rooted in the fact that we are made in the image and likeness of God, who is a Trinity of persons. The temporal, or linear level of human becoming on the horizontal plane is made genuinely possible through our fundamental faith relationship with Transcendent Being on the vertical plane. Both the horizontal and vertical together overall constitute reality, which is a whole. For us limited human beings it is difficult to see the whole with its transcendent and communal dimensions. The values which mediate it for us, therefore, call for norms in order to express and protect them.

Norms. Moral norms, commandments, principles, rules and laws are but verbal formulations articulating values in terms of human behavior. "We must start by noting that a moral norm is not so much an extrinsic limitation arbitrarily placed by religion or society, as an intrinsic demand of love."[37] Norms give verbal expression to the relational nature of the created order including human existence itself. Their purpose is to indicate for us what actions and behavior are true expressions of Absolute Good and which are not. Laws and commandments should not hedge a person in, cramping or crippling one. They are meant to free us for the truth, for salvation. "Therefore Jesus repeatedly urges consideration of the spirit and intent of the law as opposed to its juridical-causistic interpretation."[38]

Because of the original Fall there exists a human tendency toward both antinomianism and legalism. Antinomianism finds all demands of morality to be disagreeable. Legalism recognizes only the letter of the law, its extrinsic formulation, while denying that laws are indicative of any higher norm than that which is written. The New Testament clearly condemns both extremes. Jesus himself came not to abolish the law or the prophets but to fulfill them (see Mt. 5:17). Still, he rejected all legal extrinsicism as insufficient for salvation, for reaching God. For Jesus the law is fundamentally a manifestion of the will of God. According to St. Paul, "the law is holy, and the commandment is holy and righteous and good" (Rom. 7:12). Yet, a few short verses earlier he stated that "now we are released from the law, dead to what held us captive, so that we may serve in the newness of the spirit and not under the obsolete letter" (Rom. 7:6). Jesus and Paul reduce the entire law to the commandment of love of God and of one's neighbor (see Mt. 22:34-40; Gal. 5:14), which in turn is revelatory of the personal Triune God, the Absolute Good.

Norms are primarily of two types: prohibitive and goal-directed.[39] The former, such as the Ten Commandments, indicate those attitudes which absolutely contradict the gift and call of love; they protect and foster the moral or "doing" values. The latter, such as the Beatitudes, describe the spiritual or "being" values; they portray the type of person we should be. The particular value, or the spiritual-moral quality (traditionally referred to as the "moral object" as distinguished from the physical object of an act), which a norm articulates and protects, is a specification of the basic human tendency toward the good.

> A person-centered morality cannot *a priori* exclude an absolute moral norm. This implies that the essential nature and the basic values of man are inviolable. The human person is called to tend to God, not only by explicit relationships with Him, but in and through the moral act itself, which specifies the basic dynamism of love.[40]

While there is indeed one Absolute Good, we can speak of other ethical "absolutes" (in the sense that they are clearly expressive of the Absolute Good) without which "the intrinsic good of the human person would not be safe from invasion and suppression under some pretext or other."[41]

For St. Thomas Aquinas the absolutes of ethics were practically equated with the Ten Commandments "insofar as the precepts of the first table contain the very ordination towards God, and the precepts of the second table contain the order of justice among men; namely that nobody should be wronged and everyone should receive what is right."[42] The application of these universal precepts to concrete situations, however, he saw as open to change. "Thus the precepts of the Decalogue are immutable as to the very justice which they contain; but as to the determination in view of the application to individual acts (for instance whether this or that is murder, theft, adultery, or not) there is place for change."[43]

The classicist methodology of the pre-Vatican II moral manuals maintained that there are absolutes, mostly in the areas of human life and sexuality, whose deliberate violation is always sinful. Proponents of this approach tended to operate out of an absolute-physicalist interpretation of the natural law. By way of reaction, many contemporary Catholic moralists espousing the equally rationalist approach of historical relativism maintain that there are no externally defined absolutes. For them, human intentionality alone gives moral significance to an action.

From the perspective of symbolic consciousness, human actions enflesh within themselves either the basic dynamism of love or the sundering effects of evil. Such actions carried out by human beings, who are by nature responsible persons, contain a moral element irrespective of the subjective intentionality of the agent. In the Last Judgment scene from Matthew's gospel (Mt. 25:31-46), Jesus indicates that the condemned are unaware of any evil intentionality on their part. In the Parable of the Two Sons (Mt. 21:28-32), their actions speak louder than their expressed intentions. Today, we speak of "sinful social structures," such as racism, apartheid, economic injustices, etc., which incarnate evil alienation and for which we might share a moral responsibility irrespective of our subjective intentionality and culpability.

Morality is a category applicable to all human actions inasmuch as they are expressive of a free and responsible person, who can, despite one's subjective intentionality to the contrary, perform concrete actions that move the created order away from the divine plan. Certain types of actions in themselves always entail such moral evil. There are, therefore, ethical absolutes preserving certain values. Sometimes, in a conflict situation a higher and more urgent value may take precedence, and one is forced to choose a lesser moral evil. Subjective intentionality does not make that choice of the lesser evil a good in itself; it simply recognizes fully the reality of the human condition.

Subjective intentionality, however, is a determinant in judging whether or not the moral evil is a formal sin. Many contemporary moralists prefer to restrict the category of morality to the consideration of subjective intentionality and sin. Such a narrowing of the focus of morality tends to deny the incarnational aspect of human activity and too easily relieves one of responsibility, regardless of subjective culpability, for one's harmful actions. Thus, the Christian Orthodox tradition retains the concept of "involuntary sin" referring to "wrong or evil acts or events in which we are involved, but which we have not willed, nor for which we can be held morally responsible."[44]

1. Norms articulating values can take many forms depending upon their nature and source. Commandments are universal precepts considered to be of divine origin; they bind under the weight of obligation. Before assuming the form of a three-fold vow in the twelfth century and being given canonical status for consecrated religious and members of secular institutes, the **evangelical counsels** in the early Church called Christ's followers beyond the minimum of observing commandments to the fullness of life and love in Christ Jesus. The counsels show us how to respond in love to the Good News of God's unsurpassing love. They describe the essence of apostolic life, the *koinonia* or "mutual sharing" (Acts 2:42-44; Heb. 13:16). They show us how to live Christ, who "emptied himself, taking the form of a slave . . . becoming obedient to death" (Phil. 2:7-8) and for our sakes "became poor although he was rich" (2 Cor. 8:9). To some, even, is given the gift of "the Father (cf. Mt. 19:11; 1 Cor. 7:7) to devote themselves to God alone more easily with undivided heart (cf. 1 Cor. 7:32-34) in virginity or celibacy" (LG 42). Indeed, Christ himself is the only evangelical counsel who shows us how to love God more than self and to "live in love" (Eph. 5:2).

The evangelical counsels propose that following Christ is more than keeping commandments and avoiding sin. As a commitment to love they exclude all legalism. The Second Vatican Council in speaking of the universal vocation to holiness tells us that the Church's holiness finds expression in "this practice of the counsels prompted by the Holy Spirit, undertaken by many Christians whether privately or in a form or state sanctioned by the Church" (LG 39). The counsels, in other words, hold forth a new way of life for all the baptized. Rather than suggesting an "other-worldly" spirituality, "they are symbols of the whole church's call to sexual and material restraint and obedience to the Gospel. . . . Poverty, chastity, and obedience are the flip side of the coin of money, sex, and power, the three principal means by which we try to force the world to center upon ourselves."[45] They provide us with the ability to see the world and to live in it with the attitude of Jesus Christ, making us his followers not only in name but in fact.

2. While the Church has always considered the love and power of the

156

Holy Spirit to be her inner guiding principle, and while even ancient civilizations, such as Greece and Rome, recognized some higher principle of order as the foundation of their jurisprudence, all human societies have depended upon **positive law** to establish order and protect the common good. Thus St. Thomas Aquinas maintained that law must be an ordering of reason (or faith in the case of the Church). It imposes a public obligation upon society; as such, it is factual and objective, an authoritative standard of behavior declaring what "ought to be." While some philosophical schools maintained that the obligatory force of law depends on the arbitrary will of the legislator, Aquinas saw obligation dependent upon the law's correspondence to the common good.

Ecclesiastical legislation, or Canon Law, finds its roots even in the New Testament. The "Council of Jerusalem," as it is sometimes called, in Acts 15 tells of the early apostolic community settling some thorny issues concerning Gentile converts through a legislative decree sent to the missionary churches in Antioch, Syria and Cilicia (Acts 15: 28-29). St. Paul, too, did not hesitate to interpret and apply Jesus' teaching regarding divorce and remarriage for the Corinthian community (see 1 Cor. 7:12-14).

In promulgating the 1983 Code of Canon Law, Pope John Paul II stated that its specific purpose is "to create such an order in the ecclesial society that, while assigning the primacy to love, grace and charisms, it at the same time renders their organic development easier in the life of both the ecclesial society and the individual persons who belong to it."[46] Canon Law thus draws attention to some demands of the Christian vocation and fosters the building of Christian community by regulating duties, protecting rights and counteracting abuses. The role of authority in the Church is a function of service, or "*diakonia*" (Mk. 10:44-45). There is an obligation in conscience to observe the laws of the Church rightly understood.

The purpose of civil law is to promote the common good and protect citizens' rights. The "common good" as described by Vatican II is "the sum total of social conditions which allow people, either as groups or as individuals, to reach their fulfillment more fully and more easily" (GS 26). Scripture tells us that "There is one lawgiver" (Jas. 4:12). Civil law, therefore, is founded upon the divine law. During the "Age of Christendom" in medieval Europe there was no practical difference between the moral law and civil law. In our contemporary secular society, however, legal positivism basically identifies law with legislation. Here, civil law and morality often converge but do not coincide.

Civil law does not make an action good or bad, but only takes a stand as to what favors the common good in a particular situation. Before the U.S. Supreme Court's decision in ''Roe vs. Wade'' liberalizing abortion laws, abortion itself was considered to be both a crime and a serious moral evil in this country. Afterwards many people got the mistaken impression that since abortion is no longer a crime, it is not a moral evil either. Civil laws are not meant to be doctrinal declarations. ''What is forbidden by morality is *sinful* and what is forbidden by civil law is a *crime*. Many sinful acts are also criminal, but crime and sin are not identical.''[47]

We have an obligation in conscience to observe civil law. In responding to a question regarding the payment of a census tax, Jesus unequivocally states, ''Then repay to Caesar what belongs to Caesar and to God what belongs to God'' (Mt. 22:21). St. Paul tells us that we should be subject to public authorities, as a matter of conscience, because they are ''ministers of God'' (see Rom. 13:1-7). The Petrine literature counsels Christians to ''Be subject to every human institution for the Lord's sake, whether it be to the king as supreme or to governors as sent by him for the punishment of evildoers and the approval of those who do good'' (1 Pt. 2:13-14). The Second Vatican Council, too, ''exhorts Christians, as citizens of both cities, to perform their duties faithfully in the spirit of the Gospel'' (GS 43), and to pay just taxes and fulfill their other social obligations, such as abiding by ''the norms of social conduct, such as those regulating public hygiene and speed limits'' (GS 30).

All laws, ecclesiastical and civil, as well as all norms, commandments and counsels derive their power and significance inasmuch as they give expression and specification to the one Absolute and Eternal Law, the Triune God. Their primary purpose is tutorial (Gal. 4:24-25); they are meant to teach us how to respond correctly to the dynamic workings of divine grace within us, as well as point out for us the divine plan operative within the whole of creation. They are meant to protect the primary value of persons and the relational order of creation from the alienating effects of ''the law of sin and death'' (Rom. 8:2). They serve to illuminate and make explicit the will and order of God in his creation as this is made known within the depths of one's heart, that is, one's conscience.

Notes

1. *Summa Theologica*, Ia-IIae, 106, 1.

2. Rodger Charles, S.J., *The Social Teaching of Vatican II*, p. 15.

3. Ratzinger, Schürmann and von Balthasar, *Principles of Christian Morality*, p. 79.

4. Ibid., p. 79.

5. Ibid., p. 86.

6. See Joseph A. Grassi, "Discernment of Spirits: The New Testament View" in *The Genesis Effect*, pp. 327, 329-331.

7. Stanislas Lyonnet and I. de la Potterie, *The Christian Lives By the Spirit* (New York: Alba House, 1971), p. 206.

8. "Dominum et Vivificantem," no. 63.

9. Ibid., no. 37. Cardinal Joseph Ratzinger in a recent address to bishops gathered for a Dallas, Texas, meeting stated that ". . . the church believes that in the beginning was the *Logos* and that therefore being itself bears the language of the *Logos*, not just mathematical, but also aesthetical and moral reason. This is what is meant when the church insists that 'nature' has a moral expression. No one is saying that biologism should become the standard of man." [*Origins* 13, no. 40 (March 15, 1984), p. 664.]

10. Hall, *The Genesis Effect*, p. 13.

11. Lobo, *Guide to Christian Living*, p. 169.

12. "To Those Who Are Scandalized," 8. MPG 52, 479, as quoted by Harakas, *Toward Transfigured Life*, p. 131.

13. "Sermons on the Statues," 12, 3 as quoted in ibid., p. 132.

14. *Summa* I-II, q. 91, a.2.

15. Lobo, op. cit., pp. 170-171.

16. See *Summa* II-II, q. 154, a. 12: "Reason presupposes things as determined by nature . . . so in matters of action it is most grave and shameful to act against things as determined by nature."

17. Alan Bloom, *The Closing of the American Mind* (New York: Simon & Schuster, 1987), p. 29; also Rodger Charles, S.J., op. cit., pp. 91-97.

18. Bloom, op. cit., p. 181.

19. Charles, op. cit., p. 99.

20. Lobo, op. cit., p. 222.

21. Ibid., p. 179. Thus Cardinal Joseph Ratzinger, head of the Vatican's Doctrinal Congregation, told bishops attending a workshop in Dallas, Texas, in 1984: "In some way or another we are beginning to realize that materiality contains a spiritual expression and that it is not simply for calculation and use. In some way we see that there is a reason which precedes us which alone can keep our reason in balance and can keep us from falling into external

unreason." [*Origins* 13, no. 40 (March 15, 1984), p. 664.]

22. Bloom, op. cit., pp. 172, 105.

23. Ibid., p. 170.

24. James A. Fischer, C.M., "Law and Wisdom" in *Christian Biblical Ethics*, pp. 108, 112.

25. Harakas, op. cit., p. 135. The general and social character of the natural law within the Christian Orthodox tradition finds difficulty with the Roman Catholic Church's claim that "birth control is wrong because it is opposed to the natural law." (p. 131).

26. See *Summa Theologica*, IIa-IIae, 94, 4.

27. See *Summa Contra Gentes*, 3, 128, 3.

28. *De Malo*, 15, 1, 3: *Summa Theologica*, IIa-IIae, 64, 6, 7; 154, 2; 66, 3, 5; *Supplementum*, 65, 1; 67, 2.

29. James T. Burtchaell, C.S.C., "The Natural Law Revisited" in *National Catholic Reporter*, 23 (May 8, 1987), p. 13, 20.

30. See Timothy E. O'Connell, *Principles for a Catholic Morality* (New York: Seabury Press, 1978), pp. 141-142.

31. Lobo, op. cit., p. 227.

32. Daly, *Christian Biblical Ethics*, p. 101.

33. See *Summa Theologica*, Ia-IIae, q. 106-108.

34. Hall, op. cit., p. 22.

35. Ibid., p. 10.

36. Ibid., p. 169.

37. Lobo, op. cit., p. 226.

38. Schelkle, *Theology of the New Testament*, vol. 3, p. 34.

39. See Häring, *Free and Faithful in Christ*, vol. 1, p. 342.

40. Lobo, op. cit., p. 227.

41. Ibid., p. 228.

42. *Summa Theologica*, Ia-IIae, q. 100, a. 8. as quoted by Häring, *Free and Faithful in Christ*, vol. 1, p. 363.

43. Ibid., ad 3.

44. Harakas, op. cit., p. 174 and 175, where he explains that "By calling the situation a 'sin,' it acknowledges that evil has occurred. . . . By calling it 'involuntary' it both acknowledges the formal lack of responsibility, while at the same time accepting the involvement in the accident [in which someone has been maimed or killed by our car, although we were not at fault]."

45. Hunter Brown, "Counsels for the Baptized," *Commonweal* CXIV, 17 (October 9, 1987), pp. 559-560.

46. John Paul II, "Sacrae disciplinae leges" (Apostolic Constitution) in *Code of Canon Law*, Latin-English Edition, (Washington, D.C.: Canon Law Society of America, 1983), p. xiv.

47. Lobo, op. cit., p. 264.

Chapter 7

Conscience and Its Formation

Deep within his conscience man discovers a law which he has not laid upon himself but which he must obey. Its voice, ever calling him to love and to do what is good and to avoid evil, tells him inwardly at the right moment: do this, shun that. For man has in his heart a law inscribed by God. His dignity lies in observing this law, and by it he will be judged. His conscience is man's most secret core, and his sanctuary. There he is alone with God whose voice echoes in his depths. By conscience, in a wonderful way, that law is made known which is fulfilled in the love of God and of one's neighbor. — Gaudium et Spes, *#16*

Conscience is probably one of the most elusive and misunderstood realities of our spiritual-moral lives. Our childhood catechisms never defined conscience nor described it. We were merely told to "examine our conscience" in order "to receive the sacrament of Penance worthily."[1] We were further taught that we could "make a good examination of conscience by calling to mind the commandments of God and of the Church, and by asking ourselves how we may have sinned with regard to them."[2] The commandments thus provided us with a checklist for our thoughts, words, deeds and omissions. If any of these latter violated God's laws, we chalked them up as sins to be confessed and pardoned in the sacrament of Penance. The formation of conscience consisted primarily of learning about commandments and laws so that we could properly apply them to given actions, and thereby judge our culpability or lack thereof in that particular instance.

The above description of conscience, taken from the Second Vatican Council's Pastoral Constitution on the Church in the Modern World, indicates that this human faculty is something far richer and deeper than recent popular piety has perceived it to be. It is, first of all, described as the secret locus or core of my being where I am alone with the Triune God dwelling within me. There, I hear his intimate loving call to become the sort of person that he has intended me to be from all eternity. Conscience is, thus, an awareness of the divine call within one's heart of hearts to personal self-transcendence, to ongoing conversion — religious, intellectual, affective and moral. Just as the acorn "knows" the tree it shall become, so within my conscience I hear and know God's unique, individual call to become the person he wants me to be. Unlike the acorn lacking reflective knowledge and free will, human beings are gifted with self-reflection and freedom. In their conscience, therefore, they can personally respond or refuse to respond to God's call of love and thereby give shape to their own destiny. Even despite repeated deafness to his call and even rejections, God is ever patient and his voice continues to echo within our hearts calling us to faith and repentance.

This voice of God is the attraction of love, of the good. It calls us to act according to who we are (*agere sequitur esse/credere*), to do good and avoid evil by fulfilling the law written within our hearts to love God and neighbor. This call to become who we are meant to be can, thus becomes more specific and concrete as it directs us in a particular moment to do this or shun that. By these practical judgments of conscience involving the exercise of our knowledge and freedom, we respond to value, we enflesh our relationships of love and mature according to God's plan, we grow "in Christ, the Last Adam." Conscience is thus the human faculty of responsibility and discernment through which we answer God's loving call within the very depths of our being and then live out that call by enfleshing this law of love in all the practical decisions of our everyday lives.

What Conscience Is Not

Before we look further at the understanding of conscience within the Christian tradition, it is appropriate for us to consider what is often mistaken for conscience in our contemporary society. Conscience, first of all, is not a feeling, despite the example of the recent soft-drink commercial which stated that "When you make a choice, what's right is what feels right." In the late sixties in this country, conscience "made a great comeback, as the all-purpose ungrounded ground of moral determination, sufficient at its slightest rumbling to discredit all other obligations or loyalties."[3] This highly existentialist subjectivistic notion considered the individual conscience to be the creator and source of its own values and norms, answerable only to itself. All that matters is that one is sincere and means well. Here one's conscience, anchored in genuine, authentic feeling, becomes the highest court of appeal.

Our feelings, however, are not to be equated with conscience. If you have

163

made a resolution to get some physical exercise every day and after a couple of weeks fail to do it one day, you may "feel guilty," but that does not make it a matter of conscience. You know it is not wrong to miss Mass on Sunday when one is sick, but you confess the "sin" anyway because you do not "feel right" about it. Such feelings are morally neutral and have nothing to do with conscience. On the other hand, many people do not feel guilty about racial or sexual discrimination, but that does not make such practices right. As a result of original sin, our human drives, longings and feelings can all run off in their own direction because they often lack integration. Our feelings can be helpful barometers of our decisions and actions, but they cannot always be taken at face value. They cannot be the ultimate test of moral right and wrong.

Some contemporary schools of psychology, such as the Freudian, identify conscience with the superego, an automatic and prepersonal function of censorship and control that results from the socialization process beginning in childhood. The superego is actually "the ego of another superimposed on our own to serve as an internal censor to regulate our conduct by using guilt as its powerful weapon."[4] It has been compared to an attic in an old house, which instead of furniture contains the "should's" and "have-to's" we have absorbed from all the authority figures in our lives, beginning with our parents and including our teachers, police, boss, the Church, and so on. Such commands and prohibitions do not arise from our perception of the intrinsic value or disvalue of the action contemplated. Their sole origin is our need to be loved and to maintain the approval of the authority figures in our lives.

The largely unconscious mechanism of the superego is really "preconscious" or prepersonal because it does not involve our personal perception and appropriation of values. It does not involve our knowledge and freedom. In the life of an infant it is a step on the way to the development of a personal conscience. In the life of an adult, too, the superego still has a place. It relieves one of the need of constantly having to decide about routine everyday situations, but it must be integrated with a mature conscience. The commands of the moral conscience, on the other hand, are primarily oriented toward the values involved which have become personalized and internalized. They are a response to God's call, his invitation to love. A person with an overly active superego often experiences great difficulty in distinguishing what God is really calling him or her to do from what "mother said I should do."[5]

The different schools of psychology propose their own theories of conscience development. For Freudians the superego is properly developed by means of loving discipline. Behaviorism, which denies the existence of human free will and autonomy, considers conscience as a phenomenon that results from the accumulation of the appropriate learned conditioned responses. For instance, a dog will begin to salivate at the sound of a bell if this has been routinely followed by the provision of food. A modified version of this theory called "instrumental learning" strives to form conscience through the instrumentality of rewards and punishments.

The cognitive schools of psychology give more importance to intellectual development. The theories of Jean Piaget and Lawrence Kohlberg are one-sidedly rationalistic. While the latter's theory of moral development was popular with many educators, including catechists during the seventies, it has come under valid criticism for being concerned only with moral reasoning, for splitting the connection between morality and religion, and for its strictly male orientation. These theories, however, do see the development of conscience as a normal growth pattern "from a conscience subject to external control (what we are told to do by someone in authority, or what we see others do) to a more internal, self-directing conscience (what we ourselves perceive to be right and want to do). In other words, the one criterion of mature moral conscience is making up one's mind for oneself about what ought to be done. *Note*: the criterion says *for* oneself, not *by* oneself."[6] Thus the dictum "Follow your conscience" within Roman Catholic tradition means much more than simply acting upon one's subjective feeling, or obeying some psychic authority figure, or even working through a purely rationalistic process.

Conscience in Scripture and Theological Tradition

St. Paul tells us that "whatever is not from faith is sin" (Rom. 14:23). Christian tradition has always maintained the inviolability of personal conscience. It is the immediate subjective norm of morality. Conscience is right when its dictates correspond to the objective moral order; it is erroneous when it fails to do so. Thus Thomas Aquinas maintained that one also sins by not following one's erroneous conscience. To emphasize this point he provides some very pointed, even shocking examples. "Conscience," he says, "obliges in the sense that whoever acts against his conscience has the will to sin. Consequently, if someone believes that by not fornicating he commits a mortal sin, he chooses to commit a mortal sin by not committing the act. And therefore he does sin mortally."[7] The Second Vatican Council affirms this truth when it states that "it often happens that conscience goes astray through ignorance which it is unable to avoid, without thereby losing its dignity. This cannot be said of the man who takes little trouble to find out what is true and good, or when conscience is by degrees almost blinded through the habit of committing sin" (GS 16). To arrive at a better understanding of conscience and its functioning, let us now trace its development within our religious tradition.

Conscience in Sacred Scripture. A description of the functioning of conscience, although not the word itself, is found already in the Book of Genesis when it recounts the sin of Adam and Eve. The action of the couple who "hid themselves from the LORD God among the trees of the garden" (Gen. 3:8) points to the operation of a "consequent" or "judicial conscience," that is, a conscience which experiences guilt and shame after committing a sinful act. Futhermore, there is also a sense of separation from the source of good, God himself, as Adam confesses, "I heard you in the garden; but I was afraid, because I was naked, so I hid myself" (Gen. 3:10). This story also tells of the rationalization process we often resort to in order to excuse and justify our actions, "something which would be unnecessary if there was no sense of obligation to do good and avoid evil."[8] Adam thus points the finger of blame at Eve: "The woman whom you put here with me — she gave me fruit from the tree, and so I ate it" (Gen. 3: 12). And Eve, too, refuses to accept responsibility as she blames the devil: "The serpent tricked me into it" (Gen. 3:13).

The only Old Testament use of the term "conscience" is found in Wisdom 17:11 — "For wickedness . . . because of a distressed conscience, always magnifies misfortunes." Again here, we see the functioning of a consequent conscience evidenced in the pain of remorse. Other works employ "the heart" and "loins" to describe the whole inner person made by and known to God alone (see Ps. 7:10; 26:2; Jer. 12:20; 17:10; 20:12). Nowhere in the Old Testament, however, do we find an "antecedent conscience" where a person assesses beforehand the moral implications of a contemplated action.

In the gospels Jesus speaks of "the heart" as the center of the moral person (see Mk. 7:19). He called those pure of heart (that is, the single-minded and simple) "blessed" (Mt. 5:8). He teaches that our hearts should not be fixed upon earthly treasures, but upon the things of heaven (Mt.

166

6:19-21) and that sin, such as adultery, is a matter first of the heart, a lustful look, before it is an external action (Mt. 6:28). For the Hebrew in Jesus' day, "the heart was the seat of thoughts, desires and emotions, and also of the moral judgment, taking over the functions we ascribe to the conscience, for which there is no specific word in the gospels."[9] Jesus thus demands that our actions be the fruit of our inner disposition (see Lk. 6:43-45) and that our faith find authentication in moral action (see Mt. 7:21-27; 21:28-32).

St. Paul uses the Greek word "*syneidesis*" ("consciousness") some twenty times in his writings. In the Stoic understanding of the term it referred to self-consciousness passing moral judgment. For Paul, "conscience" serves as the internal coordinate to the civil power's external wrath (see Rom. 13:5); it refers to a personal awareness of moral responsibility. "The characteristic mark of this spiritual function is, of course, the personal and spontaneous reaction before or after some moral decision; but awareness of moral values is, of course, necessarily presupposed as its foundation."[10]

Most often Paul calls it a "witness" (Rom. 2:15; 9:1; 2 Cor. 1:12), which accompanies our actions and attests to the truth of our assertions. Conscience is a principle of liberty (1 Cor. 10:29) which bows, however, to a neighbor's spiritual need (1 Cor. 10:23). Ultimately, it refers to a person's whole inner vision of reality, the world and human life, as seen through the eyes of faith (Rom. 14:23). Conscience governs the "new creature's" spontaneous reaction to daily events. It is formed by examining or testing oneself ("*dokimazein*" — see 1 Cor. 11:28; 2 Cor. 13:5; Gal. 6:4), by discerning God's will (Rom. 12:2; Eph. 5:10) and discerning what is of value (Phil. 1:10), as viewed within the context of the Two Great Commandments of love of God and of one's neighbor.

Theological Developments in the Understanding of Conscience. The patristic tradition elevates conscience to an important element of the spiritual and moral life. Thus, Clement of Alexandria writes that "the conscience is an excellent means for exact choosing of the good or avoiding (evil); the correct life is its foundation."[11] St. John Chrysostom regarded it as an "adequate teacher" and as "the judge seated" within our minds.[12] Both Scripture and the Fathers speak of a "good" and a "bad" conscience. John Chrysostom also instructs us that "the good conscience comes from a life and acts which are good."[13] The Fathers, however, provide us with no systematic understanding of the functioning of conscience.

Scholastic theology spoke of two dimensions of conscience. From the twelfth century onwards the Greek word "syneidesis" (in Latin, "*conscientia*") came to mean the here and now judgment of practical reason deciding matters of right and wrong. Another Greek term "*synderesis*," taken from a text of St. Jerome,[14] was employed to describe the innate inclination within human beings to know and do the good. St. Thomas Aquinas identified faith with "*synderesis*" on the level of the supernatural life,[15] and saw in Christian conscience ("*syneidesis*") the application of practical faith to the decisions of everyday life.[16] For him the human will was an intellectual appetite oriented by its very nature toward the good comprehended by reason.[17] The morally good life was understood as "the fullness of being" ("*plentitutdo essendi*);[18] it was "the actualization of innate human capacities, with the moral virtues, the acquired and infused habits of good action under the direction of prudence as their 'eye,' conferring a connaturality with the good and, as 'second natures,' guiding in a quasi-instinctive way to the right decision."[19]

By the sixteenth century the standard manuals of moral theology came under the influence of voluntarism, which represented an approach to morality quite alien to that of the scholastic period. This approach, however, based on William of Ockham's radically different concept of the will and its freedom, would remain predominant in Catholic morality for four centuries up until Vatican II. For Nominalism, as Ockham's philosophical school was called, the human will was a purely autonomous power, completely indeterminate and free. Its regulation came not from practical reason, or the intellect directing it from within, but from law, as an extrinsic principle obligating and constraining it. Here too, the idea of law was radically deformed. Whereas, St. Thomas Aquinas saw law as an "ordinance of reason,"[20] that is, reason's own internal illumination and direction of the will, in Ockham's scheme law emerges as a gratuitous and arbitrary check upon the will. Obedience thus replaces prudence as the chief cardinal virtue. The virtues themselves, seen by Aquinas as "excellences" or powers informing and educating the passions from within, are downgraded. They now exercise the negative function of repressing the passions and keeping them out of the will's way in its obedience to the law.[21]

The influence of voluntarism proved costly for the spiritual-moral life. The all-important role of prudence in the Christian life was effectively suppressed, while the place of positive law became absolutized. "Rigid objective norms — two-and-a-half ounces; twelve minutes were prescribed to secure against abuses with the results that the claims of a particular situation were often muted because the responsibility of the individual for assessing them had been usurped."[22] There developed an ethics of avoidance or conformity to an extrinsic moral code. A great deal of time, effort and discussion was expended during this period over questions about the doubtful conscience and its binding power. The famous moral systems of probabilism, probabiliorism, and equi-probablilism were developed to respond to this dilemma (see Chapter 2). Legalism, in the end, for all practical purposes usurped the place of "right reason" (*recta ratio*), the place of "the law of the spirit of life in Christ Jesus" (Rom. 8:2).

Conscience within Catholic Tradition Today: Renewal and Return

A better understanding of the nature and functioning of conscience is possible today, if we conjoin the contemporary theological renewal within Roman Catholicism with appropriate insights from the behavioral sciences and a return to a healthier pre-Reformation tradition. Within this context we shall now, therefore, look at the various elements that come into play within the two dynamic movements of this human faculty: responding to value — transcendental and categorical values (*synderesis*), and making moral decisions according to the dictate of practical reason (*syneidesis*).

Responding to Value ("synderesis"). We saw above that St. Thomas Aquinas described *synderesis* as an innate inclination to know and do the good. According to Christian biblical revelation, God alone is the Absolute Good that calls and draws us to himself as the Supreme Value. For this reason, then, Aquinas identifies faith with *synderesis* on the level of supernatural life, and Vatican II speaks of conscience as our "most secret core and ... sanctuary," where we are "alone with God whose voice echoes in [our] depths" (GS 16). "Thus the Council presents conscience in no uncertain terms as the personal center of communion with God. It is the preconceptual recognition of the absolute call to love."[23] *Synderesis* is the immediate, intuitive attraction of value, as well as the repulsion from its opposite; it is a pre-reflective, non-categorical openness to meaning which does not have any objective content. It is a consciousness of value drawing us and motivating us to realize ourselves, to become who we are meant to be. As the faculty of ultimate personal commitment and self-transcendence, conscience on this level responds on the basis of faith.

Our recognition of this absolute call to faith-hope-love, then, seeks

169

categorization and concretization in our everyday lives as we strive to reflectively know and do the good.

> The human eros is such that we not only desire to know, love, and act, but we desire normatively to know, love, and act. It is not good enough to know just anything, to love just anything, or to do just anything; we inherently desire, and are drawn by grace, to know the truth, to love the truth, and to do the truth. In the practical life of moral action, this means that we desire normatively to know, love, and do value.[24]

The force of *synderesis* thus impels us to search out the objective moral values in each concrete case and to discover the right thing to do in each instance. On the categorical level *synderesis* through a process of reflection and analysis becomes moral knowledge.

1. Our human longing to know, love and do the truth leads to **moral knowledge**, which assumes two forms, **speculative and evaluative**. On the speculative level our knowledge of the truth is cognitive or intellectual. It is fact-oriented knowledge, that is, knowledge *about* moral values, about what is right and wrong. Memorizing the Ten Commandments, or the sayings of Jesus in the gospels, for instance, provides us with moral knowledge on this level. It is a detached, "objective" kind of knowledge like that of the mathematician or the physical scientist. It is knowledge that can be taught.

Moral knowledge of the speculative kind itself comes primarily from two sources: natural law and divine law (or Revelation). Natural law, as we have already seen, is comprised of certain self-evident principles of the moral order which provide us with an understanding of human nature. It draws upon the wisdom of human experience arrived at through the radical human capacity for self-reflection. Divine law is made known to us through Revelation, that is, through the testimony of sacred Scripture, the beliefs of our creeds, the official teachings of the Church, our theological and liturgical tradition, the lives of the saints, and so forth.

On the evaluative level we personally appropriate and integrate what we know. Here, moral knowledge is more "caught" than taught. It is affective or felt knowledge, which we acquire through personal involvement by embracing or appreciating the value that has been found. Its acquisition is not altered through rational argumentation alone, but by personal experience, interaction, discovery and appreciation of value. It is the knowledge conveyed through love, beauty, mystery and art. Growth on this level comes from involvement with persons who are close to us, who are attractive to us, who love us and trust us. The more we try to personally appropriate and live the value, the more we are attracted to it and gradually come to assimilate it.

Evaluative knowledge is moral knowledge, properly so-called. Without having arrived at this level of knowledge we act merely by hearsay, by what we are told is right or wrong, rather than on the basis of what we have discovered and believe to be valuable. Thus a small child may "know" that a particular action is considered to be gravely sinful, yet his or her mind is insufficiently developed to appreciate or evaluate the gravity of the action. Such a child will not normally have the evaluative knowledge or "sufficient reflection" necessary for committing a grave sin. Likewise, the Roman Rota has declared some marriages null because of the absence of evaluative knowledge. "The decisions were given on the score that a person, even though otherwise intelligent, was incapable of realizing the gravity of the marriage commitment."[25]

2. Our responsiveness to value (*synderesis*) thus depends not only upon moral knowledge, but also upon the moral state of the agent, that is, upon one's **character**. The "sort of person" we are or have become matters morally. Our moral behavior is "not in itself determined by the rules we adhere to or how we respond to one particular situation, but by what we have become through our past history, by our character."[26] Character identifies a person's responsive orientation toward reality. It is shaped by the pattern of our responses, which in turn are based upon the way we see and interpret the world. A person, for instance, who sees the world as a hostile place and himself or herself as ill-equipped to survive in such an atmosphere is likely to develop a shy, timid, defensive character. Another person who sees the world as a friendly place tends to develop a trusting, loving character.

We acquire character by directing our freedom and loyalty to values outside ourselves. In a very real sense, we become what we love. "Character is what results from the values that we make our own. When a value has woven its way into the fabric of our being, we delight in doing what pertains to that value."[27] The habitual doing of that value, then, becomes a virtue in us. Virtues build character. They are "concrete manifestations of the conversion process lived out on a regular and sustained basis."[28] They are rooted in our faith-hope-love responsiveness to God's gift-call (grace). Christian character results from our accepting the life, message and example of Jesus Christ as the norm of our lives.

"Character pre-disposes us to choose in certain ways, even though it does not predetermine every choice. We can act against character, and by making new choices we can change our character."[29] Our conscience warns and gnaws at us only when we go contrary to our habitual way of acting, when we go against what we know to be our "better self." Habitually acting contrary to our better self leads to a blinding of moral vision and a hardening of our moral sensibility, which in turn can deaden our conscience. By continuing to disregard our conscience or undercutting it through subtle rationalization, we fail to act as we really judge and so we come in time to judge as we act.[30] We lose the spiritual power of discernment. The total lack of conscientious response, apart from cases of severe mental deficiency, can result from faulty training, from the psychopathic lack of the affective function which responds to value, even though the intellectual function remains intact. The real world of moral choices depends more upon our character, our habits, vision, affections and countless other non-rational factors than it does upon impersonal rules, rational abstractions and logical procedures. "What sort of person ought I to become?" or being a moral person is prior to the question "What should I do?" We will further consider this aspect when we consider the formation of conscience.

Making Moral Decisions (syneidesis). The basic inclination of conscience to know and appropriate value, the good (*synderesis*), becomes very practical and concrete, when in the words of Vatican II, it tells us "inwardly at the right moment: do this, shun that" (GS 16). The specific application of the general orientation to the good along with my personal "knowledge" of what is right and wrong, flowing from "who I am," my character, produces a practical judgment of reason in a given, concrete situation. Such a moral judgment becomes a "proximate norm" for me, binding me insofar as it transmits in truth here and now the ethical values that I must realize in this particular instance. This is the functioning of conscience, traditionally so-called (*syneidesis*).

Acting according to such a moral judgment, we act true to the "self." Violating it would be violating our integrity. Thus,

... authentic moral interpretations (like religious ones) typically move from the symbolic experience of value, through affective-cognitive judgments of value, to normative (ought) claims

172

and arguments, and justifications for moral actions. This movement is cumulative and invariant and it should be considered the norm in all authentic moral decision making . . . the normativity (oughtness) derives from the inherent unfolding structure of human self-transcendence itself.[31]

Although such judgments of conscience constitute the ultimate definitive norm for individuals in the given cases in which they are made, they do not thereby become a general norm for other persons faced with similar decisions. They remain a subjective norm, that is, my personal unique free response of love to the "objective" Absolute Good — in Christian terms, the Triune God of Love — who calls me. Conscience's role, therefore is that of a "practical dictate" and "not a teacher of doctrine."[32]

Moral judgments of conscience may either precede the action (*conscientia antecedens*), restraining us from evil or urging us to do good, or follow the action (*conscientia consequens*), condemning us as bad or affirming us as good. Our moral choices can be either implicit or explicit. Most choices are actually implicit coming from the inner level of our person, the level of moral habits or virtues, of values and attitudes. "If, for example, patience has become a value for me, I will usually act patiently in a frustrating situation without any explicit awareness that I have chosen to be patient."[33] In more important matters, we generally tend to make moral decisions only after due consideration of all the facts and circumstances, as well as our own discernment of our unique, personal obligation of love in this particular instance.

1. In making a practical judgment of conscience we must first examine *all* the pertinent **facts and circumstances**. We thus try to gather and clarify all the data: the "what" (the problem, the issue involved), the "why" (the events and circumstances that presented the problem), the "who" (the persons involved), the "when and where" (time, place, etc.). After having gathered all the data, we next explore the alternatives and consequences, that is, all the possible ways of dealing with our question.

What are the various alternative courses of action open to us? What steps can we take in dealing with the problem? It is important to search out all the possible alternatives because the first couple which present themselves might not be the best ones. It is also important to estimate the probable consequences of the various alternatives. A

173

very desirable alternative may have the worst consequences.[34]

As our search continues for the best way to respond to the situation, we also consult a wide base of moral wisdom and authority. We draw upon sacred Scripture and the teachings of the Church. We seek the counsel of a spiritual director and the opinion of reputable theologians. We also turn to our own experience and that of others, and take recourse as well in our own feelings and intelligence.

2. After I have gathered and assessed all the data, I now seek to **discern** what I ought to do, my obligation, in this concrete situation. My decision must be mine, issuing from my personal values and my understanding of God's will for me. No one else is going to stand in my shoes on Judgment Day and be accountable for my choices. As a Christian, therefore, I must decide how I ought to act here and now in this particular situation so as to give a loving response to the God who is present and loving and calling me in this moment.

Discernment plays a central role in the moral decision-making process. "When taken in a religious context, discernment connotes a graced ability to detect what is the appropriate response to the invitation of God. It goes beyond the question 'Is this action morally right?' to the more personal question of appropriateness: 'Is this action consistent with who I am and want to become? What sort of person does this type of action?' "[35] Through discernment I am also able to distinguish important information from the unimportant, to see relationships between aspects of the information that enable me to comprehend how it all fits together or how it cannot fit together, and to draw inferences from it.

St. Thomas Aquinas described this discernment process under his treatment of the virtue of prudence, which he identified with the Holy Spirit's gift of counsel.[36] For him prudence was the chief cardinal virtue, which gave direction to the entire moral decision-making process by placing the trivialities of everyday living within the all-embracing dynamism of God's love. Prudence is practical wisdom, which looks to the objective and divine order of things but remains always in the service of love. Closely allied with prudence, for Aquinas, is *epikeia*, which is a part of the virtue of justice. In the application of law *epikeia* allows for an exception in a case, where it finds the concrete will of God in that source of law which is God himself, and therefore in love and goodness.[37] When *synderesis*, operating through character and moral knowledge, brings prudence to bear upon all the facts

174

and circumstances of a given situation, we are capable of making a practical judgment of reason that is morally certain.

As the supreme subjective norm of moral action, conscience arrives at moral certitude, not absolute certainty. Practical reason is actually incapable of making an exhaustive analysis of all pertinent data. But it can reflect upon all the data as imaginatively as possible and fit the data together into a reasonably coherent pattern. This is all that is humanly possible, and therefore all that is reasonably expected of us. "A person who acts on the basis of this sort of practical reason or moral certainty knows all the complexity and difficulty of life have not been eliminated. But he or she has creatively achieved sufficient conviction so as to act with true confidence."[38]

Where moral certainty cannot be attained, there arise doubts of conscience. A doubt may concern the specific meaning of a moral norm or its application in a particular situation. The basic principle in such cases is this: "In a *practical doubt* concerning what is to be done here and now, one may never act." Otherwise, a person is exposing himself to a violation of God's will. Thus, St. Paul teaches us: "whoever has doubts is condemned if he [acts], because this is not from faith" (Rom. 14:23). The most difficult situation is a conflict of conscience, or a "perplexed conscience." This latter may involve conflicting obligations and, in its most extreme form, a choice between two evils. In such situations, a person must always choose what truly seems to him or her to be the greater duty or the lesser evil. Generally speaking, practical certainty is to be striven for by personal reflection and by consultation with authoritative sources, where possible. One ought to be genuinely and ardently desirous of discovering what is good. The extent of one's effort should be measured by the importance of the matter or value involved. In the end, one is expected to exercise prudence.

The Formation of Conscience

The word "conscience" literally means "knowing with," that is, "being witness to oneself." It can also be understood to mean "a knowing together," or a partnership in discerning the will of God.[39] Although each person is ultimately responsible for his or her own decisions and actions, the formation of conscience is actually a communal effort. It is a matter of appropriating a shared vision and living one's life accordingly. A Christian conscience is formed within the context of a communal faith that sees in Jesus Christ the revelation of God's plan for the world and the ultimate meaning of human existence. As Christians we interpret our life's journey through the "eyes of faith." We personally accept Jesus' life, teachings and values, handed on to us through the tradition of the Church in creed, cult and code, as *the way* to everything that is true and good.

Together, as Church, we seek to live "in Christ" by following his example of self-emptying and reconciling love. The formation of a Christian conscience, therefore, is a matter of constantly growing in our awareness of "the way, the truth and the life" that is Christ. It means making his teachings, his vision and his values our own through an ongoing process of conversion. It is, first of all, a matter of "who we are," of becoming a faithful disciple, follower, member of his Body. We then grow together "in Christ" by sharing his life and living in the "law of Christ." The formation of Christian conscience goes far beyond the mere teaching of moral norms. "The overly scientific bent of some recent moral theology was so decision-oriented that the need to move beyond decisions to the development of moral persons was sometimes overlooked."[40] Learning moral rules, thus, is not the first task in the formation of conscience. Let us now consider in more detail some of the principal elements involved.

Developing a Christian Vision or World-view. Our choices and actions flow from the way we see reality, our "philosophy of life," our world-view. In other words, we choose what we do on the basis of what we see, and we see what we see because of who we are, our character.

> The "seeing" that is an expression of our character is more than taking a look. Seeing is interpreting and valuing as well. What we regard as worthy of our response depends on our "view" of things. What we see sets the direction and limits of what we do, generates certain choices rather than others, and disposes us to respond in one way rather than another. What is a choice for someone else may never occur to us as a choice at all, for we simply do not see the world that way.[41]

Being a follower of Christ, therefore, and living our lives in faith-hope-love (as we saw in chapter five), means that we strive to look at the world through the eyes of Christ, the eyes of faith. "Ethics, especially Christian ethics, is a discipline of vision, of seeing life as it really is. This vision, this 'seeing as' is very much an exercise of imagination."[42]

Moral knowledge, we have already seen, occurs on two levels: *speculative* (intellectual, fact-oriented) and *evaluative* (affective). As

Christians we can and must grow in the knowledge and understanding of our traditions, doctrines, beliefs, practices, moral principles and rules. We can acquire this knowledge in the same way we learn any other fact-oriented or academic discipline. On this level, also, we can learn the principles for clear objective judgment. Developmental psychologists, such as Piaget and Kohlberg, have traced a series of stages of growth in this latter process. Knowledge on this level, however, while it is necessary to give clarity and form to our system of beliefs, our faith vision, does not usually motivate us or capture our imaginations. We can memorize the Ten Commandments and still not be motivated to live their vision and values.

The cultivation of the Christian imagination, we are rediscovering today, is essential to the development of Christian character and values.

> The imagination is a powerful moral resource not to be equated with fantasy or make-believe. Our imagination shapes what we see, feel, think, judge, and act because all thinking relies on images. We are guided and formed by stories and images that dwell within us even more than we usually think ourselves to be. Our imaginations, shaped by stories and images, involve a kind of felt knowing in which we hold together both what we know about something and how we feel about it.[43]

Jesus, in his teaching, the gospels tell us, appealed first to the imaginations of his listeners by always resorting to the use of stories or parables (see Mt. 13:34). Today, the world of advertising succeeds in motivating us to buy commercial products often solely through the use of a collage of powerful audio-visual imagery. While rules and regulations address the logical intellect, stories, images and rituals appeal to the whole person. The American sociologist, Robert N. Bellah, has thus observed that, "Finding oneself means, among other things, finding the story or narrative in terms of which one's life makes sense."[44]

The development of a vision or world-view is not something we provide for ourselves by ourselves. It is a community achievement. "Social scientists tell us that as we grow the vision we acquire is in part the result of internalizing the beliefs and values of the particular communities which make up our environment. Our vision is almost wholly dependent upon our relationships, on the worlds in which we live, and on the commitments we have made."[45] Each one of us, especially in a pluralistic society, inhabits many worlds at one and the same time. In addition to family and Church, we

177

also live in and are influenced by our ethnic community, our school or professional community, as well as by the world of sports, politics, business, the social communications media, advertising and entertainment, to name but a few.

Each of these communities or worlds has its own story, communicating to us what is "good" and how life ought to be lived. The more we participate in the stories, rituals, images and symbols of a community, the more we begin to take on its way of seeing. Indeed, it is good for us to examine ourselves to ascertain which of the above worlds is most shaping our moral vision on any given issue, be it divorce, premarital sex, homosexuality; the arms race; attitudes toward the poor, immigrants, women, racial minorities; the use of drugs, abortion, euthanasia, genetic research, etc. Are we most influenced on any one, some, or even all of the above-mentioned issues by the Church? By the world of entertainment: popular songs, the TV soaps? By the media news? Politics? By our particular professional world?

"The Church is the one community directly and uniquely responsible for communicating the stories of the Christian faith which ought to shape and nurture Christian character and conscience."[46] Handing on these stories (along with rituals, images, language, convictions and forms of action), the Church evangelizes and makes disciples by forming the Christian imagination. Discipleship thus means the commitment to listen constantly to the Christian story in the depths of our heart, and to allow what we hear there to give shape to our vision and choices. Within this perspective, moral conversion or growth is a process of re-imagining, so that our vision of God's plan, his will, corresponds ever more fully with Jesus' proclamation of the Good News of God's kingdom.

The Role of the Magisterium. Living our lives as disciples of Jesus Christ, that is, according to God's plan, his vision (which alone is truth), requires that we put on the mind and attitudes of Jesus. This we cannot do alone, but only as members of his body, the Church. Through faith and baptism we enter the Christian story; we share in Christ's life through the apostolic community of faith. Cardinal Joseph Ratzinger thus points out that

"Morality" is not an abstract code of norms for behavior, but it presupposes a community way of life within which morality itself is clarified and is able to be observed. Historically considered, morality does not belong to the area of subjectivity, but is guaranteed by the

178

community and has reference to the community.[47]

Discerning "what is the will of God, what is good and pleasing and perfect" (Rom. 12:2) was in the mind of St. Paul "the object of the corporate mind's activity."[48]

1. From patristic times and even earlier we find a belief which has maintained that **the common consent of all the faithful** is an infallible index of the truth. This tradition is echoed by Vatican II:

> The whole body of the faithful who have an anointing that comes from the holy one (cf. 1 Jn. 2:20 and 27) cannot err in matters of belief. This characteristic is shown in the supernatural appreciation of the faith (*sensus fidei*) of the whole people, when, "from the bishops to the last of the faithful" [St. Augustine] they manifest a universal consent in matters of faith and morals. By this appreciation of the faith, aroused and sustained by the Spirit of truth, the People of God, guided by the sacred teaching authority (*magisterium*), and obeying it, receives not the mere word of men, but truly the word of God (cf. 1 Th. 2:13), the faith once for all delivered to the saints (cf. Jude 3). The People unfailingly adheres to this faith, penetrates it more deeply with right judgment, and applies it more fully in daily life (LG 12).

This *sensus fidelium*, sustained by the Spirit of truth, is always guided by the magisterium, the authentic teaching authority of the pope and bishops, as successors of the apostles. It necessarily includes the bishops and is never separate from them, otherwise it is not *sensus fidelium* but simply a matter of opinion.

The "supernatural appreciation of the faith of the whole people" does not consist solely or necessarily in a public consensus or even, for that matter, in a majority opinion.[49] In the post-Vatican II era there has been a tendency among some American Catholics to combine the image of the "People of God" with democratic beliefs about "individual autonomy" and "rule by public consensus." On this latter basis some Catholics, including theologians, have criticized and contradicted the sacred teaching authority of the Church (*magisterium*). "The acceptance by the community cannot be measured by an *ad hoc* sampling of opinion; indeed, on a biblical model, popular opposition may be as valid a criterion for rightness as popular acceptance."[50] Recent history regarding racial equality, social justice and world poverty clearly demonstrates that the opinion of the majority of Christians at certain times and in certain places on specific moral issues can be erroneous.[51]

The reason for erroneous opinions on the part of Christians can be found by the fact, mentioned above, that in a pluralistic society we are members of several different communities or worlds at one and the same time. The truth of revelation does not then reach believers in pure divine form, but is often filtered through or combined with the "stories" from the other communities in which we live (political philosophies, the media, cultural biases, etc.). Father Avery Dulles, S.J., points out that "Public-opinion surveys of American Catholic attitudes generally tell at least as much about the dominant values of our secular society as about the implications of the Catholic faith."[52] The supernatural sense of faith must be ascertained not from mere head counts, but through responsible discernment. Persons of faith, impelled by prayerful familiarity with the things of God, may, like good students in the classroom "often be able to hear more than the teachers are conscious of saying."[53] In such a way, the role of the *sensus fidelium* brings about genuine enrichment and is not merely passive.

2. In Catholic ecclesiology **the episcopal magisterium remains normative** when it formulates moral teaching for specific cases. The dictum "Follow your conscience," when taken by itself without further specification, can seem to suggest that a person may simply ignore an unwelcome teaching of the magisterium. Docility, or teachability, according to St. Thomas Aquinas is an integral part of prudence.[54] In making a moral decision, therefore, "factor for factor, an authentic teaching of the Church should be for a Catholic the single weightiest, even when not all-controlling, of the objective elements to consider."[55] The Second Vatican Council, thus, teaches that a

> . . . loyal submission of the will and intellect must be given, in a special way, to the authentic teaching authority of the Roman Pontiff, even when he does not speak *ex cathedra* in such wise, indeed, that his supreme teaching authority be acknowledged with respect, and that one sincerely adhere to decisions made by him, conformably with his manifest mind and intention, which is made known principally either by the character of the documents in question, or by the frequency with which a certain doctrine is proposed, or by the manner in which the doctrine is formulated. (LG 25)

180

The decisions of bishops, who teach in communion with the Roman Pontiff on matters of faith and morals, are also to be adhered to with "a ready and respectful allegiance of mind" on the part of Catholics. For someone to make a moral choice "with indifference to, or in spite of, the episcopal magisterium would be forfeiting one's claim to be acting as a loyal Catholic and according to a properly informed conscience. As 'normative,' the teaching of the episcopal magisterium deserves the presumption of the truth on the part of the faithful."[56]

The episcopal magisterium is a continuation of the pastoral mission Jesus gave to the apostles to go and teach all nations (Mt. 28:19). It is a ministry, or service (*diakonia*), of truth exercised under the guidance of the Holy Spirit. The magisterium has the resources to pull together the moral wisdom of the ages (Scripture, the teachings of the Fathers and Councils, the lives of the saints, broad human experience, scientific information, the reflections of theologians past and present), which are so numerous and complex that it is very difficult for any single person to be knowledgeable about them and capable of bringing them into play in a single moral decision. In effect, when the magisterium formulates a specific teaching, it is telling us that, over the centuries as Christians (bishops, saints and scholars) have sought to live the gospel in their daily lives and have carefully reflected upon matters such as this, their experience indicates that this specific action is either congruent or incongruent with the faith we profess.

Thus Vatican II further teaches that "in forming their consciences the faithful must pay careful attention to the sacred and certain teaching of the Church"(DH 14). An earlier version of this text presented to the Council Fathers stated that conscience must be formed "according to" the teaching of the Church. This draft of the text was rejected by the Council as being "too restrictive" and not in keeping with long-standing Catholic tradition. The approved version of "pay careful attention to" recognizes that no Catholic may rightly ignore the Church's moral teaching, or treat it as irrelevant. The teaching of the magisterium, while truly important and indispensable, is not the exclusive basis of a practical judgment of conscience. Both authority and conscience are complementary aspects of a person's search for what is true and good.

No external authority can ever take the place of conscience, yet conscience can never be properly formed without the help of the wisdom and voice of authority. "One insight of the morally and religiously converted person is that the quest for absolute autonomy in the moral life is an illusion. Commitment to, reliance on, and trust in others are all marks of the converted life. Authorities in the moral life are not a luxury but an absolute necessity."[57] The tendency today to view authority as an alien intrusion upon our rational autonomy denies both our limitedness and the social origin of our reason and experience. It denies that we are communal beings and flies in the face of the central Christian belief that individually we are but members of Christ's Body. As completely independent, autonomous individuals, we often run the danger of being dominated by our own narrow subjectivity. Therefore, as faithful Christians "we grant an antecedent credibility to the official teachings of the community because we ultimately believe that we do not save ourselves."[58]

Those who teach in the name of the Church, pastors, catechists, theologians and preachers, help form consciences through the exercise of their special ministry. They are first and foremost keepers of the Christian "story," servants of the truth as handed down by apostolic tradition. They must assist the faithful in arriving at an ever fuller understanding of that tradition. Clearly, solidly and systematically, preachers, teachers and catechists must present authentic teaching, with pride of place given to the official teachings of the Church. "Believers have an authoritative right to listen to the authentic Word of God spoken by their pastors."[59] The pulpit and the classroom are in principle not the place for contradiction of ecclesial teachings nor for subjective biases, obtuse information or controversy.

Spiritual Discernment. Making the right choice through the "discernment of spirits" has been a part of religious tradition from ancient times. Primitive cultures believed that any decision a person made was influenced by the spirits or gods. A choice that produced favorable results was believed to have been informed by good spirits, and a bad choice was made under the influence of bad spirits. The Oracle of Delphi in Greece came into prominence in the ancient world as a place of discernment, as a place to consult wise men or women before making a major decision. The Old Testament recounts the wisdom of Solomon, who, when given the opportunity by God to ask for anything he might want, requested: "Give your servant, therefore, an understanding heart to judge your people and to distinguish right from wrong" (1 Kgs. 3:9).

The New Testament speaks frequently of the need to test, examine (*dokimazein*) and for judging and discerning (*diakrisis*). In the gospels Jesus asks, "Why do you not judge for yourselves what is right?" (Lk. 12:57). When enumerating the different kinds of spiritual gifts, St. Paul includes among them "discernment of spirits" (1 Cor. 12:10). Indeed, he tells the Thessalonians, "Do not quench the Spirit. . . . Test everything; retain what is good. Refrain from every kind of evil" (1 Thes. 5:19, 21-22); and he prays for the Philippians that their "love may increase ever more and more in knowledge and every kind of perception, to discern what is of value" (Phil. 1:9-10).

In Matthew's gospel, the criterion for discernment is putting Jesus' words and commands into practice, especially his teaching in the Sermon on the Mount (chaps. 5-7). The imitation of God's own unconditional love for everyone, whether good or bad (see Mt. 5:45), is the inner basis of Jesus' teaching and commands. So important is this criterion for Matthew, that "the final judgment scene in his gospel concerns the manner in which the Sermon on the Mount has been put into practice. Those who are Christians have become identified with Christ by obeying his commands, and imitating his care and concern for the hungry, the thirsty, the naked, the stranger, the sick and those in prison" (see Mt. 25:35-36).[60] In Luke's writings, the Spirit is a gift of God that comes only after fervent prayer, and is intimately connected with the person of Jesus. In the Acts of the Apostles, the Spirit makes possible the oneness of the human race at the first Pentecost. In the Gospel according to John, the criterion is the example of Jesus' love that goes as far as giving up one's life for another (Jn. 15:12-13). The basis for such love is found "in a deep feeling of oneness and identification resulting from the divine indwelling in both Jesus and the believer" (see Jn. 17:23).[61] St. Paul lists the fruits of the Spirit, which are unifying emotions, drawing us closer to others: "love, joy, peace, patience, kindness, generosity, faithfulness, gentleness, self-control" (Gal. 5:22-23).

Christian spiritual discernment, thus, is the virtue or capacity to distinguish what pertains to the "law of Christ" and what does not. It is the capacity to see into our "hearts," to get in touch with the core level of our being where the human and divine come together in the connaturality of love. There, at the center of our being, in the deepest recesses of the self, we can examine the interior movements of the soul (our feelings, thoughts, impulses, etc.). "The purpose of such examination is to decide, as far as possible, which of the movements we experience lead to the Lord and to a more perfect service of him and our brothers, and which deflect us from this goal."[62] Some of these movements lead more toward life and some more toward death.

God calls us to fullness of life by calling us to be our true selves. God works in mysterious ways, ways that do not go against our own humanity nor against our need to act responsibly, to act as adults. God works through the natural order, leading us both as individuals and as a world to greater life. Our fates are interwoven. We are called then to live in harmony with life as it is evolving within us and in the world around us. Christians, by seeking to find and do God's will, are striving to be more fully alive and human, not less, to be truly integrated, not confined to some small realm like that of the super-ego.[63]

Discernment is really an exercise of the moral imagination. It strives to see and understand the meaning, the purpose, the truth, that lies behind our knowledge of the "letter of the law" and moral principles. "It wants to get at the deepest human meanings. It wants to keep wrestling with the mystery of God whom we can never fully express in principles."[64]

1. A key element in the spiritual discernment process is **prayer**. Meditation and contemplation lead one into the inner life of the soul and God's presence there. Through prayer and disciplined reflection we can become aware of God's will for us, of his kingdom breaking into our lives. In his *Spiritual Exercises*, for example, St. Ignatius of Loyola "taught that essential to growth in discernment was the prayerful entering into the images and messages of Scripture. This way one took on more the values of Christ and, behind them, the internal images or 'mind' of Christ."[65] Through such meditation and by seeking to live out Christ's values in our daily lives, our thoughts and feelings, minds and wills become more like Christ's. As a result, our sensitivity to God's movement in life becomes more natural and spontaneous and we can more readily discern the life-giving, integrating movements from those leading to personal dissolution and death.

American theologians, such as H. Richard Niebuhr, have shown that each of us brings to prayer and the discernment process our own unique histories which have formed us. Through the memories and symbols which have given form to our unique identity, that history continues to be present to us. Our attempts to discern the present moment, therefore, depend not only upon the objective symbols of faith, but also upon the pattern of God's previous action in our lives. Grace builds upon nature. The gift of God's presence to our lives depends upon our personal disposition to receive it. Often my own personal perception of myself, my self-identity, can get in the way.

Identity rests more on the images and metaphors of the self than on definite ideas. They provide pictures through which the unique character of the self can be glimpsed and they organize habitual ways of responding to the world. For example, if I feel myself to be a victim, I am likely to inject wariness and fear into even innocent relationships. My defensiveness may be all the more powerful if this image of being a victim remains unconscious. My spontaneous reactions will be defensive or even hostile, leading me to actions which are more appropriate to my fear of being violated again than to the actual situation, which may contain nothing objectively threatening. Discernment will be operating but it will be neurotic discernment, skewed by my inadequate self-image.[66]

Through reflective prayer we open ourselves to the loving, transforming power of God in our lives. We are able to rethink our personal histories through a new set of images which the Christian community of faith proposes as normative. If I previously conceived myself as a victim, the image of the cross and resurrection of Jesus can transform my self-perception. Viewing myself now as one who has been forgiven and empowered to forgive others, I must begin to reinterpret my history of injuries.

2. Within the context of prayer and conversion we **make an examination of conscience**. Rather than serving to provide a checklist of possible sins committed, as it often did in the recent past, this exercise probes our personal response to God's loving call in the depths of our heart. It examines our attitudes and choices within the context of the quality of our relationships to God, neighbor, self and all of creation. Our baptism into Christ and our living out his paschal mystery of self-giving, reconciling love becomes the criterion with which we measure our everyday choices and actions.

"Discernment seeks the disclosure of the whole in the part."[67] As an exercise in discernment, therefore, an examination of conscience seeks to determine whether or not the divine indwelling of the Triune God is evident in our daily lives. It seeks to determine to what degree our choices and actions correspond to the Eternal Law, that is, the relational order present at the heart of all creation. How, in other words, are our lives genuine expressions of the two great commandments of love? Our examination of conscience should thus be a loving act of gratitude which recognizes the great gifts of love and grace that are ours.

"In the light of recognizing our gifts, we become aware of how unloving, insensitive, blind, selfish, or ungrateful we have been in taking these gifts for granted, in hoarding them, or abusing them."[68] This awareness of our selfishness and sin evokes sorrow or contrition, which itself is an expression of trusting faith that God is the merciful Father ready to welcome us back. The gift of God's merciful love now fills us with hope for the future and frees us to respond anew to these gifts of love by becoming more sensitive and loving persons, and by resolving to take concrete steps to move in this new direction.

3. Discernment is also practiced when we experience the allurements of **temptation.** If discernment seeks the disclosure of the whole in the part, the "subtlety of temptation lies in the reduction of the whole to a part and the consequent lure to fanatical absorption in pursuit of the partial."[69] Good alone has the power to attract us. Uncreated Absolute Good has diffused itself through all of creation in a whole array of lesser goods. Concupiscence, a result of original sin, has made us short-sighted whereby we fail to look beyond the immediate good we seek to the evil effects we cause along with it. Temptation flows from this inner tendency to assert ourselves against God's will and decide for ourselves what is right and wrong, that is, what place of importance we will give to these lesser goods in our lives.

Because of original sin our longings, appetites and desires no longer readily work in harmony with our knowledge of right and wrong. Temptation is an urge toward evil, namely, toward sundering the proper relational order of all these goods in our lives. In our present state of earthly existence, temptations cannot be avoided. As John Shea has pointed out,

> The Spirit leads Jesus into the desert. Faith does not stay in the waters that gave it birth but it travels the deserts that challenge it. Faith in the real world is, as all the Gospels indicate, a story of encountering and overcoming the powers of destruction. If this is the case, temptation comes with the territory.[70]

Discernment allows us to recognize temptation's enticements, its masquerades and rationalizations. The fact is that our practical intellect, when making moral choices, is continually under the sway of appetite and swamped by desire.

Since Jesus' day, ascetical practices, such as prayer, fasting and works of charity, have served to foster spiritual development and awareness (see Mt. 6:1-18). Such spiritual exercises aid us in our struggle against temptations.

Not to cultivate an awareness and sensitivity to our thoughts, speech, motives, attitudes, choices and actions, "inevitably means that we will perceive evil and sin in our lives as a natural and normal condition . . . temptations exist to be struggled against. There is no 'cheap grace.' "[71] Self-control is one of the fruits of the Spirit (see Gal. 5:23). In other words, God's gift of love, his kingdom, is ultimately enjoyed only by those who "strive to enter through the narrow gate" (Lk. 13:24).

4. Scripture records that the gift of wisdom or discernment was given to Solomon by the Lord in a dream. Indeed, the Bible contains some seventy passages referring to dreams or visions of the night (for example, Gen. 28:10-12; Job 33:12-18; Dan. 1:17; Mt. 1:20; 2:12; Acts 16:9; 18:9; etc.). The Church Fathers, too, held the belief that God still spoke directly to people through dreams and visions. The second-century "Shepherd of Hermas" begins with a vision the author experiences as he begins to fall asleep one night and is carried away by the Spirit. Justin Martyr mentions that dreams are sent by spirits and Irenaeus used his understanding of dreams to refute the idea of reincarnation or transmigration of souls. Clement of Alexandria believed that true dreams come from the depth of the soul and reveal spiritual realities. Many of the Fathers used this belief as evidence for the immortality of the soul.[72]

Following the teachings of Aristotle, Aquinas and other theologians later downplayed the spiritual role of dreams. They maintained that it was impossible for us to have direct, immediate contact with spiritual reality. St. Thomas Aquinas thus criticized St. Augustine's belief in dreams which he attributed solely to the latter's acceptance of Platonist philosophy. The spiritual significance of dreams came to the forefront once again with the development of modern psychoanalysis, especially the Jungian school. Carl Jung accepted dreams as a direct participation in the collective unconscious or the objective psyche, that is, a world of spiritual reality.[73] As a psychologist, he maintained that when he speaks of "God" he is referring empirically to the existence of an archetypal image of the "self" and not making a metaphysical statement. In his later writings Jung sometimes expressed his personal conviction that God is both a transcendent God, as well as a psychological reality.[74]

A number of Christian practitioners of Jungian analysis have bridged the gap between empirical psychology and religious faith. John A. Sanford, for example, writes that "It is not too much to say that the life process which psychology perceives at work in us, and which Jung calls 'individuation,' is the restoring of the image of God within us to 'a still closer resemblance.' "[75] Through archetypal images, dreams open up for us the spiritual depths of the unconscious, which contain the image of the whole person we are to become, the "person in the mind of God." The attempts of the unconscious to realize this image over the course of our life has just as much influence upon our behavior, as does our experiences of the past.

Jungian analysis maintains that our dreams are concerned primarily with the problem of opposites, of woundedness and division, that we experience deep within ourselves. Sanford thus notes that the Bible begins with the story of the split in human nature and that the rest of the Bible can be viewed as the story of our coming to an awareness of God's recreating our wholeness on a higher level.

> To understand what wholeness means we must first understand the extreme diversities within personality. We all contain potentialities for good and evil, light and darkness, love and hate; we possess masculine and feminine attributes, logos and eros; we are constituted of two psychic principles, consciousness and the unconscious. We share an instinctual nature with the beasts and a spiritual nature with the angels; we are thinking and feeling, perceivers of an outer and inner reality. Man is, as Jung puts it, a *complexio oppositorum*, a complexity of opposites. We are in fact so complex that our dreams contain a bewildering number of human and animal figures, all of them expressing different aspects or tendencies of personality.[76]

Dream symbols and archetypes help us see, depending upon our facility to work with them, the inner workings of the soul as it responds to God's call to mature "in Christ, the Last Adam." Jung's *complexio oppositorum* finds ready correspondence with our Christian anthropology outlined in Chapter Three.

Notes

1. *Saint Joseph Baltimore Catechism*, Official Revised Edition No. 1 (New York: Catholic Book Publishing Co., 1964), q. 171.

2. Ibid., q. 174.

3. Bloom, *The Closing of the American Mind*, p. 326.

4. Gula, *To Walk Together Again*, p. 146.

5. Ibid., p. 148.

6. Ibid., p. 145.

7. *In Rom.* 14, Lect. 2.

8. Harakas, *Toward Transfigured Life*, p. 108.

9. Schnackenburg, *The Moral Teaching of the New Testament*, pp. 69-70.

10. Ibid., p. 288.

11. *Stromata*, 1.1, as cited by Harakas, op. cit., p. 109.

12. See *Homily on Genesis* 54.1 and *Homily on 2nd Corinthians* 9:3.

13. *Homily 1 on 2nd Corinthians*, 4:13, as cited by Harakas, op. cit., p. 109.

14. See *Commentary on Ezekiel*, chap. 6.

15. See *In 2 Sent.*, 41.1.1; *Summa IIa-IIae*, 10.4, a, 2; *In 1 Sent. prol.* 5.

16. See *Summa* Ia, 79.12, 13, esp. ad 3.

17. *Summa* Ia, q. 19, a. 1.

18. *Summa* Ia-IIae, q. 18, a. 1.

19. Joseph V. Dolan, S.J., "Conscience in the Catholic Theological Tradition," *Conscience: Its Freedom and Limitations*, ed. William C. Bier, S.J. (New York: Fordham University Press, 1971), p. 15.

20. *Summa* Ia-IIae, q. 90, a.4.

21. See Dolan, op. cit., pp. 14-15.

22. Ibid., pp. 15-16.

23. Lobo, *Guide to Christian Living*, p. 283.

24. Happel and Walter, *Conversion and Discipleship*, p. 162.

25. Lobo, op. cit., p. 361, where the author adds: "A series of decisions given by Felici from 1934 onward clearly distinguishes between the *cognitive faculty* and the *critical faculty*." (See *Decisiones S.R. Rotae*, vol. 33, pp. 145-56; and vol. 48, p. 468.)

26. Stanley Hauerwas, "Toward an Ethics of Character," *Theological Studies* 33, no. 4 (December 1972): p. 710.

27. Gula, op. cit., p. 158.

28. Happel and Walter, op. cit., p. 43.

29. Gula, op. cit., p. 158.

30. Dolan, op. cit., p. 18.

31. Happel and Walter, op. cit., p. 161.

32. See National Conference of Catholic Bishops, *Human Life in Our Day* (Washington, D.C.: USCC, 1968), p. 14.

33. Nicholas Lohkamp, O.F.M., *Living the Good News: An Introduction to Moral Theology for Today's Catholic* (Cincinnati: St. Anthony Messenger

Press, 1982), p. 100.

34. Ibid., p. 101.

35. William C. Spohn, S.J., "The Reasoning Heart: An American Approach to Christian Discernment," *Theological Studies* 44, no. 1 (March 1983): p. 30.

36. See *Summa* IIa-IIae, q. 47-56.

37. See Häring, *Free and Faithful in Christ*, vol. 1, p. 363, where he quotes St. Alphonsus: "*Epikeia* means the exception of a case because of the situation from which can be judged, with certainty or at least with sufficient probability, that the legislator did not intend to include it under the law. This *epikeia* has its place not only in human laws but also in natural laws where, because of the circumstances, the action could be freed from malice" (*Theologia moralis*, lib. I, n. 201). The author adds that Alphonsus' reference to "natural laws" refers only to imperfect formulations of it and not to the law written in one's heart. "Moral manuals" of the recent past took a voluntaristic approach to *epikeia* as recourse to the will of the legislator who would not wish to insist on the observance of the law in difficult circumstances.

The Orthodox Church adds an additional category of "*oikonomia*," which counterbalances "*akribeia*," a holy exactness, even strictness, in the observance of the law. *Oikonomia*, unlike *epikeia*, is not a precise norm of action nor a legal entity, and is very difficult to define. It refers to the application of the mystery of God's saving power to a particular situation. It pertains to the bishop's, or "*oikonimos*'," task of taking care of God's household. For example, "an *oikonomos* may come to the judgment that the saving strength of God may heal a sinner (say, a divorced and remarried person) to the extent that he/she can be received into Eucharistic communion. After all, the Savior who came to *forgive* sins can also *forget* the union from which nothing remains beyond sad memories. There is no limit to his saving power, and the *oikonomos* can interpret it." [Ladislas Orsy, S.J., "In Search of the Meaning of OIKONOMIA: Report on a Convention," *Theological Studies* 43, no. 2 (June 1982): p. 319].

38. Philip S. Keane, S.S., *Christian Ethics and Imagination* (New York/Ramsey: Paulist Press, 1984), p. 109.

39. Lobo, op. cit., p. 292.

40. Keane, op. cit., p. 103.

41. Gula, op. cit., p. 159.

42. Keane, op. cit., p. 100; see also Daly, *Christian Biblical Ethics*, p.

128: "Thus, the *discrimen* or imaginative, pre-discursive construal of one's individual and communal reality is the overridingly dominant element in human morality as well as Christian ethics."

43. Gula, op. cit., p. 165.

44. Bellah, *Habits of the Heart*, p. 81.

45. Gula, op. cit., p. 161. Thus, Bellah, ibid., p. 152: "Children do not grow up through abstract injunctions. They identify with their parents, they learn through role-modeling, and they are influenced by the historic specificity of their family, church, and local community."

46. Gula, op. cit., p. 166.

47. Joseph Cardinal Ratzinger, "Bishops, Theologians and Morality," *Origins* 13, no. 40 (March 15, 1984), p. 661.

48. Murphy-O'Connor, *Becoming Human Together*, p. 214.

49. See John Paul II, *Familiaris Consortio*, Apostolic Exhortation on the Christian Family in the Modern World (November 22, 1981), no. 5.

50. Daly, op. cit., p. 295.

51. See Lobo, op. cit., p. 192.

52. Avery Dulles, S.J., "*Sensus Fidelium*," *America*, 155, no. 12 (November 1, 1986): p. 242.

53. Ibid., p. 263.

54. *Summa*, IIa-IIae, q. 48, a.1.

55. Dolan, op. cit., p. 17.

56. Gula, op. cit., p. 174.

57. Happel and Walter, op. cit., p. 171.

58. Ibid., p. 189.

59. Happel and Walter, op. cit., p. 192. The National Catechetical Directory, *Sharing the Light of Faith* (Washington, D.C.: USCC, 1979), when addressing the question of conscience formation, clearly states:

"It is the task of catechesis to elicit assent to all that the Church teaches, for the Church is the indispensable guide to the complete richness of what Jesus teaches. When faced with questions which pertain to dissent from non-infallible teachings of the Church, it is important for catechists to keep in mind that the presumption is always in favor of the magisterium.

"Conscience, though inviolable, in not a law unto itself; it is a practical dictate, not a teacher of doctrine. Doctrine is taught by the Church, whose members have a serious obligation to know what it teaches and adhere to it loyally. In performing their catechetical functions, catechists should present the authentic teaching of the Church" (no. 190).

60. Joseph A. Grassi, "Discernment of Spirits: The New Testament View," *The Genesis Effect*, p. 326.

61. Ibid., p. 328.

62. Edward Malatesta, S.J. (ed.), *Discernment of Spirits* (Collegeville, Minnesota: Liturgical Press, 1970), p. 9.

63. Robert L. Schmitt, S.J., "Discernment," *The Genesis Effect*, p. 335.

64. Keane, op. cit., p. 102.

65. Schmitt, op. cit., p. 366. See Antonio T. De Nicolas, *Powers of Imagining: Ignatius de Loyola* (Albany, New York: State University of New York Press, 1986), pp. 390.

66. Spohn, op. cit., 35.

67. Ibid., p. 40.

68. Gula, op. cit., p. 181.

69. John J. Shea, "Christian Faith and the Temptations of Christ," *Chicago Studies* 25, no. 1 (April 1986): p. 75.

70. Ibid., p. 74.

71. Harakas, op. cit., pp. 248-249.

72. See Morton T. Kelsey, *God, Dreams and Revelation: A Christian Interpretation of Dreams* (Minneapolis, Minn.: Augsburg 1974), pp. 102-163.

73. Ibid., p. 175-177.

74. See. John A. Sanford, *Dreams: God's Forgotten Language* (New York: Crossroad, 1984), pp. 201-203.

75. Ibid., pp. 207-208 with reference to St. Augustine, *City of God*, Bk. XI, Ch. xxvi.

76. Ibid., p. 83.

Chapter 8

Virtue, Sin, and the Human Act: Living As a Responsible Person

> *Thus "virtue and vice" are the specifics of character; "good acts and sins" are the specifics of decision-making.* — Stanley S. Harakas[1]

Christian living is an ongoing response to the divine gift-call. Our awareness of this call comes, as we have just seen in the previous chapter, through the human faculty of conscience. There, in our heart of hearts, the deepest core of our being, we experience first the attraction of the good calling us to self-transcendence, to become the person each one of us is uniquely meant to be. This dynamic pull of value (*synderesis*) addresses our personal freedom. Our "yes" to it gives rise within us to a fundamental attitude of responsiveness to value called virtue, which is constitutive of our character or personality. Virtue is a fundamental right attitude so deep-seated as to have become a kind of second nature. Seen within this perspective, virtue is one attitude, not diverse. This strength of character, in turn, manifests itself in concrete modes of behavior (or virtues, in the plural).

Likewise, a basic attitude of unresponsiveness to the law of love, the law of Christ, written within our hearts is the essence of sin (in the singular) — "*hamartia*" in Scripture, denoting the power of sin. As a deep-seated attitude of unresponsiveness or inappropriate responsiveness, sin takes root in our character as vice. Virtues and vices give shape to who we are. They qualify our character and our exercise of fundamental freedom, which in turn informs the decision-making process (*syneidesis*). Our practical judgments of conscience are then concretized in good acts or sins.

The first fundamental element of the classical manuals of moral theology was the "human act." It was the starting point for determining whether or not a particular mode of action was a sin or a virtue. Such an approach still maintains a certain validity when an objective evaluation of a given human action needs to be made. We, therefore, will conclude this chapter by describing the elements and principles that come into play in this situation. Primarily, though, viewed within the perspective of the divine-human dialogue or relationship that we have been considering within these pages so far, human acts are the fruit of our response-ability to God's gift-call. Our good deeds and misdeeds are but the enfleshment or incarnation of the quality of our relationships to God, neighbor, self and world. They are, in varying degrees and according to their pattern, concrete expressions of our character. They symbolize who we are, or as Jesus tells us in the Sermon on the Mount, "by their fruits you will know them" (Mt. 7:20; see also 3:18; Mk. 4:20; Jn. 15:2, etc.). So, before analyzing the objective elements of the human act, we shall consider first the nature and role of virtue and sin.

Virtue

As a permanent capacity (*habitus*) of the soul, virtue is determined by value, which gives it direction. A value (as we saw in chapter 6) is a mediator or image of a deeper, inner reality which attracts and motivates us. For a Christian, the person of Christ is the supreme value and norm. Father Bernard Häring, C.Ss.R., thus wrote in *The Law of Christ*:

> Christ taught us what virtue is, above all in His own all-embracing love. What virtue is appears in the very excess of His loving sacrifice by which He offered Himself for the glory of God and the salvation of mankind. In Christ there is the most tremendous union of opposites without force or constraint.[2]

Just as the faithful, self-emptying and reconciling love of Christ is the principal value of the Christian spiritual-moral life, so the God-given capacity to love as Christ loves is the greatest virtue. It is the foundation and source of all the other virtues.

The ancient Stoics maintained that one is good in all virtues or good in none. Rooted in our fundamental option of faith, virtue manifests and promotes wholeness and salvation. Christ's reconciling love saves us and makes us whole by redeeming us, buying us back as it were, from the sundering effects of sin. Salvation is the healing power of Christ's love, his wholeness, restoring us to the proper relational order found in that selfsame love. In Christ, the new Adam, the image of God in which we were first created has been restored to the human race. The other virtues, informed by our faith-hope-love, help us conform to the "law of Christ," the law of love.

Thus, in this very real and deeply spiritual sense, law and virtue go together as call and response. The law of Christ is all grace; and virtue, our facility to respond, is initiated by the power of the Holy Spirit moving us from within. Virtue is genuine to the extent that freedom is basic to it, and "where the Spirit of the Lord is, there is freedom" (2 Cor. 3:17).

Types of Virtue. "Virtue" and "vice" are not scriptural terms. Virtue (*arete*) is common to classical Greek thought where it describes a given quality of a truly good person. For the ancients a good person was a rational being. Thus for Socrates the principal virtue was wisdom (*sophia*). Plato systematically assigned the virtues according to the human psychological functions of the intellect, passions and will. To reason he ascribed the virtue of wisdom, to affectivity courage, and to moral decision-making self-control; when wisdom guided self-control with courageous strength and ordered determination, a person arrived at justice, that is, the appropriate ordering of all one's functions. Thus, for Plato justice was the virtue of virtues. Aristotle maintained that happiness was the ultimate good, and he introduced the idea of "measure" into the discussion about virtue. The two extremes of "too little" and "too much" in relation to virtue became what was called a "vice."

From classical Greek philosophy we learn that the designation of what is a virtue or vice depends upon one's understanding or image of what it means to be truly good or truly human. The Western patristic tradition in St. Ambrose and St. Augustine adopted the Stoic scheme of four basic virtues directing the powers of the soul: prudence, justice, fortitude and temperance. In the Old Testament we read that wisdom "teaches moderation and prudence, justice and fortitude, and nothing in life is more useful for men than these" (Wis. 8:7). Thus, they came to be referred to traditionally as the "cardinal virtues," or the "hinges" of the Christian life. Interestingly, the Oriental vision of the truly good, as presented by K'ung Fu-tzu (Latin, "Confucius"), lists the four greatest gifts that heaven can bestow as benevolence, gentleness, justice and prudence.[3]

St. Augustine integrates the four cardinal virtues within the vision of Christ-like love.[4] For the Christian all of the virtues find their roots in Jesus' paschal mystery, in the self-giving and reconciling love manifested there. Thus, St. Paul states, "So faith, hope, love remain, these three; but the greatest of these is love" (1 Cor. 13:13). The Christian tradition has designated these three as the supernatural, infused theological virtues. As

195

supernatural and infused, they are totally free gifts of God's generous love, beyond all merely human capability and effort. They are called "theological" because they constitute our relationship with God; they make us *who we are* as adopted children of God and disciples of Jesus Christ. From our state of discipleship comes the continual call to become "children of the Most High" by being "merciful, just as [also] your Father is merciful" (Lk. 6:36). Christian virtue flows from *who we are* and are *called to become* in Christ. "A good tree does not bear rotten fruit, nor does a rotten tree bear good fruit. For every tree is known by its own fruit" (Lk. 6:43-44).

From our life in Christ and our vocation to become like him come certain specific Christian "eschatological virtues," as Father Bernard Häring, C.Ss.R., has named them. Found in the gospels, they pertain to our understanding of what it means to be a disciple. He lists four of them: gratitude-humility, hope, vigilance, serenity and joy. The first, gratitude-humility, are two inseparable attitudes. We humbly recognize our complete dependence on God for all his gifts by seeking to imitate Christ, the servant of all, who "did not regard equality with God something to be grasped," but "emptied himself, taking the form of a slave" (Phil. 2:6-7). Hope turns our eyes to the absolute and abiding future in God and makes us clearsighted about the necessary steps to take; it makes us eager for growth and ongoing conversion. Vigilance sets the believer free from distraction, superficiality, and wishful thinking; it helps him or her to "judge the signs of the times" (Mt. 16:3), to discover the present opportunities for following the Lord. As we enter ever more fully into Christ's paschal mystery, the Spirit fills our lives with serenity and joy, which allow us to accept the pleasures and burdens of each moment without anxiety over the future (see Mt. 6:25).[5]

The classical tradition distinguished between natural, acquired virtues and supernatural, infused virtues. The former, rooted in our corporeal-spiritual nature, were concerned with the development of our natural powers through their correct and constant practice. The latter, on the other hand, flowed directly from the dynamism of sanctifying grace. The supernatural virtues were seen as directed by faith, whereas the natural virtues were directed by reason's response to the natural law. Such a distinction, today, is not considered all that relevant, since we saw, when we considered the "law of Christ," that the natural and supernatural are not really two distinct and separate orders, but actually interpenetrate one another.

As attitudinal responses to the "law of Christ," which St. Paul tells us we fulfill by "bear[ing] one another's burdens" (Gal. 6:2), virtues "aim not only at perfecting people, they aim also at creating just conditions and relations for a just society.''[6] Virtues are directed to values, which are in themselves relational priorities. They provide us with the ready capacity to live and interrelate as persons created in the image and likeness of the Triune God. This latter fact is the source of our inviolable dignity as persons, which in turn generates an entire array of rights and duties. Virtue gives us a ready facility to carry out these duties, for a person's rights are "claims upon our behavior, which we do not have the right to ignore or violate."[7]

To every right that emanates from our inherent value and dignity as persons corresponds a duty. Rights and duties are dialogical elements concretizing the reciprocal call and response that constitute our relational and communal nature as human beings. The virtues predispose the Christian disciple regularly to implement those values and perform those duties which meet the needs of the poor and disinherited, and to work to correct situations of sin or sinful social structures. Rooted in the power of Christ's paschal mystery, virtues work to apply the effects of salvation; they work to bring about reconciliation and wholeness and to restore all things "in Christ."

The Imitation of Christ and the Saints. "Our 'being' as Christians is constituted, as we have seen by character, virtues, duties and rights. There is a further aspect of 'being' which is identified with what it is that we admire and what we imitate. 'Being' is formed by what we aspire to."[8] St. Paul thus writes: "Be imitators of me, as I am of Christ" (1 Cor. 11:1). In presenting rules for the daily conduct of Christians, the letter to the Ephesians directs us to "be imitators of God, as beloved children, and live in love, as Christ loved us and handed himself over for us as a sacrificial offering" (Eph. 5:1). The Fathers of the Church would further develop this theme. St. Basil the Great defined Christianity itself in terms of the imitation of Christ: ". . . the goal of Christianity is the imitation of Christ according to the measure of His incarnation, insofar as is conformable with the vocation of each individual."[9]

This imitation of God and of Christ is not to be a mere legalistic, external conformance. St. Basil's quote above tells us that it must correspond to the unique vocation of each individual. This imitation, in other words, flows from who we are, as made in the image and likeness of God and living now "in Christ" as God's "beloved children." The saints, too, are held up for our imitation because in heroic ways they allowed the mystery of God's love, Christ's paschal love, to shine through their daily lives and labors. Thus, monk, mother, teacher, corporate executive, student, farmer, office worker, research scientist, husband, etc. are able to live "in Christ," imitate him in their own vocations and situations. Christ and the saints serve as role models, as images that should attract and motivate us. For instance, we should want to imitate Christ's "love, His patience, mercy, kindness, gentleness, His uncompromising opposition to hypocrisy and evil. His forgiving relationships with repentant sinners, His high moral and spiritual standards. His respect for life."[10] Such imitation does not mean becoming a slavish copier of details, such as attempted by the medieval practice of self-flagellation. Scripture and the Fathers, rather, call us to imitate a whole orientation and way of life.

Sin

St. Paul provides us with the truly proper perspective from which to view sin, when he declares that "where sin increased, grace overflowed all the more" (Rom. 5:20). Sin can only be correctly appreciated when it is considered within the context of the Good News of salvation in Jesus Christ. The tendency, since medieval times, to focus primarily upon the avoidance of sin as the central thrust of a Christian's moral life has misconstrued the role sin plays in our lives. Furthermore, people today react with some justification against the notion of sin common to earlier generations, which defined it as "a deliberate transgression against the law of God." While this definition itself is not incorrect if properly understood, it needs to be modified in those instances where it paints an image of God who is not unlike a civil or ecclesiastical lawgiver and conceives God's law in terms of a codified, positive law imposed from outside.

A decade ago, an eminent psychologist, Karl Menninger, wrote a book entitled *Whatever Became of Sin?*[11] While making full allowance for the limits placed on freedom by the influence of heredity, environment, intellectual drives and subconscious motives, he insisted that there was still such a thing as moral responsibility. He further maintained from his professional standpoint that the world would be a healthier place if we showed more concern for repentance and conversion. The loss of the sense of sin in modern times can be attributed to several factors. The scientific achievements and philosophical currents of the nineteenth century espoused an overly optimistic view of evolution and human progress that allowed no room for the possibility of human failure. Ethics has been shaped, in many instances, by historical relativism. The advance of secularism lessened the sense of God and promoted a worldwide decline in respect for authority. Certain schools of psychology confused sin with neurotic feelings of guilt and frequently stressed the role of psychic determinisms at the expense of moral responsibility. Conscience has been frequently equated with subjective feelings. An overemphasis has been placed on collective responsibility for sinful social structures downplaying personal guilt. And among members of some Christian churches, especially the Catholic Church, there has been a reaction against an overemphasis on sexual sins, as well as against a legalistic, formalistic and juridical notion of sin and morality.[12]

When we turn to the pages of sacred Scripture, however, we clearly see that sin is an ever present reality. Indeed, the gospel itself makes no sense if it is not seen as the proclamation of our victory over the forces of sin and evil through the salvation won for us in Jesus Christ. In announcing his birth, the angel instructs Joseph in a dream: "Mary your wife . . . will bear a son and you are to name him Jesus, because he will save his people from their sins" (Mt. 1:20-21). John the Baptist later introduces Jesus as "the Lamb of God, who takes away the sin of the world" (Jn. 1:29). In his preaching Jesus constantly calls upon his hearers to "Repent, and believe in the gospel" (Mk. 1:15). But we cannot repent and be converted unless we take sin seriously. At his last supper on the night before he died, Jesus handed his disciples the cup and said, "this is my blood of the covenant, which will be shed on behalf of many for the forgiveness of sins" (Mt. 26:28). Deliverance from sin is the constant thrust of Jesus' life and mission. We shall now take a closer look at the development of the understanding of sin within Scripture and our theological tradition.

Biblical Perspectives of Sin. Throughout the Scriptures sin is seen, first of all, as a universal power active in our lives and within the world that is hostile to God and to his plan. It always strikes at the heart of our relationship to God, to ourselves, to others and to all of creation. It is the complete opposite of the love and reconciliation that Jesus reveals on the Cross. More than the mere violation of a law or an idea, sin is a rebellion against the person we are called to be. Our wrongful actions and transgressions, then, give expression to this power of sin that seeks to grab hold of our lives. As St. Paul explains, "if I do what I do not want, . . . it is no longer I who do it, but sin that dwells in me" (Rom. 7:16-18).

1. From the very beginning of **the Old Testament**, in the Book of Genesis, sin is presented as a rebellion against God's will. It is a deliberate action that results in a breakdown of relationships. Created in God's image

199

and gifted with freedom, Adam and Eve want to become like him deciding for themselves what is good and bad. They give in to the temptation and eat of the forbidden fruit from "the tree of knowledge of good and bad" (Gen. 2:17). Immediately their eyes are opened and they realize their nakedness and shame, so they hide from God. When God confronts them with their disobedience, Adam first attempts to justify himself by pointing the finger of blame both at Eve and at God himself: "The woman whom you put here with me — she gave me fruit from the tree, and so I ate it" (Gen. 3:12). As punishment they must toil all the days of their lives to eat the earth's yield (Gen. 3:17). Their deliberate failure to listen to God's word has resulted in harming all their relationships: to God first of all, to their deepest selves as evidenced by feeling nakedness and shame, to one another as Adam points the finger of blame at Eve whom he earlier described as "bone of my bones and flesh of my flesh" (Gen. 2:23), and to creation itself as they now have to toil to eat the fruit of the earth. This breakdown of relationships continues as Genesis describes Cain out of envy killing his brother Abel, and later presents us with the story of the Tower of Babel which results in scattering the nations and confusing their speech.

Throughout the remaining books of the Old Testament it is the covenant relationship which provides the context for the proper understanding of sin. Moses breaking the tablets with the Ten Commandments when he sees that the people have turned away from God to worship an idol symbolizes the breaking of the covenantal relationship that gave the Decalogue its whole meaning (Dt. 9:16-17). Thus, the most common Hebrew word used to describe sin is "*hatt' ah*," which means basically "to miss the mark," such as when an archer aims a bow and yet the arrow misses the target. The "mark" that is missed by sin is not the mere breaking of some law, but the covenantal relationship itself. "To sin is not simply to break a rule; it is to fail to respond to Another."[13] All sin, therefore, is in some way an expression of idolatry, because through it we set up something else other than God and his plan for us as the center of our loyalty and the goal of our heart's desire. This something else may be our own self-gratification and comfort, power, wealth, fame, another person, a pet project or political cause, etc.

Sin is also described in the Old Testament as "rebellion" ("*pesha*"). Again, the breaking of a personal relationship is implied as, for example, when Isaiah complains that the people of Judah, who had been raised and reared as sons by Yahweh, have now rebelled against him (see Is. 1:2). Sin is, therefore, frequently associated with the "heart" because it is basically a failure to love God. To sin is to harden one's heart to God's love (see Is. 29:13). The Psalmist beseeches God to create "a clean heart" for him (Ps. 51:12). Jeremiah and Ezekiel speak about the law of the new covenant that God will write on people's hearts so that they will know almost instinctively right from wrong (Jer. 31:33-34; Ezk. 36:25-27). Sin is also presented as harlotry, the violation of a spousal relationship (see Hos. 2; Jer. 3:1-5, 20; Ezk. 16:23-43). Furthermore, there is found no concept of private sin in the Old Testament. "Sin, even if committed alone, weakened the community since it affected the relationship with Yahweh, Lord of the people."[14] Catalogues of sin thoroughly incompatible with the covenant are found in Dt. 27:15-26; Ezk. 18:5-18; 22:4-13, etc.

From the Old Testament we also learn that the concept of sin includes the consequences of the act, namely the disintegration of the soul, which in turn spreads further dissolution around it. As Father Eugene H. Maly described it, "sin in the Scriptures is a movement that is begun with the conception of evil in the heart, which then moves forward to the actual doing of the deed, and then, because of the quasi-simultaneity of the sin and its consequences, ends inevitably in ruin. It might be said that the movement is almost irreversible, at least from act to consequence, on the part of the sinner."[15] Punishment for sin, therefore, is not seen as some outside retribution visited by God, but rather the "inexorable running of sin's course."[16] It is the radiation of the evil that continues on, affecting even whole communities still unborn.

Sin follows upon original innocence. In other words, the human condition is not evil in itself. "The Bible, as opposed to much other religious literature, recognizes the devil's incitement as always external to the core of the personality."[17] The New Testament alone reveals the true meaning of sin in Christ's death and resurrection, where is seen fully the final logic of grace offered and sin committed. The Old Testament, however, places before us the essential dynamic of sin: it is the refusal to love God which brings with it the perversion of the human heart. When we turn away from God, it is our own truth we reject as well.

2. In the New Testament sin is seen as a rejection of the Kingdom of God. More specifically, it is a denial of Jesus Christ who embodies in his own person God's kingdom and the truth of our own humanity (see Mt. 10:33; 12:30; Jn. 15:23-25). Sin is a refusal to repent and believe, a refusal to live by the Spirit of God, Christ's Spirit poured out upon us in his paschal mystery (Jn. 16:9; Mk. 3:29). It is a rejection of love, an unwillingness to

remain in relationship (1 Jn. 4:15-16). In the gospels Jesus announces the coming of God's reign or kingdom (Mt. 4:17), which includes *both* an offer of salvation or forgiveness (i.e., the healing power of God's love destroying sin and bringing about reconciliation) *and* an urgent call to repentance (i.e., the grace to look now at life's meaning through the eyes of God rather than through our own narrow and limited vision).

Sin, then, is the rejection of this offer and call. In his parables, Jesus makes known the loving mercy of the Father, revealing the divine plan of salvation. As Eugene Maly points out: "salvation is not only liberation from sins; it is a making whole. Whatever else the effect of sin is, it is a destruction of wholeness of being and relationships. Salvation, by destroying sin, restores this wholeness."[18] Jesus, thus, portrays sin as a wandering from the Father's house (see Lk. 15:13). In the Sermon on the Plain, where he proclaims our inherent vocation to become children of the Most High, Jesus also calls us beyond the letter of the law to its spirit, that is, to its profound intention. Here, he teaches that sin pertains to "the heart," which is the seat of our moral life (Lk. 6:45). Our victory over sin, according to the gospels, is to be obtained through total adherence to the cause of the kingdom that comes in the person of Jesus. This is a matter of cooperating with grace, rather than of human effort.

St. Paul distinguishes the power of sin in the world ("*hamartia*," in the singular) from sinful faults ("*paraptoma*") and transgressions ("*parabasis*"). He refers to sin some sixty times in his letters as a universal force that is hostile to God and his kingdom. Particular sinful acts, faults and transgressions, are viewed then as the expression or exteriorization of this power active in our lives and the world. He tells us that "Jews and Greeks alike . . . are all under the domination of sin" (Rom. 3:9). Furthermore, humanity itself is responsible for this sorry state (Rom. 5:12); it is not the result of unnatural intercourse with rebellious angels (Gen. 6:1-4), nor of God's planting evil desires within our heart (Gen. 8:21).[19] Sin entered the human world through disobedience (Rom. 5:19). For Paul, sin is a law within our "flesh," directing us toward all that is transient and perishable (see 1 Cor. 10:3; Gal. 3:3). Christ alone saves us from the tyranny of sin, justifying us through his obedience (Rom. 5:19).

Sin from the Pauline perspective is a personal, demonical being that dwells in us (see Rom. 7:20) and has enslaved us (Rom. 7:14). It strikes at the root of our personhood in such a way that we lose to it our own existence as a person.[20] It brings about a division within us (Rom. 7:19) and produces alienating, anti-social behavior. Paul's vice-lists (1 Cor. 6:9-10; Gal. 5:19-21; Rom. 1:24-32; 13:13) suggest "not only failure to recognize the other, but an active repulsion of the other."[21] Sin is thus the negation of the personal and relational, and ultimately the denial of Jesus Christ who is the concrete, personal norm of all that it means to be a human being. But Christ has redeemed us through grace (Rom. 3:24), "bought us" back from slavery to sin (see I Cor. 6:20). Through God's favor we now live "in Christ" as "a new creation" (2 Cor. 5:17); God "has reconciled us to himself through Christ . . . so that we might become the righteousness of God" (2 Cor. 5:18, 21). Through Christ, God has given us the victory over the powers of sin and death (1 Cor. 15:57).

In the Johannine view sin is primarily a refusal to believe in Christ (Jn. 16:9), to listen to his word (Jn. 15:22). "Sin is lawlessness" (1 Jn. 3:4), the rejection of God's will; it is living outside the divine life for "No one who remains in him sins" (1 Jn. 3:6). Further, it is "wrongdoing" (1 Jn. 5:17), the denial of divine righteousness and justice. Ultimately, sin is the refusal to love and to be loved (see 1 Jn. 4:16). "If we say, 'We are without sin,' we deceive ourselves, and the truth is not in us" (1 Jn. 1:8). The sinner "hates the light," namely Christ, and "does not come toward the light" (Jn. 3:20).

Throughout the New Testament sin is never viewed in a legalistic sense as the mere violation of some precept or impersonal, abstract norm. Fighting sin, which is presented as an essential component of the Christian life, therefore, "is never a question of fleeing from a taboo, but of conforming oneself to the mystery of Christ."[22] The New Testament writers always present sin within the context of our salvation, of our being reconciled in Christ, who is *the* truth and *the* light. "If then you were raised with Christ, seek what is above, where Christ is seated at the right hand of God" (Col. 3:1). "Therefore let us celebrate the feast, not with the old yeast, the yeast of malice and wickedness, but with the unleavened bread of sincerity and truth" (1 Cor. 5:8). Through sin ("*hamartano*"), one "missed the mark," or "lost one's way down the road," and thereby failed to arrive at the goal, that is, Christ.

Living in Christ, furthermore, was a communal reality. "In the New Testament, sin and community are always viewed from the perspective of mutual love and responsiveness to other's needs."[23] Sin was a sundering of relationships. One person's life influenced the lives of others (Rom. 14:7). "Thus, Paul did not simply encourage individuals to live lives worthy of their individual callings, for God's call was to a unity in Christ as a gathering of saints (cf. Eph 4:1-6; 1 Thes 4:7; Rom 1:6-7; 1 Cor 1:2, 9)."[24] Sins directly affecting the community, whether internally or externally, were the primary concern of the New Testament churches. They sought to reconcile sinful members, welcoming them back if necessary, while maintaining the holiness of the Church derived from Christ's dying and rising (Eph. 5:25) and being a temple of the Spirit (2 Cor. 6:16).

Developments in the Theological Understanding of Sin. In joining the Church, individuals left their former lives behind and bound themselves by their baptismal vows or oath (*sacramentum*) to live by the Spirit of Christ. "Even as late as the mid-second century, this experience and sense of identity as a tight community was so strong that the most serious sin seems to have been the formation of factions, particularly in opposition to the bishop or presbyters who symbolized the community's oneness."[25] While the biblical communities were aware of degrees of sin (see 1 Jn. 5:16-17), no distinction was made between sins that had to be confessed (mortal sin) and sins which may be confessed (venial sins). Jesus spoke of blaspheming against the Holy Spirit which will never be forgiven (Mk. 3:29), and St. Paul provided catalogues of sins that exclude one from the Kingdom of God (1 Cor. 6:9-10; Gal. 5:19-21, etc.). These latter were never intended to be lists compiled for the purpose of confession to a priest. They were intended to be a call to conversion. "To those who have chosen Christ, these lists of sins serve the purpose of aiding discernment. They unambiguously point to what can never be done in the name of Christ or in the name of redeemed love."[26]

1. In the **patristic era** the public or canonical form of penance developed. Modeled on the stages of the catechumenate, it was frequently referred to as a "second baptism." Again, no complete catalogue or uniform list of sins was compiled. The sins submitted for canonical penance (*exomologesis*), namely, the public ritual manifestation of penance, varied from one local church to another. "In those times it was the scandal that was important, the damage the sin would cause the credibility of the Church and her mission in the world." [27] Tertullian singled out apostasy, homicide and adultery as three sins which were irremissible — penance was to be done but reconciliation could never be granted. His influence was such that by the fourth and fifth centuries this triad became the only sins for which canonical penance was required in some churches. Describing the situation at that time, James Dallen writes:

Those who were properly called penitents were guilty not only of *peccata*, part of every Christian life, but also of *crimina* calling for great penance, *paenitentia magna*, but Augustine found it difficult to specify the precise difference. In general, these sins were not everyday sins of weakness . . . but rather sins of malice . . . sins calling for the total oblation of the contrite heart in penance.[28]

These "sins of malice," however, were not the only serious sins recognized as such by the early Church. She always proclaimed the biblical catalogues of sins opposed to the acceptance of the Kingdom of God, and these too needed to be repented with a firm resolution to overcome them before one could receive the Eucharist.

2. Due to its rigorism, the celebration of canonical penance soon began to wane. In **the Middle Ages** a new private, "tariff" form of penance was introduced to the Germanic peoples by Celtic monks. Influenced by the secular legal system with its tariffs (fines) and commutations (substitute penalties) as satisfaction made for crimes, the new form of penance centered on actions or omissions which violated written commandments and laws. Penitential Books prescribing a certain penance or tarriff for a given sin made Christian morality primarily a matter of avoiding sins. The category of sins needing to be confessed steadily broadened.

"Throughout the Middle Ages, both the frequency and fullness of confession became increasingly important as the effort was made to enforce more frequent communion and encourage proper preparation."[29] The Fourth Lateran Council in 1215 made annual confession obligatory for those who had committed mortal sin. Thus, the distinction between mortal and venial sin now took on juridical importance, and moralists soon began to turn to quantitative and objective measurements in order to distinguish between the two. They settled upon three conditions necessary for mortal sin: *serious matter, sufficient reflection,* and *full consent of the will,* the three conditions taught by our catechisms. By focusing on serious matter alone, ready catalogues of mortal sins were easily composed to aid in the examination of one's conscience. Thus, an act-centered and legalistic approach to the moral life continued within Catholicism right up until the second half of the twentieth century. The spiritual development of the moral agent, the person "in Christ," received no attention in the moral theology manuals of this period.

3. The **Second Vatican Council** in its Pastoral Constitution on the Church in the Modern World develops a Christian anthropology that is rooted in the Scriptures. Reflecting upon both the Church and the human vocation, the document first discusses the dignity of the human person as made in the image of God (GS 12). It points out that by our innermost nature we are social beings who need to enter into relationships with others in order to live and develop our talents. It is within this context, then, that it describes the role and nature of sin.

> Although set by God in a state of rectitude, man, enticed by the evil one, abused his freedom at the very start of history. He lifted himself up against God, and sought to attain his goal apart from him. ... Often refusing to acknowledge God as his source, man also upset the relationship which should link him to his last end; and at the same time he has broken the right order that should reign within himself and other men and all creatures.
>
> Man therefore is divided in himself. As a result, the whole life of men, both individual and social, shows itself to be a struggle, and a dramatic one, between good and evil, between light and darkness (GS 13).

Vatican II clearly portrays sin as a rupture in the right relational order that should exist between God and us, within ourselves, with others and with all of creation. Such division, or alienation, results from our abuse of the gift of freedom.

This same council document proceeds to describe the essential communitarian nature of the human vocation as the design of God, which reflects the very life of the Trinity (GS 24). From this communitarian nature flows the process of socialization, which while basically positive can also affect persons negatively. "As it is, man is prone to evil, but whenever he meets a situation where the effects of sin are to be found, he is exposed to further inducements to sin, which can only be overcome by unflinching effort under the help of grace" (GS 25). But this situation of sin and its influence, Vatican II affirms must always be considered within the light of Jesus Christ and the preaching of the gospel. "The good news of Christ continually renews the life and culture of fallen man; it combats and removes the error and evil which flow from the ever-present attraction of sin. It never ceases to purify and elevate the morality of peoples" (GS 58).

4. The new **Rite of Penance**, revised by decree of the Second Vatican Council (SC 72) and promulgated by Paul VI in 1973, speaks of sin and penance in terms of relationship or friendship with God (RP 5, 7) rather than in relation to legal norms. Likeness to Christ rather than conformity to a set of laws is the stated goal of our conversion from sin (RP 6a, 15). It places sin and reconciliation within the context of the new covenant established by Christ's paschal mystery (RP 1). Sin shows infidelity to one's baptismal pledge as a member of a covenant community. Reconciliation reinserts the penitent into the paschal mystery and restores him or her to the covenant community in which Christ's Spirit is active.

"The RP uses the traditional, two-category distinction of sin — grave (rather than mortal) and venial — but its descriptive definitions (RP 5, 7) bring out the relational character, just as its language throughout emphasizes social sin and the social dimensions of sin."[30] The new rite defines grave sin as a withdrawing from the communion of love with God; venial sin is described as a daily weakness which prevents us from attaining the full freedom of God's children (RP 7). Furthermore, when speaking of grave sin the "omission of the traditional reference to number, species, and circumstances also shows the RP is more concerned with sincere conversion than detailed confession, a significant shift in attitude and style of celebration."[31]

The Mystery of Sin within the Contemporary Context. The Second Vatican Council and the new Rite of Penance evidence a return to a less legalistic and more biblical understanding of sin. From a biblical perspective sin is more than just a human transgression against the law of God. Clearly, sin is a product of human freedom, but even more it is a participation in "the mystery of lawlessness" (2 Th. 2:7); it is "contact with the dark forces which, according to Saint Paul, are active in the world almost to the point of ruling it."[32] The mystery of sin as an anti-Christian current at work in the world is demonic or anti-personal in nature. It opposes the principle of divine holiness, that is, Jesus Christ as the presence of absolute love who is himself the personal concrete norm of human existence.

Sin is a de-personalizing force. "It pierces the heart of the Crucified, which represents the concreteness, in the world, of trinitarian love in its self-surrender."[33] It thereby pulls apart the relational structure which constitutes the very essence of personhood. Thus Pope John Paul II writes that "Wounded in this way, man almost inevitably causes damage to the fabric of his relationship with others and with the created world. This is an objective law and an objective reality, verified in so many ways in the human psyche and in the spiritual life, as well as in society, where it is easy to see the signs and effects of internal disorder.''[34] The effects and influence of original sin and the sin of the world upon our lives are but a concrete expression of the mystery of evil.

1. St. Paul tells us that "through one person sin entered the world, and through sin, death" (Rom. 5:12). This **original sin** affected the entire human race, **and** its history is writ large in the **"sin of the world"** (Jn. 1:29). The Church's teaching on original sin, first developed by St. Augustine, maintains that a personal actual sin of the first human being has led to the loss of sanctifying grace, or the divine self-communication, for every member of the human race. Because of Adam, God's gift of himself, which constitutes one in a state of holiness and righteousness (*justitia originale*), antecedent to that person's moral decision is lacking. This lack which ought not to exist is sin only in an analogous sense, since the individual is not culpably responsible for its absence. Yet, this situation really and intrinsically affects each and everyone. Grace is now no longer at our disposal except through our redemption by faith in Jesus Christ. Even after our baptism in which the divine self-communication is restored through the power of the Holy Spirit the woundedness of original sin remains. The garden of Eden is no longer an obtainable goal. The grace given us in baptism comes from Christ, as the goal of history, making us a "new creation," it is not a restoration of the beginning of history, or what Adam lost, but transcends that state of original righteousness.

Contemporary philosophical currents that espouse the Rousseauistic view of human nature as good, sound and whole from the start deny the existence of original sin. What defects there are within the individual or society, according to this school of thought, are wholly attributable to negative societal influences. Others tend to believe that human existence itself is irreparably flawed by its very nature and not as the result of some original sin. A number of Christians also misinterpret the doctrine of original sin by basically equating it with personal sin, which in turn gives rise to the problematic of a collective guilt produced by someone else. Original sin, too, is sometimes identified with the "sin of the world" as the sum total of all sins. Because of misinterpretations such as these, original sin has been frequently relegated to a catechism truth that has little or no bearing upon our

208

daily lives. The Johannine expression "sin of the world" is sometimes used in contemporary theology to sum up the social nature of sin or solidarity in sin. A rediscovery of the covenantal and communal nature of sin from biblical times underlines the important truth that there is really no such thing as a private sin. Every individual sin, even the most secret, harms the covenanted community's relationship to God. Pope John Paul II points out that this is the first meaning of what today is often referred to as "social sin." In opposition to the profound and splendid mystery of the "communion of saints," of solidarity in holiness, "one can speak of a *communion of sin,* whereby a soul that lowers itself through sin drags down with itself the Church and, in some way, the whole world."[35]

Since we have already seen that values are more caught than taught, the evil example of one person's sin exposes the value involved to doubt and denial; it weakens that value's appeal to the conscience of others. The persistent absence of positive testimony to a value and the continuing display of evil example exert pressure upon a whole society so that it becomes completely blind to that value. No one exists in a neutral situation.

> The accepted value-system of a society exercises a tremendous pressure, as can be attested by anyone who tries to hold out against it. What everyone does cannot be wrong, and those who protest are held up as objects of ridicule. Only the very strong can think of opposing any resistance. The majority simply acquiesce and most frequently are not even conscious of how they are manipulated.[36]

Such situations of sin result, then, from the inexorable pressure of a false value-system that permeates society. This is the "sin of the world," or even more, in the view of St. Paul it is the "world." Thus, he asks "Where is the debater of this age? Has not God made the wisdom of the world foolish?" (1 Cor. 1:20). This is "the present evil age" from which Jesus Christ rescues us (Gal. 1:4). The "world" that God reconciles (2 Cor. 5:19; Rom. 11:15) is the "world" that he will judge (Rom. 3:6).

Two other meanings of "social sin" are described by Pope John Paul II. First, all sins against love of neighbor, against justice in interpersonal relationships, offend the law of Christ and may truly be classified as social sin. Secondly, relationships between various human communities that are not always in accord with God's plan constitute situations of social evil. God intends that justice reign in the world, that freedom and peace prevail between individuals, groups and peoples. Thus, the class struggle is a social evil, as is likewise the "obstinate confrontation between blocs of nations, between one nation and another, between different groups within the same nation."[37]

It is misleading in all such situations of social sin to speak of "collective guilt." True guilt or culpability arises only out of an exercise of personal freedom. Social sin, like original sin, has an analogical meaning. It is a situation that results from the cumulative effects of many personal sins.

> At the heart of every *situation of sin* are always to be found sinful people. So true is this that even when such a situation can be changed in its structural and institutional aspects by the force of law, or — as unfortunately more often happens — by the law of force, the change in fact proves to be incomplete, of short duration, and ultimately vain and ineffective — not to say counterproductive — if the people directly or indirectly responsible for that situation are not converted.[38]

Theologians and others influenced by the Rousseauistic vision of human nature today tend to absolve the individual of personal guilt by placing all the burden upon social sin and collective guilt. Such an interpretation, however, clearly runs contrary to the understanding of sin handed down to us by Christian biblical revelation.

2. Actual or **personal sin** is an exercise of freedom on the part of the individual person by which he or she ratifies the false value-system of the "world" by choosing to act in conformity with it. Different from unavoidable failure and limitation, personal sin is "a spirit of selfishness rooted in our hearts and wills which wages war against God's plan for our fulfillment."[39] As selfishness, sin is a refusal of love, a turning away from relationships. In the parable of the Lost Son (Lk. 15:11-32), Jesus gives the message that no specific action constitutes his sinfulness, rather his sinfulness consists in the self-seeking attitude through which he isolates himself from the community to which he belongs. Likewise, in Matthew's Last Judgment scene (Mt. 25:31-46) the condemned are sent off to the eternal flames not for any deliberate act of malice, but for their basic lack of sensitivity and their underlying attitude of non-concern for the needs of others. In Luke's parable of the Pharisee and the Tax Collector (Lk. 18:9-17), the Pharisee who did everything right does not go home justified; his self-righteous attitude is his sin. Such fundamental attitudes result from an exercise of our core or

transcendental freedom, which finds expression in our concrete actions or lack thereof.

a.) **Mortal sin,** therefore, is the term used to describe this radical turning away from God's love, his gift of grace. It is "mortal" or "deadly" because it cuts us off, destroys our relationship with the Source of life. St. Thomas Aquinas wrote that when "through sin, the soul commits a disorder that reaches the point of turning away from its ultimate end — God — to which it is bound by charity, then the sin is mortal; on the other hand, whenever the disorder does not reach the point of turning away from God, the sin is venial."[40] Recently Pope John Paul II wrote that, "With the whole tradition of the Church, we call *mortal sin* the act by which man freely and consciously rejects God, his law, the covenant of love that God offers, preferring to turn in on himself or to some created and finite reality, something contrary to the divine will (*conversio ad creaturam*)."[41] According to our theological tradition such sin is comprised of three essential elements: grave matter, sufficient reflection and full consent of the will. They comprise our total refusal of God's gift-call to conversion: religious (our ultimate end) — intellectual (sufficient reflection), affective (full consent), and moral (grave matter).

1) **Serious or "grave matter"** is a moral object substantially affecting an important moral value. Grave matter alone is not the same as mortal sin. Therefore, it is incorrect to say that the main factor lies in grave matter. Many people confuse material and formal sin. Material sin is only sin in appearance, an act of objective wrongdoing in which the element of deliberation is missing. Such an act may even cause a significant amount of harm, but it is not a formal sin unless it proceeds from knowledge and freedom. Furthermore, as Pope John Paul II reminds us,

> . . . some sins are *intrinsically* grave and mortal by reason of their matter. That is, there exist acts which, *per se* and in themselves, independently of circumstances, are always seriously wrong by reason of their object. These acts, if carried out with sufficient awareness and freedom, are always gravely sinful.[42]

Giving alms, for example, as a moral object is in itself basically good. If, however, I give alms to show off, this circumstance changes the value involved making it a disvalue for me. An act of adultery, on the other hand, is always a materially grave violation of the marital covenant regardless of the circumstances and motives leading to the act.

Reacting to an over-identification of mortal sin with grave matter alone and laboring amid the subjectivistic tendencies of historical relativism, some moralists today claim that the category of "grave matter" is completely irrelevant. For them the subjective motive and circumstances are the sole determinants of the morality of an act. They argue that "The word *moral* attaches only to free human behavior."[43] Thus they speak of "pre-moral evils" and deny the existence of "intrinsically evil" actions. This overly spiritual mentality gives little or no significance to concrete human actions and the lack thereof as an external expression of one's inner attitude, of which one is not always consciously aware as Jesus teaches us in the Last Judgment scene (Mt. 25:44). Human actions are moral or immoral because they flow from persons who are radically free and fundamentally capable through grace of doing God's will. Whether one is subjectively culpable for performing a given action which does not objectively correspond to God's will depends upon various factors, including limitations placed upon one's categorical freedom and awareness thereof. The point is, however, that positing an action opposed to God's loving plan for creation (that is, an action which is harmful to the relational order, to the "divine ecology") can only be done by a creature gifted with freedom, whether that action is done with conscious knowledge of its significance or not. Herein lies the source of "objective morality" and "objective sin." Even though this latter action is not a real "formal" sin, it still pertains to the moral order and to the realm of human responsibility with regard to the consequences of it. The Orthodox tradition, thus, long ago developed the concept of "involuntary sin" to describe such an action.[44]

2) **Sufficient reflection**, the second necessary element for mortal sin, means having acquired evaluative knowledge, which we saw in the last chapter is moral knowledge properly so-called. "Evaluative knowledge is more personal, more self-involving than conceptual knowledge of facts or ideas, for it has to do with grasping the quality of a person, object, or event."[45] Unless we have an appreciation of the value in question through our personal appropriation of it, we act only on hearsay, rather than on the basis of what we have discovered to be valuable.

3) **Full consent of the will** is the third traditional element required for mortal sin. Such consent must arise from the exercise of basic or transcendental freedom (see chapter three), which differs from freedom of choice. It is a matter of the "heart" in the biblical sense, of the deepest core

of our identity. There, we say "No" to God's self-gift of life, truth and love. Our actions embody to a greater or lesser degree the fundamental orientation of our lives, yet not all actions spring from this deepest core of our being. Jesus himself points this out in the parable of the Two Sons (Mt. 21:28-31), where the first son's initial refusal is not truly indicative of his fundamental willingness to obey his Father's command, and vice versa in the case of the second son.

In recent decades Catholic moralists have introduced the category of "fundamental option" to describe our exercise of transcendental or core freedom. Much confusion has surrounded the actual meaning of the term. Many theologians feel it better explains the meaning of full consent of the will and more clearly demonstrates that mortal sin involves more than the simple performance of an action designated as grave matter. Father Bernard Häring, C.Ss.R., for example, equates it with the traditional Thomistic concept of making a basic decision regarding one's ultimate end (*finis ultimus*). Thus, he adds, "All the individual decisions and the quality of one's freedom depend on this choice."[46] He proceeds to explain how a fundamental option that leads to a loving relationship with God (traditionally, "the state of grace") may be reversed.

> We may consider two extreme types of how one loses the friendship of God. In one case it can be through the mortal sin committed by a person who is still clear-sighted, has a sharp awareness that a certain act contradicts the friendship of God, and nevertheless decides in favor of the act that reaches into the depth of his heart and shapes his whole being. The other extreme could be the result of many venial sins: through frequent abuse of God's grace, and an increasing laxity that deadens more and more the person's sensibility for the good, his gratitude to God, and responsibility for the needs of others, there finally comes the point where the fundamental option is reversed through a free act of choice, although without great sensitivity; as if a slight wind had blown out a candle that was already burnt down.[47]

This interpretation of the "fundamental option" closely parallels the description given by the Sacred Congregation for the Doctrine of the Faith in 1975 which maintained that "In reality, it is precisely the fundamental option which in the last resort defines a person's moral disposition. But it can be completely changed by particular acts, especially when, as often happens, these have been prepared for by previous more superficial acts."[48]

Surveying the contemporary scene in Catholic moral theology, Father Richard McCormick, S.J., in 1969 observed that "Increasingly one hears it said that there can be no act such that its commission or omission alone is mortally sinful."[49] He himself believes that this position portrays an unrealistic understanding of a human act. Viewed abstractly, for instance, adultery may be seen as a mere brief physical occurrence. Considered integrally, however, it "includes a larger experience: the meetings, thoughts, desires, plans, effects as foreseen, the vacillations, and so on. In other words, realistically viewed, adultery is a whole relationship brought to its culmination."[50] Still other moralists maintain that for an action to be a mortal sin it must be an expression of an explicit and formal break with God or neighbor. Pope John Paul II denies the validity of such a position when he maintains that "mortal sin also exists when a person knowingly and willingly, for whatever reason, chooses something gravely disordered."[51] Such a choice in itself already shows contempt for the divine law, God's loving plan for creation. We hurt another person not only by direct contempt and hatred, but also by our insensitivity and carelessness. The heavy influence of historical consciousness and contemporary currents within the area of psychology are clearly evident in some of these new theories.

In more than a few cases, however, personal freedom can be severely limited because of any number of external and internal factors. Even the classical manuals of moral theology listed invincible ignorance, error, inattention, violence, fear, passion and evil habits as factors that can diminish the imputability of our actions. Social pressure and the influence of one's cultural milieu may also contribute to the lessening of culpability in certain instances, as the Second Vatican Council pointed out. In all of these considerations regarding the essential elements that make up a mortal sin Catholic tradition has recognized that "it is not always easy in concrete situations to define clear and exact limits."[52] We must keep ever in mind the perspective of St. Thomas Aquinas who taught that "Although grace is lost by one act of mortal sin, still grace is not lost easily, since for one who has grace it is not easy to perform such an act because of the contrary inclination."[53]

b.) Finally, the category of **venial sin** describes those choices and actions that do not spring from the deepest level of our knowledge and freedom. Venial sin is analogous to mortal sin. Many of our daily choices do not change our fundamental commitment to be open to God, others and the world. "For example, while I may be fundamentally a caring person, my occasional acts of aloofness and causing harm do not radically change the sort of person I am, though they may weaken my commitment to goodness and love."[54] Venial sin, however, must never be considered to be of little consequence. There are different degrees of such sin, and some can be quite serious and intense, bordering very closely on mortal sin. We cannot long go through the motions of lovelessness without one day waking up to discover we have killed our love.

The Human Act

Our acts of virtue and our sins are the embodiment of our conscious free choices, of our decision-making. They are the fruits of the quality of our relationships or the lack thereof in our lives. They enflesh the values or disvalues that motivate us. When performed with sufficient reflection and full consent they are an exercise of our personal "response-ability" and express the fundamental orientation or basic direction of our lives. They are, in other words, the fruit of our faith response to the divine gift-call of grace, or of our refusal to respond to that call. There is, thus, no human act that does not involve an attitude towards the transcendental norm of morality, towards our being perfected "in Christ" and our striving after it.

Since a true human act flows from the mystery of our personal subjectivity in its relationship to the transcendent Mystery of the Triune God, it can never be the proper object of judgment by others. Jesus addresses this very reality when he commands, "Stop judging, that you may not be judged" (Mt. 7:1). Under the influence of contemporary philosophy's turn towards the subjective, many moralists today accuse an ethical analysis of the moral object of a human act to be completely irrelevant. Such an endeavor to them smacks of objectivism. From the perspective of symbolic consciousness, however, such a study is not without great merit. The same Jesus who commanded that we stop judging, also instructed us, a short fifteen verses later in the same gospel account, that "By their fruits you will know them" (Mt. 7:16, 20). This apparent contradiction shows Jesus' thorough knowledge of our corporeal-spiritual nature.

Through an objective evaluation of the human act it is possible for us to assess the act's moral significance, just as God's will and intention is "able to be understood and perceived in what he has made" (Rom. 1:20). Thus, in a very real sense "all actions are automatically and immediately inseparable

215

from the person who performs them."[55] Since morality is concerned with persons, it must always take our corporeal-spiritual nature into account. Cardinal Joseph Ratzinger therefore maintains, "It is because the body and the soul of the person interpenetrate one another that the hypothesis of a purely physical act represents a false distinction. It is precisely because of the personal involvement, with its personal goals and its personal effects, that masturbation and contraception cannot be seen as devoid of moral content in and of themselves."[56] The classical moral manuals thus singled out the personal character of the human act when they distinguished it from an "act of man." This latter category designates "all biological processes, like breathing; sensory impulses, like feeling pain; as well as spontaneous psychic reactions that precede the activity of intellect and will, like first movements of anger and sympathy."[57]

The Determinants of the Human Act. An evaluative analysis of the human act traditionally considers three components: the moral object, the relevant circumstances, and the subjective motive.

1. The **moral object** (the "*finis operis*," literally, the "end of the act") relates the human act to the value it achieves. It thus transcends the material object of the physical or biological deed. For instance, the surgical procedure of sterilization is physically the same whether it is performed on a healthy body for a contraceptive purpose or on a diseased body in order to heal or retard a pathological condition, but its moral object differs because of the situation. The moral object, the good or evil of the human act, is determined by the act's relation to the objective order established by God. Acts which destroy or interfere with God's loving plan, his relational order implanted within creation itself both in its material and spiritual components, are evil in their very selves. Acts such as blasphemy, calumny, racial prejudice, torture, child abuse and rape are always attacks upon the moral order whatever the circumstances or subjective motive of the human agent.

2. The **circumstances** are those particulars of the human act that help determine its moral nature. The sexual embrace between a man and woman who are married to each other can be a beautiful celebration and expression of their covenanted love. If however they are married to someone else or not married at all, the same physical act assumes an entirely different moral significance because it embodies different (dis)values. Just as the same

216

surgical procedure of sterilization, mentioned above, embodies different values depending whether or not its purpose is contraceptive ("direct") or therapeutic ("indirect"). Circumstances can in many instances change or modify the good or evil quality of a human act. As Jesus points out in the gospels the good act of giving alms, indeed, becomes nobler when it is done by a poor widow (Mk. 12:41-44; Lk. 21:1-4).

3. The **subjective motive** is the end or reason for which a particular person does an act. A good act such as giving alms can be vitiated if it is done just to show off. An evil intention can affect the quality of a good action. On the other hand, however, a good intention cannot justify an intrinsically evil deed. A person may not steal, for example, in order to be able to give alms to the poor. In time of war civilian populations may not be targeted in order to reduce the enemy's morale with the hope of hastening the end of the war. St. Paul has clearly stated the principle that we should not "do evil that good may come of it" (Rom. 3:8).

Principles for Situations of Conflict. While it is universally accepted that we may not do evil that good may come of it, we not infrequently find ourselves in everyday life in situations where a contemplated action will produce both a desired good effect along with certain evil consequences. Must we thus refrain from doing good in such a situation?

1. Classical moral theology developed the **principle of double effect** to guide a person caught in a situation where both good and evil effects may result from a single action. Starting with the fundamental natural law principle that we are to do good and avoid evil and its corollary that one may not do evil in order that good may come of it, classical morality maintained that there is a vital difference between a directly willed effect (*voluntarium directum*) and one that is only indirectly willed (*voluntarium indirectum* or *in causa*). Such a distinction seems to be universally admitted in spontaneous discourse. The directly willed killing of a human person is strongly condemned by all, yet it is recognized that deaths will flow from dangerous sports like auto racing and mountain climbing and from space travel, the running of big industries and so forth. These deaths are considered blameworthy only when reasonable precautions have not been taken to avoid them. The accidental killing of noncombatants is tolerated in war, but the direct killing of even a few children in order to lower the morale of the

enemy is universally condemned. The principle of double effect spells out the conditions under which an indirectly willed effect may be permissible or not imputable to the agent:

a.) **The moral object may not be evil in itself,** like torture, direct abortion or extramarital intercourse.

b.) **The good and evil effect must proceed at least equally directly from the act.** For example, morphine administered to relieve pain may endanger the life of the patient. This is quite different from the medieval practice of castrating young boys in order to maintain their beautiful soprano voices. In other words, the immediate effect must not be solely evil; the good effect should not physically result from the evil effect.

c.) **The agent may not intend or approve the evil effect.** Thus, it would be a malicious subterfuge to maintain that morphine is for relieving pain, when in fact the death of the patient is being sought.

d.) **There must be a proportionate grave reason** in order to allow the evil effect. ''Proportionate'' means that if the evil effect is slight, a slight reason suffices; if the evil effect is serious, a serious reason is required to justify the action. In the end, the virtue of prudence or discernment must be exercised.

The principle could be stated briefly: ''Undertaking an action from which a good and evil effect are foreseen is permissible if the action itself is not evil, if the bad effect is not intended, and if there is sufficiently grave reason to permit the evil effect.''[58] Many contemporary ethicists, however, who primarily identify morality with the subjective intention of the agent deny the validity of this principle of double effect or completely change its original intent. For instance, some would maintain that an action is legitimate, provided the good produced is commensurate with the evil through which it is attained. Others who have not been trained to make distinctions easily misunderstand the principle. Thus, the President's Commission for the Study of Ethical Problems in Medicine and Biomedical and Behavioral Research equates ''merely permitting foreseen evil side effects'' with actually ''intending such side effects as a means to an end.'' Such confusion is evident in the following quotation taken from a commission report:

The commission makes use of many of the moral considerations found in this doctrine (referred to as "doctrine of double effect"), but endorses the conclusion that people are equally responsible for all of the foreseeable effects of their actions, thereby having no need for a policy that separates "means" from "merely foreseen consequences."[59]

Rejecting the principle of double effect, however, drastically limits the possibilities for doing good. "If individuals had to abstain from performing good actions because of foreseen evil side effects, not only would much good remain unattempted and undone in the world, but many would be tempted to use that prospect of evil side effects as an excuse to pass up opportunities of doing good and even to shirk their duties in their personal, social and professional lives."[60]

2. The **principle of totality** was developed by classical moralists to demonstrate the licitness of certain intentional mutilations of the body, that is, surgical operations, which are necessary for the health and well-being of the whole body. According to this principle it is permissible for an injury to be done to one part of the body or organ in order that the whole individual organism may benefit. Here a mere "physical evil" (as distinct from a "moral evil") is permitted for achieving a moral good. "It is not that the surgeon's action has many aspects that might make a morally evil act morally good. It is precisely because we have prior standards or norms that tell us surgery is justified that we judge a physical infliction of pain in these circumstances morally good."[61] On the other hand, the willful infliction of physical pain for masochistic or sadistic purposes violates human dignity and thereby the law of God.

The medical breakthrough of organ transplants in recent years has brought about the need to extend the principle of totality to include the total well-being not just of the body but of the whole person. The donation of an organ for transplantation which is motivated by sacrificial love for another leads to spiritual fulfillment for the donor. Here the principle is truly personalized reflecting the "law of Christ," the inner call to self-giving love. Our human dignity and well-being lies in observing this law "which is fulfilled in the love of God and of one's neighbor" (GS 16).

3. Our human actions, furthermore, may have good or bad effects on the behavior of others. Bad effects arise from cases of **scandal and cooperation**.

219

Scandal is a human act, good or bad, or an omission which becomes a temptation or occasion of sin for another. Jesus warned us, "Woe to the world because of the things that cause sin! Such things must come, but woe to the one through whom they come" (Mt. 18:7). Even a good action can give scandal, as St. Paul notes when he teaches that indeed no food is unclean but adds, "If your brother is being hurt by what you eat, your conduct is no longer in accord with love" (Rom. 14:15). On the other hand, we cannot desist from every good action because it might give scandal to another. The principle of double effect here comes into play. Actions good in themselves which might be an occasion of sin for others need not be omitted if this would entail proportionate harm or inconvenience.

According to the authors of the classical manuals it is even permissible to counsel another to do a lesser evil in order to prevent a greater evil. "Advising a lesser sin than the one a sinner is about to commit is ordinarily allowed, if the sinner cannot otherwise be deterred from committing the greater sin."[62] Some authors, therefore, suggest that it is lawful to persuade a murderer to rob, rather than kill another, or to counsel contraception to a woman who regularly resorts to abortion and is unwilling or unable to practice natural family planning.[63] This same classic principle could be applied to a Catholic physician or counselor working with someone who is a carrier of the deadly AIDS virus and refuses to abstain from sexual activity; recommending the use of a prophylactic in this instance could be morally justified. The necessary condition for such counsel is that the patient or counselee *refuses* to practice sexual abstinence. Counseling their use in an educational or group setting on the presumption that many in the group will not practice abstinence, however, is not morally justifiable application of this same principle. This latter situation would constitute a traditional case of "scandal of the weak" which must be avoided (see Mt. 18:6; Rom. 14:21).

Cooperation is understood as any concrete help that is given to another in the commission of what one judges to be immoral. Cooperation is formal either when one who is aiding the principal agent fully agrees with the latter's intention, or when the cooperator performs an essential part of the evil action under the direction of the principal agent, for example, an assistant surgeon participating in a direct abortion. Such formal cooperation in evil is never permitted. Material cooperation is in itself a good act which is abused by another in order to do evil, for example, a taxi driver transporting someone to an abortion clinic, or a nurse preparing a patient for a morally illicit operation. Such material cooperation is licit when there is a proportionate reason and when scandal is removed as far as possible by suitable explanation.

These and other principles have been developed by classical moral theology to help us better distinguish the weeds from the wheat which will "grow together until harvest" (Mt. 13:30). They are meant to be "rules of thumb" which will aid us in responding to the good, the gift of grace, more easily. Their sole purpose, then, is to help us live "in Christ" as a new creation. Christ himself remains the sole norm. Prudence, rather than mechanical application, is thus always necessary if we are to employ these principles properly.

This analysis of the responsible human act brings our study of the "fundamental elements" of Christian living to its conclusion. Human acts are the concrete expressions of our character, of the sort of person we are and are becoming. They are the incarnations of the quality of our relationships to God and others. They flow from the way we habitually respond to the "law of Christ" written deep within our hearts, our consciences. The sundering effects of the power of sin within us and within the world, at times, can deafen and blind us to God's call and presence. Sin can so influence us that on occasion we do the evil we do not want, but through Christ and "in Christ" we have victory over sin, we are redeemed. In faith and hope the power of God's grace, his love, is making of us "in Christ" a whole new creation. This inbreaking of God's kingdom, of the eternal into time, transforms the process of our becoming; it helps us to faithfully live out the divine-human dialogue within the concrete situations and decisions of our daily lives. In the next part of this work, we shall look more closely at some of these practical everyday encounters wherein God's call continually addresses us.

Notes

1. Harakas, *The Transfigured Life*, p. 187.
2. Häring, *The Law of Christ*, vol. 1, p. 485.
3. Häring, *Free and Faithful in Christ*, vol. 1, p. 201.
4. Ibid., p. 41.
5. Ibid., pp. 201-208.
6. Happel and Walter, *Conversion and Discipleship*, p. 43.
7. Harakas, op. cit., p. 192.

8. Ibid., p. 199.

9. *The Long Rules*, cited in ibid., p. 201.

10. Harakas, op. cit., p. 201.

11. New York: Bantam Books, 1978.

12. See Lobo, *Guide to Christian Living*, pp. 374-375; also, John Paul II, *Reconciliation and Penance*, no. 18.

13. Eugene H. Maly, *Sin: Biblical Perspectives* (Dayton, Ohio: Pflaum/Standard, 1973), p. 10.

14. Ibid., p. 18.

15. Eugene H. Maly, ''Sin and Forgiveness in the Scriptures,'' *Sin, Salvation and the Spirit*, ed. Daniel Durken, O.S.B. (Collegeville, Minnesota: The Liturgical Press, 1979), p. 44.

16. Bruce Vawter, C.M., ''The Scriptural Meaning of Sin,'' *Readings in Biblical Morality*, ed. C. Luke Salm, F.S.C. (Englewood Cliffs, New Jersey: Prentice-Hall, Inc., 1967), p. 34.

17. Lobo, op. cit., p. 380.

18. Maly, *Sin: Biblical Perspectives*, p. 81.

19. See Murphy-O'Connor, *Becoming Human Together*, p. 94.

20. Schelkle, *Theology of the New Testament*, vol. 3, p. 59.

21. Murphy-O'Connor, op. cit., p. 135.

22. Lobo, op. cit., p. 116.

23. Dallen, *The Reconciling Community*, p. 7.

24. Ibid.

25. Ibid., p. 18.

26. Bernard Häring, C.Ss.R., *Sin in the Secular Age* (Garden City, N.Y.: Doubleday & Company, Inc., 1974), p. 175.

27. Ibid., pp. 179-180.

28. Dallen, op. cit., p. 61.

29. Ibid., p. 141.

30. Dallen, op. cit., p. 290.

31. Ibid., p. 283.

32. John Paul II, *Reconciliation and Penance*, no. 14.

33. Ratzinger, Schürmann, von Balthasar, op. cit., p.88.

34. John Paul II, *Reconciliation and Penance*, no. 15.

35. Ibid., no. 16.

36. Murphy-O'Connor, op. cit., p. 96.

37. John Paul II, *Reconciliation and Penance*, no. 16.

38. Ibid.

39. National Conference of Catholic Bishops, *To Live in Christ Jesus: A Pastoral Reflection on the Moral Life* (Washington, D.C.: United States Catholic Conference, 1976), p.5.

40. *Summa*, Ia-IIae, q. 72, a. 5 as cited by Pope John Paul II, *Reconciliation and Penance*, no. 17, where he adds that ". . . the ideas of death, of radical rupture with God the Supreme Good, of deviation from the path that leads to God or interruption of the journey toward him (which are all ways of defining mortal sin) are linked with the idea of the gravity of sin's objective content."

41. Ibid. John Paul II, here too, states that "in the Church's doctrine and pastoral action, *grave* sin is in practice identified with *mortal* sin." He thus rejects a contemporary theological current which proposes the reclassification of the degrees of sin into the categories of "venial," "grave," and "mortal." Some theologians who reduce mortal sin to an act of explicit and formal contempt for God and neighbor (which they identify by the term "fundamental option") have favored this threefold classification.

42. Ibid.

43. Sean Fagan, S.M., *Has Sin Changed?* (Wilmington, Delaware: Michael Glazier, Inc., 1977), p. 81.

44. Harakas, op. cit., pp. 174-175.

45. Gula, *To Walk Together Again*, p. 111.

46. Häring, *Free and Faithful in Christ*, vol. 1, p. 164.

47. Ibid., pp. 212-213.

48. Sacred Congregation for the Doctrine of the Faith, *Declaration on Certain Questions Concerning Sexual Ethics* (Washington D.C.: United States Catholic Conference, 1977), no. 10, p. 11.

49. Richard A. McCormick, S.J., *Notes on Moral Theology — 1965 through 1980* (Washington, D.C.: University Press of America, 1981), p. 204. See, for example, Louis Monden, S.J., *Sin, Liberty and Law* (New York: Sheed and Ward, 1965), p. 35: "Human action is situated historically. The fundamental option of liberty cannot be expressed adequately in one single action." Also, Josef Fuchs, S.J., *Human Values and Christian Morality* (Dublin: Gill and Macmillan, 1970), p. 96: "The free self-commitment of ourselves as persons is more than any particular action or actions and more than the sum of them; it underlies them, permeates them, and goes beyond them, without ever being actually one of them."

50. Ibid.

51. *Reconciliation and Penance*, no. 17.

52. Ibid.

53. *De Veritate*, 1, 9.

54. Gula, op. cit., p. 127.

55. Ratzinger, "Bishops, Theologians, and Morality," op. cit., p. 669.

56. Ibid.

57. Lobo, op. cit., p. 341.

58. Ibid., pp. 349-350.

59. *Deciding to Forego Life-sustaining Treatment* (Washington, D.C.: U.S. Government Printing Office, 1983), a publication of The President's Commission (cf. note 215), p. 80.

60. Orville N. Griese, *Catholic Identity in Health Care: Principles and Practice* (Braintree, Massachusetts: The Pope John Center, 1987), pp. 253-254.

61. Rodger Charles, S.J., *The Social Teachings of Vatican II*, p. 82.

62. Heribert Jone, O.F.M. Cap., *Moral Theology,* Revised English translation of the thirteenth German edition by Urban Adelman, O.F.M. Cap. (Westminster, Maryland, 1953), no. 144.3, pp. 84-85.

63. Lobo, op. cit., p. 355.

Part III

Special Questions

Chapter 9

Sexual Ethics

*In the mystery of creation — on the basis of the original and
constituent "solitude" of his being — man was endowed with a deep
unity between what is, humanly and through the body, male in him
and what is, equally humanly and through the body, female in him.*
— John Paul II[1]

Ethical determinations of concrete situations and specific cases are based
upon norms that articulate values. As we saw in chapter six, values mediate
our faith vision, our understanding of the meaning and purpose of life. As
followers of Jesus Christ and members of his Body, our vision of life's
meaning and purpose finds its fullest expression within the context of
Christian biblical revelation. As Christians, our ethical course of action flows
from our faith perception of who we are in relationship to the God who has
revealed himself to us in Jesus Christ. Our everyday moral decisions about
what is good and bad, right and wrong, therefore, cannot be based solely
upon empirical evidence nor philosophical abstractions, but rather upon
Christian anthropology and the faith experience of our Christian vocation.

Christian anthropology, as we saw in Part II of this work, has as its
foundation the principal tenet that we have been created in the image and
likeness of God, who is a Tri-unity of personal relationships. Person is thus
the basic Christian value, and love the primary virtue. Through our misuse of
God's gift of freedom, which alone allows us to stay in loving relationships
and to remain whole, the human race from its very beginning has come under
the predominant influence of the sundering effects of sin. In Jesus Christ,
however, God has become one of us and transformed our human nature
redeeming us from sin and making us a whole new creation. In every area
and aspect of our lives, therefore, the follower of Christ is called to holiness
of life, to love as Christ loves, and to live in this world as God's new creation
"in Christ."

In this chapter we shall consider some of the principal questions faced today by Christian sexual ethics. The Catholic Church is often accused of being "hung up" on sexual issues, of limiting the consideration of morality to questions about sex. Such is obviously not the case. As we shall see in chapter eleven, the popes themselves in the last one hundred years have written more on questions of social justice than on any other area of ethical concern. Yet, within the realm of general human experience a basic fascination and even preoccupation with sex always comes to the fore. And perhaps, in a very real sense this is most appropriate, for it is through the gift of human sexuality that men and women most fundamentally incarnate their relational existence and give expression to the fact that they are created in the image and likeness of God.

Male and Female

The bisexual nature of the human species is a biological fact, a primordial given. The human person is normally male or female, and there exists the most powerful attraction between the two. Is the sexual urge just for the propagation of the species as it is among the animals? Or does a sexual relationship between human beings mean something more? Before attempting to answer these questions from the perspective of Christian anthropology, let us turn first to other human reflections upon this experience.

Mythology and Philosophy. Ancient traditions tell about the original human being who was both male and female. Both the Persian and Talmudic mythologies relate how God first created a two-sexed being and later divided that being into two. This theory is most clearly expressed in Plato's *Symposium* wherein Aristophanes retells an ancient Greek myth about the original human beings, who were perfectly round, had four arms and four legs, and one head with two faces, looking in opposite ways. These human spheres possessed such marvelous intelligence and qualities that they rivaled the gods who, acting out of jealousy and fear, split the spheres in half in order to reduce their power. These original, spherical beings thus fell apart into two halves, one feminine and one masculine. Ever since then, so the story goes, the two severed parts of the original human being have been striving to reunite. "And when one of them meets his other half," Aristophanes informs us, "the actual half of himself, . . . the pair are lost in an amazement of love and friendship and intimacy, and one will not be out of the other's sight . . . even for a moment: these are the people who pass their whole lives together; yet they could not explain what they desire of one another."[2]

227

Evidence of this same belief in the sexual duality of human nature is found also in sacred Scripture. The Book of Genesis, for instance, indicates that God himself is an androgynous being, that is, someone who combines within his or her personality both male and female elements. In the first chapter we read that "God created man in his image; . . . male and female he created them" (Gen. 1:27). Thus, man and woman together are the image of God, and not man alone nor woman alone. In the second chapter of Genesis, then, we are told that when God wished to make woman, he put Adam into a deep sleep, removed a rib from his body, and made Eve from Adam's rib (Gen. 2:21-22). "Clearly the original man, Adam, was thus both male and female. From this early division of the originally whole, bisexual human being comes the longing, through sexuality, for the reunion of the severed halves."[3] The quotation from John Paul II, introducing this chapter, refers to this same original unity of male and female in "man" (Hebrew, "*adam*"). The second chapter of Genesis continues: "That is why a man leaves his father and mother and clings to his wife, and the two of them become one flesh" (Gen. 2:24).

The human being's androgynous nature has been intuited by other cultures. The American Indian Hyemeyohsts Storm wrote that "Within every man there is the Reflection of a Woman, and within every woman there is the Reflection of a Man."[4] The Russian philosopher Nicholas Berdyaev also wrote,

> Man is not only a sexual but a bisexual being combining the masculine and feminine principle in himself in different proportions and often in fierce conflict. . . . It is only the union of these two principles that constitutes a complete human being. Their union is realized in every man and every woman within their bisexual, androgynous nature, and it also takes place through the intercommunion between the two natures, the masculine and the feminine.[5]

Chinese culture has developed the images of *Yang* and *Yin* as the two cosmic principles whose interaction and relationship determine the course of events. While representing the two spiritual poles along which all life flows, the Chinese also speak of *Yang* as the masculine principle and *Yin* as the feminine existing in men and women. Ancient mythical traditions and philosophical reflection thus maintain that the attraction of male and female constitutes a primordial and fundamental urge or call to unity and completion.

Psychology. Sigmund Freud maintained that sex was a biological instinct analagous to hunger. When a person is hungry he or she seeks satisfaction, which reduces tension and in turn provides pleasure. Satisfaction of sexual desires was the most important element of human happiness. For Freud, the psychological energy or "libido" fueling the life instincts and making them work was primarily sexual energy. Other leading theorists, however, such as Alfred Adler, Carl Jung, Viktor Frankl and Abraham Maslow, see human sexuality primarily serving a social function. It is not simply a "biological need." Jung and Maslow also point out that none of us is purely feminine or purely masculine, but rather each sex contains the other within it.

1. Carl G. Jung was the first to discover empirical evidence for the psychological reality of **the human person's androgynous nature**. The feminine component in a man's personality he called the *anima* and the masculine component in a woman's personality he labelled the *animus*. These terms he derived from the Latin verb *animare*, which means "to enliven." For him the anima and animus were like enlivening souls or spirits to men and women. He also speculated that the anima and animus personify the minority of feminine and masculine genes within us.[6] On the biological level, a man derives his male physical qualities by virtue of having a slight plurality of masculine over feminine genes, and vice versa in the case of a woman. Thus, on the psychological plane, the anima personifies this minority of feminine genes, and in the case of the woman the animus personifies the minority of masculine genes. The man, thus, ordinarily identifies his ego with his masculinity and his feminine side is unconscious to him, while a woman identifies herself consciously with her femininity, and her masculine side is unconscious to her.

Psychologically our sexual yearnings are indicative of our desire for wholeness. In the words of John A. Sanford:

> As a rule of thumb, it can be said that what we yearn for sexually is a symbolic representation of what we need in order to become whole. This means that sexual fantasies symbolically complement ego consciousness in a way that points us toward wholeness. Understanding the symbolic meaning of our sexual fantasies enables us to become less compulsive regarding them, that is, instead of being driven and possessed by them, our range of consciousness can be expanded by them.
> The most frequent example of how a sexual yearning represents

what is needed to bring us wholeness is the sexual desire of a man for a woman, and of a woman for a man. Images of a woman appear in a man's sexual fantasies because she represents his missing half, the other side of his personality to which he needs to relate if he is to be complete, and vice versa with the woman. Of course this is not to say that this is all that sexual yearnings mean. There is always the desire for physical release of tension, for the meeting of body with body, and for the closeness and intimacy with another person that sexuality achieves and expresses. But it is to say that in addition to these aspects of sexuality there is also a spiritual or psychological meaning.[7]

Images possess the power to motivate and move us. We must respect our spontaneous sexual fantasies and genital stirrings as more than mere physical messages. On the psychological and spiritual plane they are calling us to personal integration and wholeness, when we make an effort to understand them. This, however, does not mean that we should try to arouse and encourage genital feelings and fantasies.[8]

Our anima or animus, our psychological other-half, is often projected onto another person creating the phenomenon of "falling in" love. Loving another person, growing in a relationship, is not something that happens in an instant; it is an ongoing process of communicating and sharing. Projection, on the other hand, is a psychological mechanism that occurs whenever a vital aspect of our personality of which we are unaware is activated. We project this aspect of ourselves outside onto someone else, as though it has nothing to do with us. Many people in our contemporary society identify love itself with this experience of projection and its attendant feelings. Thus, when the projection dies because of the personal growth process and changing psychological needs, these same people tend to believe that love also has died. The capacity to recognize and utilize these projections when they occur in one's life, as occur they must, leads to self-knowledge, personal integration, and even in many cases to mature, loving relationships with those persons who were first of all the object of our projections.

2. Freud himself distinguished between the **affectionate and genital dimensions** of human sexuality. The former corresponds to the human need for intimacy; it precedes and goes beyond the genital aim which begins with puberty. Underlying both these dimensions is the primary fact that everything we engage in — whether it be work, play, conversation, prayer, etc. — we do

it as men or women. Many psychologists maintain that the differences between masculine and feminine are not the result of socially assigned roles and conditioning, but are actual archetypal, psychological dissimilarities.[9] This primary sexuality of man and woman affects the way they perceive, think and express themselves. Affective sexuality expresses a move toward intimacy, whether it be marital love, a close friendship, or just a warm recognition. Such sexuality means we want to get close to another, to "touch" another affectively. As Dr. William Kraft points out,

> Affective sexual behavior can be an end in itself or can be in service of and part of genital behavior. For instance, a warm smile or a respectful caress can be ends in themselves, or they can lead to or be part of a genital encounter. Thus, affective sexuality can stand on its own as a way of relating to another person, or it can be a prelude to genital activity. When affective and genital sexuality are seen as identical or when affective sexuality is seen as leading to genital sex, unnecessary confusion and guilt can emerge. Consequently, some individuals might repress, unnecessarily suppress, or abuse affective sexuality — a healthy mode of sexual encounter. Intention is the primary dynamic in determining whether affective sexuality is an end in itself or a means to genital behavior.[10]

Genital sexuality refers to behavior, thoughts, fantasies, desires and feelings that involve or encourage genital behavior. A further distinction can appropriately be made between *genital behavior* and *genitality*. The former includes such explicit sexual acts as intercourse and masturbation, whereas the latter pertains to genital thoughts and feelings, and even such signs as genital erection and lubrication, that can, but need not, be actualized in personal or interpersonal genital behavior. Psychological schools that accept a wholistic view of the human person, as opposed to a merely physical or functional view, maintain that genital sexuality in and of itself is an abstraction. As Kraft states,

> Genital sexuality is an articulation of a whole person. When we try to identify with genital sex, we treat ourselves as less than we really are because genitality is one important manifestation, not the totality, of being a man or a woman. When we misuse or abuse genital sexuality, we misuse or abuse ourselves. And when we celebrate and realize genitality in a healthy way, we celebrate and actualize ourselves.[11]

The very processes of genitality, furthermore, point toward transcendent goals and values. In genital relations between a man and a woman, the two people can go out to and receive each other in ways that go beyond them. Genital experience in this situation can also point to a third person. (The very words we use to designate the sexual organs, "genitalia" or "genitals," indicate that their specific function is "to beget" or to reproduce the species.) It is a transcendent mode of communication that goes beyond a mere pleasurable physical encounter. Genital love calls upon the couple to be responsible to each other not for the moment, but for a lifetime. This is why all forms of authentic love, except that experienced in marriage, exclude genital relations.[12]

Many psychologists hold that it is extremely important for us to realize that sexual desire is not simply the need for genital relations. Rollo May, for instance, states that "for human beings the more powerful need is not for sex, *per se*, but for relationships, intimacy, acceptance, and affirmation."[13] Abraham Maslow puts it this way: "Loving at a higher need level makes the lower needs and their frustrations and satisfactions less important, less central, more easily neglected. But it also makes them more wholeheartedly enjoyed when gratified."[14] Experience bears witness to the fact that genital relations do not guarantee the development of a sense of intimacy, and that indeed intimacy itself is possible without genital expression. "The key to keeping the physical or genital dimension of a relationship in proper perspective is to develop the affective dimension of sexuality. It is possible to live fully, healthfully and happily without genital sexuality. It is not possible to do so without developed affective relationships."[15]

A Theology of the Body and Sexuality

Our understanding of sexuality depends primarily upon the way we view ourselves as persons. It flows, in other words, from our anthropology. Dr. William F. Kraft proposes that there are four basic ways that human beings experience reality: physically, functionally, spiritually, and aesthetically.[16] The physical dimension is the most fundamental and immediate. When we experience a bodily need, such as hunger or thirst, we seek immediate relief and satisfaction. Freud, we recall, said that sexual desire was just such a physical "need." St. Paul, on the other hand, completely disagreed with this viewpoint, citing the then common adage, " 'Food for the stomach and the stomach for food,' " and adding "but God will do away with both the one and the other. The body, however, is not for immorality, but for the Lord, and the Lord is for the body" (1 Cor. 6:13). Thus, when we reduce sex solely to a physical need, other persons are treated merely as sex objects who can provide us with selfish satisfaction.

Functional sex is task-oriented and rationally controlled. The popular sex manuals that have appeared in recent years view human sexuality from this perspective. While information about and analysis of sexual activity may improve sexual technique, such objective control too readily impedes the spontaneous self-giving and receiving that are essential to love and transcendence. Furthermore, it can lead to exploitation and manipulation when those who have mastered the technique feel they can seduce others in the service of their own satisfaction. Both the physical and functional images of human sexuality are abstractions that dualistically separate the physical and spiritual dimensions of human existence.

Spiritual experience introduces us to the realm of mystery and transcendence. It manifests itself in compassion, wonder, contemplation and love. At the same time, however, this most enriching dimension of human existence can also be approached in a dualistic manner, as when it is employed to deny our sexual dimension. Over the centuries various influential teachers and movements within Christianity have promoted this latter approach separating spirituality and sexuality. The aesthetic dimension of sexuality, according to Kraft, brings into harmony the physical, the functional and the spiritual. Only the aesthetic dimension respects the total human person, promoting the integration of all the aspects of his or her personhood and, therefore, one's health and wholeness. Christian biblical revelation gives continuing witness to this "aesthetic dimension." A Catholic theology of the body and sexuality, therefore, must be anchored in a genuine Christian anthropology and an integral understanding of the natural law, which respects the relational order of creation as fully revealed in the "law of Christ."

The Anthropological Vision of Genesis. When some Pharisees asked Jesus, " 'Is it lawful for a man to divorce his wife for any cause whatever?' He said in reply, 'Have you not read that from the beginning the Creator "made them male and female" and said, "For this reason a man shall leave his father and mother and be joined to his wife, and the two shall become one flesh"'? So they are no longer two, but one flesh. Therefore, what God has joined together, no human being must separate" (Mt. 19:3-6). When the Pharisees pressed him further about Moses' allowing for a decree of divorce,

233

Jesus pointed out that " 'Because of the hardness of your hearts Moses allowed you to divorce your wives, but from the beginning it was not so' " (Mt. 19:8). Pope John Paul II in his "Catechesis on the Book of Genesis" directs our attention to the significance of the expression "*from the beginning*" which Jesus repeats twice. Here, Jesus "clearly induces his interlocutors to reflect on the way in which man was formed in the mystery of creation, precisely as 'male and female,' in order to understand correctly the normative sense of the words of Genesis."[17]

Our "hardness of heart," the result of original sin, has affected our ability to see and understand God's intention and plan for human sexuality. Jesus, therefore, tells us that we must return to that primordial vision and plan of God if we want to arrive at a true and proper understanding of sexual ethics and not approach it, like the Pharisees, from a purely juridical or casuistical perspective. John Paul II in his catechesis on Genesis points out that contemporary biblical criticism informs us of two accounts of creation in this book. The first account in chapter one is chronologically later than the second account found in chapter two. This latter and more ancient "Yahwist" narrative manifests "its primitive mythical character."[18] Through its employment of symbolic consciousness this narrative provides us with an integral anthropology corresponding to the fact that "man" has been created "in the image of God."

1. Genesis tells us of the **"original solitude" of the first human being.** John Paul II draws our attention in the Yahwist account to the fact that Adam was at first alone. Thus, God said: " 'It is not good for man to be alone. I will make a suitable partner for him' " (Gen. 2:18). This verse speaks of "the solitude of 'man' (male and female) and not just the solitude of man the male, caused by the lack of woman."[19] This solitude has a double significance. First, it refers to "man's" superiority and dominion over the rest of creation. He gave names to all the creatures walking about the earth, "but none proved to be a suitable partner for the man" (Gen. 2:20). He is searching for his identity and finds what he "is not." He discovers that he is substantially different from other living beings; although by means of his body he belongs to the visible world, yet he goes beyond it. The second meaning of this original solitude, therefore, lets us see that

Corporality and sexuality are not completely identified. Although the human body, in its normal constitution, bears within it the signs of

234

sex and is, by its nature, male or female, the fact, however, that man is a "body" belongs to the structure of the personal subject more deeply than the fact that he is in his somatic constitution also male or female.[20]

The significance of this original solitude, therefore, is substantially prior to the meaning of original unity, which is based on masculinity and femininity.

2. The Yahwist account of creation next relates to us **the original unity of man and woman.** "So the LORD God cast a deep sleep on the man, and while he was asleep, he took out one of his ribs and closed up its place with flesh. The LORD God then built up into a woman the rib he had taken from the man" (Gen. 2:21-22). In his "deep sleep" Adam, by that biblical archetype, discovers as the content of his dream a "second self."[21] He awakes to find that, "This one, at last, is bone of my bones and flesh of my flesh" (Gen. 2:23). That woman is made from the rib which God took from Adam indicates the homogeneity of the whole being of both. Upon awaking, the man's recognition of the woman as "bone of my bone" despite her sexual difference gives evidence to their unity as a "communion of persons."[22] Here, "man" in the moment of communion truly becomes the image of God, "an image of an inscrutable divine communion of Persons."[23]

John Paul II in his catechetical reflection arrives here at a fundamental principal of biblical anthropology, when he points out that the expression "flesh of my flesh" seems to be saying: here is *a body that expresses the person.*[24] The body alone, furthermore, "is capable of making visible what is invisible: the spiritual and the divine."[25] The Yahwist account thus concludes: "That is why a man leaves his father and mother and clings to his wife, and the two of them become one body" (Gen. 2:24). We discover here "the 'nuptial' meaning of the body in the very mystery of creation."[26] In this total self-surrender of one person to another the married couple becomes a physical manifestation of the image of God. This "total vision of man" which was given to us by the Creator "from the beginning" must therefore guide all questions pertaining to marriage and sexual ethics. Pope John Paul II concludes his reflections by stating that

We are, in fact, children of an age in which, owing to the development of various disciplines, this total vision of man may easily be rejected and replaced by multiple partial conceptions which, dwelling on one or other aspect of the *compositum humanum*, do not reach man's *integrum*, or leave it outside their own field of vision.[27]

In Service of the Kingdom of God. Throughout the New Testament human sexuality is always discussed within the perspective of the Kingdom of God. Sex is perceived as a basic human good, a great gift of God, but it is certainly not the highest or greatest good. It is neither to be fled from nor worshipped. Jesus demands that his disciples view marriage and sexuality within the context of the mystery of creation as God intended it to be "from the beginning." In the Sermon on the Mount he forbids divorce and remarriage and says some sharp words against adultery, even that committed by desire or "with lust" in the heart. God's kingdom of love, justice and peace that Jesus proclaims is a state of grace, of relationships that are reconciled; it allows no room for treating persons as objects for one's selfish satisfaction.

Furthermore, Jesus teaches that in the resurrection "they neither marry nor are given in marriage, but they are like the angels in heaven" (Mk. 12:25). In the fullness of life with God, in his kingdom, marriage and sexuality do not exist. Thus, while the first Adam revealed the spousal significance, or "nuptial meaning" of human sexuality, Jesus as the last Adam takes us into the future of God, bringing about integration and wholeness. For the early Church, "in places as diverse as Thessalonica, Galatia, and Corinth, the fundamental determinant of sexual attitudes and behavior always remained the Christian nature of those who had accepted the gospel and were bonded by the Spirit in the developing communities."[28] Sexual ethics was based upon a wholistic anthropology that understood the dynamic relationships and tensions which existed within the human person. The Christian believer had been set free in Christ, yet was, at one and the same time, both fallen and redeemed, and an embodied spirit called to live both in time and eternity. While we shall look more closely later at the New Testament's treatment of specific sexual issues such as marriage, divorce and extramarital sex, here and now we want to consider just those questions relating to a theology of the body and sexuality that Jesus' proclamation of the kingdom of God brought to light.

1. Jesus clearly demonstrated both in his teaching and behavior **the equal dignity of women.** The Scripture scholar Rudolf Schnackenburg writes: "He did not undertake to make changes in their legal status, which in the Old Testament and Judaism was far from being one of equality of rights, but his

actual behaviour bears witness to high esteem, serious evaluation of their religious aspirations, and delicate tact, rarely encountered in later Judaism."[29] Jesus readily overstepped the bounds of Jewish customs in associating with women and welcoming them as his friends and disciples. We only have to recall his conversation with the Samaritan woman at Jacob's well (Jn. 4:27); the women who accompanied him and the Twelve, Mary Magdalene, Joanna, and Susanna "who provided for them out of their resources" (Lk. 8:3). We witness, too, his close friendship with Lazarus and his sisters, Martha and Mary (Jn. 11:5). Mary Magdalene becomes the first to meet the Risen Lord and is sent as his messenger to proclaim the news of his ascent to the Father to his "brothers" (Jn. 20:11-18). Jesus did not differentiate in his preaching between men and women. Women were to hear the word of God and participate in the future coming of the kingdom of God on a level of complete equality with men.

While the early Christian community sought to integrate Jesus' example of behavior toward women with the social customs of the day, some awkward interpretations come to the fore. St. Paul interpreting the story of creation in 1 Cor. 11:3-10, for example, teaches that a husband is "the head of his wife" because "man did not come from woman, but woman from man." Therefore, the woman should cover her head when she prays or prophesies. Paul then relativizes his instruction by adding parenthetically that "Woman is not independent of man or man of woman in the Lord. For just as woman came from man, so man is born of woman; but all things are from God" (1 Cor. 11:11-12). These latter verses hint at the great vision he portrays in Gal. 3:28, where among the baptized "there is not male and female; for you are all one in Christ Jesus." In the long run, Jesus' attitude toward the religious equality of women had its impact upon the Church and society; he "saved women from being thought of as merely sexual beings, honouring them as human beings, persons, [and] children of God."[30]

The gospels record Jesus' friendship with women and his readily accepting them as his followers. The other New Testament writings tell of their outstanding contributions in spreading the gospel and of their prominent place in some of the local churches. Yet, we find that Jesus never called women to be apostles, nor did the apostles in their turn set them apart for the apostolic ministry and the preaching of the Word of God. The Second Vatican Council in its Decree on the Apostolate of Lay People observed that "Since in our days women are taking an increasingly active share in the whole life of society, it is very important that their participation in the various sectors of the Church's apostolate should likewise develop" (AA 9). In view of this changing role of women in society and of the practice common among many Protestant communities of admitting women to the pastoral office on a par with men, a number of Catholic theologians along with others in the Church today consider the Roman Catholic Church's longstanding tradition of not ordaining women to the priesthood to be a fundamental injustice.

The Magisterium's response, upholding the Catholic Church's constant tradition on this matter, was presented by the Sacred Congregation for the Doctrine of the Faith in its "Declaration on the Admission of Women to the Ministerial Priesthood" of October 15, 1976.[31] This document appeals to apostolic tradition and to the continuing practice by both the Roman and Eastern Churches in their fidelity to Christ's manner of acting. The Declaration's theological argument centers on the sacramental nature of the priesthood. In the celebration of the Eucharist the priest does not act in his own name but *"in persona Christi."*

> The Christian priesthood is therefore of a sacramental nature: the priest is a sign . . . that must be perceptible and which the faithful must recognize with ease. The whole sacramental economy is in fact based upon natural signs, or symbols imprinted upon human psychology. . . . The same natural resemblance is required for persons as for things: when Christ's role in the Eucharist is to be expressed sacramentally, there would not be this "natural resemblance" which must exist between Christ and his minister if the role of Christ were not to be taken by a man: in such a case it would be difficult to see in the minister the image of Christ. For Christ himself was and remains a man.[32]

Some have accused the Declaration of succumbing to mere physicalism in its argumentation. Is it mere coincidence, however, that the Roman Catholic and Eastern Orthodox Churches whose ancient roots are the most deeply anchored in symbolic consciousness and sacramentality are the ones that maintain the tradition of ordaining only men? Does not the charge of archaism lodged against these churches in this matter betray rather a loss of the meaning and place of symbol in our modern world with its idolization of historical consciousness and scientific empiricism?

Psychologists and sociologists in treating of masculine-feminine development point out that for both sexes one's earliest experiences of "mother" and "father" form basic images and impressions of the nature of interpersonal relationships. While our images of "mother" and "father" vary immeasurably according to individual experiences, still for both sexes "mother" is the primary caretaker with whom the child of either sex identifies with in the first three months of life. "Father," on the other hand, represents the outside world, the completely "other" who is "out there."[33]

From the perspective of symbolic consciousness (i.e., for those who accept a real, symbolic and not just physical differentiation between masculine and feminine), we can better understand why God is called "Father" and why Jesus Christ came as a male rather than a female. It is not a question of Christianity's origins in a patriarchical society which considered women inferior. Jesus clearly acted contrary to that society's expectations. The more plausible explanation seems to be found in our primal and universal human experience of interpersonal relationships and the symbolic images of "mother" and "father" that give expression to that experience. Man and woman are equals in dignity of person. Symbolically, the experience of "father" and masculinity portrays the total "Otherness" of God. The danger, of course, always remains that in acknowledging God's utter transcendence we deny immanence and intimate closeness. In its fallen state, however, the human race is more prone towards immanentism than it is towards acknowledging the Transcendent.

2. Jesus, in proposing the state of **celibacy** for "those to whom that is granted . . . for the sake of the kingdom of heaven" (Mt. 19:11-12), ran contrary to Jewish custom with its fundamental orientation toward fertility which was emphasized throughout the Old Testament. In his proclamation of the kingdom of God, Jesus introduced the possibility of reconciliation and intimate communion with the divine Source of life and love which brought about a new spiritual marriage and fruitfulness in love. In the words of John A. Sanford, "If Jesus was not married, it was not because he was averse to sexuality or to women, but because he was conscious of a unique mission he was to perform which precluded marriage, and also because he carried his marriage *on the inside*."[34] Jesus frequently employed the symbolism of weddings to teach about the kingdom of God (see Mt. 22:1-12, 25:10; Lk. 12:36; Jn. 2:1-11) and often referred to himself as the bridegroom (Mt. 9:15, 25:1; Mk. 2:19; Jn. 3:29).

Marriage is one of the most powerful archetypes and psychic symbols. When it appears in a person's dreams, a wedding signifies that an inner unification of opposites is beginning to take place. Jesus, the last Adam, who is both the exemplar and source of human wholeness, knew the union of masculine and feminine within himself. His marriage was the marriage from within. A person, therefore, who has "renounced marriage for the sake of the kingdom of heaven" (Mt. 19:12)

> ... has sacrificed the direct, physical expression of his sexuality in order to consummate a higher union of opposites within himself. While conscious of and accepting his sexual feelings, he does not allow their direct gratification. Nor is the great eros he may feel allowed consummation in a sexual relationship with the beloved, even though the feelings of eros are not repressed but are being made conscious. The result of containing the fire within oneself is an inner development, the generation of the inner marriage which is the equivalent of the kingdom of God.[35]

The wedding as the image of the kingdom of God prevailed in the early Church. St. Paul, when teaching about Christian marriage, compares a husband's love for his wife to Christ's love for his Church (Eph. 5:21-33). The Fathers of the Church often interpreted the Old Testament Song of Songs as a symbol of Christ's unity with the Christian soul.

Celibacy in the early Church was not directed against sexuality, but was primarily intended to prepare the soul for the mystery of union in Christ. "From this union would come the birth of Christ within the personality, bringing with it incorruptibility and freedom from evil, which is, psychologically speaking, totality."[36] This inner marriage, achieved in lieu of the outer marriage, finds expression in the writings of the great mystics, such as in *The Cloud of Unknowing* and in accounts of the mystical marriage of St. Catherine of Siena. Dr. Gerald May, M.D., in his work on comtemplative psychology has observed that "The powers of genital and spiritual union are so strong and their similarities so great that it is not surprising to discover how heavily the mystics rely upon marital and sexual metaphors to describe their experiences."[37]

Human sexuality enfleshes the divine call to love and relationship, to communion of life, to totality and wholeness. Paralleling the symbolism of marriage, the figure of the androgyne also incorporated this call to wholeness and completion. Berdyaev writes, "Androgynity is the ultimate union of male and female in a higher God-like being, the ultimate conquest of decadence and strife, the restoration in man of the image and likeness of God."[38] The brilliant and shining divine youth thus became the figure through which Christ was often reported by early Christians to appear in their dreams. The virgin-boy, a man-androgyne, embodies within himself both masculine and feminine aspects of the human personality and by his strength and connection to life carries the image of totality.[39] Celibacy strives towards such completion and wholeness through union "in Christ." In a very practical way the renunciation of marriage also allows one to be totally free for the service of Christ and his gospel in this life (see 1 Cor. 7:32-35). For most Christians, though, fidelity to the vocation of marriage leads to the full fruitfulness of love and to oneness in the Lord.

Christian Marriage

Marriage between a Christian man and woman is meant to be sign or sacrament of Christ's love for his Church. The Second Vatican Council thus reaffirmed that "The Christian family springs from marriage, which is an image and a sharing in the partnership of love between Christ and the Church; it will show forth to all men Christ's living presence in the world and the authentic nature of the Church by the love and generous fruitfulness of the spouses, by their unity and fidelity, and by the loving way in which all members of the family cooperate with each other" (GS 48). This intimate partnership of life and love, the Catholic Church firmly believes, is of divine institution, and it is endowed by the Creator with its own proper laws. In this section, we shall limit ourselves to a consideration of the "unity and fidelity" of Christian marriage and the "generous fruitfulness of the spouses." The ethical issues involving these two essential aspects are the ones most often brought into question in today's secular and pluralistic society.

Unity and Fidelity. As we have already seen, Jesus shocked his contemporaries with his command against divorce and remarriage (Mt. 19:9-10). Yet, of all the ethical teachings in the New Testament, scriptural research today attests that this one comes closest to being directly attributable to Christ. Rudolf Schnackenburg writes that "What Jesus said is so unequivocal that it is possible to avoid its binding force only by interpreting his moral mission as a whole as not literally binding or by emptying it of force in some other way."[40] The unity and fidelity of marriage, Jesus instructs us, has its roots in the very mystery of creation and in the way God intended it to be "from the beginning" (Gen. 2:24; Mt. 19:5-6). Much ink has been used over the centuries in trying to explain the exception clauses found in Mt. 5:32 and 19:9. Without going into detail about all the difficulties

241

involved in their interpretation, Schnackenburg maintains that these additions found in Matthew "cannot nullify or relax Jesus' fundamental and universal prohibition of divorce."[41] Clearly, it was Jesus' intention to go beyond the law of Moses and to replace it with a new commandment from God. The Protestant and Orthodox conclusion that in Jesus' mind adultery was a true exception is, therefore, untenable.[42]

Vatican II, thus, reaffirms the constant tradition of the Roman Catholic Church when it states that "The intimate union of marriage, as a mutual giving of two persons, and the good of the children demand total fidelity from the spouses and require an unbreakable unity between them" (GS 48). This vision of marriage, rooted both in the mystery of creation and in Christ's covenant of love and fidelity with his Church, is today increasingly becoming countercultural. In an age of "no-fault" divorce the contemporary social philosopher, Allan Bloom, points out that "The possibility of separation is already the fact of separation, inasmuch as people today must plan to be whole and self-sufficient, and cannot risk interdependence. . . . The presence of choice already changes the character of relatedness."[43] The family, instead of teaching the existence of the only unbreakable bond, for better or for worse, between human beings, has in many instances become the school of conditional relationships.

Instead of experiencing the Christian story that love means staying in relationship, children are learning the contemporary secular story of conditional attachment and the primacy of self-concern over the common good. This cultural milieu is making it increasingly difficult for young couples at an immature level of Christian faith to make a genuine commitment to unity and fidelity in marriage. The Church's task is to bear witness to and proclaim evermore clearly the deep significance of our life "in Christ." Stanley Hauerwas therefore submits that "the 'prohibition' against divorce, and other negative 'absolutes,' can only be sustained and justified by showing how they are crucial as an aid to help us live more nearly faithful to the story that forms the Christian community."[44]

Generous Fruitfulness of the Spouses. The mutual love of husband and wife expressed in their physical union mirrors God's creative love through the gift of parenthood. Here again, Vatican II reaffirms the constant and traditional teaching of the Church when it states that "Marriage and married love are by nature ordered to the procreation and education of children. Indeed children are the supreme gift of marriage and greatly contribute to the

242

good of the parents themselves" (GS 50). While over the centuries the Church has given a certain primacy to the procreative end of marriage, the Second Vatican Council accorded both the unitive and the procreative aspects of marital sexuality equal status. It insisted, furthermore, upon the inseparable unity between these two ends of the conjugal act.

The Council Fathers, however, refused to say whether the love-making or the life-giving aspect of the act was the more important. They called upon married couples to regard it as their proper mission, for which they are responsible to God, to transmit life and to educate their children. Judgments in these matters must be ruled by conscience. Couples are not to simply follow their own fancy, for "When it is a question of harmonizing married love with the responsible transmission of life, it is not enough to take only the good intention and the evaluation of motives into account; the objective criteria must be used, criteria drawn from the nature of the human person and human action, criteria which respect the total meaning of mutual self-giving and human procreation in the context of true love" (GS 51).

1. When we look at the Church's attitude toward **contraception in historical perspective**, as far back as it can be traced, we find it to be negative. While the ancient Church recognized the need of limiting births for various reasons, it always rejected contraception and recommended abstinence. The Fathers of the Church, in responding to the new hedonism of the antinomian Gnostics, taught that sexual intercourse was permitted only for the sake of procreation and never solely for pleasure. St. Augustine even went further by conceding the general sinfulness of marital conduct since the Fall, unless it was entered into strictly for the purpose of conception without any subsequent consent to the carnal pleasure attending the act. In his time, the twilight years of the Roman empire, the sexual arena was "as much an emotional slaughter-house as it is in our possibly twilight years of the post-Christian West."[45]

In the Middle Ages the norm was concerned with whether or not one was yielding to sexual lust. Intercourse between spouses was only considered lawful if it was not determined by sexual pleasure. Since the sixteenth and seventeenth centuries, however, in opposition to the rigorism of the Fathers and the Jansenists, the attempt was made to overcome the strongly negative matrimonial ethics and to justify sexual intercourse when it was for the sake of married love. St. Alphonsus Liguori, for instance, taught that the conjugal act does not need an "excuse." As a genuine expression of marital love and faithfulness, it is in itself (*per se*) honorable (*bonus et honestus*). He even dares to say, "This is a matter of faith (*Hoc est de fide*)."[46] He, of course, forbids any arbitrary separation of the unitive and procreative dimensions of the conjugal act.

Pope Pius XI in 1930 published his encyclical *Casti Connubii*, occasioned by the Anglican bishops' approval in the Lambeth Conference held earlier that year of contraceptive means of birth control. Pius XI clearly condemned the use of contraceptives, but for the first time in centuries he brought to the forefront the primacy of honor due to that love (*amor* and *caritas*) which is specific to marriage, an interpersonal love that models Christ's love for his Church. He also allowed the use of periodic continence and justified the intention of avoiding conception where sufficient reason existed. In 1951, Pope Pius XII asserted that for adequate reasons married couples could be released from the duty of procreation "for long periods of time and even for the entire duration of the marriage."[47] Yet, even in such instances, Pius XII reaffirmed that marriage itself continues to have as its primary end the procreation and upbringing of new life. Contraceptive measures were again condemned. The Second Vatican Council, as we have already seen, discussed marriage and responsible parenthood in its "Pastoral Constitution on the Church in the Modern World" (GS 47-52). The Council Fathers stated that in the regulation of births Catholics "are forbidden to use methods disapproved of by the teaching authority of the Church in its interpretation of the divine law" (GS 51). By order of Pope Paul VI certain questions regarding birth control methods were left to the further investigation of the Papal Commission for the Study of Population, the Family, and Birth.

2. Pope Paul VI, on July 25, 1968, issued his encyclical on the regulation of births entitled **"Humanae Vitae."** He introduces it by describing the evolutionary changes that have taken place in our contemporary world and that pose new questions concerning the issue. He lists the expressed concerns of those who fear that the rapid increase in world population is outpacing available resources. He speaks of the new understanding of the dignity of woman and her place in society, and of the new scientific advances that allow us to rationally organize the forces of nature and to control every aspect of our lives including the regulation of births.[48] Paul VI then explains that the special papal commission established to study the question lacked complete agreement in its reports, and that certain of its recommendations were "at

variance with the moral doctrines on marriage constantly taught by the Magisterium of the Church" (HV 6).

After carefully studying the evidence sent to him, Paul VI begins his reply by first addressing the fundamental questions of Christian anthropology, the sacramentality of marriage, and the characteristics of married love. He sees a need today for the practice of "responsible parenthood," rightly understood, and he reaffirms Vatican II's positive vision of conjugal love. Within this context he points out that even when sexual activity between spouses is infertile for reasons beyond their will, it does indeed legitimately express and strengthen their marital union and love. Paul VI then states:

> The facts are, as experience shows, that new life is not the result of each and every act of sexual intercourse. God has wisely ordered the laws of nature and the incidence of fertility in such a way that successive births are already naturally spaced through the inherent operation of these laws. The Church, nevertheless, in urging men to the observance of the precepts of the natural law, which it interprets by its constant doctrine, teaches as absolutely required that *in any use whatever of marriage* there must be no impairment of its natural capacity to procreate human life (HV 11).

Paul VI proceeds to explain that this doctrine "is based on the inseparable connection, established by God, which man on his own initiative may not break, between the unitive significance and the procreative significance which are both inherent to the marriage act" (HV 12).

The encyclical clearly recognizes the responsibility of married couples to regulate the number and spacing of children. This is a primary moral decision they must make in good conscience after taking into consideration their own physical and psychological conditions and their external circumstances (see HV 16). The second moral question that then arises concerns the method to be employed. In keeping with the Church's total vision of the human person and its understanding of the natural law, Paul VI teaches that only natural family-planning methods, which "take advantage of the natural cycles immanent in the reproductive system," are morally justified. One couple thus could choose the right method but for the wrong, or selfish reasons. Another couple for appropriate reasons may select artificial contraception as the method of controlling births. Both of these choices would be morally objectionable.

3. The encyclical "Humanae Vitae" gives evidence of **a developing theology of Christian marriage** within the Catholic Church over the course of this century. Despite the accusations of many revisionist theologians that Paul VI resorts to a physicalist interpretation of the natural law, the encyclical actually builds upon the more personalistic and wholistic approach adopted by Vatican II. Whereas also, both Pius XI and Pius XII stated that procreation was the primary end of marriage and more important than the mutual support of the spouses, Paul VI followed the lead of Vatican II and abandoned any mention of primary and secondary ends. In "Humanae Vitae" both the unitive and procreative purposes are given equal status. He presents an integrated vision of married love. It is a gift from God who "is Love" and is, at one and the same time, human, total, faithful and exclusive, and creative of new life (HV 9).

By respecting the divinely established, inseparable connection between the unitive and procreative meanings of the marriage act, Paul VI maintained that the Church preserves and protects authentic human values. Artificial methods, on the other hand, seriously jeopardize important values. They can seriously hinder the mutual communication and cooperation between the spouses that the natural methods necessarily require. Paul VI thus sees artificial methods of contraception leading to certain negative consequences including conjugal infidelity, the general lowering of morality, the easy corruption of youth, and loss of respect for women (HV 17). In the decade following the encyclical's publication another important value, protected by its wholistic understanding of the natural law, came to the fore. On the tenth anniversary of "Humanae Vitae" the vice-president of the French Episcopal Conference, Archbishop Matagrin of Grenoble, pointed out that in a time of ecological awareness we ought to be sensitive to the concerns of Paul VI for "the quality of life, the biological rhythms not simply of the universe but of man himself." [49]

Challenges to the teaching of the encyclical and its theological vision were quick in coming from all sides. Living in the midst of a secular, pluralistic society with its heavy emphasis upon science and technology, empirical data, rational planning and subjective experience, many among the Catholic laity did not readily accept the moral reasoning of "Humanae Vitae." Catholic moral theologians who had shifted from the classical mentality of the manual tradition to historical consciousness, also, dissented from the encyclical's teaching. Theologizing from inductive experience, scientific evidence and a rationalistic interpretation of the natural law, the revisionist theologians dualistically separate the physical, biological processes of the human body from its personal and spiritual dimensions.[50] Since our physical processes are inherited from the subhuman world, so their reasoning goes, they can neither have nor command moral responsibility. They are subject solely to the physical, chemical and biological laws of nature, and not to the moral law. Thus one disaffected critic irreverently, yet picturesquely observed that "Sex is between persons and not between organs. It is embarassing to observe that Carl Rogers certainly perceives that and Paul VI apparently does not."[51] In a cultural atmosphere with its utilitarian attitudes and the easy availability of contraceptive technology along with ready access to abortion, it is no wonder today that available statistics show a wide gap between the Church's teaching and the actual practice of many Catholic couples. The public dissent of many Catholic theologians, capitalized upon by the secular press and the media, furthermore, has provided the "moral justification" for such practice.

In his theology of the body and human sexuality, which we looked at previously, Pope John Paul II develops more fully the basic approach taken by Vatican II and Paul VI. His vision of human sexuality is anchored in an integral Christian anthropology rooted in the fundamental belief that man and woman are created in the image and likeness of God. "For God, life and love are not separated and thus, for us, as images of God, life and love should not be separated, i.e., conjugal love and life should always be united."[52] As an embodied spirit, all a human being's free activity is an expression of one's personhood. The body expresses our personal vocation to love. When a husband and wife give themselves to one another in conjugal love, they give their persons and not merely their biological powers. In his apostolic exhortation on "The Christian Family in the Modern World," John Paul II states that "The total physical self-giving would be a lie if it were not the sign or fruit of a total personal self-giving, in which the whole person, including the temporal dimension is present."[53]

Against those who argue that natural family-planning methods separate the unitive and procreative functions of the marriage act, it must be pointed out that Paul VI already recognized this fact in "Humanae Vitae." There, he refers to the inseparable connection of the unitive "significance" and procreative "significance" of the act, and not to the biological functions or processes (see HV 12). He thus approaches the question from a symbolic understanding of the human person as an incarnate spirit, wherein the biological fecundity of human sexuality is a *personal* value, rather than a

247

mere material given. Contraceptive intervention has a different symbolic significance. It renders the act of marital union *anti*-procreative, and not merely *non*-procreative.[54] The sexual act should be the total physical surrender of spouses to one another in all their potentialities. Only in this way does it become a sign of the divine Trinitarian Love in which it is anchored. The denial of either significance, the unitive or procreative, constitutes a falsification of the act.

Extramarital Sexuality

Created in the image and likeness of God who is a tri-unity of loving relationships, the human person as an embodied spirit mirrors that image in the quality of his or her relationships. Our relational nature as a body-soul unity finds its practical expression through the gift of human sexuality which becomes progressively more incarnate through its primary, affective and genital dimensions. Because of the uniqueness of our personhood which subsumes our physical nature, human sexuality substantially differs from sex within the animal realm. Sexuality is not just a power a human person has, but is rather the incarnate mode of expression, as male or female, of who one is as a person. In 1975, the Sacred Congregation for the Doctrine of the Faith published a "Declaration on Certain Questions Concerning Sexual Ethics" (*"Persona Humana"*) which spoke to the ethical issues surrounding premarital sexual activity, homosexual relations, and autoeroticism or masturbation. The document appropriately prefaces its presentation by stating that sexuality is "one of the factors which give each individual's life the principal traits that distinguish it. In fact it is from sex that the human person receives the characteristics which, on the biological, psychological and spiritual levels, make that person a man or woman, and thereby largely condition his or her progress towards maturity and insertion into society."[55] In this section we shall consider these same three issues of sexual ethics from the perspective of this document and the theological vision we have developed thus far.

Premarital Sexual Activity. The Christian story or tradition discloses the spousal significance of the body, presented in the Book of Genesis as God's plan "from the beginning." Thus we read: "That is why a man leaves his father and mother and clings to his wife, and the two of them become one body" (Gen. 2:24). The total giving of a man and woman to each other is expressed through the genital act. Genital union is not just the momentary

248

sharing of mutual passion and pleasure. It points to transcendent goals and values that go beyond the persons involved, including the possibility of procreation. The genital act, as a personal expression of one's selfhood, requires a lifetime commitment. The Vatican Declaration thus confirms that "Experience teaches us that love must find its safeguard in the stability of marriage, if sexual intercourse is truly to respond to the requirements of its own finality and to those of human dignity" (PH 7).

The argument is frequently heard today that premarital sex is morally justifiable in cases where a couple are already engaged and truly committed to one another, or where the celebration of marriage is impeded by circumstances. Some moralists would argue that such intimate sharing is not premarital, but rather only pre-ceremonial. However firm the couple's intention may be, genital union alone cannot guarantee the fidelity such an act both expresses and requires. The transcendent nature of genital intimacy makes it a social reality, which demands the public commitment of the marriage covenant in order to protect the relationship from an individual's whims and caprices.

In a culture and society where the emphasis today is on the self and the self's needs, where young people fear commitment, where physical sex is a way of proving one's emotions and feelings towards another or is considered merely as an exciting form of recreation, the Church's teaching on the spousal significance of genital sexual behavior is easily pushed aside. Some psychologists, such as William F. Kraft, maintain that "Only a marital situation can offer the proper time and place for healthy genitality to emerge."[56] Robert N. Bellah, however, points to a basic "therapeutic attitude" that pervades the practitioners and clients of modern psychotherapy, and resonates much more broadly in the American middle class. "This therapeutic attitude," he contends, "begins with the self rather than with a set of external obligations . . . [which], whether they come from religion, parents, or social conventions, can only interfere with the capacity for love and relatedness."[57] In its pure form, it denies all forms of obligation and commitment in relationships. Only full, open, honest communication among self-actualized individuals is what matters for personal development and health. Thus "living together" and "open marriages" become the norm. Here, obviously, the contemporary secular story of individual independence and self-realization crashes head-on with the Christian story of a faithful and committed love, wherein dependence and independence are deeply related.

Homosexuality. A homosexual person may be described as someone whose fundamental sexual preference and desire is oriented toward genital intimacy with a member of the same sex. When the yearning is consistent and enduring over a long period of time it indicates the presence of a true homosexual orientation. "To have or have had some sexual desires or fantasies about the same sex or to have engaged in sexuality with the same sex," Kraft states, "does not necessarily mean, however, that a person is homosexual."[58] The Church's teaching maintains that while the homosexual orientation itself is not sinful, homogenital acts must always be judged as objective moral wrongs which are totally unacceptable. The current social and cultural milieu with its glorification of the individual's right and freedom to choose one's own lifestyle and create one's own values has produced a situation in which some homosexual persons today are publicly promoting "gay liberation" and "gay rights." They propose that homosexual behavior is just as good and moral as heterosexual expressions of love. To this end, they are exerting group pressure against government and the churches to change their laws and teachings, which, they claim, "discriminate" against their equal right to choose and live their own lifestyle.

1. The witness of **sacred Scripture and the Church's tradition** has been consistently negative towards homosexual behavior. A number of contemporary scripture scholars, nevertheless, have proposed that the biblical evidence against homosexuality is inconclusive or that its moral injunctions are culture-bound and no longer applicable to the current situation. While biblical exegesis may have legitimate problems with the exact meaning and context of a number of the antihomosexual references found in both the Old and New Testaments, the broader scriptural evidence adequately substantiates the traditional condemnation of homosexual activity.[59] Father Eugene LaVerdiere, for instance, notes that the modern distinction between a person's basic sexual orientation and sexual behavior itself was certainly unknown in New Testament times. St. Paul's warning, therefore, found in 1 Corinthians 5:19 cannot be taken as a condemnation of homosexuals, but from his writings we can conclude that "Paul does not consider homosexual behavior to be consistent with the nature of the Christian who has been freed by the gospel and whose life must unfold for the development of the community."[60]

The Vatican Congregation of the Doctrine of the Faith (CDF), in its October 1986 Letter to Bishops on "The Pastoral Care of Homosexual Persons," asserts that the Scriptures cannot be properly understood when they are interpreted in a way that contradicts the living tradition of the Church.[61] The Letter thus states that

> "The Church's doctrine regarding this issue is . . . based not on isolated phrases for facile theological argument, but on the solid foundation of a constant biblical testimony" (no. 5, par. 2). The "basic plan for understanding this entire discussion of homosexuality is the theology of creation we find in Genesis" (no. 6, par. 1). Specifically, this means that persons, "in the complementarity of the sexes, . . . are called to reflect the inner unity of the Creator" (ibid.). The human body thus has an intrinsic "spousal significance" which is not removed, however much it is obscured by original sin (ibid.).[62]

The Letter clearly anchors its treatment of homosexuality in the theology of the body and sexuality developed by Pope John Paul II. As we previously noted, his reflection upon Genesis points out that Adam the person, in his "original solitude," was created before the separation of the sexes. The Letter thus affirms that the Church today "refuses to consider the person as a 'heterosexual' or a 'homosexual' and insists that every person has a fundamental identity: the creature of God and, by grace, his child and heir to eternal life" (no. 16). It deplores all those instances wherein the homosexual person is made the object of violent malice in speech or in action.

The CDF's Letter reaffirms the fundamental moral doctrine of the Church which holds that the use of the sexual faculty can be morally good only within marriage. "To choose someone of the same sex for one's sexual activity is to annul the rich symbolism and meaning, not to mention the goals of the Creator's design" (no. 7). Interesting to note is the Letter's emphasis on Scripture and the symbolic meaning of sexuality, whereas the same Congregation's Declaration of 1975 depends more upon its interpretation of the natural law and the procreative end of the sexual act when it discusses homosexual relations. That Declaration stated that "homosexual acts are intrinsically disordered" (PH 8). The Letter goes even further by saying that "the inclination itself must be seen as an objective disorder" (no. 3), for although this particular inclination "is not a sin, it is a more or less strong tendency ordered toward an intrinsic moral evil" (ibid.).

Both documents affirm, however, that "culpability for homosexual acts should only be judged with prudence" (PH 8; Letter no.3). Operating from a true Christian anthropology, a total vision of the human person, which recognizes the redeemed, spiritual, eternal, social and radically free aspects constituting one's nature, the Letter calls upon us to avoid at all costs "the unfounded and demeaning assumption that the sexual behavior of homosexual persons is always and totally compulsive and therefore inculpable." Yet it again warns against making "generalizations in judging individual cases" (no. 11).

2. There are no conclusive theories about **the causes of homosexuality.** Psychology itself differs in its assessment of this condition. Very little is known about how a homosexual orientation develops in a given individual. Earlier theories attributing it to hereditary factors or a hormonal imbalance have recently lost credibility. Some researchers think that in a critical period of childhood a preferred sexual object or person may become firmly entrenched within the brain. More acceptable theories hold that homosexuality is a learned preference or the result of certain conditions that occurred in the course of a person's psychosocial development.[63]

Taking a Jungian approach, John Sanford suggests that a homosexual orientation can often be traced back to the developmental process wherein a boy experiences too little love from the mother, or the wrong kind of possessive or overwhelming love. Equally important, too, can be the missing love of the father, for there are times when a boy craves love from his father, including physical signs of affection. When masculine identification with the father is lacking or when the mother's animus cuts him off from his budding masculinity, "the young man's unfulfilled needs for primitive masculine development, and for the masculine affection he missed from his father, may be reflected in sexualized yearnings for closeness with other males."[64] Women, on the other hand, are shunned because he fears their sexual power and the emotionality of their animus.

A person's sexual yearnings and fantasies are indications of those aspects of the self one needs to develop in order to become whole. These needed qualities tend to get projected onto persons who mirror their images back to us. There are, thus, many expressions of male sexuality called homosexual that actually differ markedly. A yearning for contact with the male organ, for example, "represents symbolically a deep need for connection with the Self, represented by the phallus, symbol of the creative masculine spirit"[65] A middle-aged or older man may "fall in love" with a younger man bearing the image of a young Adonis, who embodies in himself both masculine and feminine virtues. The actual young man himself is not this complete person, but simply the carrier of the projection of the androgynous soul of the older man. Sanford maintains that oftentimes,

> Such emotions are not homosexuality but homoeroticism and occur in many men who are sexually well oriented. Repression of these feelings leads to repression of much that is valuable and desirable in a man. Acting them out, on the other hand, leads to guilt and unconsciousness and a negative enslavement to sexuality. It is possible, however, for a man to recognize that his feeling for another man is his longing for the Androgyne, a reflection of the deep desire to realize the union of opposites within himself, and to feel the reality of the greatest of archetypes as the foundation of his own being.[66]

Indeed, it could very well be the attraction of this Androgyne archetype that explains the much higher statistical occurrence of homosexuality in men, as compared to the lower rate in women. For women the Androgyne figure presents no problem, but in our modern society with its exaggerated cultural fear of homosexuality any erotic feelings aroused in a man for another man is considered suspect.

The CDF Declaration on Sexual Ethics distinguishes between homosexual tendencies that are "transitory or at least not incurable" and "some kind of innate instinct or a pathological constitution judged to be incurable" (PH 8). Most schools of psychology defend such a distinction. Transitory instances of homosexual behavior can be found to occur in closed environments devoid of heterosexual contact. Sometimes it also erupts in adolescence when there exsists confusion in one's affective development toward relationships with both sexes. The tenet, however, that an enduring innate instinct toward homosexuality is incurable is today being challenged in some professional circles. Ruth T. Barnhouse, in a recent work entitled *Homosexuality: A Symbolical Confusion*, claims that "thirty percent of male homosexuals who come to psychotherapy for any *reason* (not just for help with their sexual preference) can be converted to the heterosexual adaptation."[67] The author adds that the statistic just given is "well known and not difficult to verify," and suggests that homosexual persons denying that their orientation is reversible are resisting an awareness that would threaten their complacent acceptance of a gay identity.[68]

Masturbation. Psychology and sociology today show that masturbatory activity is a "normal" phenomenon, especially among the young. The CDF

Declaration of 1975 reaffirms that both the Magisterium, in the course of constant tradition, and the moral sense of the faithful have held the position that "masturbation is an intrinsically and seriously disordered act" (PH 9). The reason given for this stance is that "the deliberate use of the sexual faculty outside normal conjugal relations essentially contradicts the finality of the faculty" (ibid.). Whatever the motive, solitary sex in itself contradicts the fundamental meaning of human sexuality which is relational.

William F. Kraft holds that masturbation is a form of self-intimacy that actually impedes relational intimacy with another. It is genital pleasure without risk or responsibility. "Masturbation lends itself to fantasy where we do not have to experience anxieties such as being frightened, rejected, or impotent, but can have the illusion of being the perfect lover. In fantasy, there are no limits and the other always says yes."[69] The impulse towards masturbatory activity can also signify that the self is yearning for attention, that a person is living a too heady, a too disembodied, or overly compulsive existence. Often masturbation is engaged in just to relieve tension and to get in touch again with one's natural physical dimension.

The Vatican Declaration admits that psychology provides us with much valid and useful information that can help in judging moral responsibility and giving a pastoral response. Thus, while objectively masturbation is always intrinsically disordered, on the subjective level because of "the immaturity of adolescence (which can sometimes persist after that age), psychological imbalance or habit . . . there may not always be serious fault. But in general, the absence of serious responsibility must not be presumed; this would be to misunderstand people's moral capacity" (PH 9).

Chastity

The genuine integration of our sexual powers into the totality of who we are, into the totality of our personhood, is accomplished through the cultivation of the virtue of chastity. It is not just a vow for the consecrated religious. Chastity is a value that is essential to the personal developmental process of every human being, whether living in the single, married or religious state. It safeguards the integrity of our relational nature as persons created in the image and likeness of God. Since the advent of sin, the human body's ability to express the person has been diminished, the gift of integration has been lost. "After sin the other (usually of the opposite sex) is often looked upon not for his/her own sake, but for selfish reasons: what can he/she do for me? How can he/she satisfy my selfish desires and inclinations?"[70] Original sin attacked human nature at its most central core, in our personhood, i.e., in our ability to give of ourselves in love as an expression of the Triune God in whose image we were created.

The development of chastity as a Christian virtue depends upon the degree we subscribe to the Christian vision of the human person. This vision which holds that we are called to wholeness by keeping in their proper balance or relationship the diverse dimensions which constitute our personal existence — fallen/redeemed, body/soul, temporal/eternal, individual/social, determined/radically-free — clashes with the purely historical and empirical experience of our broken, physical, temporal, individual and predetermined existence as human beings. If sex is considered to be a mere physical appetite and the body is just a complex biological machine that a person functionally employs for one's own purposes, the virtue of chastity is looked upon as a medieval concept, a left-over attempt at archaic repression. Thus the Playboy philosophy, which considers sexual activity to be something as enjoyable and entertaining as a gourmet meal, believes that all sexual expressions between consenting adults are both healthy and morally good. Furthermore, such activity is viewed as a basic individual human right. Our popular cultural acceptance of this philosophy or "story" is clearly in evidence today, as "[s]ociety appears less and less interested in stable marriages and more tolerant of any form of sexual expression. Only rape and child molestation are matters of social concern, and, then, only as protection of individual rights."[71]

The New Testament. The witness of the gospels and other New Testaments writings place human sexuality within the context of the kingdom of God and the Creator's plan "from the beginning." Thus, in Mark's gospel Jesus' response to the Pharisees' question about divorce (Mk. 10:2-12) is situated in a long unit on discipleship as the way of Jesus' cross (Mk. 8:27 - 10:52). From this perspective then,

> Husband and wife are one (10:8) as they follow in Jesus' steps (8:34), not seeking their own importance but as servants of all (9:35). The demands of the cross thus transcend the ethic of Moses, who allowed divorce (vv. 3-5). To accept this teaching without fear, however, those who accept Jesus' call must want to see and have their blindness removed by Christ (10:46-52).[72]

Sexuality in the New Testament is presented in the light of Christ and his paschal mystery, which truly reveals the coming of God's kingdom among us. Jesus' central commandment that we love one another as he has loved us, furthermore, "does not place a major emphasis on sexual fulfillment and sexual happiness as essential components of discipleship, and certainly does not see sexual expression as essential to the love it commands."[73] Likewise for St. Paul, as we saw when we looked at celibacy, sex is not the most important thing in human existence and is not to be turned into an idol. The fundamental determinant of Pauline sexual ethics always remained the Christian nature of those who accepted the gospel.

A Universal Christian Call. Chastity as a Christian virtue is an integral part of our universal call to holiness, which we received through faith and baptism (see LG 39-40). "In Christ," we have been redeemed, healed, restored: we have been created anew. Our physical nature with its sexuality has been reintegrated into the spiritual, eternal, communal and radically-free dimensions of our life in Christ. Only within the context of this Christian story, this Christian vision, do the radical demands of the gospel in sexual matters make any sense. Christ himself is the *only* evangelical counsel. He is the norm of our lives, of whom we are called to become. For the Christian, our personal experience of him in the power of the Spirit, and not the empirical experience of our fallen human nature, is the foundation of all our behavior.

William Kraft tells us that "Chastity does not mean to be sexless, but to experience integrated and pure loving sex."[74] It promotes and nourishes healthy sexuality, for it relates to the other as a whole person. Repression of sexuality, on the other hand is unchaste.

> Simply because we do not behave sexually or indulge in genital relations does not mean we are chaste. To minimize ourselves as men or women, rigidly to control affective sexuality, and to repress genital sexuality are modes of unchaste behavior. Some frigid, rigid, and sexless people may be the greatest offenders against chastity.[75]

Chastity, thus, means employing all the dimensions of our sexuality — primary, affective and genital — to promote the development of loving relationships with other persons in an unexploitive and non-manipulative way. It is, therefore, also opposed to lust.

Lust seeks the selfish fulfillment of one's need for pleasure through the release of tension. In lust, my needs and desires are all-important with little or no thought being given to the needs, interests and desires of the other.

When we allow the gospel story of Christ's paschal mystery to form our hearts and consciences, we can learn the practice of mortification and self-discipline. Mortification, which literally means "to make dead," is healthy when it is in the service of life. Appropriating Christ's paschal mystery in our own lives means dying to our sinfulness and selfishness. When we mortify or suppress genitality, we first freely affirm genital feelings and decide not to encourage or act on them. It is different than repression or denial. "Instead of withdrawing from ourself and the other, we reject or 'kill' gratification but still remain present, along with the sexual feelings, to and for the other. Thus, we remain sexual, but freely refuse to engage in genital behavior."[76] Such mortification or self-control can be painful, yet we know it is a fruit of the Spirit given us "in Christ" (Gal. 5:23). Indeed, self-discipline is the basis of true Christian freedom.

Chastity is truly a universal vocation, as our contemporary situation itself seems to indicate. William C. Spohn, S.J. recently observed,

> AIDS reminds us of this much at least: evolution has not equipped the human species for multiple, indiscriminate sexual partnering. The human immune system has no efficient defense against the assaults of promiscuity, whether in heterosexual relations (witness the high rate of cervical cancer among female prostitutes) or homosexual ones.[77]

All persons, whatever their vocation or state in life, are called to the practice of chastity. Sexuality is the incarnational means by which human beings can relate to one another as persons. Through our sexuality we express our capacity to share God-like love. The virtue of chastity preserves the truth of this love. For vowed celibates, and single persons (including those with a homosexual orientation), chastity means the right cultivation and use of the primary and affective dimensions of sexuality along with the suppression of all genital behavior. For married couples, chastity means preserving the integrity of the genital expression of their love, as well as its exclusivity; it also means giving proper expression to the primary and affective dimensions of their sexuality. Spouses can violate chastity, not only by adultery, but also by that lust which reduces their partner to a mere sexual object. Unchaste, too, is all manipulation and exploitation of one's spouse, even outside the context of the conjugal act.

The cultivation of chastity, like all other virtues, involves a growth process. In his apostolic exhortation on "The Christian Family in the Modern

World," Pope John Paul II reminds us that we know, love and accomplish moral good by stages. The social context and other individual difficulties, such as understanding the inherent values of the moral norm, can make fulfilling the norm a real struggle. He speaks thus of "the law of gradualness" or the step-by-step advance in overcoming difficulties with constancy. This, however, he adds is not to be confused with the erroneous concept of "the 'gradualness of the law,' as if there were different degrees or forms of precept in God's law for different individuals and situations."[78]

The CDF Declaration of 1975, furthermore, recommended prudence in judging the subjective seriousness of a particular sinful act because, "It is true that in sins of the sexual order, in view of their kind and their causes, it more easily happens that free consent is not fully given" (PH 10). At the same time, it warns against holding the view that in the sexual field mortal sins are not committed. The Catholic moralist, James P. Hanigan thus concludes:

> There is no parvity of matter in sexual things in the sense that what we do sexually is not a minor matter. It matters a great deal, for the kinds of persons we are, for the kinds of relationships we establish, for the kinds of values which support and guide the social order, and most of all for our ability to love God and neighbor without conditions.[79]

The virtue of chastity brings about the genuine integration of sexuality into the person we are called to be in Christ. In our present sex-saturated culture with its self-indulgent attitudes and its glorification of subjective feeling, commitment to chastity requires we utilize all the means possible which the Church and gospel provide to help us grow "in Christ," including the sacraments, prayer, spiritual discernment, and the mutual support and encouragement which the community of faith can give. In the contemporary secular marketplace of divergent values, lifestyles, and stories about life's purpose and meaning, our hearts and consciences need to be continually converted and transformed by the Christian story, by the Good News of Jesus Christ.

Notes

1. John Paul II, *Original Unity of Man and Woman: Catechesis on the Book of Genesis*, addresses given to general audiences from September 5, 1979 through April 2, 1980 (Boston: St. Paul Editions, 1981), p. 74.

2. *The Philosophy of Plato*, The Jowett translation, ed. Irwin Edman, *Symposium* (New York: The Modern Library, 1928), p. 356 as related and cited by John A. Sanford, *The Invisible Partners* (New York/Ramsey, N.J.: Paulist Press, 1980), pp. 4-5.

3. Sanford, *The Invisible Partners*, p. 4.

4. Hyemeyohsts Storm, *Seven Arrows* (New York: Harper and Row, 1962), p. 14 cited in ibid., p. 3.

5. Nicholas Berdyaev, *The Destiny of Man* (New York: Harper Torchbooks, 1960), pp. 61-62.

6. *C. G. Jung Speaking*, ed. Wm. McGuire and R. F. C. Hull; (Princeton, N.J.: Princeton University Press, 1977), p. 296.

7. Sanford, *Invisible Partners*, p. 89.

8. See William F. Kraft, *Sexual Dimensions of the Celibate Life* (Kansas City, Kan.: Andrews and McMeel, Inc., 1979), p. 89.

9. Sanford, *Invisible Partners*, p. 7.

10. Kraft, op. cit., p. 96.

11. Ibid., p. 52.

12. Ibid., p. 63.

13. Rollo May, *Love and Will* (New York: W.W. Norton and Co., 1969), p. 311.

14. Abraham Maslow, *Motivation and Personality: Religion, Values, and Peak Experiences* (New York: Harper & Row, 1970), pp. 177-178.

15. Vincent J. Genovesi, S.J., *In Pursuit of Love: Catholic Morality and Human Sexuality* (Wilmington, Del.: Michael Glazier, Inc., 1987), p. 144, where you will also find the quotations cited in note nos. 13 and 14 above.

16. Kraft, op. cit., p. 26.

17. John Paul II, *Original Unity of Man and Woman*, p. 18.

18. Ibid., p. 28. See note no. 1 (pp. 32-33) where John Paul II analyzes the real symbolic significance of myth as interpreted by twentieth-century philosophy and science.

19. Ibid., p. 44.

20. Ibid., p. 62.

21. Ibid., pp. 64-65.

22. Ibid., p. 71, where John Paul II makes reference to Vatican II, GS 12.

23. Ibid., p. 74.

24. Ibid., p. 109 (emphasis in the original).

25. Ibid., p. 144.

26. Ibid., p. 110.

27. Ibid., pp. 173-174.

28. Eugene A. LaVerdiere, S.S.S., "The Witness of the New Testament," *Dimensions of Human Sexuality*, ed. Dennis Doherty (Garden City, New York: Doubleday & Company, Inc., 1979), p. 30.

29. Schnackenburg, *The Moral Teaching of the New Testament*, p. 133.

30. Ibid., p. 135.

31. See Austin Flannery, O.P., general ed., *Vatican Council II: More Post Conciliar Documents*, vol. 2 (Northport, New York: Costello Publishing Co., 1982), no. 97, pp. 331-345.

32. Ibid., p. 339.

33. See, for instance, Jeanine Kelsey, "Masculine-Feminine Development: A Value-Based Perspective," *The Genesis Effect*, pp. 297-298.

34. Sanford, *The Kingdom Within*, p. 166 with emphasis in the original.

35. Ibid., 170.

36. Ibid., p. 196. Paul VI presents this same vision in *Sacerdotalis caelibatus,* his encyclical letter on priestly celibacy of June 24, 1967, where he writes: "The true, deep reason for dedicated celibacy is . . . the choice of a closer and more complete relationship with the mystery of Christ and of the Church for the good of mankind: in this choice there is no doubt that those highest human values are able to find their fullest expression. The choice of celibacy does not connote ignorance or the despisal of the sexual instinct and affectivity. That would certainly do damage to the physical and psychological balance" (nos. 54-55). [Cited from *Vatican Council II: More Post Conciliar Documents*, vol. 2, p. 300.]

37. Gerald G. May, M.D., *Will & Spirit: A Contemplative Psychology* (San Francisco: Harper & Row Publishers, 1983), p. 149.

38. Nicholas Berdyaev, *The Meaning of the Creative Act*, p. 65 as cited in Sanford, *The Kingdom Within*, p. 209.

39. Sanford, *The Kingdom Within*, p. 213.

40. Schnackenburg, op. cit., p. 136.

41. Ibid., p. 137.

42. Ibid., p. 138. See pp. 138-141 where the author summarizes some of the more influential attempts at finding a solution.

43. Bloom, *The Closing of the American Mind*, p. 117.

44. Stanley Hauerwas, "The Demands of a Truthful Story: Ethics and the Pastoral Task," *Chicago Studies* 21, no. 1 (Spring 1982): p. 69.

45. Theodore Mackin, S.J., *What Is Marriage?* (New York/Ramsey, N.J.: Paulist Press, 1982), p. 131.

46. Alphonsus de Liguori, *Theol. mor.*, lib. VI, tr. VI, cap. II, n. 900 as cited by Häring, *Free and Faithful in Christ*, vol. 2, p. 521.

47. Pius XII, "Address delivered to the Union of Italian Catholic Obstetricians," Address of October 29, 1951, *Acta Apostolicae Sedis* 43 (1951), pp. 835-54.

48. Paul VI, "Humanae Vitae," no. 2 in *Vatican Council II: More Post Conciliar Documents*, vol. 2, pp. 397-416.

49. "After *Humanae Vitae*," *Tablet* 232 (1978): p. 852. See also Juli Loesch, a lay Catholic activist and founder of Prolifers for Survival, in *Commonweal* cxii (18 October 1985), 574: "Pope Paul VI asserted (actually re-asserted) that the human design is not arbitrary, but providential. In particular, our sexual design (with its pleasurability and its fertility and its bond-ability) is not sick. We don't need to be 'cured' of it. Our sexual powers are O.K. They don't need to be 'fixed.' "

50. See Hanigan, *What Are They Saying About Sexual Morality?* (New York/Ramsey, N.J.: Paulist Press, 1982), p. 52.

51. Andrew M. Greeley, *The New Agenda* (Garden City, New York: Doubleday & Co., 1973), pp. 142-143.

52. Hogan and LeVoir, op. cit., p. 55.

53. John Paul II, *Familiaris Consortio* (November 22, 1981), no. 11 in *Vatican Council II: More Post Conciliar Documents*, vol. 2, no. 122, p. 822.

54. William E. May, "An Integrist Understanding," *Dimensions of Human Sexuality*, p. 103.

55. Sacred Congregation for the Doctrine of the Faith, *Declaration on Certain Questions Concerning Sexual Ethics*, December 29, 1975 (USCC Publications Office: Washington, D.C., 1977), no. 1, p. 3.

56. Kraft, op. cit., p. 53.

57. Bellah, *Habits of the Heart*, p. 98.

58. Kraft, op. cit., p. 153.

59. See Bruce Williams, O.P., "Homosexuality: The New Vatican Statement," *Theological Studies* 48 (June 1987): 261.

60. LaVerdiere, op. cit., pp. 28-29.

61. See *Origins* 16:22 (November 13, 1986), no. 5, p. 379.

62. Williams, op. cit., p. 260.

63. Kraft, op. cit., pp. 153-154.

64. Sanford, *Invisible Partners*, 99.

65. Ibid., p. 96.

66. Sanford, *The Kingdom Within*, p. 214.

67. Ruth T. Barnhouse, *Homosexuality: A Symbolical Confusion* (New York: Seabury, 1977), p. 95; emphasis in the original.

68. Ibid., p. 109 as cited by Williams, op. cit., p. 275, fn. 32.

69. Kraft, op. cit., p. 146.

70. Hogan and LeVoir, op. cit., p.45.

71. Hanigan, op. cit., p. 112.

72. LaVerdiere, op. cit., p. 31-32.

73. James P. Hanigan, *Homosexuality: The Test Case for Christian Sexual Ethics* (New York/Mahwah: Paulist Press, 1988), p. 104.

74. Kraft, op. cit., p. 113.

75. Ibid., p. 130.

76. Ibid., p. 79.

77. William C. Spohn, S.J. "Notes on Moral Theology: The Moral Dimensions of AIDS," *Theological Studies* 49, no. 1 (March 1988): 108.

78. "Familiaris Consortio," no. 34.

79. Hanigan, Homosexuality, p. 150.

Chapter 10

Bioethics

Unless prevention, cure, and care are experienced as extensions of genuine human caring and love, they are less than they could be. They do not touch the whole person; rather, they minister to a body. They may heal a body, but we long for and need a deeper healing from each other as the body is healed, or even at times if it is to be healed. That is one good reason why persons of deep faith and religious consecration should be in health care, for in our time, it is far too easy for health care to be reduced to bodily care, in a very impersonal way. — Richard A. McCormick, S.J.[1]

The term "bioethics" refers to the application of general moral principles and rules to ethical issues pertaining to human life, health care, therapeutic practice in medicine and psychology, and to medical and biological research. As a special field of applied ethics, it actually has a much wider scope than simply being concerned with the moral decisions that surround procedures touching the health and life of individual patients. Medical ethics, in the classical sense, tended in the past to limit itself through the use of casuistry to a consideration of the moral appropriateness of particular medical interventions and procedures. Such an individualistic and act-centered approach fostered a dominant mind-set whose primary concern became the proper application of rules and norms to particular cases. This limited focus can all too easily slip into mere moralism or legalism. Norms and rules are utterly essential, but their significance must also be properly grasped and understood. We must not forget that their sole purpose is to protect critical human values that point to a holistic vision of life and its ultimate meaning.

Within the Christian tradition, therefore, bioethics, like sexual ethics, depends upon Christian anthropology, upon the gospel vision of who we are. The belief that we have been created in the image and likeness of God, who is Love or a Trinity of relationships, means that we too are primarily social beings called through the divine gift of radical freedom to share a communion of life and love with God and one another. The gospel, furthermore, reveals that we are a body-soul unity redeemed "in Christ" and called to live both in time and eternity. As such, our "wholeness" or "health" (both terms are etymological cognates) depends upon the balanced interrelationships of all these dimensions. Because we are a psychosomatic unity, for example, a deep anxiety of the soul can exact its toll upon our physical well-being. Likewise, a physical malady can weigh heavy upon our spirit.

In this chapter we dare not hope to address all of the complex issues faced by contemporary bioethics. We shall endeavor rather to discuss some of the fundamental elements, values and principles that must be taken into consideration when dealing with the various ethical issues that continually arise in the health care field in general, as well as in its many areas of specialization. We shall start by first taking a look at the Christian meaning of human life, health, suffering and death. From this perspective, then, we shall briefly reflect upon some of the critical contemporary health care issues that span the gamut from conception to the moment of death.

Of What Value — Human Life?

Life is more than the physiological processes found to occur in organic matter. Life directs the biochemical functions and communicates to them their particular development toward a definite end. Our heavily technological and utilitarian age, nevertheless, tends to look upon human life and health in functional terms. Today's secular humanist respects the deep primordial experience of being alive, fears the extinction of life, and stands in awe before it. The sanctity of life is an accepted fundamental value. The degrees of sacredness, however, vary according to the individual's capacity to exist independently. The life of a moribund patient is thus more sacred and inviolable than the life of a fetus, although we are increasingly seeing the promotion of direct euthanasia as a socially viable and suitable means of terminating the lives of those whose suffering and physical debilities no longer make their lives useful or worth living. This individualistic and functional view of life's meaning arises out of a secular culture and society that no longer believes in a divine Creator, a spiritual immortal soul, redemption or a unique divine origin and destiny for the human race. A much different vision of life's meaning and value is handed down to us through our Christian tradition.

The Witness of Sacred Scripture. The Old Testament stresses the important value of physical human life. It is the basic good without which no other good is possible. The fullness of life is found in the vigor and power of the body and its functions, its capacity for pleasure. A long life is a priceless blessing. The concept of a human being as an embodied spirit was completely foreign to the ancient Israelites. They knew only an animated body. Belief in resurrection is rarely found in the books of the Old Testament. Rather, one continued to live through one's progeny. Being childless, therefore, was considered the greatest curse.

Life, however, was not merely a physical or biological reality. It had a primary ethical and religious function. Indeed, health and vigor were believed to ultimately rest upon the integration of the human will with the divine will. Deuteronomy constantly points to the fact that life is given and maintained by the love of Yahweh and fidelity to his commandments (Dt. 4:1; 6:24; 16:20; 30:6). Thus, we read that, "not by bread alone does man live, but by every word that comes forth from the mouth of the LORD" (Dt. 8:3). The same idea appears also in the prophets. One may live by listening to the word of the Lord (Is. 55:3), by keeping his commandments (Ezk. 20:11, 13, 21). In the Wisdom literature life is the fullness of well-being; whoever pursues wisdom and righteousness will find life, honor, success, health and good fortune.

In the New Testament, Jesus reveals that the fullness of life is found in the gift of eternal life. Christ himself goes beyond the veil of physical death and makes known to the eyes of faith the eternal and spiritual dimensions that sustain all of creation in its temporal and physical dimensions. Physical death is but a passage into a new and fuller dimension of life. Human beings are more than animated bodies. They are incarnate spirits who are meant to live forever. Thus Jesus proclaims, "Amen, amen, I say to you, unless you eat the flesh of the Son of Man and drink his blood, you do not have life within you. Whoever eats my flesh and drinks my blood has eternal life, and I will raise him on the last day" (Jn. 6:53-54). Through Christ and in the Spirit we come to share a newness of life by our incorporation into Jesus' paschal mystery.

St. Paul points out that eternal life is not merely the life of the world to come. It is new life (Rom. 6:4) which we share in even now through baptism. It is death of the life according to the flesh (Rom. 8:12); it is a conferring of the life of the risen Christ (Rom. 8:11). Indeed, God bestows eternal life on "those who seek glory, honor, and immortality through perseverance in good works" (Rom. 2:7). Eternal life is "true life" (1 Tim. 6:19). Within the context of the paschal mystery, furthermore, human suffering takes on new meaning. Without belief in the resurrection the Old Testament book of Job wrestles with the question of the unmerited suffering of the innocent and its corollary, the prosperity of the wicked. The conclusion of Job is that such suffering has no rational explanation; we must live with evil and accept God as he is. Jesus reveals, however, the Son of Man was destined to suffer grievously (Mk. 8:31) so as to enter into his glory (Lk. 24:26). "Son though he was, he learned obedience from what he suffered; and when he was made perfect, he became the source of eternal salvation for all who obey him" (Heb. 5:8-9).

Throughout the gospels Jesus performs acts of healing. "Everyone in the crowd sought to touch him because power came forth from him and healed them all" (Lk. 6:19). At times Jesus affirms the Old Testament belief in the connection between illness and sin (Mt. 9:2; Mk. 2:5; Lk. 5:20). Yet, he rejects its rigid application to all circumstances. When asked about the state of the man born blind, Jesus answered, "Neither he nor his parents sinned; it is so that the works of God might be made visible through him" (Jn. 9:3). Healing and salvation are often synonymous in the New Testament as, for example, in the story of the blind beggar near Jericho to whom Jesus said, "Have sight; your faith has saved you" (Lk. 18:42). Healing is an essential part of the gospel message. It is a part of redemption, of Jesus' rescuing us from the sundering effects of evil upon our lives and bodies. Christ restores everything, all of creation, to its proper relational order and thereby brings about true health and wholeness.

Within the Christian Tradition. The Fathers of the Church hardly ever pose the question "Why does God permit such suffering in the world?" They fully believed in the New Testament's promise of the future life, that "bright promise of immortality." Their writings frequently echoed the Pauline text which states: "I consider that the sufferings of this present time are as nothing compared with the glory to be revealed for us" (Rom. 8:18). The Fathers honor Christ as the divine physician as we find, for example, in St. Ignatius of Antioch: "One is the physician, who is body and spirit, even in his death true life, born from Mary and born from God; for a time able to suffer with us, but then liberated from all suffering: our Lord Jesus Christ."[2]

Bodily life itself is considered extremely precious throughout the whole of Christian tradition. It is given to us as a sacred trust. Life is a divine gift of which we are but stewards, not owners. God alone has sovereign dominion over human life; it is thus inviolable. Bodily life, nevertheless, is not a supreme or absolute good. It has genuine value only when it is spent in the service of God and neighbor. We must not cling to it in a way that it becomes an obstacle to our vocation to love and service (see Lk. 14:26). In the quest of life's meaning, human life is altogether impossible without risk. Therefore, the risks involved in such sports as mountain climbing, auto racing, skydiving, etc., are looked upon favorably by our contemporary culture. Even more important are the risks undertaken by doctors and nurses in the course of rendering their professional services. Astronauts, too, face grave dangers in their exploration of space. The underlying principle governing such cases may be stated thus: the greater the love with which one risks one's life, and the greater the service rendered for the common good or a particular person, the purer is the witness rendered to faith and hope, and the more justifiable the risk.[3]

The inviolability of innocent human life has been attested to constantly. In more recent times, for instance Pope Pius XII affirmed: "Every human being even a child in the mother's womb, has a right to life directly from God and not from the parents or from any human activity. Hence there is no human authority, no science, no medical, eugenic, social, economic or moral 'indication' that can offer or produce a valid juridical title to a direct deliberate disposal of an innocent human life."[4] Because the sanctity of human life is anchored in the fundamental belief that we are made in the image and likeness of God, there is no such thing as a valueless life, whether in the beginning or at the end of human existence. Appealing to the fundamental dignity of and respect due the human person, the Second Vatican Council stated that "all offenses against life itself, such as murder, genocide, abortion, euthanasia and wilful suicide; all violations of the integrity of the human person, such as mutilation, physical and mental torture, undue psychological pressures; . . . all these and the like are criminal: they poison civilization" (GS 27).

Health Care: "A Profession" or "An Industry"?

The language we use to describe our work, activity and occupation is often an accurate indication of how we perceive what we are trying to accomplish. For centuries those involved in offering health care have been considered to be members of a profession. As such, all those involved in the practice of medicine have been looked upon as a vocational group that renders an irreplaceable service to the community and that is dedicated to values other than those of financial gain. They are expected to acquire a formation that is very deeply humane, helping them to unravel the sense of life, health, sickness and death. Their close personal relationships to the patient and the patient's family are thus expected to embody high professional standards.

In the contemporary situation, however, economic factors are aggressively thrusting themselves into the picture and changing the language of health care.

> Whereas we used to speak about the *profession* of medicine or health care, we now speak about the health care *industry.* Whereas we used to speak about patients, we now speak about *consumers.* Physicians, nurses, and hospital personnel have become *providers.* Health care professionals used to offer health care; they now *deliver* health care. Medicine and medical procedures and practices used to be evaluated in regard to their power to alleviate pain or to heal; now *cost effectiveness* is all important and the ultimate evaluation of medical practice is whether it enables people to become, once again, *productive members of society.*[5]

This new predominance of economics is making medical care into a commodity. Consumer demand becomes the determining factor in how and where dollars are spent. In a society that fears the natural aging process, we can buy enlarged breasts, shrunken buttocks and the removal of skin wrinkles. We can pay to have the fruit of an unwanted pregnancy excised from the womb. We can procure a disease diagnosis and its corresponding technological treatment.

This pragmatic, commodity-centered approach to health care treats persons functionally. Machines, furthermore, now can do for people what people used to do, leading to the mechanization and depersonalization of medical treatment. Rapidly disappearing is respect for the total person, as is the understanding that healing is a process involving a person's social and spiritual needs, as well as his or her physiological and psychological needs. "Thus the health care professional does not work with a biological specimen or with an isolated part of the human entity; he or she works with an integrative sensing, feeling, thinking, loving human being."[6] Concern for the whole person is not something "nice" or extraneous, but an integral element in the science and art of the healing profession. Human qualities such as wisdom, compassion, dedication and service do not translate into economic terms.

The Social Justice Dimension of Health Care. Whereas classical medical ethics concerned itself exclusively with the physician-patient relationship and the ethical appropriateness of certain decisions and individual procedures, the growth today of "for-profit" health care systems and of governmental partnership in health delivery surfaces a whole new area of ethical concerns. The social dimension of health is also critically important. The public must assume more common responsibility for social and economic structures that foster a healthy environment, along with healthy lifestyles and relationships. Contemporary health care ethics needs to concern itself with a holistic response covering all aspects that affect life and health.

Until recent decades the medical profession operated on a fee-for-service system. Physicians were dependent on no one for outside funding. Indeed, they themselves were often the major source of funding for the hospitals in which they practiced. With the appearance of third-party insurers such as Blue Cross/Blue Shield, rising health care costs, and Medicare and Medicaid legislation in the 1960s, the whole face of health financing and administration changed. Hospitals became big business and full-time administrators trained in business methods were hired to run them. The situation has now changed to the point that "administrators more than physicians . . . decide how long patients stay in hospitals, in what setting they are treated, what types of cases are 'acceptable,' and so on."[7]

In an attempt at cost-containment the Federal Government in 1985 established a prospective payment system for Medicare patients. At its heart is the Diagnostic Related Groups (DRG's) whereby patients are classed into 468 categories by virtue of their principal diagnosis necessitating their hospitalization. For each of these categories there is a predetermined length of stay and dollar reimbursement. Such action may result in short-term savings, yet in the long run we may witness an increased number of people in poorer health because hospitals may begin turning away Medicare patients who are chronically ill, decreasing the quality of care, and discharging patients as quickly as possible. It is a requirement of justice that people should not be deprived of basic health care services, yet financial, political or institutional concerns can now easily preempt the needs of the patient. This situation also poses a threat to the autonomy of the physician. It can readily become an intrusion upon the doctor-patient relationship and lead to eventual carelessness and routine in medical practice.

Other questions of social justice surround the allocation of funding and other resources towards preventive measures which promote healthy

269

environments and lifestyles. The greatest progress in health comes from efforts which raise public consciousness and improve those conditions that have an impact upon the general health, such as better housing and nutrition, prenatal and child care, clean drinking water and the like. For, "unless hospitals as a group, and society as a whole, deal with obesity, tobacco, alcohol, insufficient exercise, environmental pollutants, carcinogenic industries, etc., we will forever be cleaning up bigger and bigger messes, probably with bigger and bigger technology."[8] Efforts also need to be undertaken which will restore a sense of personal dignity and self-worth to so many among the population who resort to promiscuous sexual activity and drug abuse as forms of escapism and quick thrills. Maintaining health through promoting "a sound mind in a sound body," that is, through educating people on how to maintain a harmonious integration of our intellectual, emotional, social and spiritual life united to a healthy body, needs to become more and more a national priority. Medical schools must take the lead in training future physicians for leadership in health education, something the schools have been neglecting for too long.

The Patient-Physician Relationship. In order to protect the inviolable dignity and integrity of the patient as a person, there exist certain rights that must always be respected in the doctor-patient relationship. First of all, every human person has a basic right to adequate health care. Furthermore, the relationship between the health care professional and the patient/client is a personal covenant, which is characterized by attitudes of fidelity, reverence, respect, truthfulness and mutual trust.[9] As such, the patient has a right to be properly informed about his or her situation and to choose freely the type of treatment. The patient also has a right to confidentiality. While respecting the conscience and autonomy of the patient, the physician, too, has a right in conscience to refuse types of treatment or practices that conflict with God's vision of wholeness as proclaimed by the Church, such as abortion, contraception, sterilization, mutilation, euthanasia, etc.[10]

1. The patient's **right to adequate health care** flows from the sanctity and dignity of human life. In their 1981 pastoral letter on "Health and Health Care," the American Catholic bishops state that "Health care is so important for full human dignity and so necessary for the proper development of life that it is a fundamental right of every human being."[11] The bishops express their hope that American society will move toward establishing a national

270

policy guaranteeing adequate health care for all.[12] In this vein, the health apostolate must continue to serve the poor, the frail elderly, the powerless and the alienated. In 1983 the President's Commission For the Study of Ethical Problems in Medicine and Biomedical and Behavioral Research proposed "that everyone have access to *some* level of care: *enough care* to achieve sufficient welfare, opportunity, information and evidence of interpersonal concern to facilitate a reasonably full and satisfying life."[13] With the extremely high cost of many organ transplants and other specialized procedures, a "reasonably full and satisfying life" obviously does not permit expending exorbitant sums for the special needs of a few at the neglect of the ordinary needs of so many others.[14]

Since the beginning of the medical profession, physicians and nurses have risked their lives in treating all sorts of sickness and disease. Over the centuries health care professionals have met the challenges posed by epidemic illnesses, such as the bubonic plague, cholera, poliomyelitis, etc. They have fulfilled the highest charge of their profession. A person's right to adequate medical care demands that same dedication today. While the risk of contacting a contagious disease has been greatly reduced with the development of various immunization measures, the contemporary epidemic of acquired immune deficiency syndrome (AIDS) once again puts physicians and nurses at risk. Health care providers and institutions now confront the same moral choice that their predecessors did. In the case of AIDS, transmission in an occupational setting is rare. The risk of infection appears to be far below that of acquiring lethal hepatitis B. The provider's fear is often more a manifestation of the psychological and symbolic issues that the disease raises. Physicians and nurses are more than technicians, they are healers. They have a grave moral obligation to care for AIDS patients in addition to everyone else needing their professional service and dedication.

2. The patient's right to self-determination is protected by the **principle of informed consent**. In submitting oneself to professional care, the patient in no way abrogates his or her right of autonomy and conscience. "The ethical basis for the patient's right to choose the type of treatment is the fact that as a human being the patient is equal to the physician. When entering a healing relationship the patient does not surrender personal responsibility for determining which values are more important in a given situation."[15] Valid informed consent depends upon three prerequisites: competency, freedom from coercion, and adequate information.

271

Competency refers to the patient's capacity to judge the situation clearly "The word 'incompetent' . . . applies as a general rule to minors and to all who are delirious, unconscious, comatose, or in such an advanced state of confusion or agitation that they are unable to properly understand, appreciate and evaluate recommended life choices."[16] In the same illness, because of prolonged or intensive pain, administration of drugs, etc., a patient may be competent at certain times and doubtfully competent or incompetent at other times. Parents usually become proxies for minor children, and a husband or wife can speak for an incompetent spouse. In other instances a self-designated proxy, family members, close friends or a court-appointed guardian may be called upon to decide for an incompetent patient. Such surrogates have the obligation to make decisions based upon their knowledge of the patient and his or her personal wishes. They exercise not their own rights, but the right that belongs to another.

Freedom from coercion requires that the patient's consent or refusal of consent remains unclouded by any external pressure from health care professionals and family members. Such freedom is protected by an open, friendly and confidential relationship between physician and patient. "It is the physician above all who provides the information, the explanations, the risks, the alternatives, so that the patient can evaluate the benefits and the burdens in arriving at the free act of choice."[17] This freedom today can be easily jeopardized by the highly specialized technological and impersonal aspects of health care, particularly in its hugeness. When medical teams treat different aspects of a patient's illness, personal autonomy is easily threatened. Spouses and family members can also exercise undue emotional pressure, particularly with regard to initiating or withdrawing extraordinary means. Psychotherapists, especially, have a grave obligation not to use methods and techniques that manipulate their clients' freedom.

The principle of informed consent, furthermore, requires that the patient receive adequate information about his or her condition and about the risks attendant on certain proposed treatments. A comprehensive explanation of the various alternatives of treatment is not required, and the manner of communication must conform to the person's educational level. The general policy should be to enlighten the person as far as possible, taking into account the temperament and the best interests of the patient in the degree and manner of communication. When death is imminent or certain, the physician normally has the duty of informing the patient either by himself or through a nurse, chaplain, relative or friend. Such information may be communicated gradually; it should be done as delicately as possible. If, however, it is foreseen that it will gravely aggravate the patient's condition the information may be withheld. His or her right to know the truth so as to prepare for the solemn moment of death, however, must be respected as far as possible.

3. The health care professional's relationship to the patient is characterized by close mutual confidence and trust. The **principle of confidentiality** or professional secrecy safeguards a person's privacy and good name. The unjustifiable revelation of an entrusted secret is a violation of justice. Doctors, nurses, pharmacists, laboratory technicians and others are bound by strict secrecy regarding all knowledge acquired in the exercise of their professional services.

At times the obligation of professional secrecy may conflict with other duties towards society and oneself. In almost all countries, law requires that instances of contagious diseases be reported. When there is the possibility of serious harm to a third party, such as danger of contagion, the physician may reveal the matter if the patient refuses to fulfill an obvious obligation to make known his infectious disease. Another reason for revealing an entrusted secret could be based on the danger of serious harm to the person revealing, such as a threat to commit suicide. When serious harm might come to the physician, for example, by being falsely accused of indecent assault by a patient who has made similar charges against professional people in the past, such evidence may be revealed in self-defense if it is strictly necessary. In a court of law a physician can, on general principle, reveal confidential information only if the patient has agreed to waive his right in this particular instance. The psychotherapist-patient right to privileged communication should, however, be absolutely respected by every court. "The psychotherapist must never, before a tribunal or others, make use of any confidential material that could be prejudicial to his patient, even if the patient has explicitly waived his right to confidentiality."[18]

Confidential custody of medical records is becoming increasingly difficult in an age of computerized files and data banks. With institutional ethics committees becoming commonplace along with the frequency of malpractice suits we are witnessing the phenomenon of more and more people being given access to the record files of patients. The new process of DNA "finger-printing" complicates the picture further by possibly revealing too much confidential information about a given individual, such as a person's chances of dying from heart disease within a few years. Keeping records down to a minimum, however, could put both the patient and the health care providers at future risk, the former by not having enough information for proper diagnosis and the latter in cases of civil malpractice. Prudent record policies and regulations need to be established and monitored accordingly.[19]

Respecting Human Life at Its Beginning

Rapid developments in science and technology in recent years have made possible numerous types of intervention in the processes of human procreation. In addition to the fact that abortion and contraceptive sterilization are commonplace procedures, we also read today with increasing frequency about "test-tube" babies, i.e., conceived through *in vitro* fertilization (IVF), artificial insemination, surrogate mothers, the freezing of human embryos, genetic engineering, and the not-too-distant future possibilities of developing artificial wombs and human cloning. In February 1987 the Congregation for the Doctrine of the Faith addressed many of these issues in its "Instruction on Respect for Human Life in Its Origin and on the Dignity of Procreation." In a commentary on this instruction, Father James Burtchaell, C.S.C., of the University of Notre Dame observed that

> The Vatican is too technical, or perhaps too dainty, to state graphically enough that we have been turning procreation into science fiction and that we become monsters as a result. A society that venerates Drs. Masters and Johnson and their lab-coat lore of orgasm as advisers on the fullness of human sexuality, or that hearkens to Dr. Ruth as a *sage femme* of how men and women give themselves to one another, or that orders up children the way it uses the Land's End catalog: This is a creature feature that ought not appear on late Saturday television. Or so I take the Vatican to be telling us.[20]

Technology concerns itself with the given problem at hand. It is an applied science that manipulates the physical factors involved in order to produce the desired results. As such, the Vatican instruction maintains, "Science and technology are valuable resources for man when they promote his integral development for the benefit of all; but they cannot of themselves show the meaning of existence and of human progress."[21] Scientific research and its applications are not morally neutral.

The moral criteria for biotechnology and medicine flow from a total vision of the human person as a corporeal-spiritual unity and from the natural moral law. The human person is not just a body, a physical being, and human procreation cannot be considered just a biological process. "It is a *personal* act. As such it is a *biological and spiritual act at the same time. It has consequences going beyond the area of biology.*"[22] Bodily acts are an expression of one's personhood. The natural moral law, in this context, articulates the truth about what it means to be an integral human being. The natural law, thus, is not some mere biological law, but respects all the interlocking dynamic relationships that constitute the human person and manifest the divine ecology, or God's original plan in designing the human race and creation itself.

The natural law is the intrinsic dynamic ordering of all creation according to the divine will; it orders all things for the good. The human person gifted with reason and free will can either discern this inner principle of order and cooperate with it, or one can selfishly opt to decide on one's own what is "good for me" and proceed to act according to this wholly independent self-determination, thereby alienating oneself from the good. Since the Enlightenment, science and technology have held that there is no nature, no creation with an inherent character and order of which human purpose and choice must take cognizance and must respect. In the 1960s the ecological movement began to debunk this doctrine inasmuch as it relates to the natural environment of plants and animals. "We have yet to be persuaded that there are given, natural forces and needs in humanity ourselves that may be as uncontainable by our willful choices as are the tides of the ocean that make sport of our retaining walls and waterways."[23]

Artificial interventions regarding procreation and the origin of human life, in cases where the procedures are not strictly therapeutic, are to receive their ethical determination from the total anthropological vision of the human person, including the significance of human sexuality (as presented in chapter 9), and from the natural moral law whose fullness has been manifested to us in the "law of Christ." This vision provided us by divine revelation, the Word made flesh, makes known the human person's fundamental right to life, unique dignity and integral supernatural vocation. From this it can be deduced that "an intervention on the human body affects not only the tissues, the organs and their functions but also involves the person himself on different levels."[24] Within this perspective we shall now consider briefly the morality of abortion, sterilization procedures, and a number of other contemporary interventions in the process of procreation.

Abortion. "The Ethical and Religious Directives for Catholic Health Facilities" approved by the National Conference of Catholic Bishops in 1971, and revised in 1975, define abortion as "the directly intended termination of pregnancy before viability . . . which, in its moral context, includes the interval between conception and implantation of the embryo."[25] Such a procedure, the Directives assert, is never permitted. In this they reaffirm the humanity of the fetus and its inviolability in the womb. The Catholic Church's theological tradition has constantly maintained that, although unable to decide and speak for itself, the fetus possesses equal rights with every other human being.

1. **Within the context of the Christian tradition,** from the very earliest of times, we see a very deep respect for fetal and infant life.[26] In the ancient Mediterranean world in which Christianity appeared, abortion was a familiar practice. A leading Greco-Roman gynecologist, Soranos of Ephesus (c. A.D. 98-138), mentions abortifacients that may be used to conceal the consequences of adultery, to maintain feminine beauty, and to avoid danger to the mother when her uterus is too small to accommodate a full embryo. Plato and Aristotle looked upon abortion as a way of preventing excess population. Some physicians faithful to their Hippocratic oath, however, refused to prescribe abortifacients. Roman law punished abortion committed without the father's consent along with the giving of drugs that caused abortion, but its purpose was other than the protection of the embryo as a human person. Legally the fetus was considered to be a part of the mother.

The Old Testament itself does not mention abortion, although Philo in his first-century commentary on Exodus 21:22 said that this passage implicitly condemns it. The New Testament, especially in the "infancy narratives" of Matthew and Luke, reflects a high interest in the "fruit of the womb" (Mt. 2:1-18; Lk. 1:40, 42). "The Didache" or "Teaching of the Twelve Apostles" (c. A.D. 100 or earlier) is the first Christian work that unequivocally condemns abortion: "You shall not slay the child by abortions (*phthora*). You shall not kill what is generated" (*Didache* 2.2). "The Epistle of Barnabas" places this prohibition within the context of love of neighbor (*Barnabas* 19.5). The Fathers of the Church, including Clement of Alexandria, Minucius Felix, Cyprian, Tertullian, Jerome, Augustine, Basil, and John Chrysostom, repeated the general condemnation of abortion in their writings. When the Church emerged as a legal and social force in the fourth century, various regional Church councils imposed lifetime excommunication on women procuring abortions.

Earlier Church teaching was reiterated in the Middle Ages. The "penitentials" developed for hearing confession regularly prescribed one to ten years of penance for anyone killing an embryo. The Scholastics theorized on the time of ensoulment. St. Thomas Aquinas and others, subscribing to the Aristotelian theory of delayed hominization, considered ensoulment to occur about the fortieth day for the male fetus and about the eightieth day for the female fetus. Thus, abortion before ensoulment was not looked upon as homicide, but rather as the equally grave malice of contraception. Until 1875, medical science remained unaware of the fertilization of the ovum by the male sperm, and therefore, was also ignorant of the moment of conception.

The moral casuistry on abortion really began to develop in the fifteenth century. Antoninus (1389-1459), a Dominican bishop of Florence, refers to a thirteenth-century Dominican theologian, John of Naples, who permitted the abortion of an unensouled fetus in order to save the life of the mother. While Antoninus himself spoke of all abortion as homicide, he seems to have considered the opinion of John of Naples as probable. The great Spanish specialist on marriage, Tomas Sanchez (1550-1610), argued that the prohibition of abortion had exceptions. The subhuman character of the unensouled fetus authorized the preference of other values to its existence: if the mother otherwise would die because the fetus is invading or attacking her; if a pregnant girl's relatives would kill her if they became aware of her illegitimate pregnancy; if an engaged girl who became pregnant by another man could not end her engagement without scandal and thereby ran the risk of bearing another's child to her husband. Sanchez maintained, however, that if the fetus is at least probably ensouled no direct means may be used to kill it. Almost a century and a half later, St. Alphonsus Liguori (1696-1787) made a masterly summation of the work of the casuists. While recognizing that Sanchez's opinion permitting the intentional killing of an unformed fetus in order to save the mother was a probable opinion, St. Alphonsus himself held the "more common opinion" that it is never licit to expel the fetus. This more common opinion was "safer" and therefore to be followed.

While the casuistic examination of abortion tended to question its absolute prohibition, the legislative activity of the papacy during this time tended in the opposite direction. The reform pope, Sixtus V, issued the bull *"Effraenatam"* on October 29, 1588, in which all the penalties of both canon and civil law against homicide were applied to those producing abortion. This legislation was largely aimed at prostitution in Rome, but no exception was made for therapeutic abortion. In 1591, Gregory XIV repealed the penalties except those applying to an ensouled fetus. In 1679, Innocent XI condemned sixty-five propositions that were designated by the Holy Office as "at least scandalous and in practice dangerous," including two related to abortion:

> 34. It is lawful to procure abortion before ensoulment of the fetus lest a girl, detected as pregnant, be killed or defamed.
> 35. It seems probable that the fetus (as long as it is in the uterus) lacks a rational soul and begins first to have one when it is born; and consequently it must be said that no abortion is homicide.

The main line of casuistic thought on therapeutic abortion was unmentioned and unaffected. Outer limits on permissible teaching, however, were established in practice by this decree.

The Marquis de Sade in 1795 attacked restrictions on abortion as the result of religious superstition and actually praised the practice. Abortion became more commonplace in Western Europe, while Church teaching in the course of the next two centuries developed to an almost absolute prohibition of abortion. By the eighteenth century medical opinion had rejected the Aristotelian theory on gestation. Karl Ernest von Baer in 1827 had discovered the ovum in the human female, and by 1875 the joint action of spermatozoon and ovum in generation had been determined. In 1869, Pius IX dropped the reference to the "ensouled fetus" in the excommunication for abortion. An implicit acceptance of immediate ensoulment gained ground. The nineteenth-century German Jesuit, Augustine Lehmkuhl, taught that abortion was "true homicide." The changed view of ensoulment was part of a broader humanistic movement that developed over the nineteenth and twentieth centuries and promoted a greater sensitivity to the value of life.

The Holy Office in 1884 decided that it cannot be safely taught in Catholic schools that abortion may be performed even when without it both mother and child will die and with it at least the mother can be saved. The 1917 Code of Canon Law prescribed that anyone who successfully procures an abortion including the "mother" is excommunicated. The new 1983 Code in Canon 1398 retains this automatic excommunication for all involved in a successful abortion. In his encyclical "Casti Connubii" on December 31, 1930, Pius XI stated that "however much we may pity the mother whose health and even life is imperiled in the performance of the duty allotted to her

278

by nature, nevertheless what could ever be sufficient reason for excusing in any way the direct murder of the innocent?'' In 1951, Pius XII reaffirmed this teaching in no uncertain terms, and the Second Vatican Council taught that ''Life must be protected with the utmost care from the moment of conception: abortion and infanticide are abominable crimes'' (GS 51).

2. When does human life begin? Speculation about **the beginning of human life** has constantly fascinated us over the centuries. From Aristotle through Thomas Aquinas and beyond, the theory of successive ensoulment had strong support. When, however, the full process of fertilization was discovered in the nineteenth century, philosophers and theologians began to favor the opinion of spontaneous ensoulment at the moment of fertilization. With subsequently more accurate knowledge about embryonic development different theories about ensoulment or hominization have been proposed. Science today points to four decisive moments in the early stages of development. Reasons have been put forth to suggest that a new human person actually comes into being at any one of these moments.

a.) **Fertilization** of the ovum by the sperm marks the first decisive moment. Here begins a whole new life, distinct from that of the father and the mother, with its own unique, never-to-be-repeated genetic code (DNA). The morula or blastocyst gradually develops according to its own dynamics. After five to seven days of cell division, the zygote makes its way to the uterus and pursues its tasks of implantation and further embryonic development. Those who maintain that both human life and human personhood begin at the moment of fertilization are proponents of the theory of immediate hominization or ensoulment.

b.) **Segmentation**, the process that leads to twinning or multiple births can happen at different stages. It may happen at the morular stage, i.e, the eight-cell division in the tube, or on the zygote's way out of the tube on the fourth or fifth day of fertilization. Sometimes the division into two or more embryos does not happen until implantation. ''Twinning in the human being may occur up to the fourteenth day, when conjoined twins or triplets can still be produced. Less well known is the fact that in these first few days the twins may be recombined into one individual being.''[27] Since only a human individual can have the quality of a person, some maintain that hominization does not occur until this process is complete.

c.) **Implantation** occurs when the blastocyst is accepted by the mother's endomitrium. Scientists estimate that 30% to 50% of the fertilized cells get lost before implantation, while the rate between implantation and birth is in the ten to twenty per cent probability range.[28] It is fairly well determined now that up until sometime after its implantation the fertilized ovum is guided by the maternal RNA (ribonucleic acid), i.e., by the genetic material present in the ovum alone prior to fertilization. The sperm does not seem to play any directive part up to this point. Only after implantation does the genetic capital of the new organism become fully active, with the result that the conceptus now begins to be directed by its own RNA.[29]

d.) The **development of the cerebral cortex** to the point where brain-wave activity becomes detectable by an electroencephalogram (EEG) is clearly in evidence about eight weeks into the gestation process. Human consciousness has its indispensable substratum in the cerebral cortex. By the twelfth week the brain structure is more or less complete. "Most probably we can conclude that after the twenty-fifth or at least after the fortieth day there is no qualitative leap but only a quantitative development of the already given structure of the cerebral cortex."[30]

All of the above decisive moments in the early stages of the developing human being have given birth to theories about when ensoulment or hominization takes place. They are all, however, just theories. The origin of human life remains a mystery. Human procreation is much more than just a biological process. As John Paul II has pointed out, "A relationship between spirits which begets a new embodied spirit is something unknown to the natural order."[31] In our reflections on Christian anthropology in chapter three, we observed that by calling us forth in love God has gifted us with transcendental freedom in order that we might enter into a personal and loving relationship with him. In the deepest core of our being, in our non-categorical, unreflexive consciousness we stand open to the Transcendent, to God himself.

The precise moment of this gift-call remains hidden in the mystery of divine-human co-subjectivity. It may in all likelihood be implanted at the time of fertilization when a unique, never-to-be-repeated genetic code comes into existence. After spending four months at a l'Arche community living with and caring for a severely mentally handicapped person, Henri J. W. Nouwen wrote: "Long before our mind is able to exercise its power, our heart [by heart I mean the center of our being where God has hidden the divine gifts of trust, hope, love] is already able to develop a trusting relationship. . . . The spiritual life is given to us at the moment of conception."[32] Even if hominization were not to occur at the moment of conception, the new embryo is an incipient human being whose inherent dynamic points to human personhood and nothing else — certainly not to any other organic substance whether animal or vegetable. As such the human conceptus is deserving of the basic human right to life, of which it may not be morally deprived.[33]

3. The Catholic Church's teaching today excludes all direct abortion, that is, abortion which is either an end or a means. Cases of **indirect abortion,** however, constitute exceptions. For instance, if through an ectopic pregnancy in the fallopian tube, the tube became pathological, according to the principle of double effect it would be permissible to remove the tube surgically. Here the fetus is not the direct object of the operation; killing it would be an indirect result of an attempt to save the mother's life. Similarly a cancerous uterus may be surgically removed even if it contains a fetus, because its death would be accomplished indirectly .

As late as 1886, the German moralist, Augustine Lehmkuhl, S.J., taught that to procure an abortion to save a mother's life was "scarcely a direct abortion in a theological sense, any more than yielding a plank in a shipwreck to a friend is direct killing of oneself."[34] Lehmkuhl's opinion permitting a therapeutic abortion as indirect was rejected by the Holy Office in the decree approved July 25, 1895. The agonizing dilemma of allowing both the mother and fetus to die, when the surgical removal of the fetus can save at least the mother's life, continues to refine our understanding of direct and indirect abortion. Consider the following case that was reported to Father Bernard Häring by a gynecologist:

I was once called upon to perform an operation on a woman in the fourth month of pregnancy, to remove a benign uterine tumour. On the womb, there were numerous very thin and fragile varicose veins which bled profusely, and attempts to suture them only aggravated the bleeding. Therefore, in order to save the woman from bleeding to death, I opened the womb and removed the fetus. Thereupon the uterus contracted, the bleeding ceased, and the woman's life was saved. I was proud of what I had achieved, since the uterus of this woman, who was still childless, was undamaged and she could bear other children. But I had to find out later from a noted moralist that although I had indeed acted in good faith, what I had done was, in his eyes, *objectively* wrong. I would have been allowed to remove the bleeding uterus with the fetus itself, he said, but was not permitted to interrupt the pregnancy while leaving the womb intact. He informed me that my intervention constituted an immoral termination of pregnancy, even though the purpose was to save the mother, whereas the other way would have been a lawful direct intention . . . an action to save life, as in the case of a cancerous uterus. For him, preservation of the woman's fertility . . . played no decisive role.[35]

   While this case was a *physically* direct abortion, Häring suggests that the malice of abortion exists in "an attack on the right of the fetus to live."[36] In this situation the doctor did not attack the fetus' right to live; it was rather the woman's unfortunate pathological condition which robbed the fetus of its right to live. The doctor did not make a decision to save the mother rather than the fetus. He merely saved the only life he could under the circumstances.
   The application of the principle of double effect in such cases seems to be going through a process of refinement. George Lobo, S.J., a Catholic moralist from India, points out that in the process of removing the tube in an ectopic pregnancy, as soon as the blood vessels are clamped, the fetus already loses its life and, thus, the death of the fetus is prior to the excision of the tube.[37] Germain Grisez, a Catholic ethicist here in the United States known for his fidelity to magisterial teaching, suggests that the manualists' handling of the principle overstressed the physical causality of the act.[38] He would maintain that when an act has two effects and no other act intervenes between the action and one or other of the effects, then the effects should be said to be produced with equal immediacy. Thus, he would allow abortion to save the life of the mother, because here the removal of the fetus produces the good and bad effect with equal immediacy.[39]

   4. Many pills and intrauterine devices used for contraceptive purposes are actually **abortifacients**. Only the anti-ovulatory pills or anovulents produce a form of temporary sterilization by primarily suppressing the ovulation process. All other contraceptive pills are more likely to allow ovulation to occur regularly and avoid pregnancy by preventing uterine implantation should the fertilization of the ovum take place. These pills must

properly be regarded as abortifacients. These so-called "oral contraceptives" are misnamed. They do not prevent conception or fertilization, but are actually abortion-causing agents.

In France, a new type of pill is under development and is already being used experimentally in several countries, including the United States. Presently referred to as RU-486, it in no way claims to prevent ovulation, but rather is classified as an "anti-progesterone." It works against the hormone progesterone that prepares the uterus to receive the fertilized egg. This pill induces menstruation, thus preventing the fertilized ovum from implanting. RU-486 is being praised as a scientific breakthrough because the woman would only have to take it four days a month to ensure the onset of menstruation, and not 21 to 28 days a month, as is now required of the conventionally marketed pills. Along with the so-called "morning after" pills, RU-486 is undoubtedly an abortifacient.

Furthermore, the variously shaped intrauterine devices, commonly referred to as I.U.D.'s, are now known not to prevent fertilization. They, too, primarily prevent the implantation of the fertilized egg and must be viewed as abortifacient agents, and not as contraceptive devices.[40] The use of abortifacients along with any other direct attack upon the human embryo's or fetus' right to life is in reality anti-therapeutic because it violates the relational wholeness of the created order in which we all participate; it violates the natural law personalistically and wholistically understood. Abortion violently tears apart the essential and fundamental relationship between the mother and her offspring. The direct, intentional destruction of human life in the womb is a grave offense against the law of Christ, the law of love. It is a sign of total rejection by the mother, and as such is anti-relational and totally unloving. Direct attacks against the right to human life are always grave violations of the law of love.

Treating Victims of Rape. Understanding, compassion, respect and concern are the most basic needs innocent rape victims have. These are often denied in a society that still tends to look upon victims of rape with suspicion, as somehow guilty, or even as having "asked for it." The victims also have serious spiritual, psychological and legal needs. Catholic hospitals should be particularly equipped to handle these needs. The hospital chaplain's office, or pastoral care department, must have developed special approaches that intermesh with emergency room procedures. Sensitization programs may be especially helpful for male members of the emergency room staff, and the networking of hospitals with other caring programs such as rape crisis centers may help meet the victim's legal and psychological needs.

Catholic hospitals may have tended to avoid treating rape victims because of confusion over methods of preventing pregnancy. There is valid concern that certain methods are abortifacient. Legal liability has been another concern when a pregnancy occurred because of the hospital's refusal to take measures it considered to be immoral. Conscience clauses in the law, however, protect religious institutions from such liability. It is widely acknowledged, furthermore, that the chances of conception after rape are statistically quite low. The traumatic circumstances of rape tend to make the vaginal secretions highly spermicidal so that an insufficient number of sperm survive to make fertilization possible. The possibility, also, that rape might occur during the woman's fertile cycle is less than one out of five. In addition it is estimated that about 75% of the rapists experience sexual dysfunction during rape.[41]

Regarding the treatment of rape victims the Catholic Church maintains that it is morally permissible to prescribe medication and other treatments that can prevent fertilization from occurring, but nothing may be done to stop the implantation of a fertilized egg in the uterine wall. "With increasing clarity, the Church has focused on the contraceptive intention as being the heart of what is meant morally by contraception. In moral terms contraception is understood to be an attempt at interfering with the natural consequences of a true conjugal act. To be a true conjugal act, it must be freely and deliberately entered into by both spouses."[42] Measures thus may be taken to prevent the invading sperm's pronucleus from fusing with that of the ovum's. Unlike the sperm from a conjugal act, the rapist's sperm is unjustly deposited in the woman's vagina, and the woman has the right to treat the sperm accordingly.[43] Once fertilization has taken place, however, even the rape-conceived human possesses all the rights and dignity of any other human being. The embryo is completely innocent of the evil involved in the rape act.

Most spermicide methods, such as spermicidal douches, as well as dilation and curettage (D and C), are today recognized as not offering much hope in preventing pregnancy. Spermicidal douches are useless because some sperm may reach the oviducts within five minutes of coitus. D and C, which involves scraping the endometrium lining allows reservoirs of sperm to remain in the endocervix. It also serves to prevent implantation of the fertilized ovum and is, thus, morally equivalent to abortion. Sometimes high doses of DES (diethylstilbestrol) are given for an anovulant purpose when there is a very slight possibility of preventing implantation from occurring. It is now believed, however, that DES has high toxicity and is a carcinogenic. Ovral, a birth control pill, which is now prescribed for rape victims by some hospitals, is actually an abortifacient.[44] While very few rapes end in pregnancy, even one such instance is a tragedy. In order to help lessen the victim's fears and for the prevention of venereal disease, a spermicidal douche may be given. Research for non-abortifacient, anti-fertility treatments needs to be encouraged.

Sterilization. Because of the various side-effects and infections caused by pills and intrauterine devices, sterilization in recent years has become the most common method of contraception. Sterilization may be defined as any surgical, radiological or chemical means that renders conception impossible. Ethically, it is important to distinguish two kinds of sterilization: *direct* and *indirect*. Direct sterilization is any procedure aimed at making conception impossible. "Sterilization procedures such as tubal ligation (fallopian tubes tied or cut), its masculine counterpart, vasectomy ("vasa deferentia" tied or cut), hysterectomy (surgical removal of the uterus), oophorectomy (surgical removal of the ovaries), salphingectomy (surgical removal of the fallopian tubes), radiation of the generative organs with X-ray, etc., come under the heading of contraceptive (direct) sterilization if they are done for the purpose of rendering a person sterile."[45] As the NCCB's "Ethical and Religious Directives for Catholic Health Facilities" state: "Sterilization, whether permanent or temporary, for men or for women, may not be used as a means of contraception" (no. 18).

Indirect sterilization is a procedure aimed at treating a pathological condition, but from which sterility may result. According to the principle of double effect it is licit for a proportionate reason when a simpler treatment is not reasonably available. The U.S. bishops' Directives thus add that "Hence, for example, oophorectomy or irradiation of the ovaries may be allowed in treating carcinoma of the breast and metastasis therefrom; and orchidectomy [excision of the testicles] is permitted in the treatment of carcinoma of the prostate" (no. 20). Likewise, a hysterectomy may be performed to remove a severely damaged or cancerous uterus. In the case of menstrual disorders a woman should not too hastily request or permit a hysterectomy because it is a major and serious intervention, which can produce a wide range of complications in its aftermath. A number of Catholic moralists favor the opinion, too, that a physician may ethically opt to leave a threatening womb in place, and simply isolate it by cutting or "tying" the fallopian tubes. A 1985 study, however, indicates that a tubal ligation may lead to a worsening of the womb.[46] It can all too easily become a question of rationalizing what in effect is contraceptive sterilization.

The principle of totality allows for the removal of a healthy part of the body only when there is no other way to provide for the overall good. On the question of uterine isolation, Father Edward Bayer of the Pope John XXIII Medical/Moral Research and Education Center writes: "If a hysterectomy is morally acceptable, and if in medical reality, the isolation is likely to do less rather than more harm, it is justified. If a given physician and patient are sincerely convinced that this is so, they may resort to such a solution."[47]

The principle of totality cannot be invoked, according to the Congregation for the Doctrine of the Faith, in a case where the intention is to cure or prevent a physical or psychological ill-effect which is foreseen or feared as a result of pregnancy, for example, when the uterus is damaged due to repeated caesarian sections or when a married woman has severe pulmonary or rheumatic heart disease and there is fear a subsequent pregnancy may kill her.[48] The principle of totality does not justify such deactivation of the human reproductive system when there is some other safe way to provide for the overall good of the person, such as periodic sexual abstention.

Indirect sterilization is a therapeutic procedure that seeks to preserve health or restore wholeness when illness or disease have invaded the body. Direct sterilization, on the other hand, is a mutilation of the body and thereby of the person. As the CDF Letter observes, "Sterility induced as such does not contribute to the person's integral good, properly understood, 'keeping things and values in their proper perspective.' "[49] It is a violation of the natural law according to the "order of nature," because it is an unwarranted intervention destroying a natural physical function that is not diseased. We do not need to be cured of our sexuality. It violates the natural law according to the "order of reason" because other means are available, such as periodic abstinence, which protects in a wholistic manner all the interrelating values involved.

Artificial Intervention in Human Reproduction. Biomedical research and scientific technology in recent years have made possible an entire array of artificial interventions that can manipulate human ontogenesis from fertilization to birth. The 1987 C.D.F. Instruction on Bioethics, referred to above, points out that

> These interventions are not to be rejected on the grounds that they are artificial. As such, they bear witness to the possibilities of the art of medicine. But they must be given a moral evaluation in reference to the dignity of the human person, who is called to realize his vocation from God to the gift of love and the gift of life.[50]

Within the context of the wholistic anthropological vision handed on to us through Christian biblical revelation and the Roman Catholic tradition, therefore, we shall now consider the critical values at stake in some of these new interventions.

1. Since the birth of the first publicized "test-tube" baby, Louise Brown, in Great Britain in 1978, **in vitro fertilization** (IVF) has become a standardized technological procedure. Despite the great joy of a childless couple whose deepest desire may be fulfilled by this means, in vitro fertilization in the objective order is a moral evil. First of all, it violates the essential and fundamental relationship between the unitive and procreative significance of human sexuality. On a purely physical, functional level it separates the inseparable union between life and love. It turns the act of love-filled procreation into human manufacturing, wholly depersonalizing it.

> The human offspring is not merely another biological entity but a *person*, a spiritual being with the potential of sharing intimately the life of the Divine Persons. Consequently, the manner in which such a person is to be generated is significant and requires intimate person-to-person contact. . . .
> Granted that a husband and wife love one another, and that their intention to have a child by IVF is an expression of their mutual love, still the intervening acts, the surgical action (laparoscopy to obtain the egg), the masturbation (to obtain the sperm), the laboratory procedure (in which the egg and sperm are united), and the transcervical introduction of the developing embryo are not actions which of themselves express a personal love.[51]

The development of the practice of IVF, furthermore, introduces a second major ethical problem, namely, the destruction of numerous human embryos, as some embryos called "spares" are either destroyed or frozen. Such procedures violate human integrity and the right to life. The voluntary destruction of fertilized human eggs is the moral equivalent of direct abortion.

2. Another common medical practice today is **artificial insemination,** which is the introduction of the male sperm into the female organism without normal intercourse. Heterologous artificial insemination involves the sperm previously collected from a donor other than the husband (artificial insemination donor, or AID). Homologous artificial insemination, on the other hand, utilizes the sperm of the husband (AIH). Pope Pius XII in 1949 taught that both procedures are illicit, but he left open an unspecified kind of "assisted insemination" in the case of the husband.[52]

Artificial insemination involving a donor, often anonymous, introduces all kinds of ethical problems. Today a woman whose husband is infertile or a woman who is not even married can procure sperm from a "sperm bank." Morally, such a procedure dissociates procreation from conjugal love. It violates the child's right to be brought up in a marriage where "through the secure and recognized relationship to his own parents . . . the child can discover his own identity and achieve his own proper human development."[53] Other grave problems arise affecting the personal relationships of the child so-conceived: the woman resorting to this procedure can manipulate her husband to gain his consent; the mother can develop a possessive attitude toward "her" child; the possible emotional effect upon a teenager who learns that his or her father is a sperm-salesman; danger of intermarriage between unknown half-brothers and half-sisters with potential major hereditary consequences, etc.

In the case of homologous artificial insemination within marriage, the C.D.F. Instruction states that it "cannot be admitted except for those cases in which the technical means is not a substitute for the conjugal act but serves to facilitate and to help so that the act attains its natural response."[54] In other words, the integral connection between the unitive and procreative significance of the marital act must be safeguarded at all times, because it is an act that is inseparably physical and spiritual. Homologous IVF and embryo transfer (ET) objectively deprive human generation of its proper perfection, namely, being the result and fruit of a loving conjugal act between spouses. Such a procedure turns procreation into "manufacturing" children; technology is given precedence over love.

A new procedure called tubal ovum transfer (TOT) was first developed in 1983 at the St. Elizabeth Medical Center in Dayton, Ohio that helps women with blocked, diseased, or absent fallopian tubes to conceive and bear a child within their wombs. The procedure begins with the infertile couple having marital intercourse at home before going to the hospital outpatient facility. The day chosen coincides with the peak of the woman's ovulation process. The husband's sperm is previously collected by use of a special perforated silicon sheath which allows some sperm to enter the wife's vagina. At the hospital the woman's ova are retrieved and repositioned by laparoscopy within an hour's time under general anesthetic. The transfer of the ovum and sperm, separated by a bubble of air, is accomplished by using a catheter. Fertilization is allowed to take place, not in a test tube, but within the wife's womb. The generation of new human life occurs within the context of the marital act with medical assistance simply being used to assure the natural completion of the procreative process. A similar technique called gamete intrafallopian transfer (GIFT) developed at the University of Texas in San Antonio was reported on in 1984. As long as the husband's sperm are collected by a morally acceptable method and the repositioning of the gametes are done within the context of the conjugal union of husband and wife, the process is not morally objectionable. It is also less expensive than IVF procedures.[55]

3. Numerous couples unable to bear children and unwilling to wait for adoption have taken recourse in recent years to the practice of **surrogate motherhood**. The infamous Baby M case has made surrogacy front-page news. The process involves the artificial insemination of the surrogate mother by the husband of the contracting couple. When brought to term, the surrogate mother delivers the child to the waiting couple who pay for all medical and legal fees. The surrogate mother also receives a sizable sum for her services, as much as $10,000. Complications arose in the Baby M case when the surrogate mother refused to give up the child after she was born. On February 3, 1988, the New Jersey Supreme Court ruled "In the matter of Baby M" that such a surrogacy contract was invalid and unenforceable but agreed with the trial court that custody of the child shall go to the natural father.

Surrogacy is a gross violation of relational integrity on several counts.[56] It is a rejection of the fundamental bond of maternal love and of the child's right to be raised by his or her own parents. The surrogate mother for all practical purposes rents her womb for nine months and by contract sells the child she has raised there. No consideration is given to the natural bonding relationship that has already developed, albeit imperceptibly, between the mother and the child in the womb. Surrogacy also offends against conjugal fidelity, becoming essentially adultery as it introduces a third party into the exclusive intimacy proper to the marital relationship. The child is treated as some *thing* that is contracted, rather than seen as a gift of covenanted love. This was so pointedly verified in the Baby M case, where the child was tossed around like a plaything by the adults involved claiming to have power over her.

While we must have compassion and understanding for the suffering caused by infertility in marriage, as well as for those spouses who fear bringing a handicapped child into the world, we must also realize, in the words of the C.D.F. Instruction, that "marriage does not confer on the spouses the right to have a child, but only the right to perform those natural acts which are *per se* ordered to procreation."[57] The child always remains a *gift* of love, and can never be considered an object of ownership or an object to which one has a right. Surrogacy radically depersonalizes the most intimate and personal act a husband and wife can share.

4. Recent developments in genetic engineering raise the question of the morality of **research and experimentation on human embryos and fetuses**. The discovery of the biochemical substance deoxyribonucleic acid (DNA) as the biochemical correlate of genes in the early 1950s opened up a whole new area of medical research. Now human genes and chromosomes have become the object of experimentation and therapy. The development of techniques of amniocentesis, ultrasound, and more recently, fetoscopy allow for the diagnosis of genetic disorders while the child is still in the womb. Unfortunately, these new techniques have been touted primarily as a means of preventing genetic diseases through the employment of selective abortion upon diagnosis of a genetic or chromosomal defect. These same techniques, however, do allow for the possibility of early and beneficial treatment of some of these disorders in the prenatal stage.

A positive moral evaluation can be given to prenatal diagnosis if it "respects the life and integrity of the embryo and the human fetus and is directed towards its safeguarding or healing as an individual."[58] The free and informed consent of the parents must be acquired in all such cases. The same can be said about medical research and experimentation on human embryos and fetuses. In all instances the fruit of the womb must receive the full dignity and respect of any other human being. Any procedure that would place a human embryo or fetus at disproportionate risks would be immoral, as would be any diagnostic technique done with the thought of possibly inducing an abortion, depending upon the results.

The C.D.F. Instruction condemns as a violation of human dignity all practices of keeping human embryos alive, whether in the womb or the test-tube, for experimental or commercial purposes, as well as the IVF production of human embryos destined to be exploited as disposable "biological material." It also judges as an attack upon the supreme value of personhood all "plans for fertilization between human and animal gametes and the gestation of human embryos in the uterus of animals, or the hypothesis or project of constructing artificial uteruses for the human embryo."[59] The freezing of human embryos also constitutes an offense against human dignity by exposing them to grave risks of death and physical harm, and by temporarily depriving them of the maternal bond and shelter established during gestation. Furthermore, the embryos obtained for freezing are usually procured through IVF, a technological procedure that depersonalizes human reproduction and separates the unitive and procreative meaning of the conjugal embrace.

Ethical Decisions: Prolonging Life or Allowing To Die?

Health care ethics today is confronted with countless questions from the time of conception until the moment of death. Space in this chapter will allow us to consider only some of the most important issues. We regrettably shall not be able to consider the ethical perspectives of surgery, psychotherapy, drug and alcohol addiction, sexual reassignment, medical experimentation, etc. Yet, in all these areas respect for personal integrity and freedom within a wholistic anthropology serves as the basis for the general principles that come into play in every ethical decision. Herein we want to look now at some of the questions that health care providers face when human life has run its course and death is approaching.

The Meaning of Death. Since treatment of the whole person is the fundamental concern of medicine, health care professionals themselves must come to a personal understanding of the meaning of human life, health, suffering and death. The tendency today to look upon health as a consumer commodity rendered through ever more advanced technology depersonalizes health care by approaching it from a purely functional and physical perspective. From such a standpoint the failure to relieve pain and prevent death is the greatest failure. Only when the health care professional has personally come to grips with the mystery of suffering and death can he or she properly minister to the sick and dying. As Father Bernard Häring, C.Ss.R., points out, "The existential attitude of the doctor or nurse to death will determine not only all of his or her relationships but also the very understanding of the healing profession."[60] Suffering and death are an integral part of human life in its physical, temporal existence. Embracing the mystery of it alone allows us to integrate, transcend and thereby overcome it.

As Christians, our faith in the Good News of Jesus Christ gives a whole new meaning to the mystery of suffering and death. In the Gospel according to John, Jesus announces: "I am the resurrection and the life; whoever believes in me, even if he dies, will live, and everyone who lives and believes in me will never die" (Jn. 11:25-26). Jesus delivers us not from physical death, but from its finality. In him, suffering and death are redeemed as he reveals the spiritual and eternal dimensions that lie at the core of our being. In the words of the Eucharistic Preface "Christian Death I" we hear proclaimed that "for your faithful people life is changed, not ended. When the body of our earthly dwelling lies in death we gain an everlasting dwelling place in heaven." The New Testament itself explains the meaning of Christ's suffering and death. In the Letter to the Hebrews we read: "Now since the children share in blood and flesh, he likewise shared in them, that through death he might destroy the one who has the power of death, that is, the devil, and free those who through fear of death had been subject to slavery all their life" (Heb. 2:14-15).

Fear of death is present in every one of us. It is part of our unredeemed state. To our imaginations death can appear as ultimate futility bearing witness to the total meaninglessness of life. The thought of death can breathe deep anxiety with visions of our final annihilation. Pascal claimed that we spend all our lives trying to take our minds off death. Some of us manage more or less to repress it. What makes death and dying so horrifying is that in our unredeemed state we cannot integrate it into our lives. Viewing it from the perspective of sin, death is experienced as painful separation, rather than as ultimate communion with the Triune Mystery of Love. Christ, however, by undergoing death as the ultimate act of loving obedience to the Father, in contrast to Adam's primal disobedience, has overcome the sting of death. In Christ the last Adam, we dare ask, "Where, O death, is your victory? / Where, O death, is your sting?" (1 Cor. 15:55). Faith gives us a new understanding of the meaning of life and death.

Prolonging Life. Resuscitation procedures today can give many a second chance at life. Organ transplants can save, or at least extend, a life formerly doomed to die. We are all familiar with instances of physical life being maintained after all hope of a person's returning to consciousness was irretrievably lost. A tremendous disproportion is currently evident between disregard or even contempt for human life at its promising beginning and the great efforts undertaken to prolong death. For those who view physical death as the ultimate failure, no effort will be spared in preventing death from happening. On the other hand, for those who believe that death is a natural process in life leading one into the fullness of eternal life, every proper and reasonable effort will be made to preserve life. Subscribing to this latter vision, the Roman Catholic tradition insists that all persons have a serious responsibility to take ordinary means to preserve their lives and health, but that extraordinary measures are not morally required.

1. Catholic theology has traditionally distinguished between **ordinary and extraordinary means** of preserving life and health. Ordinary means are those which do not place excessive physical, mental, financial or spiritual burdens on the patient or on his or her family. Extraordinary means are those which do cause serious burden. What is serious burden? The answer to this question varies from situation to situation. It requires weighing all the values involved and exercising prudent judgment.

Because the health care profession readily equates "ordinary means" with standard treatment and "extraordinary means" with experimental treatment, much confusion surrounds the theologians' use of these terms in the contemporary context. The Congregation for the Doctrine of the Faith in its 1980 "Declaration on Euthanasia" speaks instead of "proportionate means" and "disproportionate means."[61] Other contemporary moralists have suggested the use of the terms "benefit" and "burden," or "beneficial vs. non-beneficial." In other words, the question that must be answered is "Does the benefit to the patient justify the burden?" It is important to avoid two extreme approaches:

1. Automatically doing everything medical science can do at any cost.
2. Judging that an individual's life is no longer "worth living" and abandoning the person or directly ending his or her life.

Neither of these extremes is morally acceptable.[62] For example, antibiotics are now the standard arsenal of medicine in treating pneumonia, yet it would be considered cruel and extraordinary to use them in treating a person dying of cancer, who is in great pain and close to death, who develops pneumonia. In a second case, it would be immoral to decide not to correct through surgery esophageal atresia in a Down's syndrome child with no other defects simply because the child will have to live his or her life with a mental impairment.

Questions of conscience frequently arise today in health care situations involving the use of drugs, the determination of terminal illness, code-no-code policies, the withdrawal of life-sustaining mechanisms, support care, truth telling, and the lack of unanimity among decision makers and their advisors in crisis situations. The obligation, however, to preserve or prolong life belongs to the person alone, or when incompetent to his or her designated proxy. This is true also in regard to the decision of whether to use or forego extraordinary means. Others, depending upon their relationship to the patient, have the obligation to provide means necessary to preserve life, and this obligation cannot be reduced to the distinction between ordinary and extraordinary means. The obligation of charity extends to any need the person alone cannot relieve. Every person has a unique dignity by being made in the image and likeness of God. This unique dignity must be respected by providing proper care and comfort in a reasonably expected manner.

2. The question of **resuscitation** presents another ethical dilemma with regard to preserving and prolonging human life. Resuscitation refers to the procedures taken to rescue a person from the brink of death by restoring heartbeat and breathing. It was first developed for otherwise healthy persons whose heartbeat or breathing ceased following surgery or near-drowning. Today it is used almost on everyone who is the victim of cardiac arrest. Indeed, cardiopulmonary resuscitation (CPR) is considered to be a medically ordinary means of preserving life.

There are situations, however, when it should not be administered: a) when it cannot be done within a few minutes (3 to 5 minutes) after cardiac arrest (useless, hence non-compulsory); b) in cases of irreversible terminal illness when death is imminent and the patient is beyond any hopeful prognosis (useless, hence non-compulsory); c) when the patient, while still competent, definitely decided against it and did not later reverse that decision.[63]

A DNR order ("Do Not Resuscitate), also known as "No Code," means that the resuscitation team in the hospital will not be called to reverse a cardiac arrest. A "Code Blue," on the other hand, calls the team into action. Hospital policies should require adequate physician-patient communication about a resuscitation decision.

Euthanasia. Catholic Church teaching defines "euthanasia" as "an action or omission which of itself or by intention causes death, in order that all suffering may in this way be eliminated."[64] Advocates of euthanasia also refer to it as "mercy-killing" and "death with dignity." The Hemlock Society, Concern for the Dying, and the Society for the Right to Die, are three euthanasia advocacy groups promoting their cause in the United States. It is currently estimated that in the Netherlands, where "euthanasia reform" has been legalized, some 8000 lethal injections are administered every year. Proponents of euthanasia feel that the same humane consideration manifested for an incurably ill and acutely-suffering animal ("Put it out of its misery") should be extended to hopelessly ill and incurable human beings. Lacking any conviction about God's dominion over human life and the existence of eternal life, these adherents of a purely secular humanist viewpoint find no redemptive value in human suffering. The Good News of Christ's paschal mystery, of our victory over suffering and death through union with him, makes absolutely no sense to many of our contemporaries.

1. The fight against legalizing euthanasia becomes somewhat confused by the longstanding Roman Catholic tradition of allowing the **withdrawal of extraordinary means** of sustaining human life. Secular society, which does not recognize the Church's moral distinction between "ordinary" and "extraordinary means," also looks upon the withdrawal of the latter as a form of euthanasia. In 1957 Pope Pius XII spoke approvingly of families who bring pressure to bear upon the attending physician "to remove the respirators so as to allow the patient, already virtually dead, to depart in peace."[65] The withdrawing of such life-support systems leads most probably to immediate death. Yet, the cessation of a no longer beneficial treatment is not killing but removing an artificial obstacle that impedes the natural death process. Withdrawing treatment, in the words of the Vatican declaration, "is not the equivalent of suicide; on the contrary, it should be considered as an acceptance of the human condition, or a wish to avoid the application of a medical procedure disproportionate to the results that can be expected, or a

desire not to impose excessive expense on the family or community."[66]

Catholic moralists today, however, are divided over the question of withholding artificial sustenance. Providing basic nutrition and hydration is an ethically ordinary means of preserving life, and as a general rule, must not be denied to the sick. Father Charles McFadden, O.S.A., summarizes what has been the mainstream position of Catholic moralists on this issue:

> Routine medical practice today utilizes intravenous feeding in a countless variety of cases. Certainly the physician regards this procedure as an *ordinary* means of preserving life. It is obviously able to be carried out, under normal hospital conditions, without any notable inconvenience. For this reason we must regard recourse to intravenous feeding, in the case of typical hospitalized patients, as an ordinary and morally compulsory procedure.
>
> The above conclusion applies, as stated, to routine hospital cases where the procedure is envisioned as a *temporary* means of carrying a patient through a critical period. Surely an effort to sustain life *permanently* in this fashion would constitute a grave hardship and not be morally compulsory.[67]

While the Vatican has issued no definitive statement on such cases, the Pontifical Academy of Sciences in a November 1985 report recommended that while treatment is not required for a patient in a permanent coma, irreversible as far as it is possible to predict, still care including feeding must be provided.

In the case of Marcia Gray, a Rhode Island woman who had been in a coma for two years, the Diocese of Providence, Rhode Island, on January 10, 1988 issued a theological statement maintaining that nutrition and hydration in this case constituted extraordinary means of care and could be removed without violating Catholic teaching. Commenting on the statement, Bishop Louis Gelineau of Providence, explained that

> The magisterium of the church has not yet issued a definitive statement regarding the need to provide nutrition and hydration to the permanently unconscious person. Within the church, however, two theological opinions are presented. The first, that nutrition and hydration can be considered extraordinary means of sustaining life in certain circumstances; the second states that fluid and nutritional support are always to be provided.[68]

Longstanding Catholic theological tradition seems to lean in favor of the first opinion, although there exists a very real danger that advocates of euthanasia and health-care planners with a cost-benefit orientation might readily use such a position against entire classes of demented, senile institutionalized patients who are not terminally ill.

2. Catholic moral tradition gives a resounding "No" to the practice of **active or positive euthanasia,** that is, the voluntary commission of a life-terminating action. Positive euthanasia is sometimes called mercy-killing. The direct intention is to put an end to a person's life. The Vatican "Declaration on Euthanasia" referring to the teaching of Pius XII, however, does allow for the administration of narcotics or painkillers to suppress undesirable pain and anxiety, even though a shortening of the terminal illness may be foreseen. The dying person is not to be deprived of consciousness unless there is a serious reason for so doing.[69] Stopping treatments with the intention to hasten death is also a form of active euthanasia.

The Moment of Death. Verification of the moment of death, according to Pius XII, "cannot be deduced from any religious and moral principle, and under this aspect, does not fall within the competence of the Church."[70] The U.S. Bishops' Ethical and Religious Directives for Catholic Health Facilities state that the determination of the time of death must be made "in accordance with responsible and commonly accepted scientific criteria" (no. 31). Medical science today equates brain death with human death. Most of the individual states in the United States have adopted a definition-of-death statute which includes the brain-death stipulation with the exact calculation of the moment of death being left to accepted medical standards and the law in each jurisdiction.

In a very real sense we are dying all the time. Life itself is paradoxically a process of dying and death is the culmination of a lifelong process. Each decision in life prepares us for the ultimate one of either definitively accepting God's loving design or rebelling in despair. As Christians, our baptism into Jesus' paschal mystery unites us with this process and takes us beyond the veil of physical death into the realm of everlasting life. Our union with Christ demands continuing conversion, an ongoing participation in his dying and rising, and ultimately offering ourselves into the Father's hands in one great final act of loving trust and obedience. As members of Christ's Body, we must help those who are dying by being there for them, caring, supporting and praying for them. We must lovingly and respectfully accompany them to the threshold of the "new Jerusalem" where God "will wipe every tear from their eyes, and there shall be no more death or mourning, wailing or pain, [for] the old order has passed away" (Rev. 21:4).

Notes

1. Richard A. McCormick, S.J., *How Brave a New World?: Dilemmas in Bioethics* (Garden City, New York: Doubleday & Company, Inc., 1981), p. 43.

2. *Letter to the Ephesians*, 7, 2 as cited in Häring, *Free and Faithful in Christ*, vol. 3, p. 42.

3. Bernard Häring, *Medical Ethics* (Notre Dame: Fides Publishers, 1973), pp. 69-70.

4. Pius XII, "Allocution to Midwives," October 29, 1951, *Acta Apostolicis Sedis* 43 (1951): 838-839.

5. Kevin D. O'Rourke, O.P., J.C.D., and Dennis Brodeur, Ph.D., *Medical Ethics: Common Ground for Understanding* (St. Louis, Missouri: The Catholic Health Association of the United States, 1986), pp. 33-34.

6. Ibid., p. 35.

7. Dena Seiden, "Prescription for a Medical Ethic: Diminishing Resources, Critical Choices," *Commonweal* cxii (March 8, 1985): 140.

8. Ibid.

9. Häring, *Medical Ethics*, pp. 199-200.

10. See Charles E. Cavagnaro, M.D. and Antonio Antonucci, obl. O.S.B., "KYRIOTIS: The Moral Authority of the Physician," *Ethics & Medics* 12 (November 1987): 2.

11. United States Catholic Conference, "Health and Health Care: A Pastoral Letter of the American Catholic Bishops" (Washington, D.C.: USCC Publications, 1982), p. 5 with reference to Pope John XXIII's encyclical *Pacem in Terris*, art. 11.

12. Ibid., p. 13.

13. The President's Commission, *Securing Access to Health Care* (Washington, D.C.: U.S. Government Printing Office, 1983), I, pp. 18-22.

14. Griese, *Catholic Health Care Identity*, p. 63.

15. O'Rourke and Brodeur, op. cit., p. 4.

16. Griese, op. cit., p. 156.

17. Ibid., p. 196.

18. Häring, *Medical Ethics*, pp. 202-203.

19. See Griese, op. cit., pp. 366-367.

20. Burtchaell, "The Natural Law Revisited," pp. 12-13.

21. Congregation for the Doctrine of the Faith, *Instruction on Respect for Human life in Its Origin and on the Dignity of Procreation*, Vatican translation (Boston, Mass.: St. Paul Editions, n.d.), p. 7.

22. Lorenzo M. Albacete, S.T.D., Commentary on *Instruction on Respect for Human Life in Its Origin and on the Dignity of Procreation* (Boston, Mass.: St. Paul Editions, 1987), p. 5.

23. Burtchaell, op. cit., p. 10.

24. CDF, "Instruction on Respect for Human Life. . .," p. 8.

25. United States Catholic Conference, *The Ethical and Religious Directives for Catholic Health Facilities* (St. Louis, Mo.: The Catholic Health Association of the United States, 24th printing, 1986), no. 12., p. 7.

26. The development of this particular section is but a brief summary of John T. Noonan, Jr., "An Almost Absolute Value in History," *The Morality of Abortion: Legal and Historical Perspectives*, ed. idem, (Cambridge, Mass.: Harvard University Press, 1970), pp. 1-59.

27. A.E. Hellegers, "Fetal Development," *Theological Studies*, 31 (1970): 4.

28. See Häring, *Medical Ethics*, p. 81.

29. Genovesi, *In the Pursuit of Love*, pp. 341-342.

30. Häring, *Medical Ethics*, p. 83.

31. John Paul II, *Love and Responsibility*, trans. H. T. Willts (New York: Farrar, Straus & Giroux, 1981), p. 55.

32. Henri J. W. Nouwen, "The Peace that is Not of this World," *Weavings* 3 (March/April 1988): 29.

33. See Congregation for the Doctrine of the Faith, "Declaration on Procured Abortion," November 18, 1974, no. 13 in *Vatican Council II: More Post Conciliar Documents*, vol. 2, pp. 445-446.

34. Augustine Lehmkuhl, S.J., *1 Theologia moralis* n. 841 (Freiburg i. Br., 5th ed., 1888) cited in Noonan, op. cit., p. 46.

35. Häring, *Medical Ethics*, p. 108.

36. Ibid.

37. Lobo, *Guide to Christian Living*, p. 352.

38. Germain Grisez, *Abortion: The Myths, the Realities, and the Arguments* (New York: Corpus, 1970), pp. 32-46.

39. See, Lobo, op. cit., p. 352.

40. See Genovesi, op. cit., pp. 222-227.

41. A. Nicholas Groth and Ann Wolbert Burgess, "Sexual Dysfunction During Rape," *New England Journal of Medicine* 297, no. 14 (October 6, 1977): 765 cited in Lloyd W. Hess, Ph. D., "Treatment For Rape Victims In Catholic Health Facilities," Part Two, Ethics & Medics 10 (December 1985): 1; and Genovesi, op. cit., p. 342.

42. Hess, op. cit., Part One, 10 (November 1985): 2.

43. See Thomas J. O'Donnell, S.J., *Medicine and Christian Morality* (New York: Alba House, 1976), p. 277.

44. Hess, op. cit., Part Two, p. 2.

45. Griese, op. cit., p. 85.

46. See John Cattanach, *The Lancet*, April 13, 1985, pp. 847-9 referred to by Edward J. Bayer, "To Tie or Not to Tie?" *Ethics & Medics* 11 (September 1986): 2.

47. Ibid.

48. See C.D.F., "*Haec sacra congregatio*" (March 13, 1975) in *Vatican Council II: More Post Conciliar Documents*, no. 107, pp. 454-455.

49. Ibid., with reference to Paul VI, *Humanae Vitae*.

50. C.D.F., "Instruction on Respect for Human Life". . ., p. 9.

51. "Human Life and Free Choice," *Ethics & Medics* 7 (March 1982): 4.

52. Pius XII, Address to Catholic Doctors, September 29, 1949, *Acta Apostolicae Sedis* 41 (1949): 559-560.

53. C.D.F., "Instruction on Respect for Human Life. . ., p. 24.

54. Ibid., p. 31.

55. Griese, op. cit., pp. 43-47; Donald G. McCarthy, "Infertility Bypassed," *Ethics & Medics* 11 (March 1986): 3-4; and Lloyd W. Hess, "Assisting the Infertile Couple," Part Three, *Ethics & Medics* 11 (February 1986): 2-4.

56. See C.D.F. "Instruction on Respect for Human Life. . .," p. 26.

57. Ibid., p. 33.

58. Ibid., p. 14.

59. Ibid., p. 19.

60. Häring, *Free and Faithful in Christ*, vol. 3, p. 77.

61. Congregation for the Doctrine of the Faith, "Declaration on Euthanasia" ("*Jura et bona*"), May 5, 1980 in *Vatican Council II: More Post Conciliar Documents*, vol. 2, no. 112, p. 515.

62. Lawrence T. Reilly, "Prolonging Life Conscience Formation," *Moral Responsibility in Prolonging Life Decisions*, ed. Donald G. McCarthy and Albert S. Moraczewski, O.P. (St. Louis: Pope John Center, 1981), p. 143.

63. Griese, op. cit., p. 165.

64. C.D.F., "Declaration on Euthanasia," in op. cit., p. 512.

65. Pius XII, Discourse to Doctors (November 24, 1957), *Acta Apostolicae Sedis* 49 (1957): 1029.

66. C.D.F. "Declaration on Euthanasia" in op. cit., pp. 515-516.

67. Charles J. McFadden, *The Dignity of Life* (Huntington, Indiana: Our Sunday Visitor, Inc., 1976), p. 152.

68. Bishop Louis Gelineau, "On Removing Nutrition and Water From Comatose Woman," *Origins* 17 (January 21, 1988): 545.

69. C.D.F., "Declaration on Euthanasia," in op. cit., p. 514.

70. Pius XII, Address to the International Congress of Anesthesiologists, November 24, 1957, *The Pope Speaks* (Spring 1958): 398.

Chapter 11

Catholic Social Teaching

The Church links human liberation and salvation in Jesus Christ, but she never identifies them, because she knows through revelation, historical experience and the reflection of faith that not every notion of liberation is necessarily consistent and compatible with an evangelical vision of man, of things and of events; she knows too that in order that God's kingdom should come it is not enough to establish liberation and to create well-being and development.

And what is more, the Church has a firm conviction that all temporal liberation, all political liberation . . . carries within itself the germ of its own negation and fails to reach the ideal that it proposes for itself whenever its profound motives are not those of justice in charity, whenever its zeal lacks a truly spiritual dimension and whenever its final goal is not salvation and happiness in God. — Paul VI[1]

Modern Catholic social teaching traces its beginnings to the writings of Pope Leo XIII. His great encyclicals on Christian philosophy, politics and the social order attempted to recapture the classical vision of St. Thomas Aquinas and to apply those teachings to current injustices in the economic order. Leo XIII's landmark encyclical of 1891, *Rerum Novarum*, began the Catholic Church's critical participation in the developments of modern social and economic life. In the last century the papacy has probably written more on social ethics than on any other single topic. The Catholic bishops of the United States, too, have addressed numerous issues of the political and social order in various policy statements and pastoral letters which they have published over the past seventy years. Yet U.S. Catholics remain virtually ignorant of this whole body of official Church teaching.

Pope Leo XIII rooted his social ethics in the supreme value of the human person. All political and social structures need to respect and respond to this primary moral claim of human dignity. The origin of the state itself, furthermore, is found in our social nature making it a natural institution. Thus

302

the Second Vatican Council maintains that "the political community and public authority are based on human nature, and therefore that they need belong to an order established by God" (GS 74). While the Church and the political community are autonomous and independent of each other in their own fields, the Church is "at once the sign and the safeguard of the transcendental dimension of the human person" (GS 76).

The Church's social teaching is thus an integral part of her essential and primary mission of evangelization. In proclaiming the Good News of Jesus Christ she makes known the truth of what it means to be fully human. Pope John Paul II emphasizes this point in his encyclical *Sollicitudo Rei Socialis* ("On Social Concern"), where he states that

> ... the Church has *something to say* today, just as twenty years ago, and also in the future, about the nature, conditions, requirements and aims of authentic development, and also about the obstacles which stand in its way. In doing so the Church fulfills her mission to *evangelize*, for she offers her *first* contribution to the solution of the urgent problem of development when she proclaims the truth about Christ, about herself and about man, applying this truth to a concrete situation.[2]

Human development, as understood by contemporary Catholic social thought, is not primarily economic. It is an integral development of the whole person which respects and promotes "human rights — personal and social, economic and political, including the *rights of nations and of peoples*."[3] The Church's espousal and promotion of these rights is part of her religious mission. For while Christ gave the Church no distinct mission in the political, economic and social order, her mission of evangelization remains a source of insight, motivation and commitment that can serve to structure and consolidate the human community according to the divine law (see GS 42).

Since it aims to guide Christian behavior, the Church's social doctrine, Pope John Paul II affirms, "belongs to the field, not of *ideology*, but of *theology* and particularly of moral theology."[4] It is concerned with our self-understanding and our vocation as seen through the light of faith. Christian anthropology, as we reflected upon it in chapter three, remains the authentic starting point of Christian social ethics as well. All structures, whether political, economic or cultural, are meant to facilitate human development, that is, our growth as conscious, free, relational beings who are made in the image and likeness of God. In other words, they are meant to serve our growth in love. Their sole task is to promote the "common good," which Vatican II defines as "the sum total of all those conditions of social life which enable individuals, families, and organizations to achieve complete and efficacious fulfilment" (GS 74).

Social structures are the concretization of human beliefs and vision; they are the natural product of right reason or the lack thereof. Catholic social teaching, therefore, is based upon our participation in the natural law according to the "order of reason" and is illumined by faith. It seeks to bring the gospel's vision of human life and its meaning to bear upon the societal structures and needs of a given historical time. While it remains constant in its fundamental principles and directives, which are rooted in the Good News of Jesus Christ, this social doctrine continues to change as it adapts to historical conditions and the unceasing flow of world events. Before surveying modern Catholic social doctrine which began with Pope Leo XIII, we shall look first at its roots in Scripture. We shall then trace its development through the Fathers of the Church and scholastic theology, demonstrating how it has addressed the circumstances and needs of changing times and events.

Biblical Foundations

The elements of biblical social doctrine are shaped by the covenantal relationship between God and his people. In the Old Testament the virtue of justice or righteousness formed the basis of all relationships in human life. Justice signified fidelity to the demands of the covenant. For the ancient Hebrews, religion included politics. The authority that ruled the state was designated by God; it constituted a theocracy that had a sacral character.

In the New Testament, Jesus reveals the new and eternal covenant of self-giving, reconciling love. Love is God's justice that surpasses all human justice. In proclaiming the coming of God's kingdom Jesus makes a distinction between secular authority and that of God. He tells us that we are to "repay to Caesar what belongs to Caesar and to God what belongs to God" (Mt. 22:21). Yet, secular authority itself, while distinct, is rooted in the divine (see Jn. 19:10-11).

The Old Testament. God's justice flows from his covenant with his people. It is a saving justice that reveals his love and mercy, his goodness, that is likened to the surging waters of an unfailing stream. For their part, the people are to reflect this holiness of God, who through the prophet Amos tells

304

them: "Your cereal offerings I will not accept, nor consider your stall-fed peace offerings. . . . But if you would offer me holocausts, then let justice surge like water, and goodness like an unfailing stream" (Amos 5:22-24). Fidelity and constancy in doing the works of love and mercy is the only sacrifice acceptable to God. This Old Testament concept of justice as goodness poured forth in an unfailing stream stands in stark contrast to the classical symbol which portrays justice as a blindfolded woman holding in her hand the balanced scales.

Justice in the Old Testament has many nuances. It describes the people's proper relationship to God which comes about through observance of his laws. The biblical concept of justice is more comprehensive than subsequent philosophical definitions. Its primary concern is manifesting God's holiness and goodness by doing what is right and good. Rather than providing a strict definition of rights and duties, biblical justice is demonstrated through love of God and neighbor. It becomes present by doing God's will, by keeping his commandments made explicit in Israel's great legal codes such as the Decalogue (Ex. 20:1-17) and the Book of the Covenant (Ex. 20:22-23:33).

> Far from being an arbitrary restriction on the life of the people, these codes made life in community possible. The specific laws of the covenant protect human life and property and demand respect for parents and the spouses and children of one's neighbor, and manifest a special concern for the vulnerable members of the community: widows, orphans, the poor and strangers in the land.[5]

These commandments tell the people how to imitate God who delivered them from slavery and oppression. They in turn must show the same fidelity, mercy and kindness to one another. When the people stray from their covenantal relationship with God to serve other idols, the prophets summon them back to the One who betrothed them "in right and in justice, in love and in mercy" (Hos. 2:21).

The New Testament. Jesus proclaims the coming of God's kingdom by word and example. In the Sermon on the Mount he teaches the universal kinship and solidarity of all who call upon God as "Our Father in heaven" (Mt. 6:9). He then proceeds to warn us against storing up for ourselves treasures on earth (Mt. 6:19) and about the impossibility of serving both God and money (Mt. 6:24). Jesus exhorts his followers to stop worrying about food, clothes and material goods. Instead, we must "seek first the kingdom [of God] and his righteousness'' (Mt. 6:33). God's kingdom, moreover, becomes evident in our works of love. Jesus' description of the Last Judgment scene teaches us that the heirs of the kingdom are those who showed compassion to those in need, to the hungry, the thirsty, the naked, the sick and the prisoner. Furthermore he enjoins us to love our enemies, to do good to those who hate us, to give without expecting return. In sum, he tells us ''Be merciful, just as [also] your Father is merciful'' (Lk. 6:36).

In the Parable of the Rich Man and Lazarus (Lk. 16:19-31), Jesus teaches us about universal human dignity as the poor man, Lazarus, is granted salvation while the rich man who shows no mercy is condemned. The Parable of the Good Samaritan (Lk. 10:29-37) is used by Jesus to instruct us that loving our neighbor means showing mercy to everyone in need. Jesus identifies himself as the one who has come to serve, not to be served, and he clearly states that his followers must likewise serve the needs of all (Mt. 20:26-28). Indeed, Jesus further specifies the commandment to love our neighbor when he says, ''love one another as I love you'' (Jn. 15:12). His paschal mystery is the ultimate ground and source of Catholic social teaching. Jesus' death, too, is a model for those who suffer persecution for the sake of justice (Mt. 5:10).

After Jesus' resurrection and ascension the early apostolic community of faith continued to demonstrate Jesus' concern for the poor. The Jerusalem church distributed its possessions so that ''there was no needy person among them'' (Acts 4:34). St. Paul, too, charges the church at Corinth to imitate Christ in its generosity to those in need (2 Cor. 8:9), and he insists that we ''are all one in Christ Jesus'' (Gal. 3:28). The Johannine community asks: ''If someone who has worldly means sees a brother in need and refuses him compassion, how can the love of God remain in him? Children, let us love not in word or speech but in deed and truth'' (1 Jn. 3:17-18). The Letter of James warns against showing any partiality based on wealth or social status (Jas. 2:1-13), and it states unequivocally that genuine religion consists of this: ''to care for orphans and widows in their affliction and to keep oneself unstained by the world'' (Jas. 1:27). It tells the rich, furthermore, to weep and wail over their impending miseries because the cries of the poor, whose wages have been withheld, and those of the defrauded harvesters have reached the ears of God (Jas. 5:1-6).

The Social Thought of the Fathers and the Scholastics

As we have already seen, in ancient Israel religion and government were one. The religious law was the law of the people and the state. In New Testament times the Christian community was but a small minority without any way or hope of influencing and shaping the public order of the Roman Empire. Besides, the coming Kingdom of God was incomparably more important. Both Jesus and St. Paul had recognized the secular power's right to demand obedience from its subjects (Mk. 12:17; Rom. 13:1-7). This recognition, however, was tempered with a spirit of inner detachment and independence since these institutions would eventually perish. Thus, while their visions regarding the role of politics and the state markedly differed, nevertheless the moral foundations and principles directing social concerns in both the Old and New Testaments found their source in the covenantal relationship between God and his people, which is faithfully kept by doing justice or righteous works of love and mercy.

The Pre-Constantinian Church. In the post-apostolic period there was no strong perception that Christians either could or should attempt to reform the structures of society. Even the New Testament did not attack the institution of slavery, but did require that Christians look upon slaves as their equals in dignity. St. Paul insisted that there was no distinction between slave and free in Christ (1 Cor. 12:13; Gal 3:28). Before the era of Constantine the Church was often cruelly persecuted as an illegal organization. As a result, it was continually on the defensive and its involvement in society was drastically curtailed.

Christians were primarily urged to practice acts of private charity in order to manifest God's goodness and love. Such charity took the form of almsgiving, which was said to be a spiritual ransom, a penance for sins. Thus, Tertullian observes: "Our care for the derelict and our active love have become our distinctive sign before the enemy . . . See, they say, how they love one another and how ready they are to die for each other."[6] It was a duty, especially of deacons, to care for the sick and visit the prisoner. Ransom was often collected for the release of captives. The same love and care were extended to victims of plague and public disasters, as well as to travelers and the dead. The Church of Rome became famous for its hospitality to strangers. Converted slaves were accorded equal status and allowed to hold ecclesiastical offices, including that of bishop. Despite persecution by the pagan state, the majority of the Fathers entertained a positive attitude toward it, affirming the obligation of taxes and military service.

From Constantine to the End of the Patristic Era. Before the Church was formally recognized by Constantine's Edict of Toleration in A.D. 313 the early Christian martyrs, in refusing to grant to Caesar what was not his to demand, gave witness to the existence of an alternative force in society capable of resisting the totalitarian state. The martyrs, in fact, laid the foundation stone for the concept of individual freedom vis-a-vis the state. By the beginning of the fourth century the disintegrating empire needed the Church's moral authority, social strength and cohesion. As a result of this alliance the Church was now free to carry on her mission openly and more effectively, and this was especially true of her works of charity. While Christian influence on legislation was now possible, the Church, as in the first three centuries, did not see itself as called to reform unjust social and economic structures. Viewed as a consequence of sin, these structures were still perceived as fixed, rigid, and ultimately insignificant. It did, however, manage to promote legislation that brought about less despotic government, better treatment of slaves, suppression of the immorality of stage and arena, help for the poor in all its forms, and an increased respect for women.[7]

1. The major political question in this period focused on **the relationship between the Church and the state.** Under Constantine a close and harmonious collaboration between the two prevailed. The emperor's authority to summon synods, to steer the course of theological discussions through his ecclesiastical advisors and to exile heretics was unquestioningly accepted. His successors, however, sought to exercise a strict control over the Church. Constantius (337-361) called himself the *episcopus episcoporum* ("the bishop of the bishops"), which designation was vigorously resisted by a number of the Church Fathers. For St. Ambrose, Bishop of Milan, "the Emperor is in the Church, not over the Church"[8] In this view the Church and the state stand in a positive relationship to each other, but the innermost sphere of the Church's life — faith, morals and ecclesiastical discipline — remain beyond the competence of the state.

Drawing upon pagan sources, especially Plato and Cicero, in addition to sacred Scripture, St. Augustine developed a political theology which put forth "the theory of the two cities." The *civitas terrena* ("earthly city") is not identified with the state, nor is the *civitas Dei* ("city of God") with the Church. Both are ideal societies, the one according to the flesh, the other according to the spirit; both are partially realized in concrete historical structures, since evil and corruption are present in their members. The state is necessary because of the social nature of the human person which makes it a natural institution. Furthermore, the existence of original sin requires the power of the state to assure order, peace and unity, as it works to guarantee the material and economic, as well as the moral and religious, interests of its citizens.[9]

This basic vision was later developed by Pope Gelasius (492-496) into the theory of "the two swords," according to which "there were two divinely instituted, separate and independent, but mutually supportive, powers in society — that of the Church for spiritual matters, that of the state for temporal."[10] This so-called Gelasian theory of the two powers remained the basic vision throughout the Middle Ages. The theocratic character of the Frankish monarchy under Charlemagne was but an interlude. The clashes between the emperor and the papacy which developed from the eleventh century on tended, however, to become the norm for the next several centuries.

2. The writings of the Church Fathers touch upon a whole range of **social relations** including slavery, work, the right of ownership, the social function of property, interest and usury, etc. While trying to improve the overall lot of the slaves, the Fathers sought to justify it as a necessary economic institution, a product of war and a consequence of sin. Indeed, members of the clergy and religious institutions themselves had slaves. They also urged Christians to work and avoid idleness. Through honest labor one procured for oneself the basic material necessities of life and could also acquire the means to assist the needy and the poor. The fourth-century *Apostolic Constitutions* included a chapter entitled "The Idle Believers Must Not Eat."

St. Ambrose, among many other Fathers, maintained that prior to the Fall of Adam private ownership was not known. It is a consequence of sin with its inequality of properties and conditions. Yet, such private property is only apparent, for strictly speaking no one owns anything. Everything is a part of God's creation and belongs to him. The right to private property is limited by others' needs. In the last decade of the fourth century with its worsening economic situation, some of the Fathers, such as Ambrose, Augustine, John Chrysostom, Gregory of Nazianzus, and Basil of Caesarea, denounced the excessive accumulation of wealth in the hands of the rich and their lack of concern for the needs of the poor. Ambrose emphasized that almsgiving on the part of the avaricious is nothing but the restitution of stolen goods. Christians were urged to aid the poor not simply because of justice but above all because Christ is identified with them. Gregory of Nyssa thus wrote: "Do not despise these men in their abjection; do not think them of no account. Reflect what they are and you will understand their dignity; they have often taken upon themselves the person of our Savior."[11]

Certain aspects of the Fathers teachings were evidently time bound, such as their attitude towards slavery, as well as towards commerce and interest-taking. They denounced greedy merchants who sold at a higher price what they had not bought or produced. Money not being productive by itself, they considered it morally objectionable for bankers to make a profit by exacting interest on loans. They condemned, too, charging a higher price for goods in times of scarcity and the buying of properties at a lower price because of bankruptcy. Many of the Fathers' social writings are but commentaries and homilies on the gospel, which are still valid today, including especially the following elements: "the affirmation of the basic equality of all human beings; the doctrine of the right of private ownership; the principle that material goods are destined by God for the use of all human beings to satisfy their basic needs; the insistence on the necessity of conversion of heart and detachment from earthly possessions; the inculcation of the duty of almsgiving not only out of charity but also out of justice; the doctrine of the identity of Christ with the poor."[12]

The Scholastic Synthesis. During the Middle Ages the Church was left to fill the vacuum created by the collapse of an effective secular authority. Because of the many social, economic and political changes that occurred, the Church was compelled to undertake the tasks of civil government. She was the only viable social organization remaining intact in the western half of the now defunct Roman Empire until the emergence of the feudal state in the twelfth century. Temporal power had passed to the popes as a result of the weakness of the Empire and the confusion of political affairs in Italy. Feudalism as the new system of social organization was based on landholding and working in return for personal service — military or agricultural. The Church during this period, because of the wealth of her labors and the extensive gifts she received from others for the service of God, found herself a major landholder inextricably bound up with the social order. Her abbots and bishops became key figures politically, economically and militarily.

As the Church found herself moving closer to the center of the civil order, she became aware that she might be able to initiate social reform within the institutions of society. "It might be possible now to promote the idea of a unified Christian civilization whose spirit would penetrate and renew the whole fabric of the social enterprise."[13] The Church had the leaders and the strength to undertake the necessary reforms and therefore worked with great courage and industry, despite a number of lapses, to make a better Europe. Thus, the Age of Christendom was born.

The relationship between the Church and the state during the Middle Ages, however, came to a head over the practice of lay investiture, wherein the secular lord "invested" the abbot or bishop with the insignia of his office. In attempting to end the corruption brought on by lay control, Pope Gregory VII excommunicated the Holy Roman Emperor, Henry IV, in 1076. This act marked the beginning of a long controversy, during which the Gelasian theory of "the two swords" was replaced by the hierocratic theory. According to this latter postulate the Church was essentially superior to the state and the pope had the right to intervene in political affairs for the salvation of souls. Thus Pope Boniface VIII in his 1302 bull *Unam Sanctam* presents the pope as the source of both powers with the duty to pass on the temporal sword.

The new situation called for a new theological vision. The medieval theologians, not finding an adequate basis for political theory in the Scriptures, turned to classical Greek philosophy as an additional source. "This combination of revealed and natural wisdom, while it did not enjoy the uncontested authority of dogma, provided a solid intellectual basis for reflection on the scope and limits of human government and on the relations between the spiritual and temporal powers."[14] The theological synthesis put forward by St. Thomas Aquinas considered the state an institution of natural law, and therefore part of the natural order. The Church belonged to the supernatural order of grace. His doctrine combined scriptural and Augustinian thought with Aristotelian and stressed the origin of both powers in God. Aquinas thus wrote that "Both powers derive from God, the spiritual and the temporal. Temporal authority, therefore, is subject to the spiritual insofar as God has subordinated it, namely in matters concerning the salvation of souls; so in these matters a man must obey the spiritual power rather than the temporal."[15]

From the Stoics, Aquinas borrowed the concept of an absolute and a relative state of nature. The former he compared to the human condition of innocence before the Fall, in which harmony existed everywhere and no laws or government were necessary. The relative state of nature he likened to the human condition after original sin, whereby government and laws were now needed to regulate the community and restrain evil. Aquinas then inserted these views of nature into a two-storey model of the universe. The *created world*, or first storey, has passed from innocence to sin and corruption. The *supernatural*, or second storey, constitutes the world of God and the heavenly court, which is the goal and fulfillment of the natural world. These two worlds are united by two social realities: law in its various forms and the institutions of Church and state. The purpose of the state is actually twofold: to provide for the common good and to actively repress evil. The Church, possessing revealed truth, is charged with the mission of directing persons and institutions to their final end, the supernatural.[16]

Regarding the actual form of political authority, Thomas Aquinas favored a constitutional government based upon the consent of the governed. From his study of the Greek experience summed up in Aristotle, the insights of Scripture and tradition, the developing institutions of the society of his times and the form of government practiced by his own Dominican Order, he believed that the common good and sound discipline could be pursued best through government by consent, expressed through the principle of representation.[17] The feudal ordering of society that prevailed in the Middle Ages, however, was based on a theory of social duties, not a theory of rights. Social duties and obligations were attached to one's social role, whether one was a serf or a feudal lord. These social obligations took priority over individual desires and wants. Each individual's fulfilling of the responsibilities of his or her place in society was expected to insure total domestic tranquility. Aquinas and other medieval philosophers and theologians subscribed to this theory. It was only after the breakup of medieval civilization that emphasis would be placed upon individual rights.

Renaissance, the Reformation, and the Modern Secular State

While the Scholastic synthesis continued to guide Catholic social thought well into the twentieth century, changing economic, political, religious, cultural and social patterns began to alter the face of Europe in the fifteenth and sixteenth centuries. Medieval civilization and the Age of Chivalry gave way to the Renaissance, first in Italy, then in France and England, with the rediscovery of classical Greek and Roman literature, art and architecture. The growth of towns through commerce and trade, the widening geographical horizons, the invention of the printing press, the emergence of powerful

312

nation-states, all tended to shift attention from thoughts about the hereafter to concern for the here and now. The Church's continued active involvement in the political arena, its exaction of taxes and the scandalous sale of indulgences were now vigorously resisted both by the rising national states seeking their own sources of revenue and by the urban bourgeoisie.

The Protestant Reformation. The Reformed churches' antipapal doctrines and moral positions proved conducive to capitalist economic expansion. While the mendicant communities and the religious orders within Catholicism gave witness to the ultimate insignificance of worldly possessions — Protestantism, and Calvinism particularly, rejected completely this otherworldly stance. It demanded instead a worldly asceticism that was to be carried into the marketplace, where one was to carry out one's duty toward God, family and community, but always with a spirit of disciplined self-control and mystical piety. The Calvinist work ethic also redefined the idea of vocation or calling. Whereas the medieval Catholic concept saw each person called to a distinct task in the world, which was to be undertaken without thought of personal gain or satisfaction, the reformers attracted the merchant class by a doctrine of calling which enjoined diligence in work, and celebrated success as a sign of God's favor.

Catholic theologians and the reformers all sought to promote the ideas of stewardship and a Christian social order. While in the gospel Christ instructs the rich young man to sell all his possessions and distribute the proceeds to the poor, he also teaches the parable of the talents. Stewardship maintains that all who possess talent or property are not owners, but stewards. They hold their talent and property as trustees and are accountable to God for their use. On this point both the Catholic and Protestant theologians agreed, promoting its practical expression in the life of the Christian community. They agreed, too, on the need for a Christian society; they were one in their conviction that the whole community enjoyed a stature and importance at least equal to that of the individual. To be a Christian was to be a member of a people "sharing the common life." The medieval Church held tenaciously to the conviction that all worldly endeavors were subject to the scrutiny of both the Church and the state. Luther in Germany and Calvin in Geneva had no argument at all with this point. The Puritans, too, desired to bring the social order in line with gospel teachings. Some worked towards a reformed Christendom by imposing Christian discipline on everyone in society.[18]

The relationship between Church and state differed significantly within

Protestantism. While John Calvin eventually saw justification for active resistance to lawful magistrates, Luther maintained that the power of the local or national prince was absolute. Luther had abandoned the idea of an authority in the Church, such as the Catholic tradition knew. Since there was obviously a need for ecclesiastical discipline, he considered it to be the task of secular rulers. Secular government became the judge of needful reform within the Church, as well as the means of securing it. The result was a National Church subject to secular authorities. The breakup of Christendom and the growth of nationalism was thus encouraged by the Reformation. The "Protestant" states were now free of the pope and increasingly in conflict with the emperor, opposition to whom Luther fully condoned. The local princes now knew practically complete political and religious autonomy. The advantages of such absolutism did not go unnoticed by the "Catholic" states, such as Spain and France, even while they continued to remain in the Catholic fold.[19]

The Enlightenment and Growing Secularization. The intellectual ferment spawned by the Renaissance ushered in the new Age of Reason and Science. Disgust, too, over the passions that continued to ignite the conflict between Throne and Altar gave birth to a class of philosophers and intellectuals who sought to construct a new social order based on scientific reasoning. The Enlightenment, as it was called, in a very real way can trace its beginning to the political philosophy of Niccolo Machiavelli (1546-1627). Blaming the political confusion that existed in Italy on the Church and the papacy, he stressed the all-importance of the absolute authority of the prince. For the ruler in the pursuit of the purpose of maintaining the state, the end justified the means. Machiavelli had no interest in justice, a natural-law morality or the common good. According to him, force itself was the origin of the state, and it was appropriate for the prince to use whatever means necessary to maintain security and order.

Machiavelli was the first significant secular political theorist. He held that modern philosophy must be politically effective, unlike the theories of Plato, Aristotle, Socrates and other ancient philosophers that went virtually ignored by the civil order. Thus, in the words of Allan Bloom, "The Enlightenment thinkers proposed a political science that could be used by founders, such as in America, in establishing principles and arrangements for a sounder and more efficient politics, and a natural science that could master nature in order to satisfy men's needs."[20] They rejected the existence of

God, at least the Christian God, as the enemy of reason. Their goal was the reconstitution of political and intellectual life totally under the supervision of philosophy and science. How far they succeeded is borne witness to by the fact that while there is no regime which one can point to as Platonic or Aristotelian, the Enlightenment itself is certainly responsible for liberal democracy, as is Marxism for communism.

The social contract theory of modern democratic societies has its roots in the political philosophy of Thomas Hobbes (1588-1679) and John Locke (1632-1704). They explored the newly discovered territory called the state of nature, where all men are free and equal and possess rights to life, liberty and the pursuit of property. "Right" here is not the opposite of *wrong*, but of duty. These inalienable natural rights belong to man as an individual prior, both in time and sanctity, to any civil society. Government exists for and acquires its legitimacy from ensuring these rights. Thus, whereas in the medieval tradition social obligations were consequent upon one's state in life, in the contract theory social obligations are the result of positive law agreed upon by individuals. Hobbes and Locke deny the efficacy of the common good as a motivator of public virtue and social behavior. Human beings are driven by selfish interests, and only the rational awareness and ordering of these self-interests according to social contract can effectively promote the common good, which means defending each person's individual rights. "Yet as new freedoms and rights were claimed by individuals, the unity of civilization began to crumble, nationalism arose, and individuals claimed a new role for themselves in the midst of social structures."[21]

Modern Catholic Social Thought

The Enlightenment gave birth to liberalism and the democratic revolutions, which began in the late eighteenth and continued through the nineteenth century. Economic liberalism with Adam Smith (1723-1790) as its chief ideologist proposed an economic system independent of any ethical norms beyond the "laws" of the market and the motive of self-interest. While Smith had no qualms about state intervention where the market did not work and supported public assistance for the poor along with public education, T. R. Malthus (1766-1834) and David Ricardo (1772-1823) saw grinding poverty as an essential feature of a productive market economy. These latter subscribers of a free market which operated according to "iron laws" fully believed that any effort to intervene on behalf of the poor would not only have disastrous economic consequences but would actually lessen the condition of the poor. These theories fueled the success of the industrial revolution and modern capitalism. A form of social Darwinism further reinforced the idea that social life, and not just biological evolutionism, was governed by the laws of competition and selection. Large corporate organizations thus began to appear in an effort to create order in the face of wild oscillations of the free market.

Nineteenth-century capitalism was truly creative in giving rise to new products, new industries and new markets. But it proved enormously destructive of land and labor. Even where material prosperity had increased, the human costs were extremely high because of the disruption of communities and cultures as villages emptied, kinship ties broke down, and vast urban aggregates grew. "[I]n reaction to the sufferings caused by the early expansion of the market economy, the ideology of socialism developed as a counterpoise to capitalism and argued, in opposition to the orthodox economists, that a state-directed economy would be more just and humane than what was currently coming into being."[22] Karl Marx (1818-1883) absolutized the determinant power of economics over all historical realities. His dialectical materialism denied the existence of God and turned over all divine functions to history, which alone would bring ultimate human fulfillment after a series of violent class struggles. Marx's philosophy found a wide hearing among the emerging labor movements of nineteenth-century Europe. Factory workers saw the Christian churches in league with their oppressors, the absolute state and irresponsible capitalists. They began staying away from churches in droves.

Papal Social Teaching. Catholic thinkers located the source of modern problems in secularism, and the overwhelming sentiment of Church leaders was that true social harmony and welfare was identical with Catholic influence and power. At the end of the nineteenth century, Pope Leo XIII wrote a series of encyclicals on Christian philosophy, politics and the social order in which he revived the classical teachings of St. Thomas Aquinas. It was a remarkable attempt on his part to bridge the catastrophic isolation of the Catholic Church from the mainstream of Western intellectual, cultural and political life. Leo XIII affirmed the supreme value of the human person, whose dignity is rooted in his or her transcendental worth, as the standard by which political, economic and social institutions are to be evaluated. In doing this he identified the basic principle of twentieth-century Catholic social teaching.

1. The first stage of modern Catholic social thought is marked by **the Church's response to the industrial revolution.** The opening paragraphs of Leo XIII's *Rerum Novarum* (1891) appealed to the principles of truth and justice which played a central role in the Church's traditional approach to the problems of conflicting rights and duties. The encyclical began with a description of the conflicts caused between workers and capitalists, rich and poor, by the process of industrialization and modernization.

> The encyclical's goal was to address these conflicts by clarifying both the demands of justice and the interrelationship between the rights of the conflicting groups. . . . The language of rights, therefore, focuses on the dignity, liberty and needs of all persons in society regarded disjunctively or one at a time. The language of justice, on the other hand focuses on the dignity, liberty and needs of all persons regarded conjunctively or as bound by obligations and duties to one another.
>
> The principles of justice are not appealed to by the tradition to resolve conflicts of rights according to an extrinsic standard. Rather, the intrinsic correlation of rights and justice reflects the fact that genuine rights exist in an ordered relationship with each other. It is the task of the principles of justice to make this order explicit.[23]

It was on the economic flank that Leo XIII made the most substantive advances in his engagement with modern society. He insisted that wages be determined not by economic considerations alone but also by taking into account the basic needs of individuals. Furthermore, while everyone has a right to possess private property, no one has the right to use that property without reference to the needs of the larger human community. The common good takes precedence over individual gain.

In the relationship between Church and state, Leo XIII followed closely the Thomistic vision. The Church had been divinely established to provide the means of salvation, and the state was bound to profess the truth of Christianity and to support the Church in its supernatural task. Politics and law, furthermore, exist to serve persons and not vice versa. The human person is never simply of functional or utilitarian value. Leo XIII, thus, attacked "both liberal capitalism, which released the individual from social and moral constraints, and socialism, which subordinated individual liberty to social well-being without respect for human rights or religious welfare."[24] He criticized all forms of democratic theory which maintain that basic values

317

and human rights are created by human choice. "As Leo saw it, once the voluntarist supremacy of human choice and liberty is made the exclusive foundation of political life there can be no defense of the person against the supremacy of the will of those who have the greater numbers."[25]

Marking the fortieth anniversary of *Rerum Novarum*, in 1931 Pope Pius XI issued his encyclical *Quadragesimo Anno* in which he continued to emphasize human dignity as the basis of all human rights. The world was now in the throes of the Great Depression, and the successful Russian revolution was consolidating itself into a communist regime while Fascist dictatorships were emerging in Italy and Germany. In the midst of these new historical developments Pius XI called for the restoration of economic self-government in order to overcome the chaotic injustice of capitalism and the regimented injustice of socialism, both of which had functionalized human persons. Nostalgia for the romantic vision of the medieval guild order with its hierarchical structure of status and rights fueled Pius XI's call for joint organizations of workers and managers, determining policy for industry as a whole. He also envisioned a council of industry representatives establishing overall national economic policy. He proposed a total reorganization of society according to a full-fledged "Christian social order" as the only appropriate middle-way between oligarchical capitalism and atheistic communism.

The critique of the economic causes of the Depression, of Fascism and Communism, in Pius XI's writings was also accompanied by his development of the concept of "social justice," by which moral reasoning takes into account the fact that relationships between persons have an institutional or structural dimension.[26] In *Quadragesimo Anno*, the pope used the term eight times. Prior to this, classical morality identified three types of justice: commutative, distributive and general or legal. Commutative justice binds individual to individual in the sphere of private transactions. It commands that exchange be of equal value and covers contracts, promises and property transactions in the private sphere including wage agreements. Commutative justice operates by the standard of strict equality and is violated by theft, fraud and unjust damage. Distributive justice determines how public social goods are to be allocated to individuals or groups. Perversions of it include all kinds of corruption, favoritism towards individuals or groups, all kinds of oppression, all unrelieved poverty. In addition to these two forms of particular justice, general or legal justice pertains both to the bearers and subjects of authority who practice it by passing and furthering legislation favorable to the common welfare.[27] Political authority, therefore, has the obligation to ensure that the common good is served, and the citizen has the duty to obey just laws once promulgated.

In his encyclical *Divini Redemptoris* (1937) Pius XI, however, provided this definition of social justice:

> It is of the essence of social justice to demand from each individual all that is necessary for the common good. But just as in the living organism it is impossible to provide for the good of the whole unless each single part and each individual member is given what it needs for the exercise of its proper functions, so it is impossible to care for the social organism and the good of society as a unit unless each single part and each individual member . . . is supplied with all that is necessary for the exercise of his social functions.[28]

Social justice demands that the institutions of society be ordered in a way that makes it possible to protect the social and personal rights of all. It is achieved by the acts of all other virtues, and particularly the acts of commutative, distributive and legal justice. Social justice is their ultimate norm, bringing into harmony all the various relationships directed by the forms of particular and general justice.

Social justice is also promoted by the principles of solidarity and subsidiarity. The former is the structural principle of every conceivable society which expresses directly the common moral responsibility to work together in order to promote the common good. This is the principle underlying the vision of society put forth by *Quadragesimo Anno*. In the same encyclical, Pius XI describes subsidiarity as the principle which never assigns "to a larger or higher society what can be performed successfully by smaller and lower communities."[29] The principle of subsidiarity thus counterbalances the principle of solidarity by protecting the vital integrity of the family, the neighborhood and the church, along with professional and labor groups and other intermediate associations.

2. The **internationalization** of Catholic social doctrine begins during World War II with Pius XII's attempts to address the growing economic and political interdependence of the world. In his Christmas Address of 1942, the pope turned to an examination of the basic principles of the internal order of nations which he saw as prerequisites for lasting international peace. It is an order that can only grow out of the basic recognition of the dignity of persons

within society. As such, it cannot be imposed mechanically by force. Rather, it is dependent upon the permanent social institutions of family, property, association and government through which the moral community of responsible persons is ordered. Pius XII began to offer a new affirmation of democratic political structures and of social reform, while Catholic anticommunism aligned the Church with the fundamental political stance of most Western governments. He downplayed Pius XI's call for the total reorganization of society into a new Christian social order.

The "law of human solidarity" dominated the political, social and economic thinking of Pius XII. He demonstrated particular concern for issues of world poverty, imperialism and growing urbanization, as well as the tragic results of war. He condemned both totalitarianism and individualism as denying human dignity. The concept of social justice was extended to relations between industry and agriculture, and to the rights of each nation to share in world markets. Trade unionism, social insurance, the welfare state, and even mixed economic arrangements of government and private enterprise, received the Church's blessing. While radical efforts such as that of the French worker-priests were rejected, positive social action and liberal reformist politics became normal. Pius XII's numerous addresses and allocutions on Catholic social teaching, however, followed the classical approach and style, which was didactic and authoritative. Viewing the Church as a strictly hierarchical society, the pope and bishops issued doctrinal pronouncements and practical directives, which were to be applied to the world by the laity. The Church was a teacher of virtue and the true interpreter of the natural law, even as it applied to secular behavior.[30]

3. In more recent years, beginning with the pontificate of Pope John XXIII and the Second Vatican Council, Catholic social teaching made a methodological shift from the deductive to the inductive approach as it sought to interpret **"the signs of the time."** The Council Fathers introduced their Pastoral Constitution on the Church in the Modern World by stating: "At all times the Church carries the responsibility of reading the signs of the time and of interpreting them in the light of the Gospel" (GS 4). John XXIII in his last encyclical, *Pacem in Terris* (1963), listed three distinctive characteristics of our age: the ascent of the working class, the new consciousness of women, and the longing of people for independence and freedom (see nos. 39-45). In this encyclical he affirmed the values of freedom and justice, and provided a systematic listing of human rights.

Many of them, such as the right to live in a dignified manner, the right to respect for one's person, and the right to religious freedom, are traditional rights which most people would accept without too much argument. But the Pope also argues for rights that might not be accepted as easily: the right to freedom in searching for the truth and in expressing one's opinions, the right to choose freely one's state of life, the right to free initiative in economics, the right to work, the right of freedom of assembly and of association, and the right to emigrate and immigrate.[31]

John XXIII extended the notion of the common good to include this totality of rights. His interpretation of the natural law no longer defended the restoration of the medieval social framework, but used it in a secular way to argue on the basis of reason that it is possible to discover a natural order which can serve as the foundation for a new sense of international order and harmony. He condemned the arms race for depriving individuals and nations of the economic goods necessary for social progress and argued that justice, reason and humanity demand that it should cease, that nuclear weapons be banned and that progressive disarmament begin.

The teaching of the Second Vatican Council demonstrates an anthropological and ecclesiological shift along with employing a new inductive methodology. "Beginning with *Gaudium et Spes*, one notices a much more empirical methodology, which includes a careful phenomenology of the present situation."[32] There is a clear recognition that Church teaching on social issues must be adapted to various situations in different parts of the world. In the Council documents, the person becomes the focal point of the Church's mission and ministry.

All human beings, since they have the same transcendent destiny, are understood as possessing the same inviolability and therefore as being essentially equal (LG 32). Each, moreover, is ruled by personal conscience, even in religious matters (DH 1; GS 41). In view of their intrinsic dignity all should, as far as possible, participate responsibly in social and political life (GS 73). Within the church, likewise, the active participation of the faithful is appropriate (SC 14). Ordained ministry is seen not as a dignity but as a call to humble service (PO 3 and 5).[33]

Vatican II's understanding of the Church itself moved away from the classical concept of a *societas perfecta* ("perfect society") alongside the secular state to a vision of a Church which takes its form and function from its relationship to the Kingdom of God. Biblical and symbolical images are used to describe this vision of the Church, rather than juridical, hierarchical definitions. "The Church is linked to the world as the sacrament of universal unity (LG 1), a sign and safeguard of the transcendence of the human person (GS 76), a defender of authentic human rights (GS 41). In a dynamically evolving world (GS 4) social and political liberation pertains integrally to the process of redemption and hence is not foreign to the mission of the church."[34]

Pope Paul VI in 1967 published his major social encyclical *Populorum Progressio* ("On the Development of Peoples") wherein he called development "the new name for peace." By development he meant not merely economic growth, but the development of the total person; it comes from a new humanism, allowing individuals to renew themselves by embracing the higher values of "love and friendship, of prayer and contemplation." Paul VI rejected unequivocally many of the basic precepts of capitalism, including unrestricted private property, the profit motive and reliance on free trade in the world economy. Freedom of trade, he insisted, must be subject to the demands of social justice, and he called upon the developed nations to share their resources and talents with those nations that are poor.

On the eightieth anniversary of *Rerum Novarum*, Paul VI published his letter *Octogesima Adveniens* ("Call to Action") in which he emphasizes that action for justice is the responsibility of every Christian and that it was up to Christian communities to analyze the situation proper to their own country in the light of the gospel. In this letter he brings contemporary Catholic social teaching to a new stage by reflecting upon, for the first time, the problems of post-industrial societies transformed by new technologies; he sees individuals facing a new loneliness as the result of the anonymity, poverty, indifference, waste and overconsumption that are often found in the cities. He also raises the question of technology's impact on the environment. In the political arena Paul VI warns against accepting ideologies and is especially critical of the inherent violence of Marxism, which he rejects as a means by which Christians may analyze their society and plan programs of reform.

The 1971 Synod of Bishops meeting in Rome published a document entitled "Justice in the World," in which after "scrutinizing the signs of the times" they identify and condemn the structures of injustice in the world; they plead the plight of the poor, the powerless, migrants, refugees, political prisoners, etc. The Synod grounds its critique in an incarnational theology and points out that justice cannot be separated from love of neighbor, for love implies a recognition of the dignity and rights of one's neighbor. Thus, "justice attains its inner fullness only in love." The Synod, furthermore, links the work of justice with the Church's primary mission of evangelization, stating that "Action on behalf of justice and participation in the transformation of the world fully appear to us as a constitutive dimension of the preaching of the Gospel, or, in other words, of the Church's mission for the redemption of the human race and its liberation from every oppressive situation." Paul VI picks up on this point in his apostolic exhortation, *Evangelii Nuntiandi* (1975) when he describes the various links between evangelization and human advancement without identifying the two, because the Church knows well "that in order that God's kingdom should come it is not enough to establish liberation and to create well-being and development" (no. 35). Even the best of human structures and the most idealized systems soon become inhuman, "if those who live in these structures or who rule them do not undergo a conversion of heart and outlook" (no. 36).

4. The anthropological and ecclesiological shifts first evidenced in the documents of the Second Vatican Council find clear expression in the writings of **Pope John Paul II**, who brought to the papacy in 1978 his own firsthand experience of having lived with the reality of a communist state in his own native Poland. In his first encyclical, *Redemptor Hominis* (1979), he develops a theological anthropology that will serve as the basis for all his future writings: "Through the incarnation, God gave human life the dimension that he intended man to have from his first beginning" (no. 1). John Paul II relies heavily upon biblical and theological symbols and imagery. Gone is the abstract systematization of classical philosophy. He confronts the real, concrete, historical situation with the gospel vision of redemption in Christ, "with the power of the truth about man and the world that is contained in the mystery of the incarnation and the redemption and with the power of the love that is radiated by that truth" (no. 13). From this perspective he critiques the dangers of uncontrolled technological development that is not accompanied by a "proportional development of morals and ethics" (no. 15). He deplores the arms race which supplies weapons of destruction instead of bread and cultural aid, and he adds that "the principle of human rights is of profound concern to the area of social justice and is the measure by which it can be tested in the life of political bodies" (no. 17). Freedom, however, does not mean doing whatever one

wishes; "Christ teaches us that the best use of freedom is charity, which takes concrete form in self-giving and service" (no. 21).

In his encyclical "On Human Labor" (*Laborem Exercens*, 1981), Pope John Paul II maintains that work is for the person, not the person for work. Human labor should bring about a sense of accomplishment in the person. He condemns "the error of economism" that considers labor only according to its economic purpose (no. 13). Furthermore, capital exists for labor, not vice versa (no. 15). He addresses the rights of workers within the broad context of human rights, as well as other issues, such as unemployment, wages and other social benefits, unions, agricultural work, the disabled person and work, and the emigration question. Richard A. McCormick, S.J. sums up both the focus and purpose of the encyclical when he observes, "The Pope is providing a prophetic vision, a way of construing the world theologically rather than providing a series of concrete answers."[35]

The pope's theological vision of the human person and the world receives fuller development in his encyclical "On Social Concern" (*Sollicitudo Rei Socialis*, 1987) commemorating the twentieth anniversary of Paul VI's *Populorum Progressio*. John Paul II begins his letter by reflecting upon his predecessor's concept of "development," the hopes for which have not been fulfilled over the last twenty years. The gap between the wealthy North and the underdeveloped, often exploited South has widened. For him, too, poverty is more than just economic. "The denial or the limitation of human rights — as for example the right to religious freedom, the right to share in the building of society, the freedom to organize and form unions or to take initiatives in economic matters — do these not impoverish the human person as much as, if not more than, the deprivation of material goods?" (no. 15). He then offers a moral critique of both liberal capitalism and Marxist collectivism, not as abstract politico-economic theories, but as concrete realities affecting negatively the lives of countless people. Thus he observes that

> It was inevitable that by developing antagonistic systems and centers of power, each with its own forms of propaganda and indoctrination, the *ideological opposition* should evolve into a growing *military opposition* and give rise to two blocs of armed forces, each suspicious and fearful of the other's domination (no. 20).

These ideological conflicts infiltrate countries which have recently achieved independence and create divisions, sometimes even provoking civil war.

The theological vision of "On Social Concern" is rooted in the dignity of the human person as enunciated in the revealed plan of God. The "supreme model of unity" for the human race is "communion," which ultimately inspires our solidarity and is "a reflection of the intimate life of God, one God in three Persons. . . . This specifically Christian communion, jealously preserved, extended and enriched with the Lord's help, is the *soul* of the Church's vocation to be a 'sacrament' " (no. 40). The moral and social attitude, indeed the "virtue" of solidarity, is not some vague feeling of compassion, but "a firm and preserving determination to commit oneself to the common good" (no. 38). This attitude is diametrically opposed to that desire for profit and that thirst for power which lead to "structures of sin." These latter, therefore, cannot be separated from the personal and individual character of sin. Greed, avarice and selfishness create the structures of sin. Social ills will not be overcome solely by political or social remedies. An authentic conversion is necessary, a conversion which is both individual and collective. This alone remains the key to a comprehensive understanding of human liberation.

Although often cited as being a foe of liberation theology, freedom from human oppression has been part of John Paul II's teaching from the start. The point he returns to repeatedly, however, is his concern for *total* liberation. Thus "the principle obstacle to be overcome on the way to authentic liberation is *sin* and the *structures* produced by sin as it multiplies and spreads" (no. 46). He reaffirms the Church's *"option or love of preference for the poor."* To ignore the immense multitudes of the hungry, the needy, the homeless, those without medical care, as well as those without hope for a better future "would mean becoming like the 'rich man' who pretended not to know the beggar Lazarus lying at his gate (cf. Lk 16:19-31)" (no. 42). The condemnation of social evils and injustices is part of the Church's prophetic role, her ministry of evangelization. "But it should be made clear that *proclamation* is always more important than *condemnation*, and the latter cannot ignore the former, which gives it true solidity and the force of higher motivation" (no. 41).

The American Catholic Pastoral Tradition

After World War I ended the Catholic Bishops of the United States converted the National Catholic War Council, founded in 1917 to aid and coordinate Catholic participation in the war effort, into a peacetime coordinating agency for Catholic affairs and eventually changed its name to the National Catholic Welfare Conference (NCWC). One of the most important of its early statements was published in 1919 in a pamphlet entitled "Social Reconstruction: A General Review of the Problems and Survey of Remedies." Authored by the director of the Social Action Department, Monsignor John A. Ryan, it "embodied a detailed set of principles and suggestions on such subjects as the need for minimum wage legislation, unemployment, health, and old-age insurance for workers, age limit for child labor, legal enforcement of the right of labor to organize, and the need for a public housing program and for a national employment service."[35] During the 1930s eleven out of the twelve major proposals in this so-called "Bishop's Program of Social Reconstruction" became law, attesting to the progressive character of Catholic leadership in this area of social concern.

In the 1930s the Great Depression brought bishops, priests and laity alike to come to terms with the dire economic situation. They began to take a serious look at sections of the papal encyclicals that condemned unrestrained liberal capitalism. In the wake of Pius XI's *Quadragesimo Anno*, the NCWC issued another programmatic pamphlet, "Organized Social Justice — An Economic Program for the United States Applying Pius XI's Great Encyclical on Social Life" (1935), which was signed by some 130 Catholic social thinkers. The pastoral letters of the U.S. Catholic bishops during this period demonstrate a fundamental concern for the quality of family life. "The 'public issues' that are addressed in the pastoral letters, including war, race, human rights, the economy and the international order, are consistently examined in connection with 'family issues,' including marriage, divorce, contraception, abortion, the education of children."[37] Throughout the 1930s and 1940s they continue to emphasize the family and family-related moral issues as the key to the common good. In 1943, for example, in response to the crisis of World War II their statement on "The Essentials of a Good Peace" extend the notion of the common good to the international context and refer broadly to the "family of nations."

The NCWC was succeeded in 1966 by two national organizations: the United States Catholic Conference (USCC), a civil entity through which the bishops issue most of their statements on political and social issues; and the National Conference of Catholic Bishops (NCCB), a canonical body which deals with the more strictly ecclesiastical concerns, such as liturgy, ecumenism, education, etc. Through these two organizations the bishops develop and issue specific policy statements for the guidance of individual citizens and policymakers.

326

Through these statements the bishops have made a commendable effort to promote human rights, justice, and peace. In the realm of foreign policy, they have opposed the violation of human rights abroad, defended both conscientious and selective conscientious objection, advocated arms control, urged the alleviation of hunger in the world, opposed the reinstitution of the draft, and condemned the use of nuclear weapons. In domestic policy, they have condemned abortion and racism, sought federal aid for parochial schools, defended the rights of farm workers, urged the government to fight inflation without causing greater unemployment, e dorsed national health insurance, and offered proposals for prison and welfare reform, the preservation of the family farm, and a more humane immigration policy.[38]

In November 1980, the bishops committed themselves to a new process of drafting pastoral letters, when they appointed a committee to undertake a fresh appraisal of the ethical issues surrounding war and peace in a nuclear age. Over a span of two years, the committee invited some sixty persons including high government officials, committed pacifists, research scientists, medical doctors, political scientists and theologians to give testimony. Each of three successive drafts was distributed widely to all who testified, to every bishop in the country and other bishops around the world, to the pope, innumerable theologians, the media and a wide variety of other interested parties, before being presented to the full body of bishops at their national meeting of May 1983, in Chicago.

1. The pastoral letter of the Catholic bishops of the United States on war and peace, entitled **"The Challenge of Peace: God's Promise and our Response"** (1983) marks a major milestone in the social teaching of the American Catholic hierarchy. It differs from previous statements because of the wide-range of consultation involved in its drafting and because it takes seriously Paul VI's instruction in "Call to Action" (*Octogesima Adveniens*) that "the Christian communities analyze with objectivity the situation which is proper to their own country" (no. 3). Written from the perspective of Catholic Faith, the bishops' letter addresses the fact that "nuclear war threatens the existence of our planet; this is a more menacing threat than any the world has known" ("Introduction"). In the letter they tackle many concrete questions concerning the arms race, contemporary warfare, weapons systems and negotiating strategies. Their treatment of these issues falls into three categories:

a) universal moral principles binding all peoples everywhere, regardless of their personal religious preferences [e.g., non-combatant immunity and proportionality]; b) formal, official teaching of the Catholic Church binding in conscience on all Catholics everywhere [e.g., the indiscriminate destruction of entire cities]; c) prudential moral judgments made by the bishops, based on their observations and their applications of moral and Church teaching to specific situations as they understand such situations, but not necessarily binding Catholics or others in conscience [e.g., the treatment of "no-first-use"].[39]

The bishops draw upon Catholic social tradition, as exemplified by Vatican II and recent papal teachings, in order to penetrate more adequately the biblical vision of peace and relate it to a world not yet at peace. Their concern is twofold: how to construct a more peaceful world and how to assess the phenomenon of war. To accomplish this they turn to the fundamental doctrines of God's transcendence and the dignity of the human person.

Peace is described as "both a gift of God and a human work. It must be constructed on the basis of central human values: truth, justice, freedom, and love" (no. 68). The bishops then explain the Church's traditional teaching on the presumption against war and the principle of legitimate self-defense. The moral criteria of the "just-war" or "limited-war" doctrine are explained. Recourse to war is permissible when the following conditions are present: a) just cause (to confront "a real and certain danger"); b) competent authority (declared by those responsible for the public order); c) comparative justice (do the rights and values involved justify killing?); d) right intention (pursuing peace and avoiding unnecessary destruction); e) last resort (all peaceful alternatives have been exhausted); f) probability of success; and g) proportionality (damage inflicted and costs incurred by war must be proportionate to the good expected by taking up arms). Furthermore, the actual conduct of such a war is governed by the two principles of proportionality and discrimination. The former principle requires that the "response to aggression must not exceed the nature of aggression" (no. 103), and the latter "prohibits directly intended attacks on non-combatants and non-military targets" (no. 107). These principles today must take into consideration, in the first instance, the possible escalation of a conventional war into a total "atomic" war; and in the second instance, the mobilization of the political, economic and social sectors in modern warfare. This part of the letter concludes with an exposition of Catholic teaching on the value of non-violence and of the Church's call for legal protection of conscientious objection to all war, as well as selective conscientious objection.

After establishing the religious and moral principles involved, the bishops offer their reflections on four major sets of issues, as "an invitation to a public moral dialogue": 1) the use of nuclear weapons; 2) the policy of deterrence in principle and in practice; 3) specific steps to reduce the danger of war; and 4) long-term measures of policy and diplomacy.[40] Regarding the initiation of nuclear war they state that "We do not perceive any situation in which the deliberate initiation of nuclear warfare, on however restricted a scale, can be morally justified" (no. 150). The bishops give their judgment on deterrence in these words:

> ... considerations of concrete elements of nuclear deterrence policy, made in light of John Paul II's evaluation, but applying it through our own prudential judgments, lead us to a strictly conditioned moral acceptance of nuclear deterrence. We cannot consider it adequate as a long-term basis for peace. . . . Nuclear deterrence should be used as a step on the way toward progressive disarmament (nos. 186 and 188.3).

They throw their support behind "immediate, bilateral verifiable agreements to halt the testing, production, and deployment of new nuclear weapons" (no. 191.1).

Citing a statement from the Holy See to the United Nations in 1976, the bishops reiterate that "the arms race is to be condemned as a danger, an act of aggression against the poor, and a folly which does not provide the security it promises" (no. 128). Public opinion needs to be formed in such a way that "there should be clear public resistance to the rhetoric of 'winnable' nuclear wars, or unrealistic expectations of 'surviving' nuclear exchanges, and strategies of 'protracted nuclear war' " (no. 140). Peace is the fruit of order. It is built up when we recognize the theological truth of "the unity of the human family— rooted in common creation, destined for the kingdom, and united by moral bonds of rights and duties" (no. 235). Peace and the values that promote it depend ultimately on "the disarmament of the human heart and the conversion of the human spirit to God who alone can give authentic peace" (no. 284). It calls for reverence for human life in all its forms.

When we accept violence in any form as commonplace, our

sensitivities become dulled. . . . Violence has many faces: oppression of the poor, deprivation of basic human rights, economic exploitation, sexual exploitation and pornography, neglect or abuse of the aged and helpless, and innumerable other acts of inhumanity. Abortion in particular blunts a sense of the sacredness of human life. In a society where the innocent unborn are killed wantonly, how can we expect people to feel righteous revulsion at the act or threat of killing non-combatants in war? (no. 285).

Peacemaking is not an optional commitment. It is a requirement of our Faith. Through prayer and penance we can turn back from the evil of total destruction and turn our hearts "toward God, toward neighbor, and toward the building of a peaceful world" (no. 300).

2. Following closely the same process and methodology they used in their peace pastoral, the Catholic bishops of the United States issued a second major letter in the fall of 1986 entitled **"Economic Justice for All: Catholic Social Teaching and the U.S. Economy."** They introduce their letter by stating that "Every perspective on economic life that is human, moral and Christian must be shaped by three questions: What does the economy do for people? What does it do *to* people? And how do people *participate* in it?" (no. 1). Taking an inductive approach they briefly describe the "signs of hope" and the failures evident in the current U.S. economy. Among the latter they describe poverty, homelessness, hunger, unemployment, dwindling social supports for family stability and farmers facing the loss of their land and way of life. Given, furthermore, the pre-eminent role of the United States in an increasingly interdependent global community, the bishops want to bring the legacy of Christian social thought into the public debate about the directions in which the U.S. economy is moving. In their "Message" accompanying the pastoral they state that "we write as pastors, not public officials. We speak as moral teachers, not economic technicians" (no. 7).

   In Chapter Two of the letter the bishops outline the Christian vision of economic life based upon "the fundamental conviction of our faith . . . that human life is fulfilled in the knowledge and love of the living God in communion with others" (no. 30). They turn to the Scriptures to show how this vision flows out of the Old Testament focal points of creation, covenant and community, as well as from Jesus' proclamation of the reign of God and his teaching of the dual command of love. The meaning of Christian discipleship is then explained with reference to Jesus' description of the Last

Judgment scene (Mt. 25:31-46), the parable of the Rich Man and Lazarus (Lk. 16:19-31), and other pertinent New Testament texts. The pastoral letter next defines the moral principles involved including respect for human dignity, the common good, solidarity, the preferential option for the poor, active participation and subsidiarity. Commutative, distributive and social justice are defined. In all this the bishops rely upon the developing body of social teaching contained in Vatican II and the papal encyclicals since Leo XIII. They invoke John Paul II's assessment of human work and the Church's traditional teaching on fair wages, labor unions, the right and duties of private ownership of property, and the government's role to guarantee human rights and justice.

After outlining the moral vision of the bishops, the letter attempts to analyze some selected aspects of the U.S. economy: employment, poverty, food and agriculture, and the U.S. role in the global economy. The bishops preface this section stating,

> Our judgments and recommendations on specific economic issues . . . do not carry the same moral authority as our statements of universal moral principles and formal church teaching; the former are related to circumstances which can change or which can be interpreted differently by people of good will. We expect and welcome debate on our specific policy recommendations. Nevertheless, we want our statements on these matters to be given serious consideration by Catholics as they determine whether their own moral judgments are consistent with the Gospel and with Catholic social teaching (no. 135).

Maintaining that employment is a basic right, the bishops call upon private enterprise and the government to work towards full employment through direct job-generation efforts. To fight poverty they propose a seven-point national strategy including job-creation and just wages, equal employment for women and minorities, stronger commitment to education for the poor and a thorough reform of the nation's welfare and income-support programs. Concern is expressed that the nation's food system may be in jeopardy "as increasing numbers of farm bankruptcies and foreclosures result in increased concentration of land ownership" (no. 217). Finally, in this section, they call for a fundamental change in the U.S. approach to the developing countries. "We want to stand with the poor everywhere, and we believe that relations between the United States and developing nations should be determined in the first place by a concern for basic human needs and respect for cultural conditions" (no. 260). The pastoral letter outlines plans for a new American experiment that would replace competition with partnership and teamwork in all areas of the economy. It concludes with a reflection upon the Christian vocation in the world today, a vocation which "consists above all in a change of heart: a conversion expressed in praise of God and in concrete deeds of justice and service" (no. 327). It is a call to holiness "achieved in the midst of the world, in family, in community, in friendships, in work, in leisure, in citizenship. Through their competency and by their activity, lay men and women have the vocation to bring the light of the Gospel to economic affairs" (no. 332). The bishops, furthermore, affirm that "all the moral principles that govern the just operation of any economic endeavor apply to the church and its agencies; indeed the church should be exemplary" (no. 347). This applies particularly to the Church's role as an employer and holder of property.

Both this pastoral letter and the one on peace evoked widespread public debate and criticism. Opposition to the general principles of social ethics contained in them was rather mild. Controversy centered rather on their practical applications, over which, the bishops themselves acknowledge, there is room for discussion and disagreement. Father Avery Dulles, S.J., however, raises the question as to whether the spirit of criticism and dissent thus unleashed by the pastorals might not spread to "strictly religious matters in which the bishops have unquestionable authority in the Church?"[41] Vatican II, furthermore, asserted that the renewal of the secular order is the special responsibility of the laity (see AA 7), and the 1971 Synod of Bishops stated: "It does not belong to the church, insofar as she is a religious and hierarchical community, to offer concrete solutions in the social, economic and political spheres for justice in the world" ("Justice in the World," 37). Yet, a good teacher often finds it necessary to give good concrete examples that will better shed the light of understanding upon the principles he or she is trying to convey. The predominantly pragmatic spirit of many, if not most Americans tends to make them impatient and non-receptive to the exposition of theories and principles that are not immediately demonstrated by practical application. Perhaps, only time will tell where wisdom lies.

Liberation Theology

Other regional churches have taken up Paul VI's challenge in *Octogesima Adveniens* to discern the appropriate response that they should give to their own particular situations. Thus a new approach to doing theology has appeared in recent years among Latin American theologians.

Liberation theology employs a strictly inductive methodology, through which it attempts to develop norms and criteria for political action and options on the basis of a concrete historical and social analysis. As a critical reflection on praxis (action), liberation theology seeks to enable persons, especially the poor, to become subjects of their own self-determination so that they can help in their own transformation and in the transformation of the social, economic and political structures in which they live. "At ecclesial community meetings, people study their own situation and the Bible, taking into account family problems, political pressures, personal limits and their own value system. Theologians attend more to the decisions people make and how they make them."[42] They aim to uncover the deepest values of the people and develop these within the Christian context.

Liberation theology is primarily an attempt to develop a theology proper to the Latin American context rather than a try to adapt European theology to the situation in Latin America. Its concern is with reality and how to respond to it appropriately, rather than with that same reality *interpreted* theologically, philosophically or culturally.[43] Brother Jeffrey Gros, the director of the Commission on Faith and Order of the National Council of Churches of Christ in the U.S.A. identifies six characteristics of this theology: 1) there is a focus on the dialectic of experience and revelation, as is apparent in the basic Christian communities with their study of Scripture, action in the world and reflection; 2) there is a focus on popular religion, using it with the tools of anthropology to understand the relationship of common spirituality to the social order; 3) the preferential option for the poor is central; 4) it is radically sacramental, seeing in the people of God the mystery of the risen Christ here on earth; 5) on the technical level, the theologies of liberation use the social sciences: economics, sociology, political science and contextual analysis; and 6) they deal seriously with the hermeneutics of suspicion developed from within the context of the Christian faith, which evaluates what *is* in light of the gospel promise of what is to be, indicating the changes necessary to close this gap.[44]

Liberation theology is based upon a dynamic concept of the human person, creatively oriented toward a social future. Oriented, therefore, toward what may be, rather than toward what is, it hopes to eliminate oppressive human relations, structures and social systems, especially the exploitative uses of power and the oppressive forms of international dependency that now exist. Liberation theology also hopes for the creation of a new person and a new sense of social solidarity rooted in liberation from sin and solidarity with

God.[45] In their general conferences at Medellin (1968) and Puebla (1979), the Latin American bishops tried to articulate a social doctrine adapted to their own time and situation by applying many of the themes of liberation theology. At Medellin, for example, they addressed the two major themes of justice and peace. The bishops suggested a variety of directions for social change and analyzed some of the elements of political reform which must be initiated to bring about greater justice. They called for decisions to be made on the basis of the common good rather than on the good of privileged persons. This requires *conscientizacion*, or the awakening of the social conscience and communal customs in all strata of society; to this end, the bishops called for the development of small basic communities. The document on peace addressed unjust situations which promote tensions and inhibit the development of peace. One source of such tensions the document called "internal colonialism," that is, the keeping of certain groups under continual domination which causes antagonism between social classes; another is the relationship between international tensions and external neocolonialism.

Although liberation theology is not a single, uniform school, but a pluralistic current, it has frequently been criticized for depending more upon socio-political analysis and solutions than upon the gospel and its proclamation of conversion for the forgiveness of sin. Critics often attack its endorsement of Marxist analysis and its unqualified advocacy of socialism. The International Theological Commission issued a long study on liberation theology in 1977.[46] This report admits that there are many "elements of great value." It warns, however, that the gospel of Jesus Christ must not be consolidated with secular history and that there are risks of uncritically accepting the assumptions of Marxism when using its sociological theories in the theological attempt to build a more humane society. The Commission maintains that while there is certainly unity between human effort and eschatological salvation, there is also a distinction. The Vatican's Congregation for the Doctrine of the Faith issued two "instructions" on liberation theology, the first in 1984 and the second in 1986.

C.D.F.'s "Instruction on Christian Freedom and Liberation" issued on March 22, 1986 limits itself to indicating the principal "theoretical" and "practical" aspects of its theme, while drawing attention to "deviations, or risks of deviation, damaging to the faith and Christian living."[47] The instruction begins by discussing the state of freedom in the world today and proceeds to show the effects of personal sin upon the human vocation to freedom. Sin, as separation from God and the root of human alienation, is identified as *the* source of division and oppression. It, then, develops the biblical theme of liberation which climaxes in Jesus' proclamation of the Good News to the poor and his paschal mystery. "Through his perfect obedience on the cross and through the glory of his resurrection, the Lamb of God has taken away the sin of the world and opened for us the way to definitive liberation" (no. 51). The instruction reaffirms that the Church "takes great care to maintain clearly and firmly both the unity and the distinction between evangelization and human promotion: unity, because she seeks the good of the whole person; distinction, because these two tasks enter, in different ways, into her mission" (no. 64). It supports the "new basic communities" and "theological reflection developed from a particular experience" as long as they interpret the experience from which they begin "in the light of the experience of the church herself" (nos. 69 and 70), and it warns against falling prey to "the myth of revolution" (no. 78).

Conclusion

This chapter on Catholic social teaching brings this entire work to an appropriate end. Our theme of *In Christ, A New Creation* is closely linked with another Pauline image, that of Christ the Last Adam, as a corporate personality. The person "in Christ," as a member of Christ's Body, is a social being called to relationships, to live in solidarity with God and neighbor. The development of Catholic social teaching over the last century, from Leo XIII to John Paul II, clearly demonstrates the anthropological shift that has occurred in contemporary Catholic theology, as well as the methodological shift from classicism to symbolic consciousness. Returning to the images and symbols of sacred Scripture, the Church is calling us again as if for the first time, to a deeper understanding of the mystery of God, human dignity and our Christian vocation. The gospel itself reveals the power of the divine plan breaking forth into our temporal existence and calling us to a conversion of heart through faith in Jesus Christ. This relationship of faith, which makes us disciples, transforms our lives according to the law of Christ, the twofold command of love.

The biblical images and symbols do not spell out concrete steps which we must follow in specific situations, rather they tease us into action, they seek to motivate us to do what is right and just. They illuminate our hearts and minds so that we can see the dimensions of life that are so frequently hidden by sin — the redeemed, the spiritual, the eternal, the social, and the gift of radical personal freedom. The shift from classicism to historical relativism within the modern secular world, a shift wholeheartedly accepted by some Christian theologians, has become a matter of either/or. The Church, on the other hand, since Vatican II strives to keep before our eyes the total vision of the human person, a wholistic vision embracing the integration of both/and — including the fallen/redeemed, the physical/spiritual, the temporal/eternal, the individual/social, and the predetermined/radically-free — dimensions of being a fully human person. The doctrines of our Faith (our creation in God's image, the Trinity, the incarnation, the paschal mystery, etc.) are symbols that "in-form" our lives and open up to us the possibility of an intimate relationship with the incomprehensible Mystery in whom we live, move and have our existence.

Jesus came to proclaim the Kingdom of God which we may enter through conversion and faith, by turning away from sin and turning to God with all our heart. Those whom Jesus called were gathered into his Church, to live as members of his Body, for the purpose of sending them forth to continue his mission of proclaiming the Good News of salvation to all the world. The Church's primary and essential mission is, like that of its founder, to proclaim the gospel both in word and deed so that it may transform the consciences and the lives of people according to God's plan. As Ernst Troeltsch saw very clearly, "The message of Jesus is not a program of social reform. It is rather a summons to prepare for the coming of the kingdom of God."[48] To which observation Avery Dulles, S.J. adds, "The followers of Jesus must live in such a way that their conduct arouses hope in the imminent coming of the kingdom. By embodying the values of the kingdom they become signs and anticipations of the new creation that is dawning in Jesus Christ."[49]

Notes

1. Paul VI, *Evangelii Nuntiandi*, no. 35.
2. John Paul II, *On Social Concern* (December 30, 1987), no. 41.
3. Ibid., no. 33.
4. Ibid., no. 41.
5. National Conference of Catholic Bishops, "Economic Justice for All: Catholic Social Teaching and the U.S. Economy," Pastoral Message and Letter (Washington, D.C.: USCC, 1986), no. 35.
6. *Apol.* 39 as cited by Phan, *Social Thought*, p. 21.
7. Rodger Charles, S.J., *The Social Teaching of Vatican II*, p. 21, fn. 28

ʍith reference to *Cambridge Medieval History* (C.U.P., 1911), vol. 1, p. 592ff.

8. *Sermo c. Auxentium*, 36 cited in Phan, op. cit., p. 25.

9. See Phan, op. cit., p. 30.

10. Charles, op. cit., p. 22.

11. *Love of the Poor*, cited in Phan, op. cit., p. 39.

12. Phan, op. cit., p. 42.

13. David J. O'Brien and Thomas A. Shannon, eds., "Introduction: Roman Catholic Social Theology," *Renewing the Earth: Catholic Documents on Peace, Justice and Liberation* (Garden City, New York: Doubleday & Co., Inc., 1977), p. 19.

14. Avery Dulles, S.J., "The Gospel, the Church and Politics," *Origins* 16 (1987): 640.

15. *II Sent.* d. 44, q. 2, a. 3 and 4.

16. O'Brien and Shannon, op. cit., pp. 19-21.

17. Charles, op. cit., p. 189.

18. O'Brien and Shannon, op. cit., pp. 23-29.

19. Charles, op. cit., p. 197.

20. Bloom, *The Closing of the American Mind*, p. 258.

21. O'Brien and Shannon, op. cit., p. 30.

22. Robert N. Bellah, "Resurrecting the Common Good: The Economics Pastoral, a Year Later," *Commonweal* CXIV, no. 22 (December 18, 1987): 739.

23. David Hollenbach, *Claims in Conflict: Retrieving and Renewing the Catholic Human Rights Tradition* (New York/Ramsey/Toronto: Paulist Press, 1979). pp. 144-145.

24. O'Brien and Shannon, op. cit., p. 35.

25. Hollenbach, op. cit., p. 44.

25. Ibid., p. 54.

27. Häring, *The Law of Christ*, vol. 1, p. 516.

28. *Acta Apostolicae Sedis* 29 (1937): 92.

29. As cited in Hollenbach, op. cit., p. 157.

30. Dulles, "The Gospel, the Church and Politics," p. 641.

31. O'Brien and Shannon, op. cit., pp. 120-121.

32. Dulles, "The Gospel, the Church, and Politics," p. 641.

33. Ibid.

34. Ibid.

35. Richard A. McCormick, S.J., "Notes on Moral Theology,"

Theological Studies 43 (March 1982): 95.

36. John Tracy Ellis, *American Catholicism*, 2nd ed. revised (Chicago and London: The University of Chicago Press, 1969), p. 144.

37. Elizabeth McKeon, "The Seamless Garment: The Bishops Letter in the Light of the American Catholic Pastoral Tradition," *The Deeper Meaning of Economic Life: Critical Essays on the U.S. Catholic Bishops' Pastoral Letter on the Economy*, ed. R. Bruce Douglass (Washington, D.C.: Georgetown University Press, 1986), p. 118.

38. J. Brian Benestad, *The Pursuit of a Just Social Order: Policy Statements of the U.S. Catholic Bishops, 1966-80* (Washington,D.C.: Ethics and Public Policy Center, 1982), pp. 3-4. A compendium of the actual statements issued during this period is found in J. Brian Benestad and Francis J. Butler, eds., *Quest for Justice* (Washington, D.C.: USCC, 1981), pp. 487.

39. Bishop John J. O'Connor, *The Challenge of Peace: An Introduction to the Bishops' Pastoral Letter* (Scranton, Pa.: The Guild Studios, n.d.), p. ll.

40. Ibid., p. 23.

41. Dulles, "The Gospel, the Church, and Politics," 644.

41. Arthur F. McGovern, S.J. and Thomas L. Shubeck, S.J., "Updating Liberation Theology," *America* 159, no. 2 (July 9-16, 1988): 34.

43. See Jon Sobrino, *The True Church and the Poor* (Maryknoll, New York: Orbis Books, 1985), pp. 15-16.

44. Jeffrey Gros, F.S.C., "Liberation Theology and Classical Theology," *Emmanuel* 93, no. 1 (January/February 1987): 22-23.

45. O'Brien and Shannon, op. cit., p. 544.

46. "Human Development and Christian Salvation," trans. Walter J. Burghardt, S.J., *Origins* 7 (1977): 305-313.

47. Congregation for the Doctrine of the Faith, "Instruction on Christian Freedom and Liberation," *National Catholic Reporter* 22 (April 25, 1986): 9-12, 41-44.

48. Ernst Troeltsch, *The Social Teaching of the Christian Churches*, vol. 1 (Chicago: University of Chicago Press, Phoenix ed., 1981), p. 61.

49. Dulles, "The Gospel, the Church and Politics," p. 640.

INDEX

Athanasius of Alexandria, St. / 50
Augustine of Hippo, St. / 11, 48, 49, 74, 78, 93, 106, 113, 143, 243, 276, 308, 309, 311
authority / 164, 165, 174, 179-182, 198
autonomy / 87, 165, 179, 181, 182

- **B** -
Babel, Tower of / 9, 200
Baby M / 289-290
baptism / 10, 16, 18, 35-38, 46, 47, 50, 53, 58, 75, 79, 88, 92-97, 116, 118, 123, 133, 178, 185, 204, 208, 265
"Barnabas, Letter of" / 45, 276
Barnhouse, Ruth T. / 253
Basil the Great, St. / 50, 98, 197, 276, 309
Bayer, Edward / 286
Beatitudes, the / 33, 106, 119, 154
beauty / 54, 68, 82, 126, 142, 151, 153, 171
Behaviorism / 86, 165
Being / 67, 68, 71, 72, 74, 81, 82, 104, 126, 150, 153, 197, 226
Bellah, Robert N. / 7, 85, 177, 249
Benedict of Nursia, St. / 50, 54
Bentham, Jeremy / 146
Berdyaev, Nicholas / 228, 240
Bernard of Clairvaux, St. / 54
Bible (see also Scripture) / 55, 62, 69, 74, 187, 188, 201, 226, 304-306
biblical morality / 19, 38, 39, 93, 100, 119, 120
bioethics (bio-medical ethics) / 147 (see Chapter 10, pages 263-301)
birth control / 244-245
bisexual / 227-228
blasphemy / 98, 216
Bloom, Alan / 147, 242, 314
body / 79, 80, 88, 92, 98, 105, 139-141, 176, 178, 179, 182, 216, 219
— and soul / 79, 216
Body of Christ, the / 16, 17, 36, 38, 48, 75, 76, 78, 82-84, 88, 99, 107, 116, 118, 121, 126, 130, 226
Bohr, Niels / 71
Bonaventure, St. / 52, 78
Boniface VIII / 311

"born-again" experience / 93
Brethren of the Common Life / 55
Burtchaell, James, C.S.C. / 274

- C -
Canon Law / 12, 53, 133, 157, 278
Calvin, John / 313-314
Calvinist work ethic / 313
capitalism / 316-325
"Casti Connubii" / 244, 278
Catherine of Siena, St. / 80, 240
Catholic social doctrine / 302-338
celibacy / 34, 128, 156, 239-241
cerebral cortex / 279
character / 143, 148, 171, 172, 174, 176-178, 180, 185, 193, 194, 197, 207, 216, 221
Charlemagne / 50
Charles Borromeo, St. / 58
chastity / 156, 254-258
Chomsky, Noam / 150
Christendom / 50, 157
Christian biblical revelation / 19, 27, 78, 86, 88, 96, 119, 124, 137, 169, 210, 226
Christian intentionality / 12
Christian marriage / 34, 127, 241-248
— theology of / 246
chronos (horizontal time) / 81
Church, the / 15-17, 19, 31, 35, 38, 42, 45, 50, 54, 56, 57, 60-62, 67, 71, 75, 78, 79, 84, 85, 88, 93, 97-99, 104, 117, 118, 120, 128, 130, 131, 133, 137, 139, 141, 146, 151, 156, 157, 162, 164, 170, 174, 176-182, 199, 204-206, 208, 209, 211, 238, 239, 241-245, 257, 276, 278, 302-338
— and State / 44, 308, 309, 313-315
— apostolic / 36, 38, 43, 92, 96, 97, 307
circumstances / 144, 150, 173, 175, 207, 211, 216, 217, 219
classicist world-view / 67, 69, 72, 119
Clement of Alexandria, St. / 47, 49, 98, 167, 187, 276
Clement of Rome, St. / 45, 97
"Cloud of Unknowing, The" / 54

Cyprian of Carthage, St. / 46, 49, 276
Cyril of Jerusalem, St. / 47

- D -
Dallen, James / 204
Darwin, Charles / 145
death / 10, 16, 30, 37, 38, 42, 49, 82, 87, 88, 95, 96, 98, 104, 107, 112, 121, 123, 124, 137, 138, 156, 158, 183, 184, 201, 203, 208, 218, 265, 273, 274, 291-298
— Christian meaning of / 119, 292
— moment of / 297-298
— physical / 80, 265
death penalty / 83
Decalogue, the (see also "Ten Commandments") / 148, 149, 154, 200, 305
Declaration on Certain Questions Concerning Sexual Ethics ("Persona Humana") / 248, 249, 251-254, 258
deification ("theosis") / 47
democracy / 315
"De Principiis" / 19, 72
despair / 119, 121, 134
Devotio moderna / 55
"Didache" / 44, 45, 96, 276
dilation and curettage (D and C) / 284
discernment / 11, 49, 57, 129, 163, 172-174, 180, 182-187, 204, 218
discipleship / 16, 33-35, 37, 38, 57, 72, 88, 96, 106, 107 (see Chapter 5, pages 111-135), 138, 178, 196
divorce / 25, 28, 149, 157, 178, 233-234, 236, 242, 255
DNR order ("Do Not Resuscitate") / 295
Dodd, C.H. / 26
dogmatic theology / 12
Dominic de Guzeman, St. / 54
doubt / 131, 133, 138, 175, 209
dream / 8, 71, 80, 82, 105, 187, 188, 199
Dulles, Avery, S.J. / 71, 180, 336

- E -
ecology / 142, 147, 149, 212
economic justice / 60, 302, 330-332

Garrigou-Lagrange, Reginald / 61
Gelasius / 309, 311
genitality / 231-232, 240, 250, 257
Germanization / 50, 53, 61, 62
Gnosticism / 47
Goldbrunner, Josef / 61
Good, the (Absolute) / 74, 142, 151-154, 169, 173, 186, 226
grace / 14-16, 19, 31, 32, 39, 48, 52, 58, 72, 78, 79, 86-88, 92, 96, 97, 99, 101, 103, 104, 106, 108, 111, 112, 115, 118, 119, 121, 123, 128, 136, 139-141, 151, 157, 158, 170, 171, 184, 185, 187, 195, 196, 198, 201-203, 206, 208, 211-215, 221
— law of / 140, 151
— teaching function of / 118, 141
Gratian's Decree / 53
grave sin (see also "sin, mortal") / 171, 207
Great Commandment of love, the / 33, 34, 37, 38, 50, 83, 125, 126
Gregory VII / 311
Gregory XIV / 278
Gregory of Nazianzus, St. / 309
Gregory of Nyssa, St. / 310
Gregory the Great, St. / 43
Grisez, Germaine / 282

- H -
hamartia / 193, 202
Hanigan, James P. / 258
Harakas, Stanley / 96
Häring, Bernard, C.Ss.R. / 12, 59, 281-282, 292
Hauerwas, Stanley / 13, 242
health / 59, 147, 219, 264
— physical / 80-82
health care / 263, 267-293
— social dimension of / 269-270
heresy / 131, 133
Hippocratic oath / 276
Hirscher, John Baptist / 58
historical world-view / 68, 69, 71
historicism / 145, 146

Industrial Revolution / 60, 316
Innocent XI / 278
International Theological Commission / 334
intimacy / 62, 82, 152
Irenaeus of Lyons, St. / 15, 46, 78
Isidore of Seville, St. / 44

- J -
Jansenism / 56, 58, 243
Jerome, St. / 168, 276
Jesus Christ / 10 and *passim*
— as the norm of Christian living / 137
John XXIII / 60, 320-321
John Cassian / 50
John Chrysostom, St. / 47, 48, 143, 167, 276, 309
John Damascene, St. / 44, 98
John of the Cross, St. / 57, 80
John Paul II / 100, 157, 207, 209, 211, 214, 226, 234-236, 247, 257, 258, 280, 303, 323-325, 329, 335
John the Baptist, St. / 34, 92, 94, 95, 101, 199
John the Evangelist, St. / 37, 38, 75, 95, 96, 112, 123, 126, 129, 138, 183
joy / 38, 45, 82, 92, 95, 100, 102, 119, 120, 125, 126, 141, 183, 196
Julian of Norwich / 54
Jung, Carl / 71, 80, 105, 187, 188, 229, 252
Justin Martyr, St. / 46, 97, 143, 187
justice / 11, 29, 30, 48, 94, 107, 115, 121, 125, 134, 149, 150, 153, 154, 174, 179, 195, 203, 209, 236, 304-305, 314
— commutative / 318
— distributive / 318
— general or legal / 318
— social (see "social justice") / 227, 318
just-war theory / 328

- K -
kairos / 81, 102
kingdom of God / 10, 32, 34, 35, 37, 38, 48, 59, 81, 82, 85, 92, 95, 100, 102, 103, 111, 118-121, 127, 129, 142, 201, 204, 205, 236-241
knowledge / 17, 27, 49, 66-72, 80, 86-88, 94, 95, 104, 106, 107, 109, 111,

123, 131, 138, 142, 144, 163, 164, 170-172, 174, 176, 183, 184, 186, 200, 211, 212, 214, 215
— evaluative / 170, 176
— moral / 170, 171, 174, 176, 212
— "objective" / 86, 170
— speculative / 170, 176
Kohlberg, Lawrence / 105, 150, 165, 177
koinonia / 36, 156
Kraft, William / 231, 232, 249-250, 254, 256

- L -
labor / 137, 315, 324
Last Judgment, the / 34, 125, 155, 210, 212
Lateran Council IV / 205
law / 10, 18, 27, 30-33, 36, 46, 50, 52, 56, 60, 72, 85, 88, 94, 105, 122, 123, 136-155, 157, 158, 162, 163, 168-170, 174, 176, 183-185, 193-196, 198-202, 207-211, 214, 217, 219, 221, 258
— civil / 52, 157, 158
— eternal / 18, 144-146, 150, 158, 185
— of Christ / 12, 74, 136, 138, 140, 141, 151, 176, 183, 193, 194, 196, 209, 219, 221, 275, 283
— of grace / 74, 139, 140, 151
— of sin and death / 87, 137
— of the spirit of life / 137
— positive / 137, 151, 157, 168, 198
laxists / 56
legalism / 47, 53, 59, 62, 74, 153, 156, 169, 263, 283
Lehmkuhl, Augustine, S.J. / 278, 281
Leo XIII / 302, 304, 316, 317, 335
Levi-Strauss, Claude / 150
lex naturale (see also "natural law") / 144
lex talionis / 122
liberalism / 59, 104, 145, 145, 315
liberation theology / 302, 332-335
libido / 229
life (see also "human life") / 7, 9, 10, 13, 16-18, 30, 56-59, 61, 62, 66, 68, 69, 71, 79, 82, 84, 85, 88, 92, 93, 95, 96, 99-101, 121-123, 126-129, 132, 136-142, 145-147, 150, 155-157, 164, 167-171, 175-179, 181, 183, 184, 187,

188, 194-196, 198, 199, 202, 203, 205, 206, 208, 211, 213, 217, 218, 226, 265-266
— bodily / 80, 263-265
— eternal / 76, 92, 102, 108, 113, 119, 139
liturgy / 20, 53, 60-62, 71, 96, 98, 100, 130, 139
Lobo, George V., S.J. / 150, 282
Locke, John / 145, 315
Lonergan, Bernard, S.J. / 102, 123
Lord's Day, the observance of / 49
Lord's Prayer, the / 33, 46, 47, 128, 129
love / 10, 14, 16, 17, 18, 28, 29, 31-38, 44, 45, 47-50, 53, 54, 58, 59, 72, 74, 78, 83, 84, 86, 87, 92, 94, 95, 96, 100-103, 105-109, 111, 113, 115, 117, 118, 120-130, 132, 134, 138-142, 146-149, 151-157, 162-164, 167, 169-171, 173, 174, 176, 183, 185-188, 193-195, 197-199, 201-204, 207, 209-211, 213, 215, 216, 219-221, 226, 232, 236, 263-264, 267, 283, 290, 304-307, 322, 323
— "falling in" love / 102, 230
lust / 96, 236, 256, 257
Luther, Martin / 55, 57, 78, 313-314

- M -
McCormick, Richard A., S.J. / 214, 263, 324
McDonagh, Enda / 13
Machiavelli, Nicolo / 314
magisterium, the / 25, 146, 147, 178 181, 238, 254, 282
male / 9, 76, 80, 82, 83, 148, 165, 226, 233, 239
— and female / 9, 27, 76, 80, 82, 83, 148, 226 - 233, 237, 239, 277
Maly, Eugene H. / 201, 202
Marcuse, Herbert / 24
marital love / 232
Marquis de Sade / 278
martyrdom / 47, 49
Marxism / 60, 315, 322, 324, 334
Marx, Karl / 132, 316
Mary / 60, 111-113, 116, 118, 199, 265
Maslov, Abraham / 229
masturbation / 216, 231, 253
materialism / 58, 66, 86, 104, 132, 133, 316
May, Gerald, M.D. / 240

Medicare / 269
— Diagnostic Related Groups (DRG's) / 269
meditation / 45, 47, 50, 55, 80, 129, 134, 184
Menninger, Karl / 198
Merton, Thomas / 61
metanoia / 32, 93, 95, 99, 100, 108
mission / 141, 181, 199, 204
— of Christ / 61, 199
— of the Church / 61, 82, 204
modern philosophy / 66, 137, 145, 149, 314-315
monasticism / 11, 50, 53, 54, 62
moral absolutes / 149, 150
moral knowledge / 84, 170, 171, 174, 176, 212, 226-227
— evaluative / 170, 176
— speculative / 170, 176
moral object / 154, 211, 215, 216, 218
moral theology / 11-14, 33, 36, 44, 45, 47, 48, 51-53, 55, 56, 58, 59, 61, 62,
66, 69, 72, 85, 92, 94, 96, 99, 102, 107, 117, 120, 123, 168, 176, 193, 205,
214, 217, 221, 303
— the "manual tradition" / 12, 18, 19, 55, 67, 72, 88
mortification (see also "self-discipline") / 148, 257
Murphy-O'Connor, Jerome / 117
Mystery / 11, 13, 15, 20, 32, 37, 58, 69, 70, 72, 75, 76, 78, 88, 98, 102, 104,
115, 124, 128, 136, 141, 152, 215, 226, 233, 292
mystical communion / 49, 50, 71, 109
mysticism / 54, 55, 57, 62, 80, 87, 102, 104, 109
myth / 8, 87, 227-228

- N -
National Catholic Welfare Conference (NCWC) / 326
National Conference of Catholic Bishops (NCCB) / 285, 326
natural family planning / 220
natural law / 38, 46, 48, 137, 141-151, 155, 170, 196, 217, 275, 304, 311, 314
nature / 54, 60, 69, 85, 92, 129, 137, 138, 141, 143-150, 153-156, 168-170,
184, 188, 193, 194, 196, 197, 206-210, 215, 216, 311-312, 315
new Adam (also "Final" or "Second") / 10, 13, 15, 46, 75, 76, 83, 116, 121,
194, 236, 239-240, 292
Newman, John Henry / 42, 61

351

Nicolas of Cusa / 78
Niebuhr, H. Richard / 184
Nietzsche, Frederick / 145 - 146
Nominalism / 53, 57-59, 62, 144, 168
norm / 16-18, 27, 136-139, 145, 153, 154, 165, 172, 173, 175, 194, 203, 207, 215, 221, 226, 263
— Christ as / 16, 137, 172, 203, 207, 221
— deontological / 17
— objective / 17
— subjective / 18, 165, 173, 175
— teleological / 17
Nouwen, Henri, J.W. / 280-281
Novatian / 46
nuclear weapons / 327

- O -
obedience / 10, 31, 34, 35, 78, 112, 119, 122-124, 136, 138, 139, 156, 168, 202
objectivism / 72, 74, 215
ordinary vs. extraordinary means / 293-294, 296
ordo bonorum / 107
ordo caritatis / 106
organ transplants / 219, 293
Origen / 47, 49, 50, 79, 97
original righteousness ("justitia originale") / 208
original sin / 48, 136, 151, 164, 186, 208, 210, 255
Orthodox Christianity / 20, 96
ovum / 83, 277 - 279, 282, 284

- P -
Papal Commission for the Study of Population, the Family, and Birth / 244
paschal mystery / 10, 37, 44, 75, 76, 97, 99, 107, 113, 116, 117, 119, 120, 123-125, 127, 128, 131, 136, 138, 139, 141, 185, 195-197, 201, 207, 257, 265, 295, 335
patient-physician relationship / 270 - 274
Paul VI / 60, 99, 101, 112, 121, 207, 244-247, 302, 322-324, 327
Paul of Tarsus, St. / 10, 12, 16, 25, 36-39, 75, 76, 83-85, 87, 96, 107, 111, 113, 117, 119, 120, 123, 125, 127, 130, 134, 137, 138, 140, 141, 143, 151,

154, 157, 158, 165, 167, 175, 179, 182, 183, 195-199, 202-204, 207-209, 217, 220, 232-233, 237, 256, 265, 292, 306, 307
peace / 38, 45, 75, 120, 121, 125, 129, 134, 153, 183, 209, 236, 327-330
peacemaking / 330
penance / 45, 50, 51, 94, 97, 100, 162, 204, 205, 207
— canonical / 50, 51, 204, 205
— sacrament of (see also "reconciliation") / 50, 51, 55, 100, 123, 162
penitential practices / 56, 94, 101, 277
Penitentials / 51
Pentecost / 35, 140, 183
person "in Christ" (see also "anthropology, Christian") / 66, 72, 76, 83
Philip Neri, St. / 58
Philo / 276
physical evil vs. moral evil / 219
Piaget, Jean / 24, 105, 149-150, 165, 177
pilgrimage / 50, 51, 118
Pius IX / 59, 278
Pius XI / 244, 246, 278, 318-320, 326
Pius XII / 59, 130, 244, 246, 267, 279, 288, 295, 319-320
Plato / 8, 79, 195, 227, 276, 308, 314-315
play / 71, 82, 153, 169, 181, 194, 220
politics / 9, 60, 178, 303-304
Polycarp of Smyrna, St. / 46
polygamy / 25, 149
Pope John XXIII Medical/Moral Research and Education Center / 286
Positivism / 58, 59, 79, 86, 145, 146, 157
poverty / 50, 54, 57, 103, 128, 152, 156, 180, 306, 325
prayer / 11, 34, 45-47, 49, 50, 54, 55, 57, 60, 97, 99, 125, 128-130, 134, 183-186, 258, 322
presumption / 134, 181, 220
priesthood / 56, 92, 238
principle / 136-138, 142, 145, 146, 148, 149, 152, 157, 167, 168, 175, 182, 207, 217-220
— of confidentiality / 273, 274
— of double effect / 217-220
— of informed consent 271-273
— of totality / 219
private property / 48

353

probabilism / 56, 169
probabiliorism / 56, 169
procreation / 49, 147, 242-243, 245-246, 274, 280, 290
prolonging life / 291-298
Protestantism / 56, 113, 144, 313, 314
prudence / 48, 133, 168, 174, 175, 180, 195, 218, 221
psychology / 49, 60, 62, 66, 71, 80, 81, 83, 84, 86, 104, 164, 165, 188, 198, 214, 229-232, 238, 239, 253, 254, 263, 283
— developmental / 105
— existential / 82
Puritans / 8, 93, 313

- Q -
"Quadragesimo Anno" / 318, 319, 326
quantum physics / 70, 75
Quietism / 58

- R -
rape / 216, 283-285
Ratzinger, Joseph Cardinal / 178, 216
reconciliation (see also "penance") / 75, 95, 121, 123, 124, 127, 134, 141, 153, 197, 199, 202, 204, 207
Reformation, the / 55, 62, 313, 314
relationship(s) / 9, 15, 17, 26, 28, 36, 44, 57, 75, 80, 83, 86, 88, 96, 99, 100-102, 105, 106, 111, 115, 120, 122, 124, 125, 127, 128, 132, 136, 137, 139, 148, 149, 151-153, 194, 196, 199-202, 206-209, 211, 213-215, 226, 232, 236
Relatio Subsistens / 75
relativism / 53, 59, 60, 69, 137, 146, 152, 155, 198, 212
religion / 8, 53, 66, 70, 125, 126, 131, 132, 150, 153, 165
religious development / 53, 55, 104-106, 115
religious experience / 93, 94, 101, 102, 109, 125
— ethical / 109
— mystical / 109
Renaissance / 55, 62, 67, 145, 312, 313
repentance (see "conversion")
responsibility / 30, 43, 81, 83, 84, 107, 155, 163, 166, 167, 169, 198, 199, 212, 213

resuscitation / 294, 295
revelation / 13, 15-17, 25, 27, 29-31, 43, 71, 76, 78, 83, 84, 88, 98, 117, 120,
124, 131, 137, 141, 151, 169, 170, 175, 180, 210, 226
revisionist theologians / 69
revivalism / 55, 93
rights / 137, 147, 153, 157, 197, 267, 276, 315
— individual / 18, 60, 303, 315
— theory of / 315
right to adequate health care / 270, 271
Rite of Christian Initiation of Adults (RCIA) / 93, 99
Rite of Penance / 100, 207
Roman Rota / 171
Rufinus of Aquileia / 97
RU-486 / 283

- S -
Sailer, John Michael / 58
salvation / 11, 13, 15-17, 27, 30, 31, 48, 55, 58, 72, 81, 88, 95, 97, 115, 117,
119, 123, 126, 127, 129, 143, 153, 154, 194, 197-199, 202, 203
Sanchez, Tomas, S.J. / 277
Sanford, John A. / 187, 188, 229, 230, 239, 252
Sartre, Jean-Paul / 24, 132
scandal / 204, 219 - 221
schism / 46, 131, 133
Scholasticism / 52, 69, 277, 304, 306, 310-312
Schnackenburg, Rudolf / 236, 237, 241, 242
science / 18, 19, 42, 58-60, 62, 66, 68, 70, 71, 75, 79, 132, 133, 147, 268,
274, 314
Scripture / 8 and *passim*
— and Tradition / 25, 130, 165, 312
Second Vatican Council (see "Vatican Council II")
secularism / 133, 198, 264, 316
secularization / 66
Self, the / 7, 8, 10, 79, 80, 86, 87
selfishness / 42, 34, 88, 105, 106, 120, 125, 141, 145, 186, 210
self-control / 106, 125, 141, 183, 187, 195
self-discipline / 97, 101, 104, 129
self-transcendence / 86, 102, 107, 163, 169, 173, 193

sensus fidelium / 179, 180
serious (or grave) matter / 205, 211-213
Sermon on the Mount / 33, 47, 183, 194, 236
service ("diakonia") / 36, 37, 88, 122, 123, 157, 181, 267, 268
sex / 50, 104, 122, 140, 141, 156, 178, 227-262, 275
— extramarital / 218, 248-254
— premarital / 178, 248, 249
sexual ethics / 20, 49, 226-262
sexual fantasies / 229
sexuality / 150, 155, 229-262
— affective / 230-232, 256
— genital / 229-232, 256
— primary / 229, 256
Shea, John / 72, 186
"Shepherd of Hermas" / 187
Siegel, Bernie S., M.D. / 80
"signs of the times" / 320, 322
sin / 9, 10, 15, 31, 33, 35-39, 42, 45, 46, 48, 50, 52, 56, 62, 72, 74, 75, 78, 79, 87, 88, 92-101, 106, 115, 119, 121-123, 129, 130, 134, 136-139, 141, 144, 151, 155, 156, 158, 164-167, 171, 186, 187 (see Chapter 8, pages 193-219), 226, 309
— actual (personal) / 208-210
— catalogues of (in Scripture) / 125, 201
— formal / 133, 155, 211, 212
— material / 211
— mortal / 56, 165, 204, 205, 211 - 215
— social dimensions of / 50, 125, 207
— venial / 49, 204, 205, 207, 215
sin of the world / 27, 199, 208, 209
situation ethics / 53, 59
Sixtus V / 277
slavery / 25, 28, 87, 88, 96, 141, 203
Smith, Adam / 315
social being / 82
social contract theory / 315
socialism / 132, 316
social justice / 60, 179, 227, 318, 319, 326
social sin / 207, 209, 210

social structures / 60, 83, 155, 197, 199, 229, 309, 315, 326
sociology / 60, 62, 66, 83, 238, 239
soul / 11, 17, 19, 54, 57, 79, 80, 92, 98, 120, 122, 129, 151, 183, 184, 187, 188, 194, 195, 201, 209, 211, 216
spiritual discernment / 182-184
spirituality / 10, 11, 13/ 49, 53-58, 60-62, 66, 80, 81, 106, 156, 232, 233, 240, 265, 283
Spohn, William C., S.J. / 257
sports / 178, 217
State, the / 60
sterilization / 216, 217, 270, 274, 275, 285, 286
— direct / 286
— indirect / 286, 287
Stoicism / 48, 79, 101, 311
story / 19, 26, 166, 177, 178, 182, 186, 188, 200
subjectivism / 58, 60, 69
subjective motive / 56, 212, 216, 217
sufficient reflection / 171, 205, 211, 212, 215
suicide / 145, 267
summae confessariorum / 53
superego / 164, 165
superstition / 55, 57, 67, 96, 133
surrogate motherhood / 274, 289, 290
symbol / 70, 71, 76, 80, 105, 106, 115, 117, 120
symbolic consciousness / 69, 71, 72, 74, 152, 155, 215
synderesis / 168-172, 174, 193
syneidesis / 167-169, 172, 193
Synod of Bishops, Rome / 60, 322, 323
synoptic gospels / 38, 119

- T -
Tanquerey, Adolfe / 61
technology / 42, 60, 68, 70, 71, 82, 147, 152, 264, 270, 274, 275, 322
Teilhard de Chardin, Pierre / 61
temptation / 50, 186, 200, 220
Ten Commandments / 29, 31, 48, 50, 148, 154, 170, 177, 200
Teresa of Avila / 57, 62, 80
Tertullian / 46, 97, 204, 276, 307